Oxford Resources for IB
Diploma Programme

T0309733

2023 EDITION
PHYSICS

Tim Kirk

STUDY GUIDE

Great Clarendon Street, Oxford, OX2 6DP, United Kingdom

Oxford University Press is a department of the University of Oxford.
It furthers the University's objective of excellence in research, scholarship, and education by publishing worldwide. Oxford is a registered trade mark of Oxford University Press in the UK and in certain other countries.

British Library Cataloguing in Publication Data
Data available

9781382016698

9781382016704 (ebook)

10 9 8 7 6 5 4 3 2 1

Paper used in the production of this book is a natural, recyclable product made from wood grown in sustainable forests.

The manufacturing process conforms to the environmental regulations of the country of origin.

Printed in China by Golden Cup.

Acknowledgements

The publisher and authors would like to thank the following for permission to use photographs and other copyright material:

Artwork: Six Red Marbles, Q2A Media, Barking Dog Art, Wearset Ltd., David Russell, and Oxford University Press.

Every effort has been made to contact copyright holders of material reproduced in this book. Any omissions will be rectified in subsequent printings if notice is given to the publisher.

Links to third party websites are provided by Oxford in good faith and for information only. Oxford disclaims any responsibility for the materials contained in any third party website referenced in this work.

Contents

Contents

Introduction

As I sit down to write this introduction, I am shocked to realize that I wrote the original introduction approximately 6.6×10^8 s ago. This length of time, more than 20 years, when rounded to the nearest order of magnitude, is a neat 10^9 or one billion seconds. Thus it is possible that some students may still be using this book a billion seconds after it was first published. If you happen to be one of these, thank you, and I wish you all the best for your studies!

Since the original publication, I have had the privilege to work in some amazing schools with many fabulous students and some exceptional colleagues—all too numerous to mention. In the intervening time, the IB syllabus has undergone three major revisions. Each time the aim of this book has remained the same—to provide an explanation (albeit very brief) of all the core concepts that are needed throughout the whole IB Physics course. As in previous editions, the structure of this book closely matches the IB Syllabus. As it focuses on physics concepts, however, the book should also prove useful to anyone following a pre-university Physics course.

Many people seem to think that you must be really clever to understand Physics, and this puts some people off studying it in the first place. So, do you really need a brain the size of a planet to cope with IB Higher Level Physics? The answer, you will be pleased to hear, is 'No'. In fact, it is one of the world's best kept secrets that Physics is easy! There is very little to learn by heart and even ideas that seem difficult when you first meet them can end up being obvious by the end of a course of study. But if this is the case, why do so many people seem to think that Physics is so hard?

I think the main reason is that there are no 'safety nets' or 'short cuts' to understanding Physics principles. You won't get far if you just learn laws by memorising them and trying to plug numbers into equations in the hope of getting the right answer. This is because most of the questions on IB examinations are targeted towards testing understanding rather than testing memory.

To really make progress, you need to be familiar with a concept and be completely happy that you understand it. This will mean that you are able to apply your understanding in unfamiliar situations. The hardest thing, however, is often not the learning or the understanding of new ideas, but the getting rid of wrong and confused 'everyday' explanations.

As ever, I would like to take this opportunity to thank the many people who have, over the years, helped and encouraged me during the writing of this book and to the many students and teachers who have commented so favourably. I am particularly grateful to those who have taken time to pass on their suggestions for improvements. Of course, the wonderful team at OUP all deserve my sincere thanks but, as ever, my heartfelt thanks go to Betsan who has given me constant support and encouragement for more than a billion seconds. Quite a feat!

Tim Kirk
July 2023

How to use this book

Overall syllabus

The full IB physics guide is published by the IB. It is intended for teachers and covers what should be taught and how it will be examined in the IB. Ask your teacher to provide you with a copy of the parts of the guide that contains the detailed syllabus content relating to your specific Standard or Higher Level course.

The syllabus content is grouped together into five different themes:

A. Space, time and motion

B. The particulate nature of matter

C. Wave behaviour

D. Fields

E. Nuclear and quantum physics

It is important to note that the way in which the syllabus content is set out in the guide is not a teaching plan or order. It details what can be assessed.

All too often, physics students concentrate on learning information in the hope that there will always be one specific equation that is the key to solving examination problems. Whilst this approach does sometimes provide a starting point, it does not help build the connected and deep understanding of the subject that is needed to succeed.

A good understanding of physics is not based on memorizing isolated facts or definitions but constructed on broader concepts and ideas. These are the links between different areas of the syllabus and the connections between prior and new knowledge. By way of an example, energy (in all its different forms) is a concept that has links to each of the five physics themes. There are many other linking concepts. Thinking conceptually helps to scaffold thinking with increasing complexity, it helps one organize and relate facts and topics. Thinking about concepts will help you to develop a deeper understanding of the material.

Syllabus breakdown

The five themes are each then split down into three smaller topics, named A.1, A.2 etc. Throughout the book you will find a dark grey box in the top corner of each page. This box contains a reference to the sub-topic covered by the content on that page. This will allow you and your teacher to match the content to the IB guide and keep track of what you know.

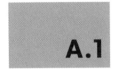

In the IB guide, each of the sub-topics has its own heading and starts with Guiding Question. The Guiding Questions are overarching questions to frame the topic. After you have studied the sub-topic in this book you should be able to think about possible ways to answer the Guiding Questions.

The material that you need to know in the IB guide is provided as Understandings, Skills, and Guidance. This is all split into Standard Level content and Additional Higher Level (AHL) content. In this book, an 'AHL' tag in a dashed box next to the heading, or a dashed outline to the box indicates that that part of the book covers additional higher level content.

Coverage of the syllabus

The first twenty-four chapters of this Study Guide cover all the underlying Physics and everything in the syllabus essentially as it is laid out in the guide. For the most part the Study Guide follows the syllabus order. Your teacher may not follow the order of the IB guide in their teaching because sometimes it's important to know concepts covered later in the syllabus to help you understand an earlier concept. Similarly, there are a few places in this book where the content is covered in a different order to make it easier for you to learn and understand the concepts.

Practice questions

At the end of each chapter there is a page of practice questions. Try answering these questions to test your understanding and practice for the exams. Then check your answers using the answers at the back of the book. These answers are not necessarily the full 'model' answers but they do contain all the information needed to score each possible mark.

Worked examples

Worked examples are provided within the chapters where they are appropriate. For example, there are worked examples for calculations you'll need to be able to complete. Worked examples are marked with a darker header so that you can find them easily. Have a go at completing the example yourself and then carefully follow the steps of the worked example to see a model example of how to do it.

Tools in the study of physics

The first twenty-four chapters of this book deal with all the physics concepts and details required by the syllabus. To understand and apply physics fully a good physicist also needs tools and an understanding of the inquiry process. Some of these are specific for a particular task and others are more general and can be used in a wide variety of applications. They will be assessed either directly or indirectly both in the written final examinations and in the internally assessed report. The IB physics guide gives information on the tools and inquiry process. These are covered in the final six chapters of this book.

A.1 Kinematics

Motion

Definitions

The motion of bodies through space and time can be described and analysed in terms of position, velocity and acceleration. These technical terms should not be confused with their "everyday" use.

- Vector quantities always have a direction associated with them.
- Generally, velocity and speed are NOT the same thing. This is particularly important if the object is not moving in a straight line.
- The units of acceleration come from its definition.

$(m\,s^{-1}) \div s = m\,s^{-2}$.

- The definition of acceleration is precise. It is related to the change in velocity (not the same thing as the change in speed). When the motion of an object changes, it is called acceleration, so this does not necessarily mean constantly increasing speed—it is possible to accelerate at constant speed if the direction changes.
- A deceleration means slowing down, i.e. negative acceleration if velocity is positive.

	Symbol	Definition	Example	SI unit	Vector or scalar?
Displacement	s	The change in position (the distance moved in a particular direction).	The displacement from London to Rome is 1.43×10^6 m southeast.	m	Vector
Velocity	v or u	The rate of change of displacement. $velocity = \dfrac{change\ of\ displacement}{time\ taken}$	The average velocity during a flight from London to Rome is $160\,m\,s^{-1}$ southeast.	$m\,s^{-1}$	Vector
Speed	v or u	The rate of change of distance. $speed = \dfrac{distance\ travelled}{time\ taken}$	The average speed during a flight from London to Rome is $160\,m\,s^{-1}$.	$m\,s^{-1}$	Scalar
Acceleration	a	The rate of change of velocity. $acceleration = \dfrac{change\ of\ velocity}{time\ taken}$	The average acceleration of a plane on the runway during take-off is $3.5\,m\,s^{-2}$ in a forwards direction. This means that on average, its velocity changes every second by $3.5\,m\,s^{-1}$.	$m\,s^{-2}$	Vector

Instantaneous vs average

The average value (over a period of time) is different from the instantaneous value (at one particular time).

In the example below, the positions of a sprinter are shown at different times after the start of a race. The average speed over the whole race is the total distance (100 m) divided by the total time (11.3 s) giving $8.8\,m\,s^{-1}$. But during the race, her instantaneous speed was changing all the time. At the end of the first 2.0 seconds, she had travelled 10.04 m, so

her average speed over the first 2.0 seconds was $5.02\,m\,s^{-1}$. During these first two seconds, her instantaneous speed was increasing—she was accelerating. If she started at rest (speed = $0.00\,m\,s^{-1}$) and her **average** speed (over the whole two seconds) was $5.02\,m\,s^{-1}$ then her instantaneous speed at 2 seconds must be more than this. In fact, the instantaneous speed for this sprinter was $9.23\,m\,s^{-1}$, but it would not be possible to work this out from the information given.

$d = 0.00\,m$ $d = 10.04\,m$ $d = 28.21\,m$ $d = 47.89\,m$ $d = 69.12\,m$ $d = 100.00\,m$

$t = 0.0\,s$ $t = 2.0\,s$ $t = 4.0\,s$ $t = 6.0\,s$ $t = 8.0\,s$ $t = 11.3\,s$

Vector mathematics must be used when calculating the instantaneous and the average values of velocity and acceleration as these are vector quantities.

Consider an object moving at a constant speed of $5\,m\,s^{-1}$ in a horizontal circle of radius 15.9 m where it takes 20 seconds do one complete circle.

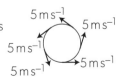

Instantaneous speed	$5\,m\,s^{-1}$
Average speed over 10 s	$5\,m\,s^{-1}$
Average speed over 20 s	$5\,m\,s^{-1}$

Instantaneous velocity	$5\,m\,s^{-1}$ along the tangent to the circle
Average velocity over 10 s	$3.08\,m\,s^{-1}$ along the diameter
Average velocity over 20 s	Zero
Instantaneous acceleration	A constant value always directed towards the centre of the circle ($1.57\,m\,s^{-2}$, see page 19)
Average acceleration over 10 s	$1\,m\,s^{-2}$ in the same direction as the tangent to the circle at $t = 10\,s$
Average acceleration over 20 s	Zero

Graphical representation of motion

The use of graphs

Graphs are very useful for representing the changes that happen when an object is in motion. There are three possible graphs that can provide useful information:

- displacement–time or distance–time graphs
- velocity–time or speed–time graphs
- acceleration–time graphs.

There are two common methods for determining particular physical quantities from these graphs. The particular physical quantity determined depends on what is being plotted on the graph.

1. Finding the gradient of the line.

To be a little more precise, you could find either the gradient of:

- a straight-line section of the graph (this finds an average value), or
- the tangent to the graph at one point (this finds an instantaneous value).

2. Finding the area under the line.

To make things simple at the beginning, the graphs are normally introduced by considering objects that are moving in one particular direction only. If this is the case, then there is not much difference between the scalar versions (distance or speed) and the vector versions (displacement or velocity) as the directions are clear from the situation. More complicated graphs can look at the component of a velocity in a particular direction.

If the object moves forwards and then backwards (or up and then down), you distinguish the two velocities by choosing which direction to call positive. It does not matter which direction you choose, but it should be clearly labelled on the graph.

Many examination candidates get the three types of graph mixed up. Always look at the axes of a graph very carefully.

Displacement–time graphs

- The gradient of a displacement–time graph is the velocity
- The area under a displacement–time graph does not represent anything useful

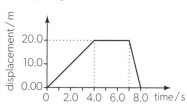

- In the first 4 seconds, the object moves at a constant speed $= \frac{20}{4} = 5\,\text{m s}^{-1}$
- The object is then stationary for 3 seconds
- The object returns at a faster speed $= \frac{20}{1} = 20\,\text{m s}^{-1}$

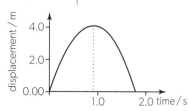

- Zero displacement is at the level of the hand throwing the object
- The object is thrown and reaches its highest point at $t = 0.9\,\text{s}$
- The object returns to the hand at $t = 1.8\,\text{s}$

Velocity–time graphs

- The gradient of a velocity–time graph is the acceleration
- The area under a velocity–time graph is the displacement

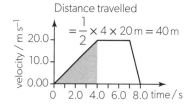

- For the first 4 seconds the object's velocity is increasing at a constant rate. Acceleration $= \frac{20}{4} = 5\,\text{m s}^{-2}$
- The object moves at a constant speed of $20\,\text{m s}^{-2}$
- Then it slows down with a constant acceleration of $-\frac{20}{1} = -20\,\text{m s}^{-2}$

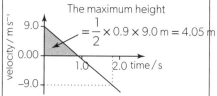

- The initial upward velocity is positive. The object has an acceleration of $-\frac{9.0}{0.9} = -10\,\text{m s}^{-2}$
- The instantaneous velocity is zero at the highest point ($t = 0.9\,\text{s}$)
- Downward velocity is negative

Acceleration–time graphs

- The gradient of an acceleration–time graph is not often useful
- The area under an acceleration–time graph is the change in velocity

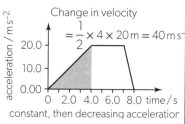

constant, then decreasing acceleration

- For the first 4 seconds the acceleration increasing at a constant rate
- The object then has a constant acceleration of $20\,\text{m s}^{-2}$
- The acceleration then decreases, but the velocity continues to increase

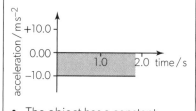

- The object has a constant acceleration of $-10.0\,\text{m s}^{-2}$
- The change in velocity is the area under the graph $= -10.0 \times 1.8\,\text{m s}^{-1} = -18\,\text{m s}^{-1}$ (change from $+9.0$ to -9.0 m s^{-1})

Uniformly accelerated motion (1)

Equations of uniform motion

These equations can only be used when the acceleration is constant—don't forget to check whether this is the case!

The list of variables to be considered (and their symbols) is as follows:

u initial velocity

v final velocity

a acceleration (constant)

t time taken

s distance travelled

The following equations link these different quantities.

$$v = u + at$$

$$s = \left(\frac{u+v}{2}\right)t$$

$$v^2 = u^2 + 2as$$

$$s = ut + \frac{1}{2}at^2$$

$$s = vt - \frac{1}{2}at^2$$

The first equation is derived from the definition of acceleration. In terms of these symbols, this definition would be

$$a = \frac{(v-u)}{t}$$

This can be rearranged to give the first equation.

$$v = u + at$$

The second equation comes from the definition of average velocity.

$$\text{average velocity} = \frac{s}{t}$$

Since the velocity is changing uniformly, you know that this average velocity must be given by

$$\text{average velocity} = \frac{(v+u)}{2}$$

$$\text{or } \frac{s}{t} = \frac{(u+v)}{2}$$

This can be rearranged to give

$$s = \frac{(u+v)t}{2}$$

The other equations of motion can be derived by using these two equations and substituting for one of the variables (see below for an example of their use).

Worked example

A car accelerates uniformly from rest. After 8 s it has travelled 120 m.
Calculate: (i) its average acceleration (ii) its instantaneous speed after 8 s.

(i) $s = ut + \frac{1}{2}at^2$

$$\therefore 120 = 0 \times 8 + \frac{1}{2}a \times 8^2$$

$$a = 3.75 \, \text{m s}^{-2}$$

(ii) $v^2 = u^2 + 2as$

$$= 0 + 2 \times 3.75 \times 120$$

$$= 900$$

$$\therefore v = 30 \, \text{m s}^{-1}$$

Using the equations and common mistakes

Each equation connects four of the five variables together. A good approach is to list the values given in the question (using "?" for anything you don't know or want to calculate). In the question above, you have

$u = 0$ [question says it starts from rest]

$v = ?$ [asked for in part (ii)]

$a = ?$ [asked for in part (i)]

$t = 8 \, \text{s}$

$s = 120 \, \text{m}$

So part (i) needs to use an equation that links u, a, t and s and part (ii) needs to use an equation that links u, v, a, and s OR v, a, t and s

As stated in the top box, the equations of uniformly accelerated motion can only be used when the acceleration is constant (or if the **average** acceleration is fixed). All too often, however, people try to use the

equations in situations when this is not the case. As acceleration is a vector quantity, uniform acceleration means a fixed numerical value of acceleration **and** a fixed direction. Common mistakes include using the equations to solve problems involving:

- circular motion (the direction of acceleration is changing all the time—see page 19)

- a mass connected to a spring (the acceleration depends on the spring extension—see page 14)

- an object moving some distance away from a planet (the acceleration near the surface is approximately constant but if the object moves a significant distance, then the gravitational force and hence the acceleration will be affected)

- an object feeling a resistive force moving through a fluid (e.g. air resistance—see page 6).

Uniformly accelerated motion (2)

Practical calculations

To determine how the velocity (or the acceleration) of an object varies in real situations, it is often necessary to record its motion. Possible laboratory methods are listed below.

Light gates

A light gate is a device that senses when an object cuts through a beam of light. The time for which the beam is broken is recorded. If the length of the object that breaks the beam is known, the average speed of the object through the gate can be calculated.

Alternatively, two light gates and a timer can be used to calculate the average velocity between the two gates. Several light gates and a computer can be joined together to make direct calculations of velocity or acceleration.

Strobe photography

A strobe light gives out very brief flashes of light at fixed time intervals. If a camera is pointed at an object and the only source of light is the strobe light, then the developed picture will have captured the object's motion.

$t = 0.0$ s
$t = 0.1$ s
$t = 0.2$ s

$t = 0.3$ s

$t = 0.4$ s

Ticker timer

A ticker timer can be arranged to make dots on a strip of paper at regular intervals of time
$t = 0.5$ s

(typically every fiftieth of a second). If the piece of paper is attached to an object, and the object is allowed to fall, the dots on the strip will have recorded the distance moved by the object in a known time.

Falling objects

A very important example of uniformly accelerated motion is the vertical motion of an object in a uniform **gravitational field**. If you ignore the effects of air resistance, this is known as being in **free-fall**.

Taking downwards as positive, the graphs of the motion of any object in free-fall are as follows.

In the absence of air resistance, all falling objects have the SAME acceleration of free-fall, INDEPENDENT of their mass.

Air resistance will (eventually) affect the motion of all objects. Typically, the graphs of a falling object affected by air resistance become the shapes shown below.

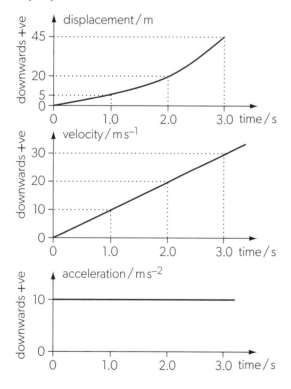

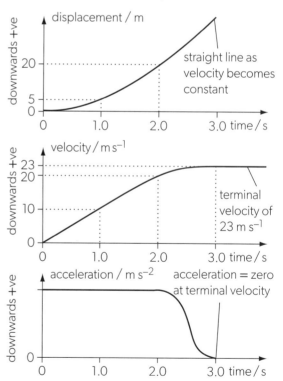

As the graphs show, the velocity does not keep on rising. It eventually reaches a maximum or **terminal velocity**. A piece of falling paper will reach its terminal velocity in a much shorter time than a falling book.

Projectile motion

Components of projectile motion

If two children are throwing and catching a tennis ball between them, the path of the ball is always the same shape. This motion is known as **projectile motion** and the shape is called a **parabola**.

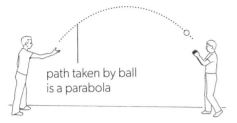

path taken by ball is a parabola

The only forces acting during its flight are gravity and friction. In many situations, air resistance can be ignored.

It is moving horizontally and vertically **at the same time** but the horizontal and vertical components of the motion are **independent** of one another. Assuming that the gravitational force is constant, this is always true.

Horizontal component

There are no forces in the horizontal direction, so there is no horizontal acceleration. This means that the horizontal velocity must be constant.

ball travels at a constant horizontal velocity

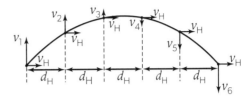

Vertical component

There is a constant vertical force acting down, so there is a constant vertical acceleration. The value of the vertical acceleration is approximately $10\,m\,s^{-2}$, which is the acceleration due to gravity.

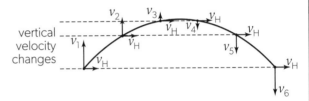

vertical velocity changes

Mathematics of parabolic motion

The graphs of the components of parabolic motion are shown on the right.

Once the components have been worked out, the actual velocities (or displacements) at any time can be worked out by vector addition.

The method of solving any problem involving projectile motion is as follows:

- Use the angle of launch to resolve the initial velocity into components.
- The time of flight will be determined by the vertical component of velocity.
- The range will be determined by the horizontal component (and the time of flight).
- The velocity at any point can be found by vector addition.

Useful "short-cuts" in calculations include the following facts:

- For a given speed, the greatest range is achieved if the launch angle is 45°.
- If two objects are released together, one with a horizontal velocity and one from rest, they will hit the ground at the same time.

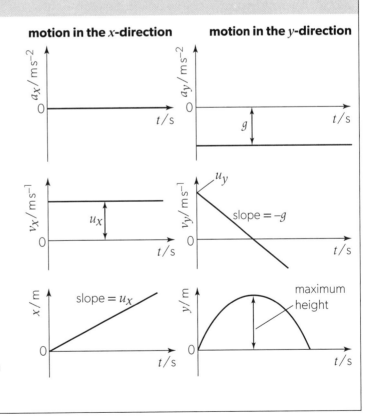

motion in the x-direction   **motion in the y-direction**

Fluid resistance and free-fall

Fluid resistance

When an object moves through a fluid (a liquid or a gas), there will be a frictional fluid resistance that affects the object's motion. An example of this effect is the terminal velocity that is reached by a free-falling object, e.g. a spherical mass falling through a liquid or a parachutist falling towards the Earth. See page 4 for how the motion graphs will be altered in these situations.

Modelling the precise effect of fluid resistance on moving objects is complex, but simple predictions are possible. Page 11 introduces a mathematical analysis of the frictional drag force that acts on a perfect sphere when it moves through a fluid. Key points to note are that:

- viscous drag acts to oppose motion through a fluid
- the drag force is dependent on:
  - relative velocity of the object with respect to the fluid
  - the shape and size of the object (whether the object is aerodynamic or not)
  - the fluid used (and a property called its viscosity).

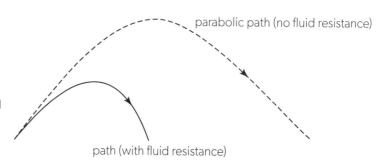
parabolic path (no fluid resistance)

path (with fluid resistance)

For example, page 5 shows how, in the absence of fluid resistance, an object that is in projectile motion will follow a parabolic path. When fluid resistance is taken into account, the vertical and the horizontal components of the velocity will both be reduced. The effect will be a reduced range and, in the extreme, the horizontal velocity can be reduced to near zero.

Experiment to determine free-fall acceleration

All experiments to determine the free-fall acceleration for an object are based on the use of a constant acceleration equation with recorded measurements of displacement and time. Some experimental set-ups will be more sophisticated and use more equipment than others. This increased use of technology potentially brings greater precision but can introduce more complications. Simple equipment often means that, with a limited time available for experimentation, it is easier for many repetitions to be attempted.

If an object free-falls a height, h, from rest in a time, t, the acceleration, g, can be calculated using $s = ut + \frac{1}{2}at^2$ which rearranges to give $g = \frac{2h}{t^2}$. Rather than just calculating a single value, a more reliable value comes from taking a series of measurement of the different times of fall for different heights $h = \frac{1}{2}gt^2$. A graph of h on the y-axis against t^2 on the x-axis will give a straight-line that goes through the origin with a gradient equal to $\frac{1}{2}g$, making g twice the gradient.

Possible experimental set-ups are given in the following table.

Set-up	Comments
Direct measurement of a falling object, e.g. ball bearing with a stop watch and a metre ruler	Very simple set-up meaning many repetitions can be easily achieved, so random errors can be eliminated. If the height of fall is carefully controlled, great precision is possible even though the equipment is standard. For a simple everyday object such as a ball bearing, the effect of air resistance will be negligible in the laboratory whereas the effect of air resistance on a ping-pong ball will be significant.
Electromagnet release and electronic timing version of the above	The increased precision of the timing can improve accuracy but the set-up will take longer. Introduction of technology can mean that systematic errors are harder to identify.
Motion of falling object automatically recording on ticker-tape attached to falling object	The physical record allows detailed analysis of motion and thus allows the object's entire fall to be considered (not just the overall time taken) and for the data to be graphically analysed. However, the addition of moving paper tape introduces friction to the motion.
Distance sensor and data logger	All measurements can be automated and very precise. Software can be programmed to perform all the calculations and to plot appropriate graphs. The experimenter needs to understand how to operate the data logger and associated software.
Video analysis of falling object	Capturing a visual record of the object's fall against a known scale allows detailed measurements to be taken. Timing information from the video recording is needed, which often involves IT.

1. An object is projected horizontally, at a velocity u_H, from the top of a vertical cliff of height, h and lands on the ground below. Taking the acceleration due to gravity as $10\,m\,s^{-2}$, write expressions for:

   a. the time taken before the object hits the ground (3)

   b. the distance from the bottom of the cliff to the place where the object lands (2)

   c. the vertical component of the velocity of the object when it hits the ground. (3)

2. A pupil cycles uphill from their home to their school at a speed of $5.0\,m\,s^{-1}$. At the end of the day, they cycle downhill from their school to their home at $10\,m\,s^{-1}$.

   a. Calculate the average speed for the pupil's journey to and from school. (3)

   b. Explain why the average speed for the whole journey is not $7.5\,m\,s^{-1}$. (2)

   c. State the average velocity for the pupil's journey to and from school. (2)

3. A weather research rocket is launched vertically from rest. For the first 6.0 seconds of flight (until all the fuel is used up), it has a uniform vertical acceleration of $110\,m\,s^{-2}$. It then falls back to the ground. Assume that the gravitational acceleration is constant.

   a. Calculate the maximum speed of the rocket. (3)

   b. Calculate the maximum height that the rocket reaches. (3)

   c. Calculate the time taken:

   i. to reach maximum height (3)

   ii. for the whole flight. (3)

   d. Sketch graphs for:

   i. the variation of acceleration with time for the rocket (3)

   ii. the variation of speed with time for the rocket. (3)

4. A projectile is launched at a velocity of $380\,m\,s^{-1}$ from a horizontal surface at an angle of $25°$ to the horizontal. Air resistance is negligible.

   a. Calculate:

   i. the horizontal component of the projectile's motion (2)

   ii. the vertical component of the projectile's motion (2)

   iii. the total time of the flight (2)

   iv. the horizontal range (total horizontal displacement) of the projectile. (2)

b. The launch velocity, u, and the angle of launch, θ, can be changed.

   i. Estimate the minimum value of u needed to achieve the range calculated in (a)(iv). (3)

   ii. The acceleration due to gravity is g. Show that the horizontal range, R, of the projectile is given by the relationship: (3)

$$R = \frac{2u^2}{g}\sin\theta\cos\theta$$

   c. Discuss the effect that non-negligible air resistance would have on the projectile's path. (2)

5. A bullet leaves the barrel of a gun at a height of $1.50\,m$ from the ground with a velocity of $300\,m\,s^{-1}$. Air resistance is negligible.

   a. The gun is aimed directly at the centre of a target positioned $50.0\,m$ away and fired horizontally. Calculate the distance between the arrival point of the bullet and the centre of the target. (3)

   b. The target is removed, and another bullet is fired horizontally. Calculate the time taken before the bullet hits the ground. (2)

   c. An identical bullet is held next to the gun and released at the same instant the gun is fired. Discuss which bullet, the one fired from the gun or the one released next to the gun, will hit the ground first. (3)

   d. The gun is now aimed vertically into the air.

   i. Calculate the height that the bullet reaches. (3)

   ii. Outline an assumption needed to answer (d)(i). (2)

   iii. Calculate the time taken for the bullet to arrive back at the point of firing. (3)

6. Discuss whether each of the situations described is a physical possibility. If the situation is possible, suggest an example. If the situation not possible, explain why.

   a. An object has a varying velocity and a constant speed. (3)

   b. An object has a varying speed and a constant velocity. (3)

   c. An object has zero velocity and a constant acceleration. (3)

   d. An object has a constant acceleration and a constant speed. (3)

7. An object is thrown at an angle downwards from the top of a $12.0\,m$ high vertical cliff towards the horizontal ground below. The object's initial velocity is $15\,m\,s^{-1}$ at an angle of $40°$ to the horizontal. Calculate:

   a. the time taken before it hits the ground (3)

   b. the location where the object hits the ground. (3)

A.2 Forces and momentum

Forces and free-body diagrams

Forces—what they are and what they do

In the examples below, a force (the kick) can cause deformation (the ball changes shape) or a change in motion (the ball gains a velocity). There are many different types of forces, but in general you can describe any force as "the cause of a deformation or a velocity change". The SI unit for the measurement of forces is the newton (N).

deformation   **change in velocity**

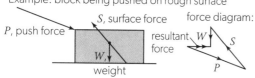

kick causes deformation of football

kick causes a change in motion of football

▲ Effect of a force on a football

- A (resultant) force causes a CHANGE in velocity. If the (resultant) force is zero, then the velocity is constant. Remember that a change in velocity is called an acceleration, so you can say that **a force causes an acceleration**. A (resultant) force is NOT needed for a constant velocity (see page 2).

- The fact that a force can cause deformation is also important, but the deformation of the ball was not caused by just one force—there was another from the wall.

- One force can act on only one object. To be absolutely precise the description of a force should include:

  o its magnitude

  o its direction

  o the object on which it acts (or the part of a large object)

  o the object that exerts the force

  o the nature of the force.

A description of the force shown in the example would thus be "a 50 N push at 20° to the horizontal acting ON the football FROM the boot".

Different types of forces

The following words all describe the forces (the pushes or pulls) that exist in nature. The origin of these forces is either gravitational or electromagnetic. Most everyday effects that we observe are due to electromagnetic forces.

Normal force F_N Elastic restoring force F_H Buoyancy F_b Electric force F_e

Surface frictional force F_f Viscous drag force F_d Gravitational force F_g Magnetic force F_m

One way of categorizing these forces is whether they result from the contact between two surfaces or whether the force exists even if a distance separates the objects.

Forces as vectors

Since forces are vectors, vector mathematics must be used to find the resultant force from two or more other forces. A force can also be split into its components. See page 176 for more details.

(a) by vector mathematics
Example: block being pushed on rough surface

P, push force S, surface force   force diagram:

resultant force

W, weight

▲ Vector addition

(b) by components
Example: block sliding down a smooth slope

R, reaction

component into slope $= W \cos \theta$

W, weight

component down slope $= W \sin \theta$

resultant down slope $= W \sin \theta$
resultant into slope $= W \cos \theta - R$
$=$ zero

Free-body diagrams

In a **free-body diagram**:

- one object (and ONLY one object) is chosen
- all the forces on that object are shown and labelled.

For example, if you consider the simple situation of a book resting on a table, you can construct a free-body diagram for either the book or the table.

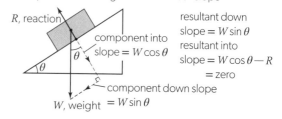

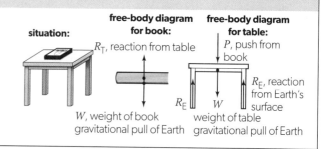

situation:

free-body diagram for book:
R_T, reaction from table

W, weight of book
gravitational pull of Earth

free-body diagram for table:
P, push from book

R_E, reaction from Earth's surface

W
weight of table
gravitational pull of Earth

Newton's first law

Newton's first law

Newton's first law of motion states that "an object continues in uniform motion in a straight line or at rest unless a resultant external force acts". On first reading, this can sound complicated but it does not really add anything to the description of a force given on page 8. It just says that a resultant force causes acceleration. No resultant force means no acceleration—i.e. "uniform motion in a straight line".

Book on a table at rest

acceleration = zero
resultant force = zero
$\therefore R - W$ = zero

Parachutist in free fall

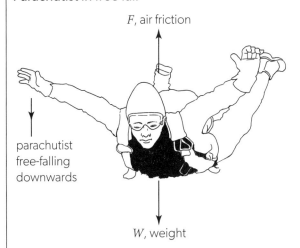

F, air friction

parachutist
free-falling
downwards

W, weight

If $W > F$ the parachutist accelerates downwards.
As the parachutist gets faster, the air friction increases until $W = F$
The parachutist then moves with constant velocity (the *acceleration* is zero).

Lifting a heavy suitcase

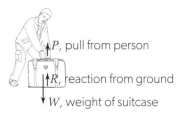

P, pull from person
R, reaction from ground
W, weight of suitcase

If the suitcase is too heavy
to lift, it is not moving:
$\therefore$ acceleration = zero
$\therefore P + R = W$

Car travelling in a straight line

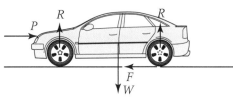

F is force forwards, due to engine
P is force backwards due to air resistance

At all times force up $(2R)$ = force down (W).
If $F > P$ the car accelerates forwards.
If $F = P$ the car is at constant velocity (zero acceleration).
If $F < P$ the car decelerates (i.e. there is negative acceleration and the car slows down).

Person in a lift that is moving upwards

lift moving upwards

The total force up from the floor of the lift = R.
The total force down due to gravity = W.
If $R > W$ the person is accelerating upwards.
If $R = W$ the person is at constant velocity (acceleration = zero).
If $R < W$ the person is decelerating (acceleration is negative).

Equilibrium and force types

Equilibrium

If the resultant force on an object is zero, then it is said to be in **translational equilibrium** (or just in equilibrium). Mathematically this is expressed as

$$\sum F = \text{zero}$$

From Newton's first law, you know that the objects in the following situations must be in equilibrium.

1. An object that is constantly at rest.
2. An object that is moving with constant (uniform) velocity in a straight line.

Since forces are vector quantities, a zero resultant force means no force IN ANY DIRECTION.

For two-dimensional problems it is sufficient to show that the forces balance in any two non-parallel directions. If this is the case, then the object is in equilibrium.

Translational equilibrium does NOT mean the same thing as being at rest. For example, if the child in the previous example is allowed to swing back and forth, there are times when they are instantaneously at rest but they are never in equilibrium.

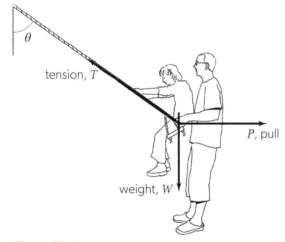

if in equilibrium:
$T \sin \theta = P$ (since no resultant horizontal force)
$T \cos \theta = W$ (since no resultant vertical force)

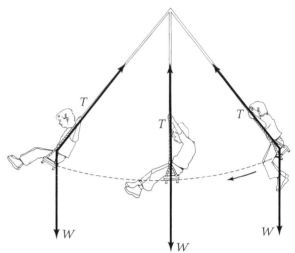

At the end of the swing the forces are not balanced but the child is instantaneously at rest.

Forces are not balanced in the centre as the child is in circular motion and is accelerating (see page 19).

Different types of forces

Name of force	Description
Normal force F_N	The component of the contact force between two surfaces that acts at right angles to the surfaces. If two surfaces are smooth, then this is the only force that acts between them.
Surface frictional force F_f	The force that opposes the relative motion of two surfaces and acts parallel to the plane of contact between the surfaces.
Elastic restoring force F_H	When a spring is stretched, it exerts an equal and opposite force on the objects attached to each end of the spring. The force is directly proportional to the extension, according to **Hooke's law**.
Viscous drag force F_d	The force opposing the motion of an object through a viscous fluid. See page 11.
Buoyancy F_b	This is the upward force that acts on an object when it is submerged in a fluid, due to the displacement of fluid. It is the buoyancy force that causes some objects to float in water (see page 11).
Gravitational force F_g	The force between objects as a result of their masses. This is sometimes referred to as the **weight** of the object.
Electric force F_e	The force between objects as a result of their electric charges.
Magnetic force F_m	The force between magnets and/or electric currents.

Viscosity and buoyancy

Definition of viscosity

An ideal fluid does not resist the relative motion between different layers of fluid. As a result, there is no conversion of work into thermal energy during laminar flow and no external forces are needed to maintain a steady rate of flow. Ideal fluids are non-viscous, whereas real fluids are viscous. In a viscous fluid, a steady external force is needed to maintain a steady rate of flow (no acceleration). Viscosity is an internal friction between different layers of a fluid that are moving with different velocities.

The definition of the viscosity of a fluid, η, (Greek letter nu) is in terms of two new quantities, the **tangential stress**, τ, and the **velocity gradient**, $\dfrac{\Delta v}{\Delta y}$.

The coefficient of viscosity η is defined as

$$\eta = \frac{\text{tangential stress}}{\text{velocity gradient}} = \frac{F/A}{\Delta v/\Delta y}$$

- The units of η are $N\,s\,m^{-2}$ or $kg\,m^{-1}\,s^{-1}$ or $Pa\,s$
- Typical values at room temperature:
  - Water: $1.0 \times 10^{-3}\,Pa\,s$
  - Thick syrup: $1.0 \times 10^{2}\,Pa\,s$
- Viscosity is very sensitive to changes of temperature.

For a class of fluids, called **Newtonian fluids**, experimental measurements show that tangential stress is proportional to velocity gradient (e.g. many pure liquids). For these fluids, the coefficient of viscosity is constant provided external conditions remain constant.

Tangential stress

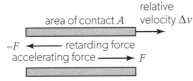

This is defined as $\tau = \dfrac{F}{A}$. Units are $N\,m^{-2}$ or Pa.

Velocity gradient

Velocity gradient $= \dfrac{\Delta v}{\Delta y}$. Units are s^{-1}.

Stokes' law

Stokes' law predicts the viscous drag force F_d that acts on a perfect sphere when it moves through a fluid:

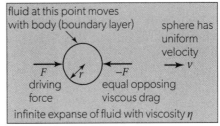
fluid at this point moves with body (boundary layer) • sphere has uniform velocity → v • F driving force • $-F$ equal opposing viscous drag • infinite expanse of fluid with viscosity η

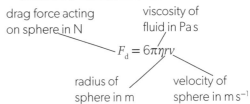
drag force acting on sphere in N • viscosity of fluid in Pa s • $F_d = 6\pi\eta r v$ • radius of sphere in m • velocity of sphere in $m\,s^{-1}$

Stokes' law assumes that:

- The speed of the sphere is small so that:
  - the flow of fluid past the sphere is streamlined
  - there is no slipping between the fluid and the sphere.
- The fluid is infinite in volume. Real spheres falling through columns of fluid can be affected by the proximity of the walls of the container.
- The size of the particles of the fluid is very much smaller than the size of the sphere.

The forces on a sphere falling through a fluid at terminal velocity are as shown below:

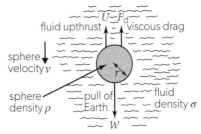
fluid upthrust U • viscous drag F_d • sphere velocity v • sphere density ρ • pull of Earth • fluid density σ • W

At terminal velocity v_t,

$$W = U + F_d$$
$$F_d = U - W$$

$$6\pi\eta r v_t = \frac{4}{3}\pi r^3 (\rho - \sigma) g$$

$$\therefore v_t = \frac{2r^2 (\rho - \sigma) g}{9\eta}$$

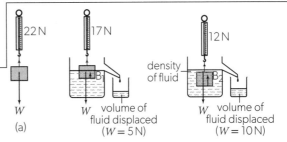
(a) $22\,N$ • W • $17\,N$ • W volume of fluid displaced ($W = 5\,N$) • density of fluid • $12\,N$ • W volume of fluid displaced ($W = 10\,N$)

A consequence of this principle is that a floating object displaces its own weight of fluid.

Buoyancy and Archimedes' principle

Archimedes' principle states that when a body is immersed in a fluid, it experiences a buoyancy upthrust equal in magnitude to the weight of the fluid displaced.

$$F_b = \rho V g$$

Newton's second law

Newton's second law of motion

Newton's first law states that a resultant force causes an acceleration. His second law provides a means of calculating the value of this acceleration. The best way of stating the second law is to use the concept of the **momentum** of an object. This concept is explained on page 16.

A correct statement of Newton's second law using momentum is "the resultant force is proportional to the rate of change of momentum". If you use SI units (and you always should), then the law is even easier to state—"the resultant force is equal to the rate of change of momentum". In symbols, this is expressed as follows.

In SI units, $F = \dfrac{\Delta p}{\Delta t}$

or, in full calculus notation, $F = \dfrac{dp}{dt}$

where p is the symbol for the momentum of a body.

Until you have studied what this means it will not make much sense, but this version of the law is given here for completeness.

An equivalent (but more common) way of stating Newton's second law applies when you consider the action of a force on a single mass. If the amount of mass stays constant, you can state the law as follows. "The resultant force is proportional to the acceleration."

If you use SI units, then "the resultant force is equal to the product of the mass and the acceleration".

In symbols, in SI units,

$$F = ma$$

resultant force measured in newtons — mass measured in kilograms — acceleration measured in $m\,s^{-2}$

Note:

- The "$F = ma$" version of the law only applies if you use SI units—for the equation to work the mass must be in **kilograms** rather than in grams.
- F is the resultant force. If there are several forces acting on an object (and this is usually true), then you need to work out the resultant force before applying the law.
- This is an experimental law.
- There are no exceptions—Newton's laws apply throughout the Universe. (To be absolutely precise, Einstein's theory of relativity takes over at very large values of speed and mass.)

The $F = ma$ version of the law can be used whenever the situation is simple—for example, a constant force acting on a constant mass giving a constant acceleration. If the situation is more difficult (e.g. a changing force or a changing mass), then you need to use the $F = \dfrac{dp}{dt}$ version.

Worked examples

1. Use of $F = ma$ in a simple situation

no friction between block and surface

If a mass of 3 kg is accelerated in a straight line by a resultant force of 12 N, the acceleration must be $4\,m\,s^{-2}$.

$$F = ma, \quad a = \frac{F}{m} = \frac{12}{3} = 4\,m\,s^{-2}$$

2. Use of $F = ma$ in a slightly more complicated situation

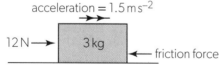

If a mass of 3 kg is accelerated in a straight line by a force of 12 N, and the resultant acceleration is $1.5\,m\,s^{-2}$, then you can work out the friction that must have been acting.

$$F = ma$$

$$\text{resultant force} = 3 \times 1.5$$

$$= 4.5\,N$$

$$\text{resultant force} = \text{forward force} - \text{friction}$$

$$\text{therefore, friction} = \text{forward force} - \text{resultant force}$$

$$= 12 - 4.5\,N$$

$$= 7.5\,N$$

3. Use of $F = ma$ in a two-dimensional situation

A mass of 3 kg feels a gravitational pull towards the Earth of 30 N.

What will happen if it is placed on a 30° slope given that the maximum friction between the block and the slope is 8.0 N?

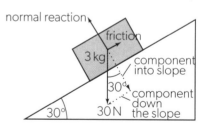

Into slope: normal reaction = component into slope
The block does not accelerate into the slope.

Down the slope:

$$\text{component down slope} = 30\,N \times \sin 30°$$

$$= 15\,N$$

$$\text{maximum friction force up slope} = 8\,N$$

$$\therefore \text{resultant force down slope} = 15 - 8$$

$$= 7\,N$$

$$F = ma$$

$$\therefore \text{acceleration down slope} = \frac{F}{m}$$

$$= \frac{7}{3} = 2.3\,m\,s^{-2}$$

Newton's third law

Statement of the law

Newton's second law is an experimental law that allows you to calculate the effect of a force. Newton's third law highlights the fact that forces always come in pairs. It provides a way of checking to see if you have remembered all the forces involved.

It is very easy to state. "When two bodies A and B interact, the force that A exerts on B is equal and opposite to the force that B exerts on A". Another way of saying the same thing is that "for every action on one object there is an equal but opposite reaction on another object".

In symbols,

$$F_{AB} = -F_{BA}$$

Key points to notice include:

- The two forces in the pair act on different objects—this means that equal and opposite forces that act on the same object are NOT Newton's third law pairs.
- Not only are the forces equal and opposite, but they must be of the same type. In other words, if the force that A exerts on B is a gravitational force, then the equal and opposite force exerted by B on A is also a gravitational force.

Examples of the law

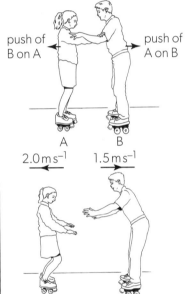

push of
B on A

push of
A on B

A   B
2.0 m s^{-1} 1.5 m s^{-1}

A   B

If one roller-skater pushes another, they both feel a force. The forces must be equal and opposite, but the acceleration will be different (since they have different masses).

The person with the smaller mass will gain the greater velocity.

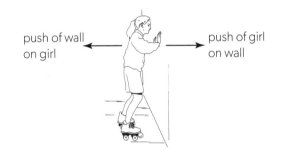

push of wall
on girl

push of girl
on wall

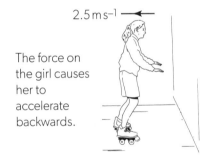

2.5 m s^{-1}

The force on the girl causes her to accelerate backwards.

The mass of the wall (and Earth) is so large that the force on it does not effectively cause any acceleration.

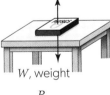

R, reaction from table

W, weight

These two forces are *not* third law pairs. There must be another force (on a different object) that pairs with each one:

R

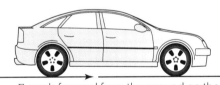

F, push forward from the ground on the car

In order to accelerate, there must be a forward force *on the car*. The engine makes the wheels turn and the wheels push on the ground.

force from car on ground $= -$ force from ground on car

W
EARTH

If the table pushes upwards on the book with force R, then the book must push down on the table with force R.

If the Earth pulls the book down with force W, then the book must pull the Earth up with force W.

Mass and weight

Weight

Mass and **weight** are two very different things. Unfortunately their meanings have become muddled in everyday language. Mass is the amount of matter contained in an object (measured in kg) whereas the weight of an object is a force (measured in N).

If an object is taken to the Moon, its mass would be the same, but its weight would be less (the gravitational forces on the Moon are less than on the Earth). On the Earth the two terms are often confused because they are proportional.

 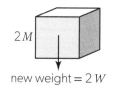

▲ Double the mass means double the weight

To make things worse, the term "weight" can be ambiguous even to physicists. Some people choose to define weight as the gravitational force on an object. Other people define it to be the reading on a supporting scale. Whichever definition you use, you weigh less at the top of a building compared with at the bottom—the pull of gravity is slightly less!

 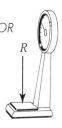

Weight can be defined as either
(a) the pull of gravity, W or
(b) the force on a supporting scale R.

▲ Two different definitions of "weight"

Although these two definitions are the same if the object is in equilibrium, they are very different in non-equilibrium situations. For example, if both the object and the scale were put into a lift and the lift accelerated upwards, then the definitions would give different values.

The safe thing to do is to avoid using the term weight if at all possible! Stick to the phrase "gravitational force" or force of gravity and you cannot go wrong.

gravitational force $= mg$

On the surface of the Earth, g is approximately $10\,N\,kg^{-1}$, whereas on the surface of the moon, $g \approx 1.6\,N\,kg^{-1}$

If the lift is accelerating upwards:
$R > W$

Measuring forces: mass and weight

The simplest experimental method for measuring the size of a force is to use the **extension** of a spring. When a spring is in tension it increases in length. The difference between the natural length and stretched length is called the extension of a spring.

Hooke's law states that, up to the elastic limit, the extension, x, of a spring is proportional to the tension force, F. The constant of proportionality k is called the spring constant. The SI units for the spring constant are $N\,m^{-1}$. Thus, by measuring the extension, you can calculate the force.

A spring under compression also obeys Hooke's law up until the point where the individual coils come into contact with each other.

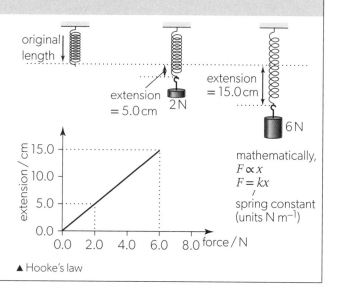

mathematically,
$F \propto x$
$F = kx$
spring constant (units $N\,m^{-1}$)

▲ Hooke's law

Solid friction

Factors affecting friction—static and dynamic

Friction is the force that opposes the relative motion of two surfaces. It arises because the surfaces involved are not perfectly smooth on the microscopic scale. If the surfaces are prevented from relative motion (they are at rest), then this is an example of **static friction**. If the surfaces are moving, then it is called **dynamic friction** or **kinetic friction**.

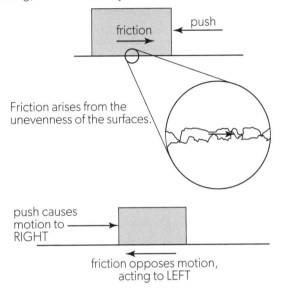

Friction arises from the unevenness of the surfaces.

push causes motion to RIGHT

friction opposes motion, acting to LEFT

A key experimental fact is that the value of static friction changes depending on the applied force. Up to a certain maximum force, F_{max}, the resultant force is zero. For example, if you try to get a heavy block to move, any value of pushing force below F_{max} would fail to get the block to accelerate.

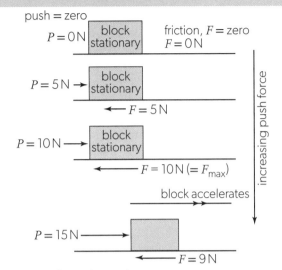

The value of F_{max} depends upon:

- the nature of the two surfaces in contact
- the normal reaction force between the two surfaces.

The maximum frictional force and the normal reaction force are proportional.

If the two surfaces are kept in contact by gravity, the value of F_{max} does NOT depend upon the area of contact.

Once the object has started moving, the maximum value of friction slightly reduces. In other words,

$$F_k < F_{max}$$

For two surfaces moving over one another, the dynamic frictional force remains roughly constant even if the speed changes slightly.

Coefficient of friction

Experimentally, the maximum frictional force and the normal reaction force are proportional. You use this to define the **coefficient of friction**, μ.

coefficient of friction $= \mu$

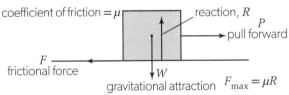

gravitational attraction $F_{max} = \mu R$

The coefficient of friction is defined from the maximum value that friction can take

$$F_{max} = \mu R$$

where R = normal reaction force

Note that:

- Since the maximum value for dynamic friction is less than the maximum value for static friction, the values for the coefficients of friction will be different $\mu_d < \mu_s$
- The coefficient of friction is a ratio between two forces—it has no units.
- If the surfaces are smooth, then the maximum friction is zero, i.e. $\mu = 0$.
- The coefficient of friction is less than 1 unless the surfaces are stuck together. $F_f \leq \mu_s R$ and $F_f = \mu_d R$

Worked example

If a block is placed on a slope, the angle of the slope can be increased until the block just begins to slide down the slope. This turns out to be an easy experimental way to measure the coefficient of static friction.

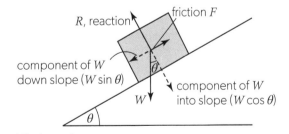

If balanced,

$$F = W \sin \theta$$
$$R = W \cos \theta$$

θ is increased.
When block just starts moving,

$$F = F_{max}$$

$$\mu_{static} = \frac{F_{max}}{R}$$

$$= \frac{W \sin \theta}{W \cos \theta}$$

$$= \tan \theta$$

Momentum and impulse

Definitions—linear momentum and impulse

Linear momentum (always given the symbol p) is defined as the product of mass and velocity.

$$\text{momentum} = \text{mass} \times \text{velocity}$$

$$p = mv$$

The SI units for momentum must be kg m s^{-1}. Alternative units of N s can also be used (see below). Since velocity is a vector, momentum must be a vector. In any situation, particularly if it happens quickly, the change of momentum Δp is called the **impulse** ($J = \Delta p = F\Delta t$).

Newton's second law states that the resultant force is proportional to the rate of change of momentum. Mathematically, you can write this as

$$F = \frac{(\text{final momentum} - \text{initial momentum})}{\text{time taken}} = \frac{\Delta p}{\Delta t}$$

Worked examples

1. $F = \dfrac{(\text{final momentum} - \text{initial momentum})}{\text{time taken}} = \dfrac{\Delta p}{\Delta t}$

   A jet of water leaves a hose and hits a wall where its velocity is brought to rest. If the cross-sectional area of the hose is 25 cm^2, the velocity of the water is 50 m s^{-1} and the density of the water is 1000 kg m^{-3}, what is the force acting on the wall?

   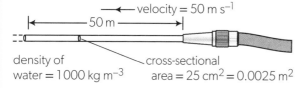

   density of water = 1000 kg m^{-3}
   cross-sectional area = 25 cm^2 = 0.0025 m^2

   In one second, a jet of water 50 m long hits the wall. So, each second:

   volume of water hitting wall =
   $0.0025 \times 50 = 0.125\text{ m}^3$

   mass of water hitting wall = $0.125 \times 1000 = 125\text{ kg}$

   momentum of water hitting
   wall = $125 \times 50 = 6250\text{ kg m s}^{-1}$

   This water is all brought to rest,
   $\therefore$ change in momentum, $\Delta p = 6250\text{ kg m s}^{-1}$

   $\therefore$ force $= \dfrac{\Delta p}{\Delta t} = \dfrac{6250}{1}\ 6250\text{ N}$

2. The graph below shows the variation with time of the force on a football of mass 500 g. Calculate the final velocity of the ball.

   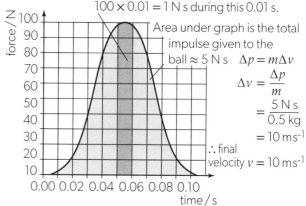

   The football was given an impulse of approximately $100 \times 0.01 = 1\text{ N s}$ during this 0.01 s.

   Area under graph is the total impulse given to the ball $\approx 5\text{ N s}$

   $\Delta p = m\Delta v$

   $\Delta v = \dfrac{\Delta p}{m}$

   $= \dfrac{5\text{ N s}}{0.5\text{ kg}}$

   $= 10\text{ m s}^{-1}$

   $\therefore$ final velocity $v = 10\text{ m s}^{-1}$

Conservation of momentum

The law of conservation of linear momentum states that "the total linear momentum of a system of interacting particles remains constant **provided there is no resultant external force**".

To see why, you start by imagining two isolated particles A and B that collide with one another.

- The force from A onto B, F_{AB} will cause B's momentum to change by a certain amount.
- If the time taken is Δt, then the momentum change (the impulse) for B will be given by
  $\Delta p_B = F_{AB}\ \Delta t$

- By Newton's third law, the force from B onto A, F_{BA} will be equal and opposite to the force from A onto B, $F_{AB} = -F_{BA}$.
- Since the time of contact for A and B is the same, the momentum change for A is equal and opposite to the momentum change for B, $\Delta p_A = F_{AB}\ \Delta t$.
- This means that the total momentum (momentum of A plus the momentum of B) will remain the same. Total momentum is conserved.

This argument can be extended up to any number of interacting particles as long as the system of particles is still isolated. If this is the case, the momentum is still conserved.

Elastic and inelastic collisions (1)

Elastic and inelastic collisions

The law of conservation of linear momentum is not enough to always predict the outcome after a collision (or an explosion). This depends on the nature of the colliding bodies. For example, a moving railway truck, m_A, velocity v, collides with an identical stationary truck m_B. Possible outcomes are:

(a) **elastic collision**

(b) **totally inelastic collision**

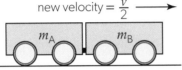

(c) **inelastic collision**

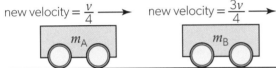

In (a), the trucks would need to have elastic bumpers. If this were the case, then no mechanical energy at all would be lost in the collision. A collision in which no mechanical energy is lost is called an **elastic collision**. In reality, collisions between everyday objects always lose some energy—the only real example of elastic collisions is the collision between molecules. For an elastic collision, the relative velocity of approach always equals the relative velocity of separation.

In (b), the railway trucks stick together during the collision (the relative velocity of separation is zero). This collision is what is known as a **totally inelastic collision**. A large amount of mechanical energy is lost (as heat and sound), but the total momentum is still conserved.

In energy terms, (c) is somewhere between (a) and (b). Some energy is lost, but the railway trucks do not join together. This is an example of an **inelastic collision**. Once again the total momentum is conserved.

Linear momentum is also conserved in explosions.

Worked example—elastic collisions

Two identical molecules are heading towards one another with identical speeds, u. Their collision is elastic. What are their speeds after the collision?

momentum before = momentum after
momentum before = $mu - mu$
$= 0$

$\therefore$ momentum after $= 0$
$$v_1 = v_2 \,(= v)$$
Elastic collision so no KE lost.

KE before $= \frac{1}{2}mu^2 + \frac{1}{2}mu^2$

KE after $= \frac{1}{2}mv^2 + \frac{1}{2}mv^2$

$$v = u$$

(relative velocity of approach = relative velocity of separation)

Worked example—inelastic collisions

A gun of mass 2 kg fires a bullet of mass 4 g. The bullet leaves the barrel of the gun at $100\,\mathrm{m\,s^{-1}}$. Calculate the recoil velocity of the gun.

momentum before = momentum after
$$0 = (0.004 \times 100) + (2 \times -v)$$

$$\therefore v = -\frac{0.4}{2} = -0.2\,\mathrm{m\,s^{-1}}$$

The recoil velocity is $0.2\,\mathrm{m^{-1}}$ in the opposite direction to the bullet.

Elastic and inelastic collisions (2)

Worked example—2D collision

Two hockey pucks collide.

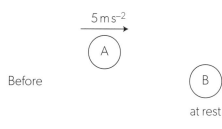

Before

B at rest

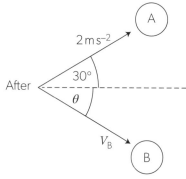

After

V_B

mass of each puck $= m$

momentum before = momentum after

Resolving horizontally:

$$(m \times 5) + (m \times 0) = m \times 2\cos 30 + mV_B\cos\theta$$

$$5m = m \times 1.7321 + mV_B\cos\theta$$

$$\therefore V_B\cos\theta = 3.2679 \quad (1)$$

Resolving vertically:

$$0 \times m = m \times 2\sin 30 - mV_B\sin\theta$$

$$V_B\sin\theta = 1.0 \quad (2)$$

$(2) \div (1)$

$$\frac{\sin\theta}{\cos\theta} = \frac{1.0}{3.2679} = 0.3060$$

$$\theta = \tan^{-1}(0.3060) = 17.01°$$

$(1)^2 + (2)^2$

$$V_B^2\cos^2\theta + V_B^2\sin^2\theta = 3.2679^2 + 1.0^2$$

$$\therefore V_B^2(\cos^2\theta + \sin^2\theta) = 11.679$$

$$\therefore V_B^2 = 11.679$$

$$V_B = 3.417\,\text{m s}^{-1}$$

Check:

Initial momentum from L to R $= 5m$

Final momentum from L to R
$$= m \times 2\cos 30 + mV_B\cos\theta$$

$$= 1.7321m + 3.2679m$$

$$= 5.00m \quad \checkmark$$

Final momentum up the page $= m \times 1.0$

Final momentum down the page
$$= m \times 3.417 \times \sin 17.01$$

$$= m \times 1.0 \quad \checkmark$$

Worked example—impulse

A ball of mass 60 g is travelling horizontally at a speed of 1.5 m s^{-1}. It hits a vertical wall and rebounds horizontally at a speed of 1.1 m s^{-1}. Calculate:

a) the percentage energy lost in the collision

b) the impulse given to the ball by the wall.

a) KE lost $= 0.5 \times 0.06 \times (1.5^2 - 1.1^2) = 0.0312\,\text{J}$

% energy lost $= \dfrac{0.0312}{(0.5 \times 0.06 \times 1.5^2)} = 2.7\%$

b) Impulse = change in momentum
$$= 0.06 \times 2.6 = 0.156\,\text{N s}$$

Uniform circular motion

Mechanics of circular motion

The phrase "uniform circular motion" is used to describe an object that is going around a circle at constant speed. Most of the time this also means that the circle is horizontal. An example of uniform circular motion would be the motion of a small mass on the end of a string, as shown.

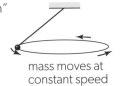

mass moves at constant speed

▲ Example of uniform circular motion

It is important to remember that even though the speed of the object is constant, its direction is changing all the time. This constantly changing direction means that the velocity of the object is constantly changing. The word "acceleration" is used whenever an object's velocity changes. This means that an object in uniform circular motion MUST be accelerating even if the speed is constant.

The acceleration of a particle travelling in circular motion is called the **centripetal acceleration**. The force needed to cause the centripetal acceleration is called the **centripetal force**.

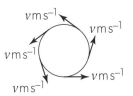

▲ Circular motion—speed is constant, but the direction of motion is changing all the time

Mathematics of circular motion

The diagram below allows you to work out the direction of the centripetal acceleration—which must also be the direction of the centripetal force. This direction is constantly changing.

The object is shown moving between two points A and B on a horizontal circle. Its velocity has changed from v_A to v_B ($v = \frac{2\pi r}{T}$). The magnitude of velocity is always the same, but the direction has changed. Since velocities are vector quantities you need to use vector mathematics to work out the average change in velocity. This vector diagram is also shown above.

situation diagram   **vector diagram**

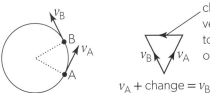

change in velocity directed towards centre of circle

v_A + change = v_B

In this example, the direction of the average change in velocity is towards the centre of the circle. This is always the case and so is true for the instantaneous acceleration.

For a mass m moving at a speed v in uniform circular motion of radius r,

centripetal acceleration $a_{centripetal} = \frac{v^2}{r}$ (in towards the centre of the circle).

A force must have caused this acceleration. The value of the force is worked out using Newton's second law:

centripetal force $F_{centripetal} = ma_{centripetal}$

$$= \frac{mv^2}{r} \text{ [in towards the centre of the circle]}$$

For example, if a car of mass 1500 kg is travelling at a constant speed of 20 m s⁻¹ around a circular track of radius 50 m, the resultant force is

$$F = \frac{1500(20)^2}{50} = 12\,000 \text{ N}$$

It is really important to understand that centripetal force is NOT a new force that starts acting on something when it goes in a circle. It is a way of working out what the total force must have been. This total force must result from all the other forces on the object. See the examples below for more details.

Note that the centripetal force does NOT do any work. (Work done = force × distance **in the direction of the force**.)

Examples

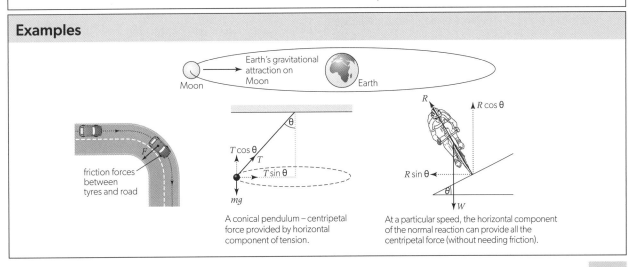

friction forces between tyres and road

A conical pendulum – centripetal force provided by horizontal component of tension.

At a particular speed, the horizontal component of the normal reaction can provide all the centripetal force (without needing friction).

Angular velocity and vertical circular motion

Radians

Angles measure the fraction of a complete circle that has been achieved. They can, of course, be measured in degrees (symbol: °) but in studying circular motion, the radian (symbol: rad) is a more useful measure.

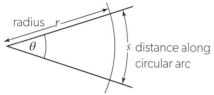

The fraction of the circle that has been achieved is the ratio of arc length s to the circumference:

$$\text{fraction of circle} = \frac{s}{2\pi r}$$

In degrees, the whole circle is divided up into 360° which defines the angle θ (in degrees) $= \dfrac{s}{2\pi r} \times 360$

In radians, the whole circle is divided up into 2π radians which defines the angle θ (in radians) as $\dfrac{s}{2\pi r} \times 2\pi = \dfrac{s}{r}$

For small angles (less than about 0.1 rad or 5°), the arc and the two radii form a shape that approximates to a triangle. Since radians are just a ratio, the following relationship applies if working in radians:

$$\sin\theta \approx \tan\theta \approx \theta$$

Angle / °	Angle / radian
0	0.00
5	0.09
45	$0.74 = \dfrac{\pi}{4}$
60	1.05
90	$1.57 = \dfrac{\pi}{2}$
180	$3.14 = \pi$
270	$4.71 = \dfrac{3\pi}{2}$
360	$6.28 = 2\pi$

Angular velocity, ω, and time period, T

An object travelling in circular motion must be constantly changing direction. As a result, its velocity is constantly changing even if its speed is constant (uniform circular motion). The average **angular velocity**, symbol ω (omega) is defined as $\omega_{average} = \dfrac{\text{angle turned}}{\text{time taken}} = \dfrac{\Delta\theta}{\Delta t}$

The units are radians per second (rad s^{-1}).

The instantaneous angular velocity is the rate of change of angle: $\omega = \text{rate of change of angle} = \dfrac{d\theta}{dt}$

1. Link between ω and v

   In a time Δt, the object rotates an angle $\Delta\theta$

   $$\theta = \frac{s}{r} \therefore s = r\Delta\theta$$

   $$v = \frac{s}{\Delta t} = \frac{r\Delta\theta}{\Delta t} = r\omega$$

   $$v = r\omega$$

2. Link between ω and time period T

   The time period T is the time taken to complete one full circle. In this time, the total angle turned is 2π radians, so:

   $$\omega = \frac{2\pi}{T} \text{ or } T = \frac{2\pi}{\omega}$$

3. Circular motion equations

   Substitution of the above equations into the formulae for centripetal force and centripetal acceleration (page 19) provide versions that are sometimes more useful:

   centripetal acceleration, $a = \dfrac{v^2}{r} = \omega^2 r = \dfrac{4\pi^2 r}{T^2}$

   centripetal force, $F = \dfrac{mv^2}{r} = mr\omega^2 = \dfrac{4\pi^2 mr}{T^2}$

Circular motion in a vertical plane

Uniform circular motion of a mass on the end of a string in a horizontal plane requires a constant centripetal force to act and the magnitude of the tension in the string will not change. Circular motion in the vertical plane is more complicated as the weight of the object always acts in the same vertical direction. The object will speed up and slow down during its motion due to the component of its weight that acts along the tangent to the circle. The maximum speed will be when the object is at the bottom and the minimum speed will occur at the top. The tension in the string will also change during one revolution.

In a vertical circle, the tension of the string will always act at 90° to the object's velocity so this force does no work in speeding it up or slowing it down. The conservation of energy means that $mgy + \dfrac{1}{2}mv^2 = \text{constant}$

situation diagram

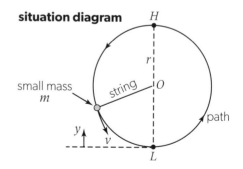

free-body diagram

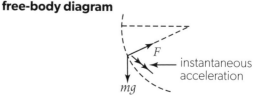

instantaneous acceleration

End of topic questions—A.2 Forces and momentum

1. A mass of 1.0 kg is at rest on a friction free surface. A force of 1.0 N acts on the mass for exactly 1.0 s.

   a. Determine how far the mass will move in the first second. (2)

   b. Determine how far the mass will move in the first ten seconds. (2)

2. An insect jumps vertically into the air from rest by pushing against the ground with its legs. The speed of the insect at take-off is 3.5 m s^{-1}. During take-off the body is accelerated over a distance of 42 mm and the mass of the insect is 2.8 g. Calculate:

   a. the average force exerted by the ground on the legs of the insect (3)

   b. the maximum height that the insect reaches above the ground. (3)

3. A car of mass 1 200 kg is travelling at a constant velocity of 50 km h^{-1}. After travelling a distance of 100 m, it makes a 90° turn to the right by following a circular path of radius of radius 22 m. It maintains a constant speed of 50 km h^{-1} during the turn.

   a. Sketch a free-body diagram to represent the forces acting on the car when travelling in a straight line. (4)

   b. Explain the origin of each of the forces you have identified in your answer to (a). (4)

   c. Calculate the time taken for the car to complete the turn. (2)

   d. Calculate the change in the car's momentum as it completes the turn. (2)

   During the turn, an additional force acts on the car.

   e. Explain the origin of this additional force. (2)

   f. Sketch a diagram to represent the direction in which this additional force acts. (2)

   g. Calculate the value of this additional force. (3)

   h. Calculate the minimum value for the coefficient of static friction between the car tyres and the ground for the car to avoid skidding as it makes the turn. (3)

4. A railway truck of mass 800 kg is moving at a constant velocity of 3 m s^{-1}. It collides with a stationary truck of mass 1 200 kg. The two trucks couple and move together after the collision.

   a. State whether this collision is elastic or inelastic. (1)

   b. Calculate the combined velocity of the trucks after the collision. (2)

   c. Find the value of the impulse received by the 800 kg railway truck. (2)

   d. Estimate the energy lost in this collision. (2)

5. Coal falls vertically onto a conveyor belt at a rate of 4.5 kg s^{-1}. The horizontal speed of the conveyor belt is 2.5 m s^{-1}.

   a. Estimate the minimum force required to maintain the speed of the conveyor belt. (3)

   b. Explain why the actual force will be larger than your answer to (a). (2)

6. A block of mass M rests on a horizontal surface. The surface is slowly tilted upwards, and when it makes an angle θ with the horizontal, the block just starts to slide down the slope.

   a. Sketch a free body diagram to show the forces acting on the block when the angle is less than θ. (3)

   b. Determine an expression for the coefficient of static friction. (3)

   c. Discuss whether the block will slide at a constant velocity down the slope or whether it will accelerate. (2)

7. An oil drop of radius r and density 8.9×10^2 kg m^{-3} falls through a gas. The viscosity of the gas is 14 μPa s and the drop reaches a terminal velocity of 18 cm s^{-1}. Determine the radius of the drop. (4)

8. A fairground ride begins with people standing against the wall of a large hollow cylindrical room of radius 2.5 m. The room starts to rotate around its central vertical axis. The people in the room experience a force pushing them against the wall.

   a. Explain the original of any horizontal force acting on the people in the room when it is rotating. (2)

   b. Draw a free-body diagram to represent all the forces acting on a person in the rotating room when it is rotating at constant speed. (4)

   The speed of rotation is increased until the linear speed of the wall reaches 9.0 m s^{-1}. At this speed, the floor of the room is lowered. The people remain suspended against the wall and do not slip down the wall.

   c. Estimate the minimum coefficient of friction that will prevent a person from slipping down the wall. (4)

9. A mass of 4.0 kg is connected to a mass of 6.0 kg by a light string. The string passes vertically over a pulley with negligible friction at the axle. Each mass is supported and then they are released together.

   a. Calculate the acceleration of each of the masses. (4)

   b. Calculate the tension force in the string. (3)

10. A small mass on the end of a string is moving in a vertical circle of radius r in a region of uniform gravitational acceleration g. Deduce:

    a. the minimum speed that the object must have at the top of the circle (4)

    b. the minimum speed that the object must have at the bottom of the circle. (4)

A.3 Work, energy and power

Energy and power

Concepts of energy and work

Energy and work are linked together. When you do work on an object, it gains energy and you lose energy. Energy is a measure of the amount of work done. **The amount of energy transferred is equal to the work done**. This means that the units of energy must be the same as the units of work—joules.

Energy transformations—conservation of energy

In any situation, you must be able to account for the changes in energy. If it is "lost" by one object, it must be gained by another. This is known as the **principle of conservation of energy**. There are several ways of stating this principle:

- Overall the total energy of any closed system must be constant.
- Energy is neither created nor destroyed, it just changes form.
- There is no change in the total energy in the Universe.

Energy types

Kinetic energy	Gravitational potential	Elastic potential energy
Radiant energy	Electrostatic potential	Thermal energy
Nuclear energy	Solar energy	Chemical energy
Electrical energy	Internal energy	Light energy

Equations for the first three types of energy are given below.

Kinetic energy $E_k = \frac{1}{2}mv^2$ where m is the mass (in kg), v is the velocity (in m s^{-1})
$= \frac{p^2}{2m}$ where p is the momentum (in kg m s^{-1}), and m is the mass (in kg)

Gravitational potential energy $\Delta E_p = mg\Delta h$ where m represents mass (in kg), g represents the Earth's gravitational field (10 N kg^{-1}), h represents the height change (in m)

Elastic potential energy $E_H = \frac{1}{2}k\Delta x^2$ where k is the spring constant (in N m^{-1}), Δx is the extension (in m)

Mechanical energy is defined as the sum of kinetic energy, gravitational potential energy and elastic potential energy. In the absence of frictional, resistive forces, the total mechanical energy of a system is conserved.

Power and efficiency

1. Power
Power is defined as the RATE at which energy is transferred. This is the same as the rate at which work is done.

$$\text{Power} = \frac{\text{energy transferred}}{\text{time taken}} \qquad \text{Power} = \frac{\text{work done}}{\text{time taken}} = \frac{\Delta W}{\Delta t}$$

The SI unit for power is the joule per second (J s^{-1}). Another unit for power is the watt (W). 1 W = 1 J s^{-1}.

If something is moving at a constant velocity v against a constant frictional force F, the power P needed is $P = Fv$

2. Efficiency
Depending on the situation, you can categorize the energy transferred (work done) as useful or not useful. In a light bulb, the useful energy is light energy; the "wasted" energy is thermal energy (and non-visible forms of radiant energy).

You define efficiency η as the ratio of useful energy to the total energy transferred:

$$\eta = \frac{E_{output}}{E_{input}} = \frac{P_{output}}{P_{input}}$$

Since this is a ratio it does not have any units.
Often it is expressed as a percentage.

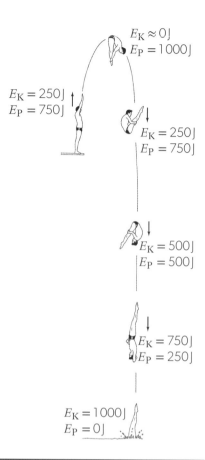

$E_K \approx 0$ J
$E_P = 1000$ J

$E_K = 250$ J
$E_P = 750$ J

$E_K = 250$ J
$E_P = 750$ J

$E_K = 500$ J
$E_P = 500$ J

$E_K = 750$ J
$E_P = 250$ J

$E_K = 1000$ J
$E_P = 0$ J

Worked examples

1. A grasshopper (mass 8 g) uses its hind legs to push for 0.1 s and as a result jumps 1.8 m high. Calculate (i) its take off speed, (ii) the power developed.

   (i) PE gained $= mg\Delta h$

   KE at start $= \frac{1}{2}mv^2$

   $\frac{1}{2}mv^2 = mg\Delta h$
   (conservation of energy)

   $v = \sqrt{2g\Delta h} = \sqrt{2 \times 10 \times 1.8}$
   $= 6$ m s^{-1}

   (ii) Power $= \frac{mg\Delta h}{t}$

   $= \frac{0.008 \times 10 \times 1.8}{0.1}$
   ≈ 1.4 W

2. A 60 W lightbulb has an efficiency of 10%. How much energy is wasted every hour?

   Power wasted = 90% of 60 W
   $= 54$ W

   Energy wasted $= 54 \times 60 \times 60$ J
   $= 194$ kJ

Work

When is work done?

Work is done when a force moves its point of application in the direction of the force. If the object moves at right angles to the direction of the force, then no work has been done.

(1) **before**   **after**

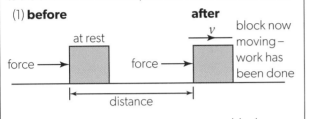

(2) **before**   **after**

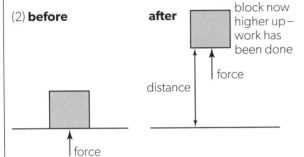

(3) **before**

after

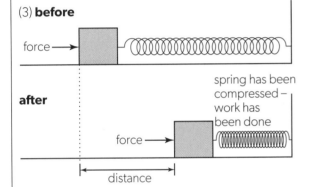

(4) **before**   **after**

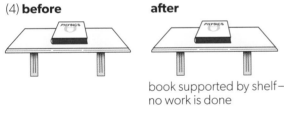

book supported by shelf –
no work is done

(5) **before**   **after**

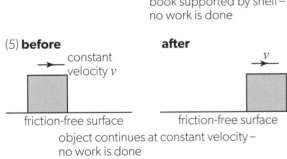

object continues at constant velocity –
no work is done

In these examples, the work done has different results.

- In (1) the force has made the object move faster.
- In (2) the object has been lifted higher in the gravitational field.
- In (3) the spring has been compressed.
- In (4) and (5) NO work is done. Note that even though the object is moving in the last example, there is no force moving along its direction of action so no work is done.

Definition of work

Work is a scalar quantity. Its definition is as follows.

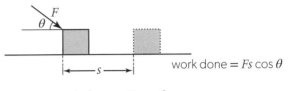

work done $= Fs \cos \theta$

work done $= Fs \cos \theta$

If the force and the displacement are in the same direction, this can be simplified to

work done = force × distance

From this definition, the SI unit for work done is N m. A new unit is defined, called the joule: $1\,J = 1\,N\,m$.

The change in the total energy of a system = work done on the system

Examples

(1) **lifting vertically**

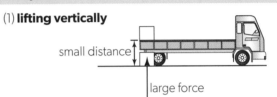

(2) **pushing along a rough slope**

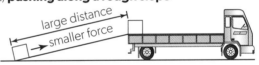

The task in (2) is easier to perform (it involves less force) but overall it takes more work since work has to be done to overcome friction. In each case, the useful work is the same.

If the force doing work is not constant (for example, when a spring is compressed), then graphical techniques can be used.

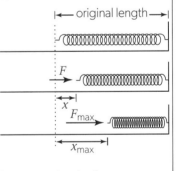

The total work done is the area under the force–displacement graph.

Useful equations for the work done include:

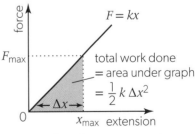

- work done when lifting something vertically $= mg\Delta h$

  where m represents mass (in kg), g represents the Earth's gravitational field strength ($10\,N\,kg^{-1}$) and Δh represents the height change (in m)

- work done in compressing or extending a spring

  $= \dfrac{1}{2}k\Delta x^2$

Energy and power generation—Sankey diagrams

Energy conversions

The production of electrical power around the world is achieved using a variety of different systems, often starting with the release of thermal energy from a fuel. In principle, thermal energy can be completely converted to work in a single process, but the continuous conversion of this energy into work implies the use of machines that are continuously repeating their actions in a fixed cycle. Any cyclical process must involve the transfer of some energy from the system to the surroundings that is no longer available to perform useful work. This unavailable energy is known as **degraded energy**, in accordance with the principle of the second law of thermodynamics (see page 73).

Energy conversions are represented using **Sankey diagrams**. An arrow (drawn from left to right) represents the energy changes taking place. The width of the arrow represents the power or energy involved at a given stage. Created or degraded energy is shown with an arrow up or down.

Note that Sankey diagrams are to scale. The width of the useful electrical output in the diagram on the right is 2.0 mm compared with 12.0 mm for the width of the total energy from the fuel. This represents an overall efficiency of 16.7%.

Electrical power production

In all electrical power stations the process is essentially the same. A fuel is used to release thermal energy. This thermal energy is used to boil water to make steam. The steam is used to turn turbines and the motion of the turbines is used to generate electrical energy.

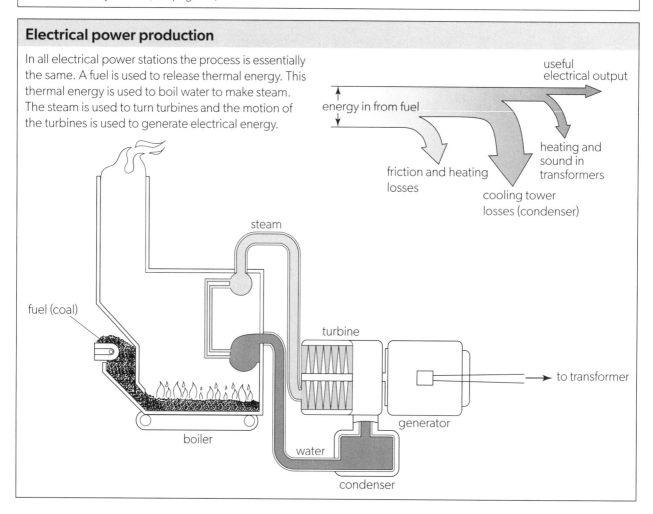

Energy sources

Energy density of fuel sources

Energy density is defined as the energy liberated per unit volume of fuel consumed. The unit is $J\,m^{-3}$. Specific energy is defined as the energy liberated per unit mass of the fuel consumed. The unit is $J\,kg^{-1}$.

$$\text{specific energy} = \frac{\text{energy released from fuel}}{\text{mass of fuel consumed}}$$

Comparison of energy sources

Fuel	Renewable?	CO_2 emission?	Energy density $(MJ\,m^{-3})$	Advantages	Disadvantages
Coil	No	Yes	23 000	• High specific energy and energy density • Relatively easy to transport • Cheap when compared to other sources. • Power stations can be located anywhere with good transport links and water availability	• Combustion products can produce pollution, notably acid raid. • Combustion products contain greenhouse gases. • Extraction of fossil fuels can damage the environment. • Non-renewable. • Large scale energy production requires large amounts of fuel.
Oil	No	Yes	36 500		
Gas	No	Yes	37		
Solar power (photovoltaic)	Yes	No	n/a	• Very "clean" production – no harmful chemical by-products. • Renewable source of energy. • Source of energy is free • Low maintenance cost	• Can only be utilized during the day. • High initial cost. • Source of energy is unreliable – dependent of weather and location. • A very large area is needed for a significant amount of power.
Hydro—water stored in dams	Yes	No	n/a	• Very "clean" production – no harmful chemical by-products. • Renewable source of energy. • Source of energy is free. • **Pumped storage** is one of the few large-scale methods of storing energy.	• Can only be utilized in particular areas. • Construction of dams will involve land being submerged under water. • **Pumped storage** is not a source of new electrical energy but a method of energy storage.
Tidal	Yes	No	n/a		
Pumped storage	n/a	No	n/a		
Wind power	Yes	No	n/a	• Very "clean" production – no harmful chemical by-products. • Renewable source of energy. • Source of energy is free.	• Source of energy is unreliable – could be a day without wind. • A very large area is needed for a significant amount of power. • Some consider wind turbines to spoil the countryside. May harm wildlife. • Can be noisy. • Best positions for wind generators are often far from centres of population.
Wave power	Yes	No	n/a	• Very "clean" production – no harmful chemical by-products. • Renewable source of energy. • Source of energy is free.	• Source of energy is unreliable – could be few waves. • A very large area is needed for a significant amount of power. • Can only be located offshore or by the coast.
Geothermal	Yes	No	n/a	• Very "clean" production – no harmful chemical by-products. • Renewable source of energy. • Source of energy is free.	• Can only be utilized in particular areas.
Nuclear (uranium)	No	No	1.5×10^{12}	• Hydrogen as fuel widely available effectively renewable. • Few harmful radioactive by-products (unlike fission)	• Technical challenges (particularly containment of plasma) of building large-scale fusion reactors have not yet been solved.

End of topic questions—A.3 Work, energy and power

1. A force F acts at 30° to the horizontal and pulls a mass of 12 kg along a horizontal rough surface at a constant velocity of 20 cm s⁻¹, as shown below.

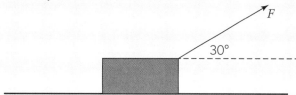

The magnitude of F is 45 N.

a. Calculate the value of the frictional force acting on the block. (2)

b. Calculate the work done by F in one minute. (2)

c. F is doing work on the block, but it is not gaining any kinetic energy or any gravitational potential energy. Explain how conservation of energy applies to this situation. (2)

d. While the block is in motion, F is changed to become horizontal, but its magnitude stays the same. Suggest the subsequent motion of the block. (4)

2. A tennis ball with a mass of 50 g is dropped from a height of 3.0 m onto a horizontal floor. After bouncing off the floor it reaches a maximum height of 2.2 m above the floor.

a. Calculate:
   i. the speed of the tennis ball just before it hits the floor (2)
   ii. the speed of the tennis ball just after it leaves the floor (2)
   iii. the energy lost by in the ball in the collision with the floor. (2)

b. Explain how the law of the conservation of energy applies to this situation if energy has been lost. (2)

3. A spring has a natural length of 20.0 cm and negligible mass. Its spring constant is 1.25 N cm⁻¹. The spring obeys Hooke's law when stretched and when compressed.

a. The spring is horizonal with its left end attached to a rigid support. A 500 g mass is attached to the free end of the spring and can move on a friction free horizontal surface. The mass is pulled 4.0 cm to the right and held in position.
   i. Calculate the force on the mass from the spring when held in position. (2)
   ii. Calculate the elastic energy stored in the spring when held in position. (3)
   iii. The mass is released. Calculate the speed of the mass when it returns to its original position. (3)

b. The spring is turned to be **vertical** with the top end attached to a rigid support. The 500 g mass is attached to the bottom of the spring causing it to extend. The mass is at rest in its equilibrium position.
   i. Calculate the extension of the spring. (2)
   ii. Calculate the elastic energy stored in the spring. (2)

c. The mass is now pulled down a further 4 cm from the equilibrium position and held in position.
   i. State the total extension of the spring in this new position. (1)
   ii. Calculate the total elastic energy stored in the spring (2)

The mass is released and accelerates up and reaches the equilibrium position with a vertical speed.

   iii. Calculate the increase in gravitational potential energy gained by the mass as it moves to the equilibrium position. (3)
   iv. Calculate the increase in kinetic energy gained by the mass as it moves to the equilibrium position. (3)
   v. Calculate the speed of the mass when it returns to its original position. (3)

d. Discuss your answers to (a)(iii) and (c)(v). (2)

4. A petrol car is driving at a constant velocity.

a. Use the data below to estimate the frictional force acting on the car from the air. (6)

Energy density of petrol	45 MJ kg⁻¹
Density of petrol	750 kg m⁻³
Petrol consumption of car	8.0 litres of petrol per 100 km (1 litre = 1 000 cm³)
Efficiency of petrol engine	20%

b. Outline two assumptions you have made in your calculation above. (2)

5. A power station burns coal of energy density 31 MJ kg⁻¹ to generate electrical energy. For every 1 000 kg of coal burned, the following three energy losses occur:

- 13 690 MJ is lost heating up the cooling water.
- 4 650 MJ is lost as a result of radiation and convection from the boiler.
- 1 550 MJ is lost as a result of friction in the generator.

a. Calculate the amount of useful electrical energy generated for every 1 000 kg of coal burned. (3)

b. Show that efficiency of the power station is approximately 30%. (2)

c. Sketch, to scale, a Sankey diagram to represent this process. (3)

In one year, the total electrical energy generated by the power station is 7.8×10^9 kWh. (1 kWh is the energy transferred in one hour by a constant power of 1 kW).

d. Show that 1 kWh is equivalent to 3.6 MJ. (2)

e. Estimate the total mass of coal burned in one year. (3)

The power station supplies approximately 500 000 homes.

f. Estimate the average mass of coal burned each day per household. (3)

A.4 Rigid body mechanics

Translational and rotational motion (1)

Concepts

The complex motion of a rigid body can be analysed as a **combination** of two types of motion: translation and rotation. These types of motion are studied separately in this book.

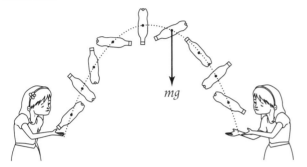

A bottle thrown through the air—the centre of mass of the bottle follows a path as predicted by projectile motion. In addition, the bottle rotates about one (or more) axes.

Translational motion is described using displacements, velocities and linear accelerations; all of these quantities apply to the **centre of mass** of the object. Rotational motion is described using angles (angular displacement), angular velocities and angular accelerations; all of these quantities apply to circular motion about a given axis of rotation.

The concept of angular velocity, ω, has already been introduced with the mechanics of circular motion (see page 20) and is linked to the frequency of rotation by the following formula:

$$\omega = 2\pi f$$

angular velocity   frequency

Translational motion	Rotational motion
Every particle in the object has the same instantaneous velocity	Every particle in the object moves in a circle around the same axis of rotation
Displacement, s, measured in m	Angular displacement, θ, measured in radians (rad)
Velocity, v, is the rate of change of displacement measured in m s^{-1} $$v = \frac{ds}{dt}$$	Angular velocity, ω, is the rate of change of angle measured in rad s^{-1}. This also sometimes referred to as angular speed. $$\omega = \frac{d\theta}{dt}$$
Acceleration, a, is the rate of change of velocity measured in m s^{-2} $$a = \frac{dv}{dt}$$	Angular acceleration, α, is the rate of change of angular velocity measured in rad s^{-2} $$\alpha = \frac{d\omega}{dt}$$

▲ Comparison of linear and rotational motion

Equations of uniform angular acceleration

The definitions of average linear velocity and average linear acceleration can be rearranged to derive the constant acceleration equations (page 3). An equivalent rearrangement derives the equations of constant angular acceleration.

Translational motion		Rotational motion	
Displacement	s	Angular displacement	θ
Initial velocity	u	Initial angular velocity	ω_i
Final velocity	v	Final angular velocity	ω_f
Time taken	t	Time taken	t
Acceleration	a	Angular acceleration	α
$v = u + at$		$\omega_f = \omega_i + \alpha t$	
$s = ut + \frac{1}{2}at^2$		$\theta = \omega_i t + \frac{1}{2}\alpha t^2$	
$v^2 = u^2 + 2as$		$\omega_f^2 = \omega_i^2 + 2\alpha\theta$	
$s = \frac{(v+u)t}{2}$		$\theta = \frac{(\omega_f + \omega_i)t}{2}$	

Combined motion

When a block slides down a slope, its motion is only the translation motion of the mass down the slope. The initial PE is converted to translational KE and work done against the frictional force.

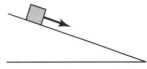

When a cylinder rolls down a slope **without slipping**, its motion is a combination of the translational motion of the mass down the slope **AND** the rotational motion about an axis through its centre. The initial PE is converted into translational KE and rotational KE. The frictional force does no work.

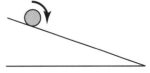

AHL Translational and rotational motion (2)

Example: Bicycle wheel

When a bicycle is moving forward at constant velocity v, the different points on the wheel each have different velocities. The motion of the wheel can be analysed as the addition of the translational and the rotational motion.

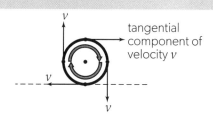

tangential component of velocity v

(a) Translational motion

The bicycle is moving forward at velocity v so the wheel's centre of mass has forward translational motion of velocity v. All points on the wheel's rim have a translational component forward at velocity v.

translational component of velocity v

(b) Rotational motion

The wheel is rotating around the central axis of rotation at a constant angular velocity ω. All points on the wheel's rim have a tangential component of velocity $v \,(= r\omega)$

(c) Combined motion

The motion of the different points on the wheel's rim is the vector addition of the above two components:

Point at top of wheel is moving with instantaneous velocity of $2v$, forward

Point in contact with ground is at rest. Instantaneous velocity is zero

Point at side of wheel is moving with instantaneous velocity of $\sqrt{2}v$, at 45° to the horizontal

AHL Translational and rotational relationships

Relationship between linear and rotational quantities

When an object is just rotating about a fixed axis, and there is no additional translational motion of the object, all the individual particles that make up that object have different instantaneous values of linear displacement, linear velocity and linear acceleration. They do, however, all share the same instantaneous values of angular displacement, angular velocity and angular acceleration. The link between these values involves the distance from the axis of rotation to the particle.

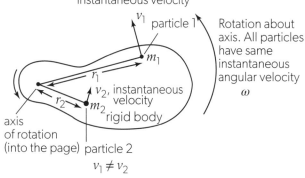

instantaneous velocity

v_1 particle 1

Rotation about axis. All particles have same instantaneous angular velocity ω

v_2, instantaneous velocity

rigid body

axis of rotation (into the page) particle 2

$v_1 \neq v_2$

(a) Displacements

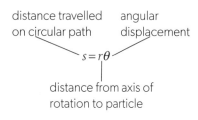

distance travelled on circular path

angular displacement

$s = r\theta$

distance from axis of rotation to particle

(b) Instantaneous velocities

linear instantaneous velocity (along the tangent)

angular velocity

$v = r\omega$

distance from axis of rotation to particle

(c) Accelerations

The total linear acceleration of any particle is made up of two components:

1. The **centripetal acceleration**, a_r, (towards the axis of rotation—see page 19); also known as the **radial acceleration**.

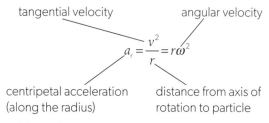

tangential velocity

angular velocity

$$a_r = \frac{v^2}{r} = r\omega^2$$

centripetal acceleration (along the radius)

distance from axis of rotation to particle

2. An additional **tangential acceleration**, a_t, which results from an angular acceleration taking place. If $\alpha = 0$, then $a_t = 0$.

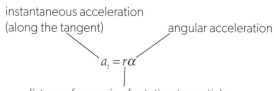

instantaneous acceleration (along the tangent)

angular acceleration

$$a_t = r\alpha$$

distance from axis of rotation to particle

The total acceleration of the particle can be found by vector addition of these two components: $a = r\sqrt{\omega^4 + \alpha^2}$

AHL Translational and rotational equilibrium

The moment of a force: the torque τ

A particle is in equilibrium if its acceleration is zero. This occurs when the vector sum of all the external forces acting on the particle is zero (see page 10). In this situation, all the forces pass through a single point and sum to zero. The forces on real objects do not always pass through the same point and can create a turning effect about a given axis. The turning effect is called the **moment of the force** or the **torque**. The symbol for torque is the Greek letter tau, τ.

The moment or torque τ of a force, F about an axis is defined as the product of the force and the perpendicular distance from the axis of rotation to the line of action of the force.

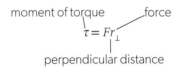

$$\tau = Fr_{\perp}$$

$$\tau = Fr\sin\theta$$

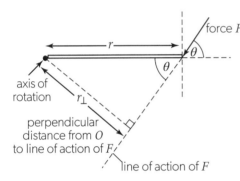

Note:

- The torque and energy are both measured in N m, but only energy can also be expressed as joules.

- The direction of any torque is clockwise or anticlockwise about the axis of rotation that is being considered. For the purposes of calculations, this can be treated as a vector quantity with the direction of the torque vector considered to be along the axis of rotation. In the example above, the torque vector is directed into the paper. If the force F is applied in the opposite direction, the torque vector will be directed out of the paper.

Rotational and translational equilibrium

If a resultant force acts on an object, then it must accelerate (page 9). When there is no resultant force acting on an object, then you know it to be in translational equilibrium (page 10) as this means its acceleration must be zero.

Similarly, if there is a resultant torque acting on an object, then it must have an angular acceleration, α. Thus an object will be in **rotational equilibrium** only if the vector sum of all the external torques acting on the object is zero.

Couples

A **couple** is a system of forces that has no resultant force but which does produce a turning effect. A common example is a pair of equal but anti-parallel forces acting with different points of application. In this situation, the resultant torque is the same about all axes drawn perpendicular to the plane defined by the forces.

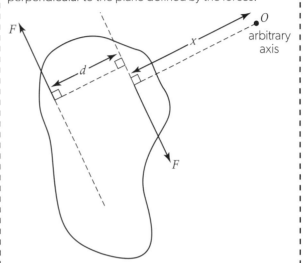

Torque of forces $= F(x + d) - F_x$
$$= F_d \text{ clockwise}$$
This result is independent of position of axis, O

If an object is not moving and not rotating, then it is said to be in **static equilibrium**. This must mean that the object is in both rotational and translational equilibrium. For rotational equilibrium:

$$\alpha = 0 \qquad \therefore \sum \tau = 0$$

In 2D problems (in the x–y plane), it is sufficient to show that there is no torque about any **one** axis perpendicular to the plane being considered (parallel to the z-axis). In 3D problems, three axis directions (x, y and z) would need to be considered.

For translational equilibrium:

$$a = 0 \qquad \therefore \sum F = 0$$

In 2D problems, it is sufficient to show that there is no resultant force in **two** different directions. In 3D problems, three axis directions (x, y and z) would need to be considered.

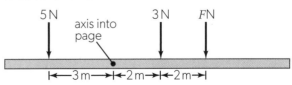

In the example above, for rotational equilibrium:
$$F = 2.25\,\text{N}$$

AHL Equilibrium examples

Centre of gravity

The effect of gravity on all the different parts of the object can be treated as a single force acting at the object's **centre of gravity**.

If an object is of uniform shape and density, the centre of gravity will be in the middle of the object. If the object is not uniform, then finding its position is not trivial—it is possible for an object's centre of gravity to be outside the object. Experimentally, if you suspend an object from a point and it is free to move, then the centre of gravity will always be below the point of suspension.

(a) plank balances if pivot is in middle

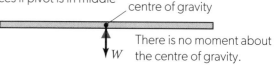

There is no moment about the centre of gravity.

(b) plank rotates clockwise if pivot is to the left

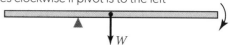

(c) plank rotates anticlockwise if pivot is to the right

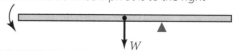

Worked example

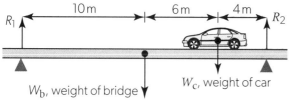

W_b, weight of bridge

W_c, weight of car

When a car goes across a bridge, the forces (on the bridge) are as shown.

Taking moments about right-hand support:
clockwise moment = anticlockwise moment
$$(R_1 \times 20\,\text{m}) = (W_b \times 10\,\text{m}) + (W_c \times 4\,\text{m})$$
Taking moments about left-hand support:
$$(R_2 \times 20\,\text{m}) = (W_b \times 10\,\text{m}) + (W_c \times 16\,\text{m})$$
Also, since bridge is not accelerating:
$$R_1 + R_2 = W_b + W_c$$

When solving problems about rotational equilibrium remember:

• All forces at an axis have zero moment about that axis.

• You do not have to choose the pivot as the axis about which you calculate torques, but it is often the simplest thing to do.

• You need to remember the sense (clockwise or anticlockwise).

• When solving two-dimensional problems it is sufficient to show that an object is in rotational equilibrium about any ONE axis.

• Newton's laws still apply. Often an object is in rotational AND in translational equilibrium. This can provide a simple way of finding an unknown force.

• The weight of an object can be considered to be concentrated at its centre of gravity.

• If the problem only involves three non-parallel forces, the lines of action of all the forces must meet at a single point in order to be in rotational equilibrium.

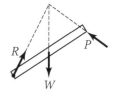

Worked examples

A ladder of length 5.0 m leans against a smooth, frictionless wall at an angle of 30° to the vertical.

a) Explain why the ladder can only stay in place if there is friction between the ground and the ladder.

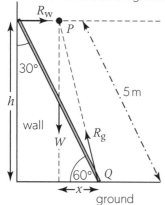

The reaction from the wall, R_w and the ladder's weight meet at point P. For equilibrium the force from the ground, R_g, must also pass through this point (for zero torque about P).
∴ R_g is as shown and has a horizontal component (i.e. friction must be acting)

b) What is the minimum coefficient of static fraction between the ladder and the ground for the ladder to stay in place?

Equilibrium conditions:
$(\uparrow)$
$(\rightarrow)$
$$W = R_v \quad ①$$
moments about Q
$$R_H = R_w \quad ②$$
$$R_w h = W x \quad ③$$
$$F_f \leq \mu_s R$$
$$\therefore R_H \leq \mu_s R_v$$

using ① & ② $\Rightarrow \mu_s \geq \dfrac{R_w}{W}$

③ $\Rightarrow \mu_s \geq \dfrac{x}{h} = \dfrac{2.5\cos 60}{5.0\sin 60}$

$$\therefore \mu_s \geq 0.29$$

AHL Moment of inertia

Newton's second law—definition of moment of inertia

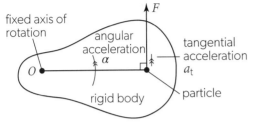

▲ Newton's second law as applied to one particle in a rigid body

Newton's second law applies to every particle that makes up a large object and must also apply if the object is undergoing rotational motion. In the diagram above, the object is made up of lots of small particles each with a mass m. F is the **tangential component** of the resultant force that acts **on one particle**. The other component, the radial component, cannot produce angular acceleration so it is not included. For this particle you can apply Newton's second law:

$$F = ma_t = mr\alpha$$

so torque $\tau = (mr\alpha)r = mr^2\alpha$

Similar equations can be created for all the particles that make up the object and summed together:

$$\sum \tau = \sum mr^2\alpha$$

or $\sum \tau = \alpha \sum mr^2$ (1)

Note that:

- Newton's third law applies and, when summing up all the torques, the internal torques (which result from the internal forces between particles) must sum to zero. Only the external torques are left.

- Every particle in the object has the same angular acceleration, α.

The moment of inertial, I, of an object about a particular axis is defined by the summation below:

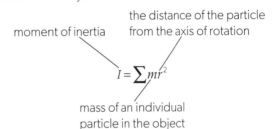

$$I = \sum mr^2$$

Note that moment of inertia, I, is:

- a scalar quantity
- measured in kg m^2 (not kg m^{-2})
- dependent on:
  - o the mass of the object
  - o the way this mass is distributed
  - o the axis of rotation being considered.

Using this definition, equation (1) becomes:

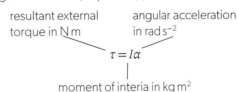

$$\tau = I\alpha$$

This is Newton's second law for rotational motion and can be compared with $F = ma$.

Moments of inertia for different objects

Equations for moments of inertia in different situations do not need to be memorized.

Object	Axis of rotation	Moment of inertia	Object	Axis of rotation	Moment of inertia
thin ring (simple wheel)	through centre, perpendicular to plane	mr^2	sphere	through centre	$\frac{2}{5}mr^2$
thin ring	through a diameter	$\frac{1}{2}mr^2$			
disc and cylinder (solid flywheel)	through centre, perpendicular to plane	$\frac{1}{2}mr^2$	rectangular lamina	through the centre of mass, perpendicular to the plane of the lamina	$m\left(\frac{l^2+h^2}{12}\right)$
thin rod, length d	through centre, perpendicular to rod	$\frac{1}{12}md^2$			

AHL Rotational dynamics

Energy of rotational motion

Energy considerations often provide simple solutions to complicated problems. When a torque acts on an object, work is done. In the absence of any resistive torque, the work done on the object will be stored as rotational kinetic energy.

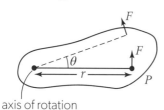

▲ Calculation of work done by a torque

In the situation above, a force F is applied and the object rotates. As a result, an angular displacement of θ occurs. The work done, W, is calculated as shown below:

$$W = F \times (\text{distance along arc}) = F \times r\theta = \tau\theta$$

Using $\tau = I\alpha$ you know that $W = I\alpha\theta$

You can apply the constant angular acceleration equation to substitute for $\alpha\theta$:

$$\omega_f^2 = \omega_i^2 + 2\alpha\theta$$

$$\therefore W = I\left(\frac{\omega_f^2}{2} - \frac{\omega_i^2}{2}\right) = \frac{1}{2}I\omega_f^2 - \frac{1}{2}I\omega_i^2$$

This means that you have an equation for rotational KE:

$$E_k = \frac{1}{2}I\omega^2$$

work done by the torque acting on object = change in rotational KE of object

The total KE is equal to the sum of translational KE and the rotational KE:

total KE = translational KE + rotational KE

$$\text{total KE} = \frac{1}{2}mv^2 + \frac{1}{2}I\omega^2$$

Angular momentum

For a single particle
The linear momentum of a particle of mass m which has a tangential speed v is $p = mv$.

The angular momentum, L, is defined as the moment of the linear momentum about the axis of rotation

angular momentum, $L = (mv)r = (mr\omega)r = (mr^2)\omega$

For a larger object
The angular momentum L of an object about an axis of rotation is defined as

angular momentum, $L = \sum(mr^2)\omega$

$$L = I\omega$$

Note that total angular momentum, L, is:

- a vector (in the same way that a torque is considered to be a vector for calculations)

- measured in $kg\,m^2\,s^{-1}$ or $N\,m\,s$

- dependent on all rotations taking place. For example, the total angular momentum of a planet orbiting a star would involve:

  o the spinning of the planet about an axis through the planet's centre of mass

  o the orbital angular momentum about an axis through the star.

Conservation of angular momentum

Newton's laws can be applied to linear motion to derive:

- the concept of the impulse of a force

- the relationship between impulse and change in momentum

- the law of conservation of linear momentum.

In exactly the same way, Newton's laws can be applied to angular situations to derive the following.

- The concept of **angular impulse**:

  Angular impulse is the product of torque and the time for which the torque acts: angular impulse $= \tau\Delta t$

  If the torque varies with time, then the total angular impulse given to an object can be estimated from the area under the graph showing the variation of torque with time. This is analogous to estimating the total impulse given to an object as a result of a varying force (see page 16).

- The relationship between angular impulse and change in angular momentum:

  angular impulse applied to an object = change of angular momentum experienced by the object

- The law of conservation of angular momentum:

  The total angular momentum of a system remains constant provided no resultant external torque acts.

A skater spinning on a vertical axis down their body can reduce their moment of inertia by drawing in their arms. This allows their mass to be redistributed so that the mass of the arms is no longer at a significant distance from the axis of rotation, which thus reduces $\sum mr^2$.

AHL Solving rotational problems

Summary comparison of equations of linear and rotational motion

Every equation for linear motion has a corresponding angular equivalent.

	Linear motion	Rotational motion
Physics principles	A resultant external force on a point object causes acceleration. The value of the acceleration is determined by the mass and the resultant force.	A resultant external torque on an extended object causes rotational acceleration. The value of the angular acceleration is determined by the moment of inertia and the resultant torque.
Newton's second law	$F = ma$	$\tau = I\alpha$
Work done	$W = Fs$	$W = \tau\theta$
Kinetic energy	$E_k = \dfrac{1}{2}mv^2$	$E_k = \dfrac{1}{2}I\omega^2$
Momentum	$p = mv$	$L = I\omega$
Conservation of momentum	The total linear momentum of a system remains constant provided no resultant external force acts.	The total angular momentum of a system remains constant provided no resultant external torque acts.
Symbols used	Resultant force F Mass m Acceleration a Displacement s Velocity v Linear momentum p	Resultant torque τ Moment of inertia I Angular acceleration α Angular displacement θ Angular velocity ω Angular momentum L

Problem solving and graphical work

When analysing any rotational situation, the simplest approach is to imagine the equivalent linear situation and use the appropriate equivalent relationships.

a) Graph of angular displacement vs time

This graph is equivalent to a graph of linear displacement vs time. In the linear situation, the area under the graph does not represent any useful quantity and the gradient of the line at any instant is equal to the instantaneous velocity (see page 2). **Thus the gradient of an angular displacement vs time graph gives the instantaneous angular velocity.**

b) Graph of angular velocity vs time

This graph is equivalent to a graph of linear velocity vs time. In the linear situation, the area under the graph represents the distance moved and the

gradient of the line at any instant is equal to the instantaneous acceleration (see page 2). **Thus the area under an angular velocity vs time graph gives the total angular displacement and the gradient of an angular velocity vs time graph gives the instantaneous angular acceleration.**

c) Graph of torque vs time

This graph is equivalent to a graph of force vs time. In the linear situation, the area under the graph represents the total impulse given to the object which is equal to the change of momentum of the object (see page 16). **Thus the area under the torque vs time graph represents the total angular impulse given to the object, which is equal to the change of angular momentum.**

Worked examples

A fly wheel has a moment of inertial of $1.2\,\text{kg m}^{-2}$ and is rotating at a constant $9.5\,\text{rad s}^{-1}$. A second stationary fly wheel has a moment of inertia of $1.5\,\text{kg m}^{-2}$. The two fly wheels are coupled together with the same axis of rotation. Calculate:

a) the angular velocity of the combination

b) the energy lost during the coupling.

a) Conservation of angular momentum:

$1.2 \times 9.5 = (1.2 + 1.5) \times \omega_f \therefore \omega_f = 4.2\,\text{rad s}^{-1}$.

b) Energy lost $= 0.5 \times 1.2 \times 9.5^2 - 0.5 \times 2.7 \times 4.2^2 = 30.1\,\text{J}$

End of topic questions—A.4 Rigid body mechanics

1. A sphere of mass m and radius r rolls, without slipping, from rest down an inclined plane. The moment of inertia for the sphere is $\frac{2}{5}mr^2$. When it reaches the base of the plane, it has fallen a vertical distance h. Show that the speed of the sphere, v, when it arrives at the base of the incline is given by

$$v = \sqrt{\frac{10gh}{7}}$$

   (4)

2. A flywheel of moment of inertia $0.75\,\text{kg}\,\text{m}^2$ is accelerated uniformly from rest to an angular speed of $8.2\,\text{rad}\,\text{s}^{-1}$ in $6.5\,\text{s}$.
   a. Calculate the resultant torque acting on the flywheel during this time. (2)
   b. Calculate the rotational kinetic energy of the flywheel when it rotates at $8.2\,\text{rad}\,\text{s}^{-1}$.
   c. The radius of the flywheel is $15\,\text{cm}$. A breaking force is applied on the circumference and brings it to rest from an angular speed of $8.2\,\text{rad}\,\text{s}^{-1}$ in exactly 2 revolutions. Calculate the value of the breaking force. (2)

3. The angular speed of a car engine is increased uniformly from $120\,\text{rad}\,\text{s}^{-1}$ to $400\,\text{rad}\,\text{s}^{-1}$ in $14\,\text{s}$. Calculate:
   a. the angular acceleration (2)
   b. the angular displacement during this time. (2)

4. A car has wheels of radius $0.35\,\text{m}$ and is travelling at $31\,\text{m}\,\text{s}^{-1}$ in a straight line.
   a. Calculate the angular speed of the wheels about the axle. (2)
   b. Analyse the variation in velocity of a point on the circumference of the wheel. (4)
   c. Sketch the path followed by a point on the rim of the wheel. (3)
   The car is brought to rest and the wheels complete 40 revolutions during this time.
   d. Calculate the angular acceleration of the wheels. (2)
   e. Calculate the distance covered during braking. (2)

5. A rotating wheel in the form of solid disc is slowed down by a frictional torque of $12\,\text{N}\,\text{m}$ which acts on the axle. It has a mass of $80\,\text{kg}$, radius $0.50\,\text{m}$ and is initially rotating at $200\,\text{rad}\,\text{s}^{-1}$. The moment of inertia I of a solid disc of mass m and radius r rotating around an axis through its centre is given by $I = \frac{1}{2}mr^2$. Calculate:
   a. the time taken before the wheel stops (3)
   b. the angular displacement during stopping. (3)

6. An engine shaft is rotating at $400\,\text{rad}\,\text{s}^{-1}$ and is transmitting a power of $25\,\text{kW}$. Calculate the magnitude of the torque that is acting on the shaft. (2)

7. A wheel with all its mass distributed at the rim rotates around an axis through its centre. The angular speed is increased from $40\,\text{rad}\,\text{s}^{-1}$ to $100\,\text{rad}\,\text{s}^{-1}$ in $5.0\,\text{s}$. The mass of the wheel is $10\,\text{kg}$ and its radius is $45\,\text{cm}$. Calculate:
   a. the work done by the torque acting on the wheel (3)
   b. the average power applied to the wheel during this time. (2)

8. A horizontal disc is rotating about a vertical axis through its centre with a uniform rotational frequency of 1.0 revolution per second. A $8.0\,\text{g}$ mass is dropped onto the disc and sticks at a distance of $50\,\text{mm}$ from the centre. The speed changes to 0.80 revolutions per second. Calculate the moment of inertia of the disc. (3)

9. A torque of $30\,\text{N}\,\text{m}$ acts on a wheel with moment of inertia $600\,\text{kg}\,\text{m}^2$. The wheel starts at rest. Calculate:
   a. the angular acceleration produced (2)
   b. the speed at which a point on the rim is moving after one minute. The mass of the wheel is $200\,\text{kg}$. (3)

10. The Earth–Moon system produces tides in the oceans. As a result of the relative movement of water, friction exists between the oceans and Earth. This provides a torque that acts to reduce the Earth's spin on its own axis.
   Deduce the effect that this torque will have on:
   a. the Earth's angular momentum on its own axis (2)
   b. the total angular momentum of the Earth–Moon system (2)
   c. the Moon's angular momentum about the Earth (2)
   d. the separation of the Earth and the Moon. (2)

A.5 Galilean and special relativity

Reference frames

Observers and frames of reference

The proper treatment of large velocities involves an understanding of Einstein's theory of relativity and this means thinking about space and time in a completely different way. The reasons for this change are developed in the following pages, but they are surprisingly simple. They logically follow from two straightforward assumptions. To see why this is the case, you first need to consider what is meant by an object in motion.

A person sitting in a chair will probably think that they are at rest. Indeed from their point of view this must be true, but this is not the only way of viewing the situation. The Earth is in orbit around the Sun, so from the Sun's point of view the person sitting in the chair must be in motion. This example shows that an object's motion (or lack of it) depends on the observer.

The calculation of relative velocity like all the mechanics in this book so far, assumes that the velocities are small enough to be able to apply Newton's laws to different frames of reference.

 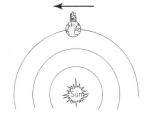

Is this person at rest...   ...or moving at great velocity?

Galilean transformations

Measurements in one frame of reference can be used to work out the measurements that would be recorded in another. The equations that do this without taking the theory of relativity into consideration are called **Galilean transformations**.

The simplest situation is two frames of reference (S and S') with frame (S') moving past frame (S) as shown below.

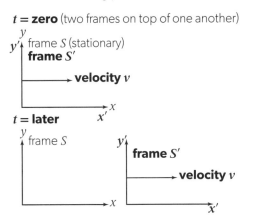

Each frame of reference can record the position and time of an event. Since the relative motion is along the x-axis, most measurements will be the same:

$$y' = y;\ z' = z;\ t' = t$$

If an event is stationary according to one frame, it will be moving according to the other frame—the frames will record different values for the x measurement. The transformation between the two is given by

$$x' = x - vt$$

You can use these equations to formalize the calculation of velocities. The frames will agree on any velocity measured in the y or z direction, but they will disagree on a velocity in the x-direction. Mathematically,

$$u' = u - v$$

For example, if the moving frame is going at $4\,\mathrm{m\,s^{-1}}$, then an object moving in the same direction at a velocity of $15\,\mathrm{m\,s^{-1}}$ as recorded in the stationary frame will be measured as travelling at $11\,\mathrm{m\,s^{-1}}$ in the moving frame.

Newton's three laws of motion describe how an object's motion is affected. An assumption (Newton's postulates) underlying these laws is that the time interval between two events is the same for all observers. Time is the same for all frames and the separation between events will also be the same in all frames. As a result, the same physical laws will apply in all frames.

Failure of Galilean transformation equations

Experimental evidence shows that the speed of light has the same value for all observers. This means that the Galilean transformations equations cannot work for light.

In 1964, an experiment at the European Centre for Nuclear Research (CERN) measured the speed of gamma-ray photons that had been produced by particles moving close to the speed of light and found these photons also to be moving at the speed of light. This is consistent with the speed of light being independent of the speed of its source, to a high degree of accuracy.

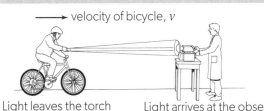

velocity of bicycle, v

Light leaves the torch at velocity c with respect to the person on the bicycle.

Light arrives at the observer at velocity c (not $v + c$).

AHL Special relativity

Maxwell and the constancy of the speed of light

In 1864, James Clerk Maxwell presented a new theory at the Royal Society in London. His ideas were encapsulated in a mathematical form that elegantly expressed not only what was known at the time about the magnetic field B and the electric field E, but it also proposed a unifying link between the two—electromagnetism. The "rules" of electromagnetic interactions are summarized in four equations known as Maxwell's equations. These equations predict the nature of electromagnetic waves.

Most people know that light is an electromagnetic wave, but it is quite hard to understand what this actually means. A physical wave involves the oscillation of matter, whereas an electromagnetic wave involves the oscillation of electric and magnetic fields. The diagram below attempts to show this.

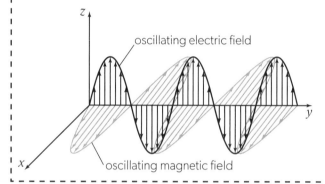

The changing electric and magnetic fields move through space—the technical way of saying this is that the fields **propagate** through space. The physics of how these fields propagate allows the speed of all electromagnetic waves (including light) to be predicted. It turns out that this can be done in terms of the electric and magnetic constants of the medium through which they travel.

$$c = \sqrt{\frac{1}{\varepsilon_0 \mu_0}}$$

This equation does not need to be understood in detail. The only important idea is that the speed of light is **independent** of the velocity of the source of the light. In other words, a prediction from Maxwell's equations is that the speed of light in a vacuum has the same value for all observers.

This prediction of the constancy of the speed of light highlights an inconsistency that cannot be reconciled with Newtonian mechanics (where the resultant speed of light would be equal to the addition of the relative speed of the source and the relative speed of light as measured by the source). Einstein's analysis forced long-held assumptions about the independence of space and time to be rejected.

Postulates of special relativity

The special theory of relativity is based on two fundamental assumptions or **postulates**. If either of these postulates could be shown to be wrong, then the theory of relativity would be wrong. When discussing relativity you need to be even more precise than usually with the use of technical terms.

One important technical phrase is an **inertial frame of reference**. This means a frame of reference in which the laws of inertia (Newton's laws) apply. Newton's laws do not apply in accelerating frames of reference so an inertial frame is a frame that is either stationary or moving with constant velocity.

An important idea to grasp is that there is no fundamental difference between being stationary and moving at constant velocity. Newton's laws link forces and accelerations. If there is no resultant force on an object, then its acceleration will be zero. This could mean that the object is at **rest** or it could mean that the object is **moving at constant velocity**.

The two postulates of special relativity are:

- the speed of light in a vacuum is the same (constant) for all inertial observers
- the laws of physics are the same for all inertial observers.

The first postulate leads on from Maxwell's equations and can be experimentally verified. The second postulate seems completely reasonable—particularly since Newton's laws do not differentiate between being at rest and moving at constant velocity. If both are accepted as being true, then you need to start thinking about space and time in a completely different way. If in doubt, you need to return to these two postulates.

Simultaneity

Simultaneity

One example of how the postulates of relativity disrupt our everyday understanding of the world around us is the concept of simultaneity. If two events happen together you say that they are simultaneous. You would normally expect that if two events are **simultaneous** to one observer, then they should be simultaneous to all observers—but this is not the case! A simple way to demonstrate this is to consider an experimenter in a train.

The experimenter is positioned **exactly** in the middle of a carriage that is moving at constant velocity. She sends out two pulses of light towards the ends of the train. Mounted at the ends are mirrors that reflect the pulses back towards the observer. As far as the experimenter is concerned, the whole carriage is at rest. Since she is in the middle, the experimenter will know that:

- the pulses were sent out simultaneously
- the pulses hit the mirrors simultaneously
- the pulses returned simultaneously.

pulses leave together

pulses arrive at mirrors together

pulses return together

The situation will seem very different if watched by a stationary observer (on the platform). This observer knows that light must travel at constant speed—both beams are travelling at the same speed as far as he is concerned, so they must hit the mirrors at different times. The left-hand end of the carriage is moving

towards the beam and the right hand end is moving away. This means that the reflection will happen on the left-hand end first.

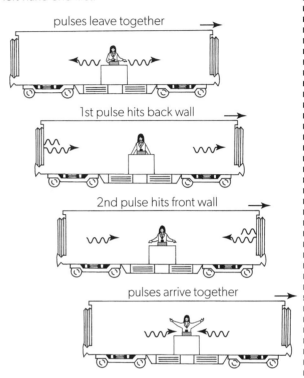

pulses leave together

1st pulse hits back wall

2nd pulse hits front wall

pulses arrive together

Interestingly, the observer on the platform does see the beams arriving back at the same time. The observer on the platform will know that:

- the pulses were sent out simultaneously
- the left-hand pulse hit the mirror before the right-hand pulse
- the pulses returned simultaneously.

In general, simultaneous events that take place at the same point in space will be simultaneous to all observers whereas events that take place at different points in space can be simultaneous to one observer but not simultaneous to another!

Do not dismiss these ideas because the experiment seems too fanciful to be tried out. The use of a pulse of light allowed us to rely on the first postulate. This conclusion is valid whatever event is considered.

Lorentz transformations (1)

Lorentz factor

The formulas for special relativity all involve a factor that depends on the relative velocity between different observers, v.

The Lorentz factor, γ, is defined as: $\gamma = \dfrac{1}{\sqrt{1 - \dfrac{v^2}{c^2}}}$.

At low velocities, the Lorentz factor is approximately equal to one—relativistic effects are negligible. It approaches infinity near the speed of light.

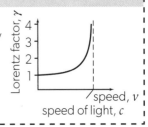

AHL Lorentz transformations (2)

Lorentz transformations

An observer defines a frame of reference and different **events** can be characterized by different coordinates according to the observer's measurements of space and time. In a frame S, an event will be associated with a given position (x, y and z coordinates) and take place at a given time (t). Observers in relative uniform motion disagree on the numerical values for these coordinates.

Clock in frame S and clock in frame S' are synchronized to $t = t' =$ zero when frames coincide.

(two frames on top of one another)

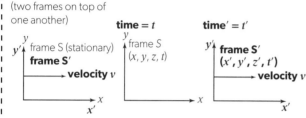

The Galilean transformations equations allow you to calculate what an observer in a second frame will record if you know the values in one frame but assume that the measurement of time is the same in both frames. Einstein showed that this is incorrect.

Because the frames were synchronized, the observers agree on the measurements of y and z. To switch between the other measurements made by different observers you need to use the Lorentz transformations.

$x' = \gamma(x - vt)$; $\Delta x' = \gamma(\Delta x - v\Delta t)$;

$t' = \gamma\left(t - \dfrac{vx}{c^2}\right)$; $\Delta t' = \gamma\left(\Delta t - \dfrac{v\Delta x}{c^2}\right)$

These all involve the Lorentz factor, γ, as defined above. The derivation of these equations is not required.

The reverse transformations also apply.

$x = \gamma(x' + vt')$; $t = \gamma\left(t' + \dfrac{vx'}{c^2}\right)$

The relative velocity of frame S (with respect to frame S') is in the opposite direction.

Worked example

You can apply the Lorentz transformation equations to the situation shown on page 37. Suppose the experiment on the train measures the carriage to be 50.0 m long and the observer on the platform measures the speed of the train to be 2.7×10^8 m s^{-1} (0.90c) to the right. In this situation, you know that the times (t) and locations (x) are measured according to the experimenter on the train (frame S) and that the experimenter on the platform is in frame S'.

1. According to the experimenter on the train (frame S), time taken for each pulse to reach mirror at end of carriage is $\Delta t = \dfrac{25.0}{3.0 \times 10^8} = 8.33 \times 10^{-8}$ s

   Total time taken for each pulse to complete the round journey to the experimenter is:

   $$\Delta t_{total} = \dfrac{50.0}{\left(3.0 \times 10^8\right)} = 1.67 \times 10^{-7}\,\text{s}$$

2. According to the experimenter on the platform (frame S'),

   $$\gamma = \dfrac{1}{\sqrt{1 - \dfrac{v^2}{c^2}}} = \dfrac{1}{\sqrt{1 - \dfrac{(0.9c)^2}{c^2}}} = \dfrac{1}{\sqrt{1 - 0.81}} = \dfrac{1}{\sqrt{0.19}} = 2.29$$

   Time taken for left-hand (LH) pulse to reach mirror at end of carriage is $\Delta t'_{(LH\,pulse)} = \gamma\left(\Delta t - \dfrac{v\Delta x}{c^2}\right)$

   where $\Delta t = 8.33 \times 10^{-8}$ s, $v = -2.7 \times 10^8$ m s^{-1} (relative velocity of platform is moving to the left) and $\Delta x = -25.0$ m (pulse moving to left)

   $$\Delta t'_{(LH\,probe)} = 2.29\left(8.33 \times 10^{-8} - \dfrac{\left(-2.7 \times 10^8\right) \times (-25.0)}{\left(3.0 \times 10^8\right)^2}\right)$$

$= 1.91 \times 10^{-7} - 1.72 \times 10^{-7} = 1.9 \times 10^{-8}$ s

Time taken for right-hand (RH) pulse to reach mirror at end of carriage is $\Delta t'_{(RH\,probe)} = \gamma\left(\Delta t - \dfrac{v\Delta x}{c^2}\right)$

$$= 2.29\left(8.33 \times 10^{-8} - \dfrac{\left(-2.7 \times 10^8\right) \times 25.0}{\left(3.0 \times 10^8\right)^2}\right)$$

$= 1.91 \times 10^{-7} + 1.72 \times 10^{-7} = 3.63 \times 10^{-7}$ s

Note that the time taken by each pulse is different—they do not arrive simultaneously according to the experimenter on the platform.

The return time for the LH pulse is the same as the time taken for the RH pulse to reach the mirror (in each case, $\Delta x = 25.0$ m and $\Delta t = 8.33 \times 10^{-8}$ s)

So total time taken for LH pulse to return to centre of carriage is:

total $\Delta t'_{(LH\,probe)} = 1.9 \times 10^{-8} + 3.63 \times 10^{-7}$
$= 3.82 \times 10^{-7}$ s

This is the same as the total time taken for the RH pulse, so both experimenters observe the return of the pulses to be simultaneous.

Check: For frame S', the total time taken for the round trip is 3.82×10^{-7} s. The Lorentz transformation can also be applied to the pulse's journey: Δx (in frame S) = 0 as the pulse returns to its starting position.

total $\Delta t'_{(either\,pulse)} = \gamma\left(\Delta t - \dfrac{v\Delta x}{c^2}\right) = \gamma\Delta t$

$= 2.29 \times 1.67 \times 10^{-7} = 3.82 \times 10^{-7}$ s

AHL Velocity addition

Velocity addition

When two observers measure each other's velocity, they will always agree on the value. However, calculation of relative velocity is not normally straightforward. For example, an observer might see two objects approaching one another, as shown below.

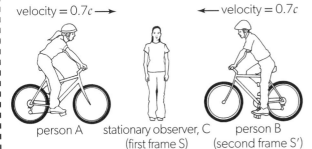

velocity = 0.7c →   ← velocity = 0.7c

person A   stationary observer, C   person B
(first frame S)   (second frame S')

If each object has a relative velocity of 0.7c, the Galilean transformations would predict that the relative velocity between the two objects would be 1.4c. This cannot be the case as the Lorentz factor can only be worked out for objects travelling at less than the speed of light.

The situation considered is one frame moving relative to another frame at velocity v.

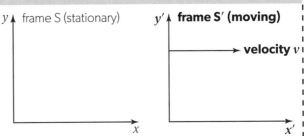

Application of the Lorentz transformation gives the equation used to move between frames:

$$u' = \frac{u - v}{1 - \dfrac{uv}{c^2}}$$

u' is the velocity under consideration in the x-direction as measured in the second frame, S'

u is the velocity under consideration in the x-direction as measured in the first frame, S

v is the velocity of the second frame, S', as measured in the first frame, S

In each of these cases, a positive velocity means motion along the positive x-direction. If something is moving in the negative x-direction, then a negative velocity should be substituted into the equation.

Worked example

In the example above, two objects approach each other with 70% of the speed of light. So u' is person A's velocity as measured in person B's frame of reference.

u' = relative velocity of approach—to be calculated

$u = 0.7c$

$v = -0.7c$

$u' = \dfrac{1.4c}{(1 + 0.49)}$ (note the sign in the brackets)

$= \dfrac{1.4c}{1.49c} = 0.94c$

Comparison with Galilean equation

The top line of the relativistic addition of velocities equation can be compared with the Galilean equation for the calculation of relative velocities.

$$u' = u - v$$

At low values of v these two equations give the same value. The Galilean equation starts to fail at high velocities only.

At high velocities, the Galilean equation can give answers of greater than c, while the relativistic one always gives a relative velocity that is less than the speed of light.

AHL Invariant quantities

Spacetime interval

Relativity has shown that our Newtonian ideas of space and time are incorrect. Two inertial observers will generally disagree on their measurements of space and time but they will agree on a measurement of the speed of light. Is there anything else upon which they will agree?

In relativity, a good way of imagining what is going on is to consider everything as different "events" in something called **spacetime**. From one observer's point of view, three coordinates (x, y and z) can define a position in space. One further "coordinate" is required to define its position in time (t). An event is a given point specified by these four coordinates (x, y, z, t).

As a result of the Lorentz transformation, another observer would be expected to come up with totally different numbers for all four of these measurements—(x', y', z', t'). The amazing thing is that these two observers will agree on something. This is best stated mathematically:

$$(ct)^2 - x^2 - y^2 - z^2 = (ct')^2 - x'^2 - y'^2 - z'^2$$

On normal axes, Pythagoras's theorem shows us that the quantity $\sqrt{\left(x^2 + y^2 + z^2\right)}$ is equal to the length of the line from the origin, so $(x^2 + y^2 + z^2)$ is equal to (the length of the line)^2. In other words, it is the separation in space.

(separation in space)$^2 = (x^2 + y^2 + z^2)$

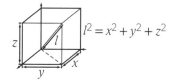

$$l^2 = x^2 + y^2 + z^2$$

The two observers agree about something very similar to this, but it includes a coordinate of time. This can be thought of as the separation in imaginary four-dimensional spacetime.

(separation in spacetime)$^2 = (ct)^2 - x^2 - y^2 - z^2$

or (separation in spacetime)$^2 = $ (time separation)$^2 - $ (space separation)^2

In one dimension, this simplifies to
$(ct')^2 - (x')^2 = (ct)^2 - (x)^2$

Other invariant quantities

In addition to the spacetime interval between two events (see box above), all observers agree on the values of three other quantities associated with the separation between two events or with reference to a given object. These are:

- proper time interval Δt_0
- proper length L_0
- rest mass m_0

These four quantities are said to be **invariant** as they are always constant and do not vary with a change of observer. There are additional quantities, not associated with mechanics, that are also invariant, e.g. electric charge.

Proper time, proper length and rest mass

(a) Proper time interval Δt_0

When expressing the time taken between events (for example, the length of time that a firework is giving out light), the **proper time** is the time as measured in a frame where the events take place at the same point in space. It turns out to be the shortest possible time that any observer could correctly record for the event.

Measuring how long a firework lasts

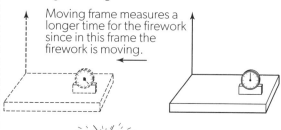

Moving frame measures a longer time for the firework since in this frame the firework is moving.

Clock that is stationary with the firework measures the proper time for which it lasted.

If A is moving past B, then B will think that time is running slowly for A. From A's point of view, B is moving past A. This means that A will think that time is running slowly for B. Both views are correct!

(b) Proper length L_0

As before, different observers will come up with different measurements for the length of the same object depending on their relative motions. The **proper length** of an object is the length recorded in a frame where the object is at rest.

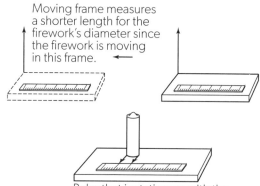

Moving frame measures a shorter length for the firework's diameter since the firework is moving in this frame.

Ruler that is stationary with the firework measures the *proper length* for its diameter.

(c) Rest mass m_0

The measurement of mass depends on relative velocity. Once again it is important to distinguish the measurement taken in the frame of the object from all other possible frames. The **rest mass** of an object is its mass as measured in a frame where the object is at rest. A particle's rest mass does not change.

AHL Time dilation

Light clock

A **light clock** is an imaginary device. A beam of light bounces between two mirrors—the time taken by the light between bounces is one "tick" of the light clock.

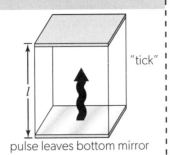

"tick"

pulse leaves bottom mirror

As shown in the derivation, the path taken by light in a light clock that is moving at constant velocity is longer. You know that the speed of light is fixed so the time between the "ticks" on a moving clock must also be longer. This effect—that moving clocks run slow—is called **time dilation**.

"tick"

pulse bounces off top mirror

The time between bounces Δt_0 is the proper time for this clock in the frame where the clock is at rest.

"tick"

pulse returns to bottom mirror

Derivation of effect from Lorentz transformation

If frame S is a frame where two events take place at the same point in space, then the time interval between these two events must be the proper time interval, Δt_0. Time dilation is then a direct consequence of the Lorentz transformation:

$$\Delta t' = \gamma \left(\Delta t - \frac{v \Delta x}{c^2} \right)$$

where $\Delta t = \Delta t_0$, (the proper time interval) and $\Delta x =$ zero (same point in space).

∴ Time interval in frame S′, $\Delta t' = \gamma \Delta t_0$

Derivation of the effect from first principles

If you imagine a stationary observer with one light clock, then t is the time between "ticks" on their stationary clock. In **this stationary frame**, a moving clock runs **slowly** and t' is the time between "ticks" on the moving clock: t' is greater than t.

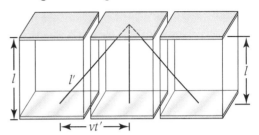

In the time t',

the clock has moved on a distance $= vt'$

Distance travelled by the light, $l' = \sqrt{\left((vt')^2 + l^2 \right)}$

$$t' = \frac{l'}{c}$$

$$= \frac{\sqrt{(vt')^2 + l^2}}{c}$$

$$\therefore \quad t'^2 = \frac{v^2 t'^2 + l^2}{c^2}$$

and $t'^2 \left(1 - \frac{v^2}{c^2} \right) = \frac{l^2}{c^2}$

but $\quad \frac{l^2}{c^2} = t^2$

$$\therefore \quad t'^2 \left(1 - \frac{v^2}{c^2} \right) = t^2$$

or $t' = \dfrac{1}{\sqrt{1 - \dfrac{v^2}{c^2}}} \times t \quad$ or $t' = \gamma t$

This equation is true for all measurements of time, even if they have not been made using a light clock.

Length contraction and evidence to support special relativity

Effect of length contraction

Time is not the only measurement that is affected by relative motion. There is another relativistic effect called **length contraction**. According to a (stationary) observer, the separation between two points in space contracts if there is relative motion in that direction. The contraction is in the same direction as the relative motion.

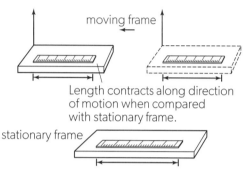

Length contracts by the same proportion as time dilates—the Lorentz factor is once again used in the equation, but this time there is a division rather than a multiplication:

$$L = \frac{L_0}{\gamma}$$

Derivation of length contraction from Lorentz transformation

When you measure the length of a moving object, then you are recording the position of each end of the object at one given instant in time according to that frame of reference. In other words, the time interval measured in frame S between these two events will be zero, $\Delta t = 0$. In this case, the length measured Δx is the length of the moving object L_0.

Length contraction is then a direct consequence of the Lorentz transformation. If you move into the frame S′, where the object is at rest, you will be measuring the proper length L_0:

$$\Delta x' = \gamma (\Delta x - v\Delta t)$$

where $\Delta x' = L_0$ (the proper length) and Δt = zero (simultaneous measurements of position of end of object).

∴ Length in frame S′, $L_0 = \gamma (L)$

$$L = \frac{L_0}{\gamma}$$

The muon experiment

Muons are a type of fundamental particle. A muon can be thought of as a more massive version of an electron. They can be created in the laboratory but they quickly decay. Their average lifetime is 2.2×10^{-6} s as measured in the frame in which the muons are at rest.

Muons are also created high up (10 km above the surface) in the atmosphere. Cosmic rays from the Sun can cause them to be created with huge velocities—perhaps $0.99c$. As they travel towards the Earth, some of them decay but there is still a detectable number of muons arriving at the surface of the Earth.

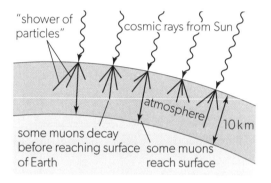

Without relativity, no muons would be expected to reach the surface at all. A particle with a lifetime of 2.2×10^{-6} s that is travelling near the speed of light (3×10^8 m s^{-1}) would be expected to travel less than a kilometre before decaying ($2.2 \times 10^{-6} \times 3 \times 10^8$ = 660 m).

The moving muons are effectively moving "clocks". Their high speed means that the Lorentz factor is high:

$$\gamma = \sqrt{\frac{1}{1 - 0.99^2}} = 7.1$$

Therefore an average lifetime of 2.2×10^{-6} s in the muons' frame of reference will be time dilated to a longer time as far as a stationary observer on the Earth is concerned. From this frame of reference, they will last, on average, 7.1 times longer. Many muons will still decay but some will make it through to the surface—this is exactly what is observed.

In the muons' frame they exist for 2.2×10^{-6} s on average. They make it down to the surface because the atmosphere (and the Earth) is moving with respect to the muons. This means that the atmosphere will be length-contracted. The 10 km distance as measured by an observer on the Earth will only be $\frac{10}{7.1} = 1.4$ km. A significant number of muons will exist long enough for the Earth to travel this distance.

Spacetime diagrams (1)

Spacetime diagrams

Spacetime separation was introduced on page 40. A spacetime diagram (sometimes called a Minkowski diagram) is a visual way of representing the geometry. Measurements can be taken from the diagram to calculate actual values.

You cannot represent all four dimensions on the one diagram, so you usually limit the number of dimensions of space that you represent. The simplest representation has only one dimension of space and one of time, as shown below.

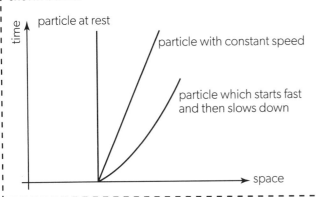

An object (moving or stationary) is always represented as a line in spacetime.

Note that:

- The values on the spacetime diagram are as would be measured by an observer whose worldline is represented by the vertical axis.

- The vertical axis in the above spacetime diagram is time t. An alternative is to plot (speed of light × time), ct. This means that both axes can have the same units (m, light years or equivalent).

- Whatever axes are being used, by convention, the path of a beam of light is represented by a line at 45° to the axes.

- The advance of proper time for any traveller can be calculated from the overall separation in spacetime. In the traveller's frame of reference, they remained stationary so the separation between two events can be calculated as shown below.

Example of spacetime diagrams

The advance of proper time for the journey between the events
$A \rightarrow B \rightarrow C \rightarrow D$
can be calculated from the values on the spacetime diagram.

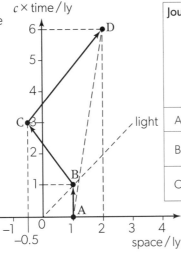

Journey	Space separation (x) / ly	Time separation (ct) / ly	(Spacetime separation)^2 $(ct)^2 - (x)^2$ / ly^2	Advance of proper time according to traveller / years $t' = \sqrt{\dfrac{(ct)^2 - (x)^2}{c}}$
A→B	0.0	1.0	$1^2 - 0^2 = 1$	$\sqrt{1.00} = 1.00$
B→C	1.5	2.0	$4 - 2.25 = 1.75$	$\sqrt{1.75} = 1.32$
C→D	2.5	3.0	$9 - 6.25 = 2.75$	$\sqrt{2.75} = 1.66$

The total advance of proper time for the traveller is $1.00 + 1.32 + 1.66 = 3.98$ years. This compares with the advance of 6.0 years according to an observer whose worldline is a vertical line on this spacetime diagram. This difference is an example of **time dilation** (see page 41).

The alternative journey directly from A to D shows a greater elapsed proper time. This is always true. A direct worldline always has a great amount of elapsed proper time than an indirect worldline.

Journey	Space separation (x) / ly	Time separation (ct) / ly	(Spacetime separation)^2 $(ct)^2 - (x)^2$ / ly^2	Advance of proper time according to traveller / years $t' = \sqrt{\dfrac{(ct)^2 - (x)^2}{c}}$
A→D	1.0	6.0	$36 - 1 = 35$	$\sqrt{35} = 5.92$

Spacetime diagrams (2)

Calculation of time dilation and length contraction

Time dilation and length contraction are quantitatively represented on spacetime diagrams. Refer to diagram on page 43.

a) **Time dilation**: In the journey directly from B → C, the relative velocity between the traveller and the stationary observer is $\dfrac{1.5 \text{ ly}}{2.0 \text{ yrs}} = 0.75c$. The Lorentz gamma factor is:

$$\gamma = \frac{1}{\sqrt{1-\dfrac{v^2}{c^2}}} = \frac{1}{\sqrt{1-0.75^2}} = 1.51$$

The journey takes 2 years according to the observer at rest. This means that the proper time as measured by the traveller (see table on page 43) will be:

$$\Delta t = \gamma \Delta t_0 \Rightarrow \Delta t_0 = \frac{\Delta t}{\gamma} = \frac{2.0}{1.51} = 1.32 \text{ years}$$

b) **Length contraction**: The observer at rest measures the journey length from B → C to be 1.5 ly. The journey will be length contracted to:

$$L = \frac{L_0}{\gamma} = \frac{1.5}{1.51} = 0.99 \text{ ly}$$

The relative velocity of travel is $0.75c$, and the time taken to go from B → C, in the traveller's frame of reference, is 1.32 yr. This makes the distance according to the traveller to be $0.75c \times 1.32$ years = 0.99 ly, as shown.

Curved worldline

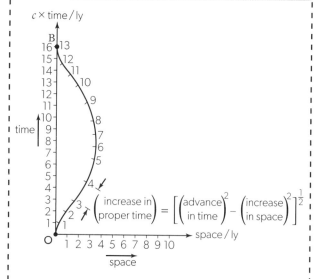

$$\left(\begin{array}{c}\text{increase in}\\\text{proper time}\end{array}\right) = \left[\left(\begin{array}{c}\text{advance}\\\text{in time}\end{array}\right)^2 - \left(\begin{array}{c}\text{increase}\\\text{in space}\end{array}\right)^2\right]^{\frac{1}{2}}$$

Proper time along a curved worldline from event O to event B is smaller than the proper time along the straight line from O to B.

The twin paradox

As mentioned on page 41, the theory of relativity gives no preference to different inertial observers—the time dilation effect (moving clocks run slowly) is always the same. This leads to the "**twin paradox**". In this imaginary situation, you compare the passage of time for identical twins in different reference frames.

One twin undergoes a very fast trip out to a distant star and back again while the other twin remains on Earth.

- In the reference frame of the twin on Earth, the twin in the rocket is in motion and time will run more slowly on the rocket.

- In the reference frame of the twin in the rocket, the twin on Earth is in motion and time will run more slowly on Earth.

When the rocket returns to Earth, both twins should expect the other twin to have experienced less time and therefore be younger than they are now; this strange expectation is the twin paradox. Both twins cannot be correct.

The solution to the paradox comes from the realization that the equations of special relativity are only symmetrical when the two observers are in constant relative motion. For the twins to meet back up again, one of them would have to turn around. This would involve external forces and acceleration. If this is the case, then the situation is no longer symmetrical for the twins. The twin on the Earth has not accelerated so their view of the situation must be correct.

AHL : Spacetime diagrams (3)

Resolving the twin paradox using spacetime diagrams

The diagram below is a spacetime diagram for a journey to a distant planet followed by an immediate return.

According to the twin remaining on Earth:

- the distance to the planet = 3.0 ly
- relative velocity of traveller is 0.6c
- each leg of the journey takes $\frac{3.0}{0.6}$ = 5.0 years
- total journey time = 10.0 years

The gamma factor is

$$\gamma = \frac{1}{\sqrt{1-\dfrac{v^2}{c^2}}} \frac{1}{\sqrt{1-0.6^2}} = 1.25$$

So according to the twin undertaking the journey:

- each leg of the journey takes $\frac{5.0}{1.25}$ = 4.0 years
- total journey time = 8.0 years
- the distance to the planet = $\frac{3.0}{1.25}$ = 2.4 ly
- relative velocity of Earth = $\frac{4.8}{8.0}$ = 0.6c

To check whose version of time "is correct", **they agree to send light signals every year.** The spacetime diagram for this situation in the Earth's frame of reference is shown on the below (left).

Note that there is no paradox; they agree on the number of signals sent and received; the travelling twin has aged less than the twin that stayed on Earth.

A more complicated spacetime diagram can be drawn for the reference frame of the outbound traveller (below right). Note that:

- The first four years has the travelling twin's worldline vertical i.e. stationary.
- When the travelling twin turns round, she leaves her original frame of reference and changes to a frame where the Earth is moving towards her at $\frac{3}{5}c$ (= 0.6c).
- Her relative velocity towards the Earth with respect to her original frame of reference can be calculated from the velocity transformation equations as $\frac{15}{17}c$ (= 0.88c) back.
- In this frame of reference, the total time for the round trip would be measured as 12.5 years

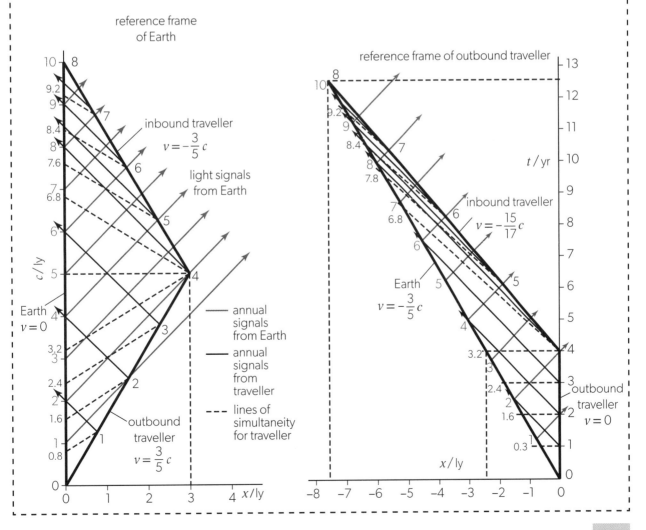

Spacetime diagrams (4)

Representing more than one inertial frame on the same spacetime diagram

The Lorentz transformations describe how measurements of space and time in one frame can be converted into the measurements observed in another frame of reference. The situation in each frame of reference can be visualized by using separate spacetime diagrams for each frame of reference (see page 45 for examples).

It is also possible to represent two inertial frames on the same spacetime diagram. A frame S' (coordinates x' and ct') is moving at relative constant velocity $+v$ according to a frame S (coordinates x and ct). The principles are as follows:

- The same worldline applies to both sets of coordinate axes (that is, to x and ct, as well as to x' and ct').

- The Lorentz transformation is made by *changing the coordinate system for frame S'* rather than the position of the worldline.

- The spacetime axes for frame S has x and ct at right angles to one another as normal.

- The spacetime axes for frame S' has its x' and ct' axes both angled in towards the $x = ct$ line (which represents a path of a beam of light).

- The coordinates of a spacetime event in S are read from the x and ct axes directly.

- The coordinates of a spacetime event in S' are measured by drawing lines parallel to the ct' and x' axes until they hit the x' and ct' axes.

2. Events C and D occur at same location in frame S'.
   Events C and D occur at different locations in frame S.

3. A pulse of light emitted by event A arrives at event D according to both frames of reference. It cannot arrive at events B or C.

Mathematically, for the above process to agree with the Lorentz transformation calculations, the following must apply:

- The angle between the ct' axis (the worldline for the origin of S') and the ct axis is the same as the angle between the x' axis and the x axis. It is:

$$\theta = \tan^{-1}\left(\frac{v}{c}\right)$$

- The scales used by the axes in S' are different from the scales used by the axes in S.

- A given value is represented by a greater length on the ct' axis when compared with the ct axis.

- A given value is represented by a greater length on the x' axis when compared with the x axis.

- The ratio of the measurements on the axes depends on the relative velocity between the frames. The equation (which does not need to be recalled) is:

$$\text{ratio of units } \frac{ct'}{ct} = \sqrt{\frac{1+\dfrac{v^2}{c^2}}{1-\dfrac{v^2}{c^2}}}$$

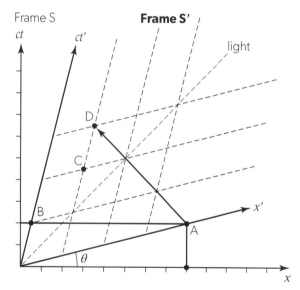

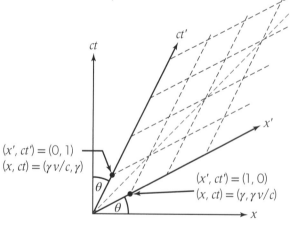

1. Events A and B are simultaneous in frame S but are not simultaneous in frame S' (A occurs before B)

$$\tan\theta = \frac{2}{8} = 0.25$$

∴ relative velocity of frames S' and S $= 0.25\,c$

Summary

- At greater speed:
  - the S' axes swing towards the $x = ct$ line as the angle θ increases.
  - the ct' and x' axes are more stretched when compared with the ct and x axes.

- Events that are simultaneous in S are on the same horizontal line.

- Events that are simultaneous in S' are on a line parallel to the x' axis.

1. Two inertial observers are moving with respect to one another. One observer records two separate events as happening simultaneously. Explain under what conditions the second observer would agree that two separate events occurred simultaneously. (4)

2. An inertial observer S is at rest. According to this observer, a second observer, S', is moving at a constant velocity v. The origins of two coordinate systems, S and S', coincide when all clocks show zero. According to S, an event takes place 4.0 ly from the origin of S when $t = 5.0\,\text{ly}\,c^{-1}$.

   a. Explain what is meant by the space–time interval between this event and the origin of S at $t =$ zero. (2)

   b. Calculate the space–time interval between this event and the origin of S at $t =$ zero. (2)

   According to S', the same event takes place at the origin of S'.

   c. Calculate the time of this event according to S'. (3)

   d. Use your answer to (c) to explain the concept of time dilation. (3)

   e. Determine the velocity v. (3)

3. The spacetime diagram below shows two events, A and B, as observed in a reference frame S. Each event emits a light signal.

   Use the diagram to calculate, according to frame S:

   a. the time between event A and event B (2)

   b. the time taken for the light signal leaving event A to arrive at the position of event B (2)

   c. the location of a stationary observer who receives the light signal from event A simultaneously with receiving the light signal from event B (2)

   d. the velocity of a moving frame of reference in which event A and event B occurred simultaneously. (4)

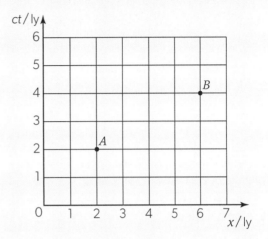

4. An unstable particle has a lifetime of $4.0 \times 10^{-8}\,\text{s}$ in its own rest frame. If it is moving at 98% of the speed of light, calculate:

   a. its lifetime in the laboratory frame (2)

   b. the length travelled in both frames. (3)

Thermal concepts

Temperature and heat flow

Hot and cold are just labels that identify the direction in which thermal energy (heat) will be naturally transferred when two objects are placed in thermal contact. The direction of the natural flow of thermal energy between two objects is determined by the "hotness" of each object. Thermal energy naturally flows from hot to cold.

The temperature of an object is a measure of how hot it is. In other words, if two objects are placed in thermal contact, then the temperature difference between the two objects will determine the direction of the natural transfer of thermal energy. Thermal energy is naturally transferred "down" the temperature difference—from high temperature to low temperature. Eventually, the two objects would be expected to reach the same temperature. When this happens, they are said to be in **thermal equilibrium**.

Heat is not a substance that flows from one object to another. What has happened is that thermal energy has been transferred. Thermal energy refers to the non-mechanical transfer of energy between a system and its surroundings.

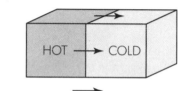

direction of transfer of thermal energy

Kelvin and Celsius

Most of the time, there are only two sensible temperature scales to choose between—the Kelvin scale and the Celsius scale.

In order to use them, you do not need to understand the details of how either of these scales has been defined, but you do need to know the relationship between them. Most everyday thermometers are marked with the Celsius scale and temperature is quoted in degrees Celsius (°C).

There is an easy relationship between a temperature T as measured on the Kelvin scale and the corresponding temperature t as measured on the Celsius scale. The approximate relationship is:

$$T(K) = t(°C) + 273$$

This means that the units used on each scale are identical in "size", but they have different zero points.

The Kelvin scale is an absolute thermodynamic temperature scale and a measurement on this scale is also called the **absolute temperature**.

Zero kelvin is called **absolute zero** (see page 64).

Kelvin temperature is a measure of the average kinetic energy of the particles as given by $E_k = \frac{3}{2} k_B T$ (see page 66 for more details).

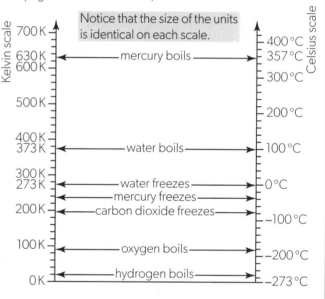

Notice that the size of the units is identical on each scale.

Examples: gases

For a given sample of a gas, the *pressure*, the *volume* and the *temperature* are all related to one another.

- The pressure, P, is the force per unit area from the gas acting at 90° on the container wall:

$$P = \frac{F}{A}$$

  The SI units of pressure are $N\,m^{-2}$ or Pa (Pascals).
  $1\,Pa = 1\,N\,m^{-2}$
  Gas pressure can also be measured in atmospheres.
  $(1\,atm \approx 10^5\,Pa)$

- The volume, V, of the gas is measured in m^3 or cm^3.
  $(1\,m^3 = 10^6\,cm^3)$

- The temperature, t, of the gas is measured in °C or K.

In order to investigate how these quantities are interrelated, you choose:

- one quantity to be the independent variable (the thing you alter and measure)

- another quantity to be the dependent variable (the second thing you measure).

The third quantity needs to be controlled (i.e. kept constant). The specific values that will be recorded also depend on the mass of gas being investigated and the type of gas being used, so these need to be controlled as well.

The density ρ of a substance can be found from its mass, M, and volume, V, using the equation $\rho = \frac{m}{V}$ (see page 64).

Heat and internal energy

Microscopic vs macroscopic

When analysing something physical, you have a choice.

- The **macroscopic** point of view considers the system as a whole and sees how it interacts with its surroundings.
- The **microscopic** point of view looks inside the system to see how its component parts interact with each other.

So far, you have looked at the temperature of a system in a macroscopic way, but all objects are made up of **atoms** and **molecules**.

According to **kinetic theory** these particles are constantly in random motion—hence the name. See below for more details. Although atoms and molecules are different things (a molecule is a combination of atoms), the difference is not important at this stage. The particles can be thought of as little "points" of mass with velocities that are continually changing.

Internal energy

If the temperature of an object changes, then it must have gained (or lost) energy. From the microscopic point of view, the molecules must have gained (or lost) this energy.

The two possible forms are kinetic energy and potential energy.

- The molecules have kinetic energy because they are moving. To be absolutely precise, a molecule can have either translational kinetic energy (the whole molecule is moving in a certain direction) or rotational kinetic energy (the molecule is rotating about one or more axes).

speed in a random direction——
∴ molecule has KE

- The molecules have potential energy because of the **intermolecular** forces. If you imagine pulling two molecules further apart, this would require work against the intermolecular forces.

equilibrium position

resultant force back towards equilibrium position due to neighbouring molecules ∴ molecule has PE

The total energy that the molecules possess (random kinetic plus intermolecular potential) is called the **internal energy** of a substance. Whenever you heat a substance, you increase its internal energy.

Temperature is a measure of the average kinetic energy of the molecules in a substance.

If two substances have the same temperature, then their molecules have the same average kinetic energy.

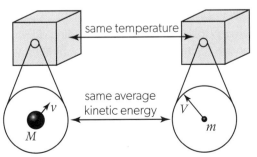

same temperature

same average kinetic energy

molecules with large mass moving with lower average speed

molecules with small mass moving with higher average speed

Kinetic theory

Molecules are arranged in different ways depending on the **phase** of the substance (i.e. solid, liquid or gas).

Solids
Macroscopically, solids have a fixed volume and a fixed shape. This is because the molecules are held in position by bonds. However, the bonds are not absolutely rigid. The molecules vibrate around a mean (average) position. The higher the temperature, the greater the vibrations.

Liquids
A liquid also has a fixed volume but its shape can change. The molecules are also vibrating, but they are not completely fixed in position. There are still strong forces between the molecules. This keeps the molecules close to one another, but they are free to move around each other.

Gases
A gas will always expand to fill its container. The molecules are not fixed in position, and any forces between the molecules are very weak. This means that the molecules are essentially independent of one another, but they do occasionally collide. More detail is given on page 67.

Heat and work

Many people have confused ideas about heat and work. In answers to examination questions it is very common to read, for example, that "heat rises"—when what is meant is that the transfer of thermal energy is upwards.

- When a force moves through a distance, you say that work is done. Work is the energy that has been transmitted from one system to another from the macroscopic point of view.
- When work is done on a microscopic level (i.e. on individual molecules), you say that heating has taken place. Heat is the energy that has been transmitted. It can either increase the kinetic energy of the molecules or their potential energy or, of course, both.

In both cases, energy is being transferred.

Specific heat capacity

Definitions and microscopic explanation

In theory, if an object could be heated up with no energy loss, then the increase in temperature ΔT depends on:

- the energy given to the object Q,
- the mass, m, and
- the substance from which the object is made.

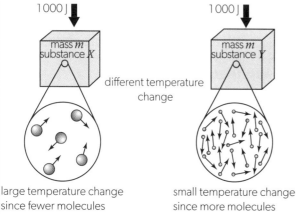

large temperature change since fewer molecules

small temperature change since more molecules

▲ Two different blocks with the same mass and same energy input will have a different temperature change

The **thermal capacity** C of an object is defined as the energy required to raise its temperature by 1 K. Different objects (even different samples of the same substance) will have different values of heat capacity. **Specific heat capacity** is the energy required to raise a unit mass of a substance by 1 K. "Specific" here just means "per unit mass".

In symbols,

thermal capacity $C = \dfrac{Q}{\Delta T}$ (J K^{-1} or J °C^{-1})

specific heat capacity $c = \dfrac{C}{(m\Delta T)}$ (J kg^{-1} K^{-1} or J kg^{-1} °C^{-1})

or $Q = mc\Delta T$

- A particular gas can have many different values of specific heat capacity—it depends on the conditions used—see page 51.

- These equations refer to the **temperature difference** resulting from the addition of a certain amount of energy. In other words, it generally takes the same amount of energy to raise the temperature of an object from 25 °C to 35 °C as it does for the same object to go from 402 °C to 412 °C. This is only true as long as energy is not lost from the object.

- If an object is raised above room temperature, it starts to lose energy. The hotter it becomes, the greater the rate at which it loses energy.

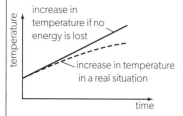

▲ Temperature change of an object being heated at a constant rate

Methods of measuring heat capacities and specific heat capacities

There are two basic ways to measure heat capacity.

1. Electrical method

The experiment would be set up as below:

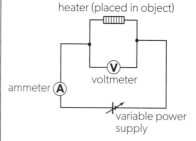

- the specific heat capacity $c = \dfrac{ItV}{m(T_2 - T_1)}$.

Sources of experimental error:

- Loss of thermal energy from the apparatus.
- The container for the substance and the heater will also be warmed up.
- It will take some time for the energy to be shared uniformly through the substance.

2. Method of mixtures

The known specific heat capacity of one substance can be used to find the specific heat capacity of another substance.

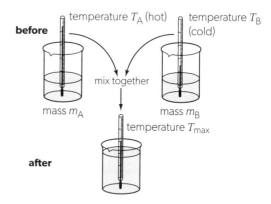

Procedure:

- Measure the masses of the liquids m_A and m_B.
- Measure the two starting temperatures T_A and T_B.
- Mix the two liquids together.
- Record the maximum temperature of the mixture T_{max}.

If no energy is lost from the system then,

energy lost by hot substance cooling down = energy gained by cold substance heating up

$$m_A c_A (T_A - T_{max}) = m_B c_B (T_{max} - T_B)$$

Again, the main source of experimental error is the loss of thermal energy from the apparatus; particularly while the liquids are being transferred. The changes in temperature of the container also need to be taken into consideration for a more accurate result.

Phases (states) of matter and latent heat

Definitions and microscopic view

When a substance changes phase, the temperature remains constant even though thermal energy is still being transferred.

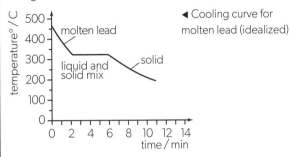

◀ Cooling curve for molten lead (idealized)

The amount of energy associated with the phase change is called the **latent heat**. The technical term for the change of phase from solid to liquid is **fusion** and the term for the change from liquid to gas is **vaporization**. The change in phase from liquid to solid is **condensing**.

The energy given to the molecules does not increase their kinetic energy so it must be increasing their potential energy. Intermolecular bonds are being broken and this takes energy. When the substance freezes, bonds are created and this process releases energy.

It is a very common mistake to think that the molecules must speed up during a phase change. The molecules in water vapour at $100\,°C$ must be moving with the same average speed as the molecules in liquid water at $100\,°C$.

The **specific latent heat** of a substance is defined as the amount of energy per unit mass absorbed or released during a change of phase.

In symbols,

$$\text{specific latent heat } L=\frac{Q}{m}\ (\text{J kg}^{-1}) \qquad Q=mL$$

In the idealized situation of no energy loss, a constant rate of energy transfer into a solid substance would result in a constant rate of increase in temperature until the melting point is reached:

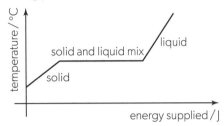

▲ Phase-change graph with temperature vs energy

In the example above, the specific heat capacity of the liquid is less than the specific heat capacity of the solid as the gradient of the line that corresponds to the liquid phase is greater than the gradient of the line that corresponds to the solid phase. A given amount of energy will cause a greater increase in temperature for the liquid when compared with the solid.

Methods of measuring

The two possible methods for measuring latent heats shown below are very similar in principle to the methods for measuring specific heat capacities (see page 50).

1. A method for measuring the specific latent heat of vaporization of water

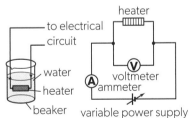

The amount of thermal energy provided to water at its boiling point is calculated using electrical energy $= ItV$. The mass vaporized needs to be recorded.

- The specific latent heat $L=\dfrac{ItV}{(m_1-m_2)}$.

Sources of experimental error:

- Loss of thermal energy from the apparatus.
- Some water vapour will be lost before and after timing.

2. A method for measuring the specific latent heat of fusion of water

Providing you know the specific heat capacity of water, you can calculate the specific latent heat of fusion for water. In

the example below, ice (at $0\,°C$) is added to warm water and the temperature of the resulting mix is measured.

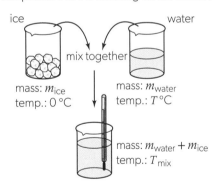

If no venergy is lost from the system then,

energy lost by water cooling down $=$ energy gained by ice

$$m_{water}c_{water}\left(T_{water}-T_{mix}\right)=m_{ice}L_{fusion}+m_{ice}c_{water}T_{mix}$$

Sources of experimental error:

- Loss (or gain) of thermal energy from the apparatus.
- If the ice had not started at exactly zero, then there would be an additional term in the equation in order to account for the energy needed to warm the ice up to $0\,°C$.
- Water clinging to the ice before the transfer.

Thermal energy transfer

Processes of thermal energy transfer

There are several processes by which the transfer of thermal energy from a hot object to a cold object can be achieved. Three very important processes are called **conduction**, **convection** and **radiation**. Any given practical situation probably involves more than one of these processes happening at the same time. There is a fourth process called **evaporation**. This involves the faster-moving molecules leaving the surface of a liquid that is below its boiling point. Evaporation causes cooling.

Conduction

In thermal conduction, thermal energy is transferred along a substance without any bulk (overall) movement of the substance. For example, one end of a metal spoon soon feels hot if the other end is placed in a hot cup of tea.

Conduction is the process by which kinetic energy is passed from molecule to molecule.

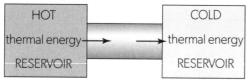
macroscopic view

Thermal energy flows along the material as a result of the temperature difference across its ends.

microscopic view

The faster-moving molecules at the hot end pass on their kinetic energy to the slower-moving molecules as a result of intermolecular collisions.

- Poor conductors are called thermal **insulators**.
- Metals tend to be very good thermal conductors. This is because a different mechanism (involving the electrons) allows quick transfer of thermal energy.
- All gases (and most liquids) tend to be poor conductors.

Examples:

- Most clothes keep us warm by trapping layers of air—a poor conductor.
- If you walk around a house in bare feet, the floors that are better conductors (e.g. tiles) will feel colder than the floors that are good insulators (e.g. carpets) even if they are at the same temperature. (For the same reason, on a cold day a piece of metal feels colder than a piece of wood.)
- When used for cooking food, saucepans conduct thermal energy from the source of heat to the food.

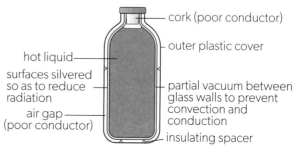
cork (poor conductor)
outer plastic cover
hot liquid
surfaces silvered so as to reduce radiation
air gap (poor conductor)
partial vacuum between glass walls to prevent convection and conduction
insulating spacer

▲ A thermos flask prevents heat loss

Convection

In convection, thermal energy moves between two points because of a bulk movement of matter. This can only take place in a **fluid** (a liquid or a gas). When part of the fluid is heated it tends to expand and thus its density is reduced. The colder fluid sinks and the hotter fluid rises up. Central heating causes a room to warm up because a **convection current** is set up as shown below.

Cool air is denser and sinks downwards.   Hot air is less dense and is forced upwards.

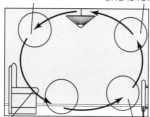

The flow of air around a room is called a convection current.   Air is warmed by the heater.

▲ Convection in a room

Convection cannot take place in a solid.

Examples:

- The pilots of gliders (and also many birds) use naturally occurring convection currents to stay above the ground.
- Sea breezes (winds) are often due to convection. During the day the land is hotter than the sea. This means hot air will rise from above the land and there will be a breeze towards the shore. During the night, the situation is reversed.
- Lighting a fire in a chimney will mean that a breeze flows in the room towards the fire.

Radiation

Radiation

Matter is not involved in the transfer of thermal energy by radiation. All objects (that have a temperature above zero kelvin) radiate **electromagnetic waves**. If you hold your hand up to a fire to "feel the heat", your hands are receiving the radiation.

For most everyday objects this radiation is in the **infra-red** part of the **electromagnetic spectrum**. For more details of the electromagnetic spectrum, see page 90.

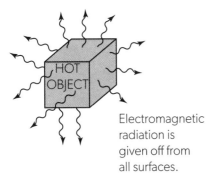

Electromagnetic radiation is given off from all surfaces.

- An object at room temperature absorbs and radiates energy. If it is at constant temperature (and not changing state), then the rates are the same.
- A surface that is a good radiator is also a good absorber.
- Surfaces that are light in colour and smooth (shiny) are poor radiators (and poor absorbers).
- Surfaces that are dark and rough are good radiators (and good absorbers).
- If the temperature of an object is increased, then the frequency of the radiation increases. The total rate at which energy is radiated will also increase.
- Radiation can travel through a vacuum (space).

Examples:

- The Sun warms the Earth's surface by radiation.
- Clothes in summer tend to be white—so as not to absorb the radiation from the Sun.

Inverse square law of radiation

As the distance of an observer from a point source of light increases, the power received by the observer will decrease as the energy spreads out over a larger area. A doubling of distance will result in the reduction of the power received to a quarter of the original value.

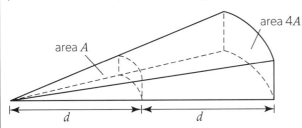

The surface area A of a sphere of radius r is calculated using:

$$A = 4\pi r^2$$

If the point source radiates a total power P in all directions, then the power received per unit area (the **intensity** I) at a distance r away from the point source is:

$$I = \frac{P}{4\pi r^2}$$

For a given area of receiver, the intensity of the received radiation is inversely proportional to the square of the distance from the point source to the receiver. This is known as the **inverse square law** and applies to all waves.

$$I \propto x^{-2}$$

Mathematics of conduction

Mathematics of conduction

The amount of energy that a substance **absorbs** when it changes its temperature depends on a different physical property to the ease with which thermal energy can be **conducted through** a substance.

- The link between *energy absorbed* and *temperature change* depends on the *specific heat capacity* of the substance (see page 50).
- The link between the rate of flow of thermal energy and temperature gradient depends on the *thermal conductivity* of the substance (see below).

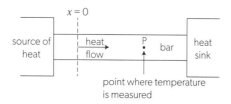

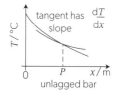 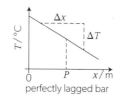

The diagrams above show the variation of temperature along a bar of material as thermal energy flows along the bar. The graphs show the situation after **steady state** conditions have been established. This is when the temperature at any point along the bar does not vary with time.

For the perfectly lagged bar, the temperature gradient is defined to be $\dfrac{\Delta T}{\Delta x}$ and is constant along the bar. This is because there is no loss of heat from the sides of the bar so there is a constant rate of flow of thermal energy and the lines of heat flow are parallel along the bar. The units of temperature gradient are $K\,m^{-1}$ or $°C\,m^{-1}$.

When considering the flow of thermal energy through a section of material,

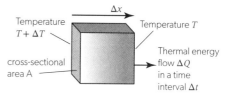

Experiments show that, for small values of ΔT and Δx,

ΔQ is proportional to ΔT and inversely proportional to Δx when Δt and A are fixed.

Thus, you can define a constant for the material called the thermal conductivity k

$$\frac{\Delta Q}{\Delta t} = kA\frac{\Delta T}{\Delta x}$$

$\dfrac{\Delta Q}{\Delta t}$ is the rate of flow of thermal energy through the substance, measured in $J\,S^{-1}$ or W

k is the thermal conductivity, measured in $W\,m^{-1}\,K^{-1}$

A is the cross-sectional area, measured in m^2

$\dfrac{\Delta T}{\Delta x}$ is the temperature gradient, measured in $K\,m^{-1}$

Technically, the equation above should have a negative sign on the RHS. This is because thermal energy flows from hot to cold so, as x increases, T goes down. This means $\dfrac{\Delta T}{\Delta x}$ is negative for a positive $\dfrac{\Delta Q}{\Delta t}$. k is a positive number. The equation in the IB Physics data booklet leaves out the negative sign so it has been left out here.

The thermal conductivity k is numerically equal to the rate of heat flow ($J\,S^{-1}$) through a unit cross-section ($1\,m^2$) across which there is a unit temperature gradient ($1\,K\,m^{-1}$). Typical values are:

Substance	$k\,/\,W\,m^{-1}\,K^{-1}$
Copper	3.9×10^2
Building bricks	6.0×10^{-1}
Asbestos insulation	8.0×10^{-2}
Air	2.4×10^{-2}

Compound materials

When heat flows through two materials that are in series, **once steady state conditions have been established**, the rate of flow of thermal energy must be the same in both materials.

$$\frac{\Delta Q}{\Delta t} = k_1 A\left(\frac{T_3 - T_2}{x_1}\right) = k_2 A\left(\frac{T_2 - T_1}{x_2}\right)$$

The temperature gradient is greater across the poorer conductor.

Comparison between thermal and electrical conduction

Electrical conductivity equation: $\dfrac{\Delta q}{\Delta t} = \sigma A \dfrac{\Delta V}{\Delta l}$

Thermal conductivity equation: $\dfrac{\Delta Q}{\Delta t} = kA \dfrac{\Delta T}{\Delta x}$

Thermal conduction			Electrical conduction
Rate of flow of thermal energy	$\dfrac{\Delta Q}{\Delta t}$	$\dfrac{\Delta q}{\Delta t}$	Rate of flow of charge
Temperature gradient	$\dfrac{\Delta T}{\Delta x}$	$\dfrac{\Delta V}{\Delta l}$	Potential gradient (= size of the electric field)
Thermal conductivity	k	σ	Electrical conductivity (= $\dfrac{1}{\text{resistivity}}$)

Radiation: Wien's law and the Stefan–Boltzmann law

Black-body radiation: Stefan-Boltzmann law

In general, the radiation given out from a hot object depends on many things. It is possible to come up with a theoretical model for the "perfect" emitter of radiation. The "perfect" emitter will also be a perfect absorber of radiation—a black object absorbs all of the light energy falling on it. For this reason the radiation from a theoretical "perfect" emitter is known as **black-body radiation**.

Black-body radiation does not depend on the nature of the emitting surface, but it does depend upon its temperature. At any given temperature there will be a range of different wavelengths (and hence frequencies) of radiation that are emitted. Some wavelengths will be more intense than others. This variation is shown in the graph below.

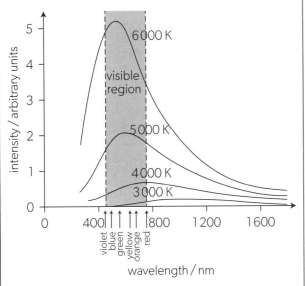

To be absolutely precise, it is not correct to label the y-axis on the above graph as the intensity, but this is often done. It is actually something that could be called the intensity function. This is defined so that the area under the graph (between two wavelengths) gives the intensity emitted in that wavelength range. The total area under the graph is thus a measure of the total power radiated. The power radiated by a black-body is given by:

total power radiated in W $\quad$ surface area in m² $\quad$ absolute temperature in K

$$P = \sigma A T^4$$

Stefan-Boltzmann constant

The value of the Stefan-Boltzmann constant is $\sigma = 5.67 \times 10^{-8}\,\mathrm{W\,m^{-2}\,K^{-4}}$.

Although stars and planets are not perfect emitters, their radiation spectrum is approximately the same as black-body radiation.

Worked example

Find the total power radiated by the Sun.

radius of the Sun = $6.96 \times 10^8\,\mathrm{m}$.

surface area = $4\pi r^2 = 6.09 \times 10^{10}\,\mathrm{m^2}$

temperature = $5\,800\,\mathrm{K}$

power radiated = $\sigma A T^4$

$\quad = 5.67 \times 10^{-8} \times 6.09 \times 10^{18} \times (5\,800)^4$

$\quad = 3.9 \times 10^{26}\,\mathrm{W}$

Wien's law

Wien's displacement law relates the wavelength at which the intensity of the radiation is a maximum λ_{max} to the temperature of the black body T. This states that:

$$\lambda_{max} T = \text{constant}$$

The value of the constant can be found by experiment. It is $2.9 \times 10^{-3}\,\mathrm{m\,K}$. It should be noted that in order to use this constant, the wavelength should be substituted into the equation in metres and the temperature in kelvin.

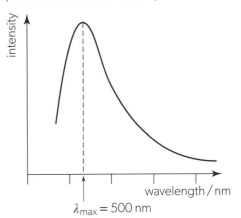

You can analyse light from a star and calculate a value for its surface temperature. This will be much less than the temperature in the core. Hot stars will give out all frequencies of visible light and so will tend to appear white in colour. Cooler stars might well only give out the higher wavelengths (lower frequencies) of visible light—they will appear red. Radiation emitted from planets will peak in the infra-red.

Intensity, I

The intensity of radiation is the power per unit area that is received by the object. The unit is $\mathrm{W\,m^{-2}}$.

$$I = \frac{\text{Power}}{A}$$

Stellar spectra

Absorption lines

The radiation from stars is not a perfect continuous spectrum—there are particular wavelengths that are "missing".

bands of wavelengths
emitted by the Sun

"missing" wavelength

wavelength ◄———
red ——► violet

The missing wavelengths correspond to the absorption spectra of a number of elements. Although it seems sensible to assume that the elements concerned are in the Earth's atmosphere, this assumption is incorrect. The wavelengths would still be absent if light from the star was analysed in space.

The absorption is taking place in the outer layers of the star. This means that there is a way of telling what elements exist in the star—at least in its outer layers.

A star that is moving relative to the Earth will show a Doppler shift in its absorption spectrum. Light from stars that are receding will be **red shifted**, whereas light from approaching stars will be **blue shifted**.

Classification of stars

Different stars give out different spectra of light. This allows stars to be classified by their **spectral class**. Stars that emit the same type of spectrum are allocated to the same spectral class. Historically, these were just given a different letter, but we now know that these different letters also correspond to different surface temperatures.

The seven main spectral classes (in order of **decreasing** surface temperature) are O, B, A, F, G, K and M. The main spectral classes can be subdivided.

Class	Effective surface temperature / K	Colour
O	30 000–50 000	blue
B	10 000–30 000	blue-white
A	7 500–10 000	white
F	6 000–7 500	yellow-white
G	5 200–6 000	yellow
K	3 700–5 200	orange
M	2 400–3 700	red

Many Hertzsprung–Russell diagrams (see page 164) in astronomy articles or text books use Stellar classification on the x-axis as opposed to decreasing surface temperature. The table above demonstrates that these two approaches are equivalent to one another.

Summary

If you know the distance to a star you can analyse the light from the star and work out:

- the chemical composition (by analysing the absorption spectrum)
- the surface temperature (using a measurement of λ_{max} and Wien's law—see page 55)
- the luminosity (using measurements of the brightness and the distance away)
- the surface area of the star (using the luminosity, the surface temperature and the Stefan–Boltzmann law).

Luminosity

Luminosity and apparent brightness

The total power **radiated** by a star is called its **luminosity** (L). The SI units are watts. This is very different from the power received by an observer on the Earth. The power **received** per unit area is called the apparent brightness of the star. The SI units are $W\,m^{-2}$.

If two stars were at the **same distance** away from the Earth, then the one with the greater luminosity would be brighter. Stars are, however, at different distances from the Earth. The brightness is inversely proportional to the (distance)^2.

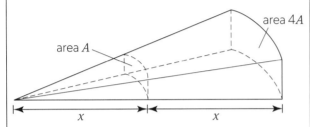

area A

area $4A$

x x

As distance increases, the brightness decreases since the light is spread over a bigger area.

distance	brightness	
x	b	
$2x$	$\dfrac{b}{4}$	
$3x$	$\dfrac{b}{9}$	inverse square
$4x$	$\dfrac{b}{16}$	
$5x$	$\dfrac{b}{25}$	

apparent brightness $b = \dfrac{L}{4\pi r^2}$

It is thus possible for two very different stars to have the same apparent brightness. It all depends on how far away the stars are.

close star
(small luminosity)

distant star
(high luminosity)

Two stars can have the same apparent brightness even if they have different luminosities

Worked example

The star Betelgeuse has a parallax angle of 7.7×10^{-3} arc seconds and an apparent brightness of $2.0 \times 10^{-7}\,W\,m^{-2}$. Calculate its luminosity.

Distance to Betelgeuse d:

$$d = \frac{1}{\text{parallax angle}}$$

$$= \frac{1}{7.7 \times 10^{-3}}\,pc$$

$$= 129.9\,pc$$

$$= 129.9 \times 3.08 \times 10^{16}\,m$$

$$= 4.0 \times 10^{18}\,m$$

$$L = b \times 4\pi d^2 = 2.0 \times 10^{-7} \times 4\pi \times (4.0 \times 10^{18})^2$$
$$= 4.0 \times 10^{31}\,W$$

Black-body radiation

Stars can be analysed as perfect emitters, or black bodies. The luminosity of a star is related to its brightness, surface area and temperature according to the Stefan–Boltzmann law. Wien's law can be used to relate the wavelength at which the intensity is a maximum to its temperature. See page 55 for more details.

e.g. our sun's temperature is $5\,800\,K$.

The wavelength at which the intensity of its radiation is

at a maximum is $\lambda_{max} = \dfrac{2.9 \times 10^{-3}}{5\,800} = 500\,nm$

Alternative units

The SI units for luminosity and brightness have already been introduced. Luminosities of different stars are often stated in comparison with the luminosity of our sun, $L_\odot$. For example, a luminosity of $2.3\,L_\odot = 2.3 \times$ the Sun's luminosity.

In practice, astronomers often compare the brightness of stars using the **apparent magnitude** scale. A magnitude 1 star is brighter than a magnitude 3 star. This measure of brightness is sometimes shown on star maps.

The magnitude scale can also be used to compare the luminosity of different stars, provided the distance to the star is taken into account. Astronomers quote values of **absolute magnitude** to compare luminosities on a familiar scale.

End of topic questions—B.1 Thermal energy transfers

1. The latent heat of vaporization of water is $2\,300\,kJ\,kg^{-1}$. How long would it take a 2.6 kW electric kettle containing 600 g of boiling water to boil off all the water? (3)

2. A sheet of insulating material is 3.0 mm thick. The temperature drop across the sheet is 100 K. The rate of flow of thermal energy through each square metre of the material is 800 W. Calculate the thermal conductivity of the material. (2)

3. A cylindrical rod of cross-sectional area $5.0\,mm^2$ and length 42 cm consists of a 30 cm rod of silver joined to a 12 cm rod of nickel and insulated. The silver end is maintained at 27 °C and the nickel end at 167 °C. The following data is also available.

   Thermal conductivity of silver: $0.42\,kW\,m^{-1}\,K^{-1}$

   Thermal conductivity of nickel: $91\,W\,m^{-1}\,K^{-1}$

   a. Explain which metal, silver or nickel, is the better conductor. (2)

   b. Calculate the temperature of the join once steady state conditions have been established. (4)

   c. Calculate the rate of conduction of thermal energy along the rod. (3)

4. Estimate the mean kinetic energy of an atom of argon in a sample of the gas kept at room temperature. (4)

5. The Sun has a radius of 696 km and a surface temperature of $5.80 \times 10^3\,K$. The distance from the Earth to the Sun is $1.49 \times 10^8\,km$.

   a. Calculate value of the wavelength at which the radiated energy from the Sun has its maximum intensity. (2)

   b. State the region of the electromagnetic spectrum in which the radiated energy from the Sun has its maximum intensity. (1)

   c. Calculate the luminosity of the Sun. (3)

   d. Calculate the power received at the edge of the Earth's atmosphere by an area of $1.00\,m^2$ that is normal to the Sun's radiation. (3)

6. The temperature inside a room is maintained at 19 °C when the temperature outside is 1 °C. The glass windows in the room have a total area of $6.0\,m^2$ and a thickness of 4.0 mm. The thermal conductivity of the glass windows is $0.8\,W\,m^{-1}\,K^{-1}$.

   a. Estimate the power needed to maintain the room temperature as a result of heat loss through the windows.

   b. Explain whether your answer is likely to be an underestimate or an overestimate.

B.2 Greenhouse effect

Equilibrium temperature of a planet

Equilibrium and emissivity

If the temperature of a planet is constant, then the power being absorbed by the planet must equal the rate at which energy is being radiated into space. The planet is in **thermal equilibrium**. If it absorbs more energy than it radiates, then the temperature must go up, and if the rate of loss of energy is greater than its rate of absorption, then its temperature must go down.

To estimate the power absorbed or emitted, the following concepts are useful.

Emissivity

The Earth and its atmosphere are not a perfect black body. Emissivity, e, is defined as the ratio of power radiated per unit area by an object to the power radiated per unit area by a black body at the same temperature. It is a ratio and so has no units.

$$e = \frac{\text{power radiated by object per unit area}}{\text{power radiated per unit area by black body at same temperature}}$$

$$= \frac{\text{power radiated per unit area}}{\sigma T^4}$$

Therefore $P = eA\sigma T^4$

A perfect black body has an emissivity of 1.

Albedo

Some of the radiation received by a planet is reflected straight back into space. The fraction that is reflected back is called the **albedo**.

The Earth's albedo varies daily and is dependent on season (cloud formations) and latitude. Oceans have a low value but snow has a high value. The global annual mean albedo is 0.3 (30%) on Earth.

$$\text{albedo} = \frac{\text{total scattered power}}{\text{total incident power}}$$

Mean intensity of incoming radiation

The intensity (power per unit area) of the radiation arriving from the Sun is called the solar constant, S (see page 60).

At any given instance of time, the total projected area of the planet of radius r that absorbs this radiation is given by:

projected area $= \pi r^2$

So, power absorbed by the planet $= S \times \pi r^2$

The planet rotates on its axis and this power is spread over the entire surface area of the planet:

surface area of planet $= 4\pi r^2$

$\therefore$ mean value of incoming intensity $= \dfrac{S \times \pi r^2}{4\pi r^2}$

$$= \frac{S}{4}$$

Solar power

Solar constant

The amount of power that arrives from the Sun is measured by the solar constant. It is defined as the amount of solar energy that falls per second on an area of $1 \, m^2$ above the Earth's atmosphere that is at right angles to the Sun's rays. Its average value is about $1400 \, W \, m^{-2}$.

This is not the same as the power that arrives on $1 \, m^2$ of the Earth's surface. Scattering and absorption in the atmosphere mean that often less than half of this arrives at the Earth's surface. The amount that arrives depends greatly on the weather conditions.

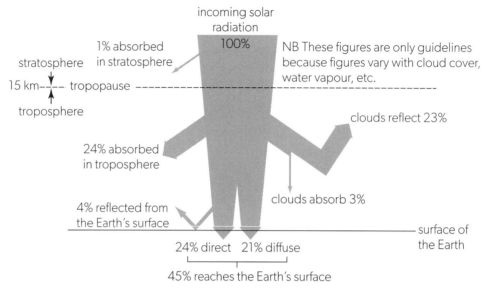

incoming solar radiation 100%

1% absorbed in stratosphere

stratosphere

15 km — tropopause

troposphere

NB These figures are only guidelines because figures vary with cloud cover, water vapour, etc.

clouds reflect 23%

24% absorbed in troposphere

clouds absorb 3%

4% reflected from the Earth's surface

24% direct   21% diffuse

45% reaches the Earth's surface

surface of the Earth

▲ Fate of incoming radiation

Different parts of the Earth's surface (regions at different latitudes) will receive different amounts of solar radiation.

The amount received will also vary with the seasons since this will affect how spread out the rays have become.

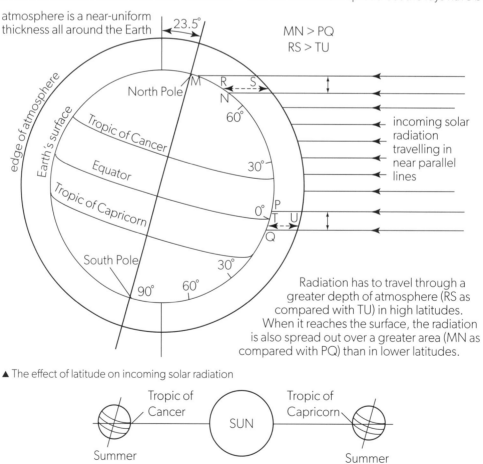

atmosphere is a near-uniform thickness all around the Earth

23.5°

MN > PQ
RS > TU

edge of atmosphere

Earth's surface

North Pole

Tropic of Cancer

Equator

Tropic of Capricorn

South Pole

M R S
N
60°

30°

0° P
T U
Q

30°

90° 60°

incoming solar radiation travelling in near parallel lines

Radiation has to travel through a greater depth of atmosphere (RS as compared with TU) in high latitudes. When it reaches the surface, the radiation is also spread out over a greater area (MN as compared with PQ) than in lower latitudes.

▲ The effect of latitude on incoming solar radiation

Tropic of Cancer

Tropic of Capricorn

SUN

Summer in northern hemisphere

Summer in southern hemisphere

▲ The Earth's orbit and the seasons

The greenhouse effect

Physical processes

Short wavelength radiation is received from the Sun and causes the surface of the Earth to warm up. The Earth will emit infrared radiation (longer wavelengths than the radiation coming from the Sun) because the Earth is cooler than the Sun. Some of this infrared radiation is absorbed by gases in the atmosphere and re-radiated in all directions.

This is known as the **greenhouse effect** and the gases in the atmosphere that absorb infrared radiation are called **greenhouse gases**. The net effect is that the upper atmosphere and the surface of the Earth are warmed. The name is potentially confusing, as real greenhouses are warm as a result of a different mechanism.

The temperature of the Earth's surface will be constant if the rate at which it radiates energy equals the rate at which it absorbs energy. The greenhouse effect is a natural process and without it the temperature of the Earth would be much lower; the average temperature of the Moon is more than 30 °C colder than the Earth.

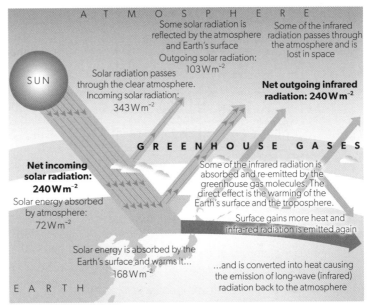

Sources: Okanagan University College in Canada; Department of Geography, University of Oxford; United States Environmental Protection Agency (EPA), Washington; Climate change 1995, The science of climate change, contribution of working group 1 to the second assessment report of the Intergovernmental Panel on Climate Change, UNEP and WMO, Cambridge Press, 1996

Greenhouse gases

The main greenhouse gases are naturally occurring but the balance in the atmosphere can be altered as a result of their release due to industry and technology. They are:

- **Methane**, CH_4. This is the principal component of natural gas and the product of decay, decomposition or fermentation. Livestock and plants produce significant amounts of methane.

- **Water**, H_2O. The small amounts of water vapour in the upper atmosphere (as opposed to clouds which are condensed water vapour) have a significant effect. The average water vapour levels in the atmosphere do not appear to alter greatly as a result of industry, but local levels can vary.

- **Carbon dioxide**, CO_2. Combustion releases carbon dioxide into the atmosphere which can significantly increase the greenhouse effect. Overall, plants (providing they are growing) remove carbon dioxide from the atmosphere during photosynthesis. This is known as **carbon fixation**.

- **Nitrous oxide**, N_2O. Livestock and industries (e.g. the production of nylon) are major sources of nitrous oxide. Its effect is significant as it can remain in the upper atmosphere for long periods.

In addition, the following gases also contribute to the greenhouse effect:

- **Ozone**, O_3. The **ozone layer** is an important region of the atmosphere that absorbs high-energy UV photons which would otherwise be harmful to living organisms. Ozone also adds to the greenhouse effect.

- **Chlorofluorocarbons** (CFCs). Used as refrigerants,

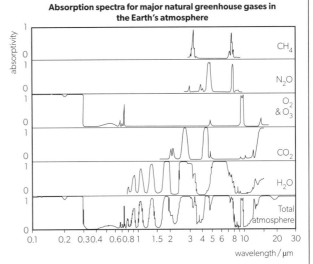

Absorption spectra for major natural greenhouse gases in the Earth's atmosphere

[After J.N. Howard, 1959: *Proc. I.R.E. 47*, 1459: and R.M. Goody and G.D. Robinson, 1951: *Quart. J. Roy Meteorol. Soc. 77*, 153]

propellants and cleaning solvents. They also have the effect of depleting the ozone layer.

Each of these gases absorbs infrared radiation as a result of resonance (see page 105). The natural frequency of oscillation of the bonds within the molecules of the gas is in the infrared region. If the driving frequency (from the radiation emitted from the Earth) is equal to the natural frequency of the molecule, resonance will occur. The amplitude of the molecules' vibrations increases and the temperature will increase. The absorption will take place at specific frequencies depending on the molecular energy levels.

Global warming

Possible causes of global warming

Records show that the mean temperature of the Earth has been increasing in recent years.

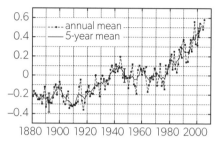

All atmospheric models are highly complicated. Some possible suggestions for this increase include:

- Changes in the composition of greenhouse gases in the atmosphere.

- Changes in the intensity of the radiation emitted by the Sun linked to, for example, increased solar flare activity.

- Cyclical changes in the Earth's orbit and volcanic activity.

The first suggestion could be caused by natural effects or could be caused by human activities (e.g. the increased burning of fossil fuels). An **enhanced greenhouse effect** is an increase in the greenhouse effect caused by human activities.

The Intergovernmental Panel on Climate Change (IPCC) is the United Nations body for assessing the science related to climate change. At the time of the publication of this book (2023), its most recent report concluded that "Human influence has **unequivocally** warmed the atmosphere, ocean and land." The report goes on to state that "*Climate change is an unequivocal threat:* it is already *causing irreversible damage* to our well-being and planetary health. *Further warming will increase losses and damages* from climate change, *often beyond our –* and our planet's *– ability to adapt.*"

The scientifically accepted view is that that the increased combustion of fossil fuels has released extra carbon dioxide into the atmosphere, which has enhanced the greenhouse effect.

Evidence for global warming

One piece of evidence that links global warming to increased levels of greenhouse gases comes from ice core data. The ice core has been drilled in the Russian Antarctic base at Vostok. Each year's new snowfall adds another layer to the ice.

Isotopic analysis allows the temperature to be estimated and air bubbles trapped in the ice cores can be used to measure the atmospheric concentrations of greenhouse gases. The record provides data from over 400 000 years ago to the present. The variations of temperature and carbon dioxide are very closely correlated.

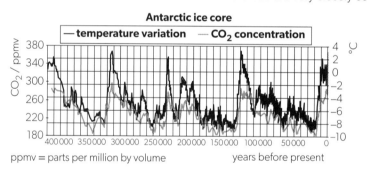

ppmv = parts per million by volume   years before present

Mechanisms

Predicting the future effects of global warming involves a great deal of uncertainty, as the interactions between different systems in the Earth and its atmosphere are extremely complex.

There are many mechanisms that may increase the rate of global warming.

- Global warming reduces ice/snow cover, which, in turn, reduces the albedo. This will result in an increase in the overall rate of heat absorption.

- Temperature increase reduces the solubility of CO_2 in the sea and thus increases atmospheric concentrations.

- Continued global warming will increase both evaporation and the atmosphere's ability to hold water vapour. Water vapour is a greenhouse gas.

- Regions with frozen subsoil exist (called tundra) that support simple vegetation. An increase in temperature may cause a significant release of trapped CO_2.

- Not only does deforestation result in the release of further CO_2 into the atmosphere, but the reduction in number of trees reduces carbon fixation.

The first four mechanisms are examples of processes whereby a small initial temperature increase has gone on to cause a further increase in temperature. This process is known as **positive feedback**. Some people have suggested that the current temperature increases may be "corrected" by a process that involves negative feedback, and that temperatures may fall in the future.

End of topic questions—B.2 Greenhouse effect

1. The radius of the Earth is r, and its albedo is α. The Solar constant is S.
   a. Explain what is meant by the *Solar constant*. (2)
   b. Explain what is meant by the *Earth's albedo*. (2)
   c. Assuming that the Earth behaves as a black body radiator, show that the Earth is predicted to reach a temperature of T given by
   $$T = \sqrt[4]{\frac{S(1-a)}{4\sigma}}$$
   where σ is the Stefan-Boltzmann constant. (4)
   d. The Earth with its atmosphere is not a perfect black body and has an emissivity of e.
      i. Explain what is meant by emissivity. (2)
      ii. The mean temperature of the Earth is 15 °C. The solar constant is $S = 1400\,W\,m^{-2}$ and the average albedo is $a = 0.3$. Calculate the emissivity of the Earth. (2)

2. This question is about the greenhouse effect.
   a. State the four main greenhouse gases. (4)
   b. By reference to molecular energy levels, outline the process by which a greenhouse gas absorbs infrared radiation. (3)
   c. Outline a primary cause of the enhanced greenhouse effect. (3)

3. Solar radiation passes through the Earth's atmosphere before being absorbed by the Earth's surface. The Earth's surface radiates some of this energy away from the Earth's surface.
   a. Outline the differences between the radiation being received by the Earth and the radiation being emitted by the Earth. (4)
   b. Explain what is meant by the *greenhouse effect*. (4)

4. The following data is available about the Earth and the planet Mercury (which has no atmosphere):
   The intensity of the solar radiation arriving to the top of the Earth's atmosphere $= 1400\,W\,m^{-2}$
   The average distance from the Sun to Earth $= 1\,AU$
   The average distance from the Sun to Mercury $= 0.4\,AU$

   Mercury's average albedo $= 0.10$
   Mercury's emissivity $= 0.98$
   Calculate:
   a. the intensity of the solar radiation arriving at Mercury's location (3)
   b. the average intensity of solar radiation arriving per m^2 of Mercury's surface (assume that Mercury is spherical and, at any given time, only half its surface area is receiving solar radiation) (4)
   c. the average intensity of solar radiation that is absorbed by each m^2 of Mercury's surface. (2)
   The temperature of Mercury is constant.
   d. State the average intensity of radiation that must be emitted by each m^2 of Mercury's surface. (1)
   e. Predict the temperature of the surface of Mercury. (4)

5. a. Explain what is meant by the statement that the Earth's average albedo is 0.30. (2)
   Five different significant regions of the Earth's surface are listed below:
   - Oceans
   - Deserts (sand)
   - Forests
   - Concrete (cities)
   - Snow
   b. Discuss which of the above surfaces will have:
      i. the largest albedo (3)
      ii. the smallest albedo. (3)
   c. Suggest an order for the five regions in terms of decreasing albedo. (5)
   d. Clouds in the Earth's atmosphere also contribute to the Earth's overall albedo. Explain whether the presence of clouds would be expected to increase or decrease the Earth's surface albedo. (3)

B.3 Gas laws

The gas laws (1)

Definitions of density and pressure

The symbol representing density is the Greek letter rho, ρ. The average density of a substance is defined by the following equation:

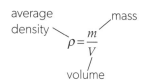

$$\rho = \frac{m}{V}$$

average density — $\rho = \dfrac{m}{V}$ — mass, volume

- Density is a scalar quantity.
- The SI units of density are $kg\,m^{-3}$
- Densities can also be quoted in $g\,cm^{-3}$
- The density of water is $1\,g\,cm^{-3} = 1000\,kg\,m^{-3}$

Pressure at any point in a fluid (a gas or a liquid) is defined in terms of the force, ΔF, that acts normally (at 90°) to a small area, ΔA, that contains the point.

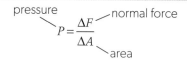

pressure $P = \dfrac{\Delta F}{\Delta A}$ — normal force, area

- Pressure is a scalar quantity—the force has a direction but the pressure does not. Pressure acts equally in all directions.
- The SI unit of pressure is $N\,m^{-2}$ or pascals (Pa). $1\,Pa = 1\,N\,m^{-2}$
- Atmospheric pressure $\approx 10^5\,Pa$
- Absolute pressure is the actual pressure at a point in a fluid. Pressure gauges often record the **difference** between absolute pressure and atmospheric pressure. Therefore if a difference pressure gauge gives a reading of $2 \times 10^5\,Pa$ for a gas, the absolute pressure of the gas is $3 \times 10^5\,Pa$.

Gas laws

The variation of pressure, volume and temperature of a gas can be investigated using the procedures outlined on the next page. In summary:

constant volume

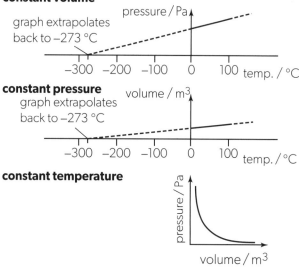

graph extrapolates back to −273 °C

pressure / Pa, temp. / °C, −300 −200 −100 0 100

constant pressure

graph extrapolates back to −273 °C

volume / m³, temp. / °C, −300 −200 −100 0 100

constant temperature

pressure / Pa, volume / m³

constant volume

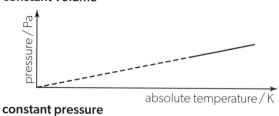

pressure / Pa, absolute temperature / K

constant pressure

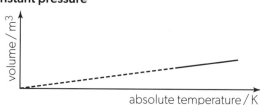

volume / m³, absolute temperature / K

constant temperature

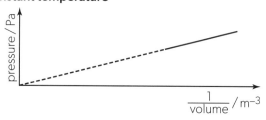

pressure / Pa, $\dfrac{1}{\text{volume}}$ / m⁻³

Points to note:

- Although pressure and volume both vary linearly with Celsius temperature, neither pressure nor volume is proportional to Celsius temperature.
- A different sample of gas would produce a different straight-line variation for pressure (or volume) against temperature but both graphs would extrapolate back to the same low temperature, −273 °C. This temperature is known as **absolute zero**.
- As pressure increases, the volume decreases. In fact, they are inversely proportional.

The trends can be seen more clearly if this information is presented in a slightly different way.

From these graphs, for a fixed mass of gas you can say that:

1. At constant V, $P \propto T$ or $\dfrac{P}{T}$ = constant (the pressure law)

2. At constant P, $V \propto T$ or $\dfrac{V}{T}$ = constant (Charles's law)

3. At constant T, $P \propto \dfrac{1}{V}$ or PV = constant (Boyle's law)

These relationships are known as the **ideal gas laws**. The temperature is always expressed in Kelvin (see page 48). These laws do not always apply to experiments done with real gases. A real gas is said to "deviate" from ideal behaviour under certain conditions (e.g. high pressure).

The gas laws (2)

Equation of state

The three ideal gas laws can be combined together to produce one mathematical relationship.

$$\frac{PV}{T} = \text{constant}$$

If you compare the value of this constant for different masses of different gases, it turns out to depend on the number of molecules that are in the gas—not their type. In this case, you use the definition of the mole to state

that, for n moles of ideal gas

$$\frac{PV}{nT} = \text{a universal constant}$$

The universal constant is called the molar gas constant R. The SI unit for R is J mol^{-1}K^{-1}: $R = 8.31$ J mol^{-1}K^{-1}

Summary: $\dfrac{PV}{nT} = R$ or $PV = nRT$

Worked example

a) What volume will be occupied by 8 g of helium (mass number 4) at room temperature (20 °C) and atmospheric pressure (1.0×10^5 Pa)?

$$n = \frac{8}{4} = 2 \text{ moles}$$

$$T = 20 + 273 = 293 \text{ K}$$

$$V = \frac{nRT}{P} = \frac{2 \times 8.31 \times 293}{1.0 \times 10^5} = 0.049 \text{ m}^3$$

b) How many atoms are there in 8 g of helium (mass number 4)?

$$n = \frac{8}{4} = 2 \text{ moles}$$

$$\begin{aligned} \text{number of atoms} &= 2 \times 6.02 \times 10^{23} \\ &= 1.2 \times 10^{24} \end{aligned}$$

Experimental investigations

1. Temperature T is the independent variable; P is the dependent variable; V is the control.

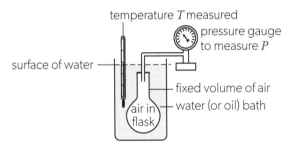

- Fixed volume of gas is trapped in the flask. Pressure is measured by a pressure gauge.

- Temperature of gas altered by temperature of bath—time is needed to ensure bath and gas at same temperature.

2. Temperature T is the independent variable; V is the dependent variable; P is the control.

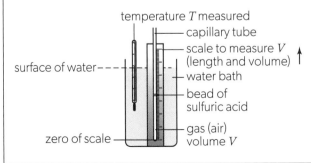

- Volume of gas is trapped in capillary tube by bead of concentrated sulfuric acid.

- Concentrated sulfuric acid is used to ensure gas remains dry.

- Heating gas causes it to expand and move the bead.

- Pressure remains equal to atmospheric.

- Temperature of gas altered by temperature of bath; time is needed to ensure that bath and gas are at same temperature.

3. P is the independent variable; V is the dependent variable; T is the control.

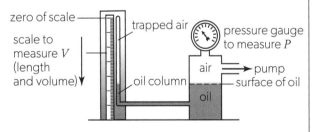

- Volume of gas measured against calibrated scale.

- Increase of pressure forces oil column to compress gas.

- Temperature of gas will be altered when volume is changed; time is needed to ensure gas is always at room temperature.

The gas laws (3)

Link between the macroscopic and microscopic

The equation of state for an ideal gas, $PV = nRT$, links the three macroscopic properties of a gas (P, V and T). Kinetic theory (page 49) describes a gas as being composed of molecules in random motion and, for this theory to be valid, each of these macroscopic properties must be linked to the microscopic behaviour of molecules.

A detailed analysis of how a large number of randomly moving molecules interact beautifully predicts another formula that allows the links between the macroscopic and the microscopic to be identified. The derivation of the formula uses only Newton's laws and a handful of assumptions. These assumptions describe what is meant by an ideal gas from the microscopic perspective.

The detail of this derivation is outlined on the following page. The result of this derivation is that the pressure and volume of the idealized gas are related to just two quantities:

$$PV = \frac{2}{3}N\overline{E_k}$$

where the number of molecules present is N and the average random kinetic energy per molecule is $\overline{E_k}$.

Equating the right-hand side of this formula with the right-hand side of the macroscopic equation of state for an ideal gas shows that:

$$nRT = \frac{2}{3}N\overline{E_k}$$

$$\text{But } n = \frac{N}{N_A}, \text{ so}$$

$$\frac{N}{N_A}RT = \frac{2}{3}N\overline{E_k}$$

$$\therefore \overline{E_k} = \frac{3}{2}\frac{R}{N_A}T$$

R (the molar gas constant) and N_A (Avogadro constant) are fixed numbers so this equation shows that the absolute temperature is proportional to the average KE per molecule:

$$T \propto \overline{E_k}$$

The ratio $\dfrac{R}{N_A}$ is called the Boltzmann's constant k_B.

$$\overline{E_k} = \frac{3}{2}k_B T = \frac{3}{2}\frac{R}{N_A}T$$

Using Boltzmann's constant, the ideal gas equation can be written in the form:

$$PV = Nk_B T$$

Definitions

The concepts of the **mole**, **molar mass** and the **Avogadro constant** are all introduced so as to be able to relate the mass of a gas (an easily measurable quantity) to the number of molecules that are present in the gas.

Ideal gas

An ideal gas is one that follows the gas laws for all values of P, V and T (see page 64).

Mole

The mole is the basic SI unit for "amount of substance". One mole of any substance is equal to the amount of that substance that contains the same number of particles as 0.012 kg of carbon-12 (^{12}C). When writing the unit it is (slightly) shortened to the mol.

Avogadro constant, N_A

This is the number of atoms in 0.012 kg of carbon-12 (^{12}C). It is 6.02×10^{23}.

Molar mass

The mass of one mole of a substance is called the molar mass. A simple rule applies. If an element has a certain mass number, A, then the molar mass will be A grams.

$$n = \frac{N}{N_A}$$

$$\text{number of moles} = \frac{\text{number of atoms}}{\text{Avogadro constant}}$$

Ideal gases and real gases

An ideal gas is a one that follows the gas laws for all values of P, V and T, so ideal gases cannot be liquefied. The microscopic description of an ideal gas is given on page 64. Real gases, however, can approximate to ideal behaviour providing that the intermolecular forces are small enough to be ignored. For this to apply, the pressure/density of the gas must be low and the temperature must be moderate.

Internal energy U of an ideal monatomic gas

The derivations in the box on the left relate the average kinetic energy per molecule in an ideal gas to the Boltzmann's constant k_B and the temperature T:

$$\overline{E_k} = \frac{3}{2}k_B T$$

Since there are no intermolecular forces in an ideal gas, it has zero potential energy. The internal energy, U, is thus all kinetic energy.

Total internal energy $U =$ number of molecules $\times \overline{E_k}$

$$U = \frac{3}{2}Nk_B T = \frac{3}{2}nRT$$

These two formulas are given in the data booklet.

Molecular model of an ideal gas (1)

Kinetic model of an ideal gas

Assumptions:

- Newton's laws apply to molecular behaviour
- there are no intermolecular forces except during a collision
- the molecules are treated as points
- the molecules are in random motion
- the collisions between the molecules are elastic (no energy is lost)
- there is no time spent in these collisions.

The pressure of a gas is explained as follows:

- When a molecule bounces off the walls of a container its momentum changes (due to the change in direction—momentum is a vector).
- There must have been a force on the molecule from the wall (Newton II).
- There must have been an equal and opposite force on the wall from the molecule (Newton III).

- Each time there is a collision between a molecule and the wall, a force is exerted on the wall.
- The average of all the microscopic forces on the wall over a period of time means that there is effectively a constant force on the wall from the gas.
- This force per unit area of the wall is called pressure.

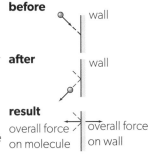

▲ A single molecule hitting the walls of the container.

$$P = \frac{F}{A}$$

The temperature of a gas is a measure of the average kinetic energy of the molecules, so if the temperature is lowered the molecules will move more slowly. At absolute zero, the molecules have zero kinetic so the temperature cannot go any lower.

Extra derivation

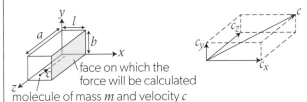

face on which the force will be calculated

molecule of mass m and velocity c

Consider N molecules inside a rectangular box of dimensions $a \times b \times l$. A typical molecule has velocity c. The components of the velocity are c_x, c_y and c_z.

In the x-direction, a molecule has a velocity c_x before it hits a wall and a velocity $-c_x$ after it hits the wall. The molecule has the same speed but is travelling in the opposite direction.

Since the collision is elastic,

$$\text{momentum change} = -mc_x - (mc_x) = -2mc_x$$
$$\text{impulse on wall} = +2mc_x \text{ (to the right)}$$

The time interval, Δt, before the same molecule returns to make another collision is

$$\Delta t = \frac{2l}{c_x} \text{ (assuming the molecule is a point)}$$

∴ average force due to this molecule

$$= \text{rate of change of momentum} = 2mc_x \div \frac{2l}{c_x} = \frac{mc_x^2}{l}$$

The total force due to the N molecules is the addition of the forces due to each molecule:

$$\text{total force} = \frac{m}{l} \times \left[\left(c_x^2\right)_1 + \left(c_x^2\right)_2 + \left(c_x^2\right)_3 + \ldots \left(c_x^2\right)_N \right]$$

$$= \frac{Nm}{l} \times \overline{c_x^2} \quad (1)$$

where $\overline{c_x^2}$ is the mean (average) value of $\left(c_x^2\right)$.

Note that the average value of $\overline{c_x^2}$ is **not** the same as the (average value of c_x^2)

For any given molecule, $c^2 = c_x^2 + c_y^2 + c_z^2$

Since N is large and the molecules are in random motion,

$$\overline{c_x^2} = \overline{c_y^2} = \overline{c_z^2} \text{ so } \overline{c_x^2} = \frac{1}{3}\overline{c^2}$$

Equation 1 becomes: total force $F = \frac{Nm}{l} \times \frac{1}{3}\overline{c^2} = \frac{1}{3}\frac{Nm\overline{c^2}}{l}$

$$\text{pressure } P = \frac{F}{A} = \frac{F}{a \times b} = \frac{1}{3}\frac{Nm\overline{c^2}}{l \times a \times b} \quad (2)$$

But $N \times m = $ total mass of gas, M

$l \times a \times b = $ total volume, V

$$\therefore \frac{Nm}{abl} = \frac{M}{V} = \text{density of gas, } \rho$$

So equation 2 becomes $P = \frac{1}{3}\rho\overline{c^2}$

The Physics Data Booklet quotes this formula as:

pressure of the gas ⟍ $P = \frac{1}{3}\rho v^2$ ⟋ average translational speed of the gas

⟍ density of the gas

v is a "typical" translational speed as it is not the mathematical average speed; it is known as the root mean squared (rms) velocity, which is the square root of the mean of the (velocity)^2: $v_{rms} = \sqrt{\text{mean of (velocity)}^2}$

Molecular model of an ideal gas (2)

Pressure law

Macroscopically, at a constant volume the pressure of a gas is proportional to its temperature in kelvin (see page 64). Microscopically this can be analysed as follows:

- If the temperature of a gas goes up, the molecules have more average kinetic energy—they are moving faster on average.
- Fast-moving molecules will have a greater change of momentum when they hit the walls of the container.
- Thus the microscopic force from each molecule will be greater.
- The molecules are moving faster so they hit the walls more often.

- For both of these reasons, the total force on the wall goes up.
- Thus the pressure goes up.

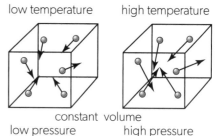

▲ Microscopic justification of the pressure law

Charles's law

Macroscopically, at a constant pressure, the volume of a gas is proportional to its temperature in kelvin (see page 64). Microscopically this can be analysed as follows:

- A higher temperature means faster moving molecules.
- Faster moving molecules hit the walls with a greater microscopic force.
- If the volume of the gas increases, then the rate at which these collisions take place on a unit area of the wall must go down.
- The average force on a unit area of the wall can thus be the same.
- Therefore the pressure remains the same.

▲ Microscopic justification of Charles's law

Boyle's law

Macroscopically, at a constant temperature, the pressure of a gas is inversely proportional to its volume (see page 64). Microscopically this can be seen to be correct.

- The constant temperature of gas means that the molecules have a constant average speed.
- The microscopic force that each molecule exerts on the wall will remain constant.
- Increasing the volume of the container decreases the rate with which the molecules hit the wall—average total force decreases.
- If the average total force decreases, then the pressure decreases.

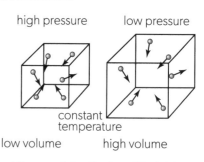

▲ Microscopic justification of Boyle's law

End of topic questions—B.3 Gas laws

1. A helium balloon has an initial volume of $0.30\,m^3$ and pressure of $1.0 \times 10^5\,Pa$. Its temperature is $18\,°C$. The balloon reaches a maximum height where the temperature has fallen to $-10\,°C$ and the pressure is $6.0 \times 10^4\,Pa$.

   a. Calculate the new volume of the balloon. (3)

   b. Calculate the number of moles of helium in the balloon. (2)

   c. Estimate the velocity of a typical helium atom when the balloon is at its maximum height. The mass of one helium atom is 6.65×10^{-27}. (4)

   d. Determine the **change** in the internal energy of the helium that has taken place during its flight. (3)

   e. Explain where this energy has gone. (2)

   f. State two assumptions that have been made about the helium. (2)

2. This question is about ideal gases and real gases.

   a. Explain the difference between an ideal gas and a real gas. (2)

   b. Under certain conditions, the behaviour of a real gas can be a good approximation of an ideal gas. Explain the conditions necessary in terms of:

      i.   temperature (2)

      ii. pressure (2)

      iii. density. (2)

   c. State three assumptions that are made about the particles of an ideal gas in kinetic theory. (3)

   d. Explain why the internal energy of an ideal gas is only kinetic energy. (2)

   e. A fixed mass of an ideal gas has a volume of $670\,cm^3$ at a pressure of $1.00 \times 10^5\,Pa$ and a temperature of $25\,°C$. The gas is heated at constant pressure to a temperature of $30\,°C$. Calculate the **change** in volume of the gas. (3)

3. In an experiment, the volume of air was recorded at different pressures. The following data was recorded.

Volume of trapped air, V/cm^3	Pressure of trapped air, P/kPa
34.0	120
29.0	140
25.5	160
22.5	180
20.0	200
18.0	220
16.5	240
15.0	260
14.0	280
13.0	300

   Sketch a graph to show the variation of the inverse of P with V using the above data.

   a. Suggest whether this data is consistent with the ideal gas equation. (3)

   b. Use your graph to explain the concept of systematic error. (2)

4. This question is about the kinetic model of an ideal gas.

   a. Explain how Newton's laws of motion can be applied to the movement of the particles of an ideal gas to understand why a gas exerts a pressure on the walls of its container. (6)

   b. Predict, in terms of the motion of the particles of ideal gas, what will happen to:

      i. the pressure of a fixed mass of ideal gas when its volume is decreased at constant temperature (3)

      ii. the temperature of an isolated sample of a fixed mass of ideal gas when the gas is compressed. (3)

B.4 Thermodynamics

Thermodynamic systems and concepts

Definitions

Historically, the study of the behaviour of ideal gases led to some very fundamental concepts that are applicable to many other situations. These laws, otherwise known as the laws of **thermodynamics**, provide the modern physicist with a set of very powerful intellectual tools. The terms used are explained below.

Thermodynamic system	Most of the time when studying the behaviour of an ideal gas in particular situations, you focus on the macroscopic behaviour of the gas as a whole. In terms of work and energy, the gas can gain or lose thermal energy and it can do work or work can be done on it. In this context, the gas can be seen as a **thermodynamic system**. A **closed** system is one in which no mass can be transferred in or out, but energy can be transferred in both directions as heat or work. An **isolated** system is one in which neither mass nor energy can be transferred in or out.
The surroundings	If you are focusing your study on the behaviour of an ideal gas, then everything else can be called its **surroundings**. For example the expansion of a gas means that work is done by the gas on the surroundings (see below).
Heat Q	In this context, heat refers to the transfer of a quantity of thermal energy between the system and its surroundings. This transfer must be as a result of a temperature difference. 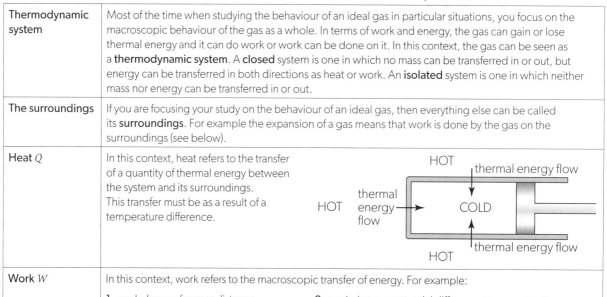
Work W	In this context, work refers to the macroscopic transfer of energy. For example: 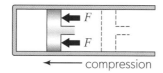 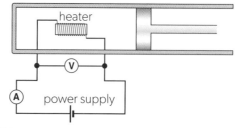 When a gas is compressed, work is done on the gas by the surroundings. When a gas expands, it does work on the surroundings. This is just another example of work being done on the gas.
Internal energy U (ΔU = change in internal energy)	The internal energy can be thought of as the energy held within a system. It is the sum of the PE due to the intermolecular forces and the kinetic energy due to the random motion of the molecules (see page 66). The total energy of a system is not the same as its internal energy. The total energy of the system also includes the overall motion of the system and any PE due to external forces. In thermodynamics, it is the changes in internal energy that are being considered. If the internal energy of a gas is increased, then its temperature must increase. A change of phase (e.g. liquid → gas) also involves a change of internal energy. 
Internal energy of an ideal monatomic gas	The internal energy of an ideal gas depends only on temperature. When the temperature of an ideal gas changes from T to $(T + \Delta T)$ its internal energy changes from U to $(U + \Delta U)$. The same ΔU always produces the same ΔT. Since the temperature is related to the average kinetic energy per molecule (see page 66), $\overline{E_k} = \frac{3}{2}k_B T = \frac{3}{2}\frac{R}{N_A}T$, the internal energy U is the sum of the total random kinetic energies of the molecules: $U = \frac{3}{2}Nk_B T = \frac{3}{2}RnT$ (where n = number of moles and N_A = Avogadro's constant) The change in internal energy of a system is related to its change in temperature: $\Delta U = \frac{3}{2}Nk_B \Delta T = \frac{3}{2}nR\Delta T$

AHL Work done by an ideal gas

Work done during expansion at constant pressure

Whenever a gas expands, it is doing work on its surroundings. If the pressure of the gas is changing all the time, then calculating the amount of work done is complex. This is because we cannot assume a constant force in the equation of work done (work done = force × distance). If the pressure changes, then the force must also change. If the pressure is constant, then the force is constant and you can calculate the work done.

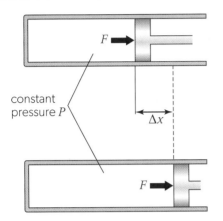

constant pressure P

Δx

Work done W = force × distance

$$= F\Delta x$$

Since pressure $= \dfrac{\text{force}}{\text{area}}$

$$F = PA$$

therefore

$$W = PA\Delta x$$

but $A\Delta x = \Delta V$

so work done $W = P\Delta V$

So if the volume of a gas increases (ΔV is positive), then the gas does work (W is positive)

P–V diagrams and work done

It is often useful to represent the changes that happen to a gas during a thermodynamic process on a P–V diagram. An important reason for choosing to do this is that the area under the graph represents the work done.

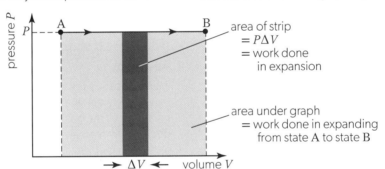

area of strip
= $P\Delta V$
= work done
in expansion

area under graph
= work done in expanding
from state A to state B

This turns out to be generally true for any thermodynamic process.

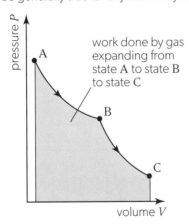

work done by gas expanding from state A to state B to state C

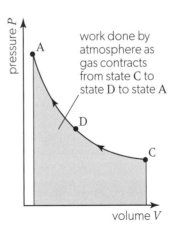

work done by atmosphere as gas contracts from state C to state D to state A

AHL The first law of thermodynamics

First law of thermodynamics

There are three fundamental laws of thermodynamics. The first law is simply a statement of the principle of energy conservation as applied to the system. If an amount of thermal energy Q is given to a system, then one of two things must happen (or a combination of both). The system can increase its internal energy ΔU or it can do work W.

As energy is conserved,

$$Q = \Delta U + W$$

It is important to remember what the signs of these symbols mean. They are all taken from the system's "point of view".

Q If this is **positive**, then thermal energy is going into the system.
If it is **negative**, then thermal energy is going out of the system.

ΔU If this is **positive**, then the internal energy of the system is **increasing**. (The temperature of the gas is increasing.)
If it is **negative**, the internal energy of the system is **decreasing**. (The temperature of the gas is decreasing.)

W If this is **positive**, then the **system is doing work** on the surroundings. (The gas is expanding.)
If it is **negative**, then the **surroundings are doing work** on the system. (The gas is contracting.)

Ideal gas processes

A gas can undergo any number of different types of change or process. Four important processes are considered below. In each case, the changes can be represented on a pressure–volume diagram and the first law of thermodynamics must apply. To be precise, these diagrams represent a type of process called a reversible process.

1. Isovolumetric

In an isovolumetric process, the gas has a constant volume. The diagram below shows an **isovolumetric decrease** in pressure.

Isovolumetric change:

V = constant, or

$\dfrac{P}{T}$ = constant

Q negative, ΔU negative ($T\downarrow$), W zero

2. Isobaric

In an isobaric process, the gas has a constant pressure. The diagram below shows an **isobaric expansion**.

Isobaric change:

P = constant, or

$\dfrac{V}{T}$ = constant

Q positive, ΔU positive ($T\uparrow$), W positive

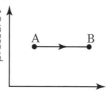

3. Isothermal

In an isothermal process the gas has a constant temperature. The diagram below shows an **isothermal expansion**.

Isothermal change:

T = constant, or

PV = constant

Q positive, ΔU zero, W positive

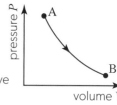

4. Adiabatic

In an adiabatic process there is no thermal energy transfer between the gas and the surroundings. This means that if the gas does work it must result in a decrease in internal energy. A rapid compression or expansion is approximately adiabatic. This is because, done quickly, there is not sufficient time for thermal energy to be exchanged with the surroundings. The diagram below shows an **adiabatic expansion**.

Adiabatic change:

Q zero, ΔU negative ($T\downarrow$), W positive

For a monatomic gas, the equation for an adiabatic process is $PV^{\frac{5}{3}}$ = constant

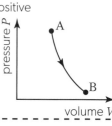

Worked example

A monatomic gas doubles its volume as a result of an adiabatic expansion. What is the change in pressure?

$$P_1 V_1^{\frac{5}{3}} = P_2 V_2^{\frac{5}{3}} \text{ so } \frac{P_2}{P_1} = \left(\frac{V_1}{V_2}\right)^{\frac{5}{3}} = 0.5^{\frac{5}{3}} = 0.31$$

∴ final pressure = 31% of initial pressure

AHL Second law of thermodynamics and entropy

Second law of thermodynamics

Historically, the **second law of thermodynamics** has been stated in many different ways. All of these versions can be shown to be equivalent.

In principle, there is nothing to stop the complete conversion of thermal energy into useful work. In practice, a gas cannot continue to expand forever—the apparatus sets a physical limit. Thus **the continuous conversion of thermal energy into work requires a cyclical process**—a heat engine.

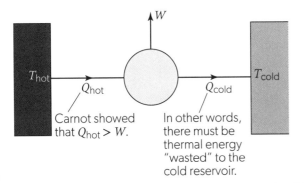

Carnot showed that $Q_{hot} > W$.

In other words, there must be thermal energy "wasted" to the cold reservoir.

This realization leads to possibly the simplest formulation of the second law of thermodynamics (the **Kelvin–Planck** formulation).

> No heat engine, operating in a cycle, can take in heat from its surroundings and totally convert it into work.

Other possible formulations include the following:

> No heat pump can transfer thermal energy from a low-temperature reservoir to a high-temperature reservoir without work being done on it (Clausius).

> Heat flows from hot objects to cold objects.

The concept of **entropy** leads to one final version of the second law.

> **The entropy of the Universe can never decrease.**

Technically, many thermodynamic equations assume the change is undertaken **reversibly**. This means that any change to the system happens very gradually, so that the system is always effectively in thermodynamic equilibrium. Real changes can be **irreversible**.

Entropy and energy degradation

Entropy is a property that expresses the disorder in the system.

The details are not important but the entropy S of a system is linked to the number of possible arrangements Ω of the system. $S = k_B \ln(\Omega)$, where k_B is the Boltzmann constant and Ω is the number of possible microstates of the system.

Because molecules are in random motion, you would expect roughly equal numbers of gas molecules in each side of a container.

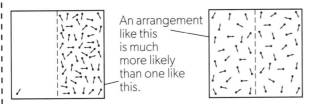

An arrangement like this is much more likely than one like this.

Probability that one given molecule is on the RHS $= \dfrac{1}{2}$

Probability that N molecules are all on the RHS $= \left(\dfrac{1}{2}\right)^N$

The number of ways of arranging the molecules to get the set-up on the right is greater than the number of ways of arranging the molecules to get the set-up on the left. This means that the entropy of the system on the right is greater than the entropy of the system on the left.

In any random process, the amount of disorder will tend to increase. In other words, the total entropy will always increase. The entropy change ΔS is linked to the thermal energy change ΔQ and the temperature T. $\left(\Delta S = \dfrac{\Delta Q}{T}\right)$

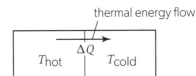

thermal energy flow

$$\text{decrease of entropy} = \frac{\Delta Q}{T_{hot}}; \quad \text{increase of entropy} = \frac{\Delta Q}{T_{cold}}$$

When thermal energy flows from a hot object to a colder object, overall the total entropy has increased.

In many situations the idea of energy **degradation** is a useful concept. The more energy is shared out, the more degraded it becomes—it is harder to put it to use. For example, the internal energy that is "locked" up in oil can be released when the oil is burned. In the end, all the energy released will be in the form of thermal energy—shared among many molecules. It is not feasible to get it back.

AHL Heat engines and heat pumps

Heat engines

A central concept in the study of thermodynamics is the **heat engine**. A heat engine is any device that uses a source of thermal energy in order to do work. It converts heat into work. The internal combustion engine in a car and the turbines that are used to generate electrical energy in a power station are both examples of heat engines. A block diagram representing a generalized heat engine is shown below.

In this context, the word **reservoir** is used to imply a constant temperature source (or sink) of thermal energy. Thermal energy can be taken from the hot reservoir

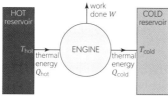

▲ Heat engine

without causing the temperature of the hot reservoir to change. Similarly, thermal energy can be given to the cold reservoir without increasing its temperature.

An ideal gas can be used as a heat engine. The $P-V$ diagram on the right represents a simple example. The four-stage cycle returns the gas to its starting conditions, but the gas has done work. The area enclosed by the cycle represents the amount of work done.

To do this, some thermal energy must have been taken from a hot reservoir (during the isovolumetric increase in pressure and the isobaric expansion). A different amount of thermal energy must have been ejected to a cold reservoir (during the isovolumetric decrease in pressure and the isobaric compression).

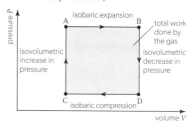

The thermal efficiency of a heat engine is defined as

$$\eta = \frac{\text{work done}}{\text{thermal energy taken from hot reservoir}}$$

This is equivalent to

$$\eta = \frac{\text{rate of doing work}}{\text{thermal power taken from hot reservoir}}$$

$$\eta = \frac{\text{useful work done}}{\text{energy input}}$$

The cycle of changes that results in a heat engine with the maximum possible efficiency is called the **Carnot cycle**.

Heat pumps

A **heat pump** is a heat engine being run in reverse. A heat pump causes thermal energy to be moved from a cold reservoir to a hot reservoir. In order for this to be achieved, mechanical work must be done.

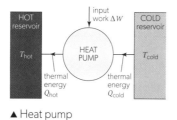

▲ Heat pump

Once again, an ideal gas can be used as a heat pump. The thermodynamic processes can be exactly the same as those used in the heat engine, but the processes are all opposite. This time, an anticlockwise circuit will represent the cycle of processes.

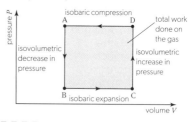

Carnot cycles and the Carnot theorem

The Carnot cycle represents the cycle of processes for a theoretical heat engine with the maximum possible efficiency. Such an idealized engine is called a **Carnot engine**.

The cycle consists of an ideal gas undergoing the following processes.

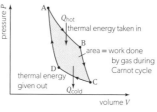

▲ Carnot cycle

- Isothermal expansion (A → B)
- Adiabatic expansion (B → C)
- Isothermal compression (C → D)

- Adiabatic compression (D → A)

The temperatures of the hot and cold reservoirs fix the maximum possible efficiency that can be achieved.

The efficiency of a Carnot engine can be shown to be:

$$\eta_{\text{Carnot}} = 1 - \frac{T_{\text{cold}}}{T_{\text{hot}}} \text{ (where } T \text{ is in kelvin)}$$

An engine operates at 300 °C and ejects heat to the surroundings at 20 °C. The maximum possible theoretical efficiency is:

$$\eta_{\text{Carnot}} = 1 - \frac{293}{573} = 0.49 = 49\%$$

End of topic questions—B.4 Thermodynamics

1. An ideal monatomic gas of volume $3.5 \times 10^5 \, cm^3$ expands to double its volume. The initial pressure of the gas is $4.2 \times 10^5 \, Pa$. This doubling of volume can be isobaric, isothermal or adiabatic.

   a) When the change is isobaric:
      i.   calculate the final pressure of the gas (2)
      ii. sketch a P–V graph for the change (2)
      iii. calculate the work done by the gas. (2)

   b) When the change is isothermal:
      i.   calculate the final pressure of the gas (2)
      ii. sketch a P–V graph for the change. (2)

   c) When the change is adiabatic:
      i.   calculate the final pressure of the gas (2)
      ii. sketch a P–V graph for the change (2)
      iii. calculate the work done by the gas. (2)

2. A kitchen contains two electrical devices—an oven and a fridge. When they are switched on, the fridge and the oven both maintain a constant temperature inside the device. Explain why the kitchen can be warmed by opening the door to the oven, but cannot be cooled by opening the door of the fridge. (6)

3. A car engine operates at $110\,°C$ when the outside temperature is $15\,°C$.

   a. Calculate the maximum efficiency of this engine assuming that it operates a Carnot cycle. (3)

   b. Discuss why the actual efficiency will be lower than this. (3)

4. Calculate the following entropy changes:

   a. $1\,kJ$ of thermal energy flows from a hot reservoir at $500\,°C$ to a cold reservoir at $20\,°C$. (4)

   b. $500\,g$ of ice melts at $0\,°C$. The specific latent heat of fusion of ice $= 334\,kJ\,kg^{-1}$. (4)

   c. A $3.5\,kW$ electrical emersion heater is switched on for $15\,s$ in a large tank of water at $10\,°C$. (4)

5. A Carnot cycle heat engine has an output power of $50\,kW$. It takes thermal energy from a heat source at $1\,500\,°C$ and rejects heat to a cold reservoir at $100\,°C$. Calculate the rate of transfer of heat to the cold reservoir. (4)

6. Outline how an entropy change can be calculated:
   i.   from the microscopic perspective of the number of different possible microstates of a system of interacting particles (3)
   ii. from the macroscopic quantities of thermal energy and temperature when temperature is held constant (3)
   iii. from the macroscopic quantities of thermal energy and temperature when temperature is not constant. (3)

B.5 Current and circuits

Electric current

Electrical currents and energy

An electrical current involves the flow of charge (positive or negative). The name given to the thing that is moving and transporting the charge is the **charge carrier**. Often the charge carriers are electrons (e.g. a current along a metal wires), but they can also be ions (e.g. in a solution) or even the absence of electrons, i.e. "holes" (e.g. in a semiconductor). Whenever a current flows, electric energy is used up, so the charge carriers entering a device must have more electrical energy than when they leave. Remember that it is electrical energy that is used up, not kinetic energy. The charge carriers enter and leave at the same velocity (see page 78). Different sources of electrical energy have different advantages and disadvantages (see page 25).

The energy difference between two points in a circuit depends on the amount of charge being moved. If twice as much charge is moved between two points in a circuit, then the total energy difference will be twice as much. The basic electrical unit used to compare two points in a circuit is thus the energy difference **per unit charge**. This is called the **potential difference** or **pd**, between the points.

potential difference between two points = energy difference per unit charge moved

$$= \frac{\text{energy difference}}{\text{charge}} = \frac{\text{work done}}{\text{charge}}$$

$$V = \frac{W}{q}$$

The basic unit for potential difference is the joule per coulomb, JC^{-1}. This is given a new name, the volt, V.

$$1 \text{ volt} = 1\,JC^{-1}$$

Voltage and potential difference are different terms for the same thing. Potential difference is probably the better name to use as it reminds you that it is measuring the difference between two points.

The name potential difference is used because technically this quantity is just a measure of the difference between two points of something called electrical **potential**. Potential difference means the difference in potential. See page 124 for more detail.

It helps to get the language right. Potential difference **across** a device causes current **through** the device.

Current

Current is defined as the **rate of flow of electrical charge**. It is always given the symbol, I. The definition of current is expressed as follows:

$$\text{current} = \frac{\text{charge flowed}}{\text{time taken}}$$

$$I = \frac{\Delta Q}{\Delta t} \text{ or (in calculus notation) } I = \frac{dQ}{dt}$$

$$1 \text{ ampere} = \frac{1\,\text{coulomb}}{1\,\text{second}} \qquad 1\,A = 1\,Cs^{-1}$$

If a current flows in just one direction, then it is known as a **direct current**. A current that constantly changes direction (first one way then the other) is known as an **alternating current** or ac.

In SI units, the ampere is the base unit and the coulomb is a derived unit: $1\,C = 1\,As$

Electrical conduction in a metal

Whenever charges move you say that a current is flowing. A current is the name for moving charges and the path that they follow is called the **circuit**. Without a complete circuit, a current cannot be maintained for any length of time.

Current flows THROUGH an object when there is a potential difference ACROSS the object. A battery (or power supply) creates the potential difference.

By convention, currents are always represented as the flow of positive charge. Thus **conventional current**, as it is known, flows from positive to negative. Although currents can flow in solids, liquids and gases, in most everyday electrical circuits the currents flow through wires. In this case, the things that actually move are the negative electrons—the **conduction electrons**. The direction in which they move is opposite to the direction of the representation of conventional current. As they move the

interactions between the conduction electrons and the lattice ions means that work needs to be done. Therefore, when a current flows, the metal heats up. The speed of the electrons due to the current is called their **drift velocity**.

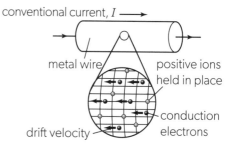

conventional current, $I \longrightarrow$

metal wire — positive ions held in place

conduction electrons

drift velocity

▲ Electrical conduction in a metal

The **drift speed equation** is $I = nAvq$

The typical drift speed of an electron is $10^{-4}\,m\,s^{-1}$ (5 A current in metal conductor of cross section $1\,mm^2$)

Internal resistance and cells

Electromotive force and internal resistance

When a 6 V battery is connected in a circuit some energy will be used up inside the battery itself. In other words, the battery has some **internal resistance**. The TOTAL energy difference per unit charge around the circuit is still 6 volts, but some of this energy is used up inside the battery. The energy difference per unit charge from one terminal of the battery to the other is less than the total made available by the chemical reaction in the battery.

For historical reasons, the TOTAL energy difference per unit charge around a circuit is called the **electromotive force (emf)**. However, remember that it is not a force (measured in newtons) but an energy difference per charge (measured in volts).

In practical terms, emf is exactly the same as potential difference if no current flows.

$$\varepsilon = I(R + r)$$

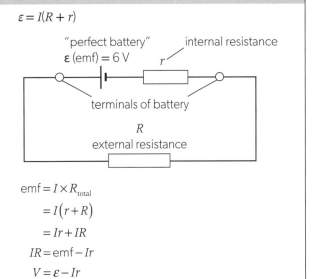

$$\text{emf} = I \times R_{total}$$
$$= I(r + R)$$
$$= Ir + IR$$
$$IR = \text{emf} - Ir$$
$$V = \varepsilon - Ir$$

Cells and batteries

An electric **battery** is a device consisting of one or more cells joined together. In a cell, a chemical reaction takes place, which converts stored chemical energy into electrical energy. There are two different types of cell: primary and secondary.

A **primary** cell cannot be recharged. During the lifetime of the cell, the chemicals in the cell get used in a non-reversible reaction. Once a primary cell is no longer able to provide electrical energy, it is thrown away. Common examples include zinc–carbon batteries and alkaline batteries.

A **secondary** cell is designed to be recharged. The chemical reaction that produces the electrical energy is reversible. A reverse electrical current charges the cell allowing it to be reused many times. Common examples include a lead–acid car battery, or nickel–cadmium and lithium–ion batteries.

The **charge capacity** of a cell is how much charge can flow before the cell stops working. Typical batteries have charge capacities that are measured in amp-hours (A h). 1 A h is the charge that flows when a current of 1 A flows for one hour, i.e. 1 A h = 3 600 C.

Determining internal resistance experimentally

The circuit below can be used to experimentally determine the internal resistance r of a cell (and its emf ε).

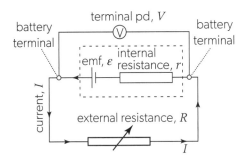

Procedure:

- Vary external resistance R to get a number (ideally 10 or more) of matching readings of V and I over as wide a range as possible.

- Repeat readings.
- Do not leave current running for too long (especially at high values of I).
- Take care that nothing overheats.

Data analysis:

- The relevant equation, $V = \varepsilon - Ir$ was introduced above.
- A plot of V on the y-axis and I on the x-axis gives a straight line graph with
  - gradient $= -r$
  - y-intercept $= \varepsilon$

Electric circuits

Ohm's law—ohmic and non-ohmic behaviour

The graphs show how the current varies with potential difference for some typical devices.

If current and potential difference are proportional, the device is said to be **ohmic** (e.g. a metal at constant temperature). Devices where current and potential difference are not proportional are said to be **non-ohmic** (e.g. a filament lamp or a diode).

Ohm's law states that the current flowing through a piece of metal is proportional to the potential difference across it providing the temperature remains constant.

(a) metal at constant temperature

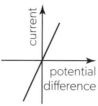

(b) filament lamp

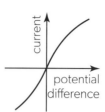

(c) diode

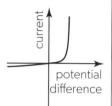

In symbols,

$$V \propto I \text{ (if temperature is constant)}$$

A device with constant resistance (i.e. an ohmic device) is called a **resistor**.

The symbols that are used when representing electrical circuits are all shown on page 5 of the Physics Data booklet.

Power dissipation

Since potential difference $= \dfrac{\text{energy difference}}{\text{charge flowed}}$

and current $= \dfrac{\text{charge flowed}}{\text{time taken}}$

then that potential difference × current

$= \dfrac{\text{energy difference}}{\text{charge flowed}} \times \dfrac{\text{charge flowed}}{\text{time taken}} = \dfrac{\text{energy difference}}{\text{time}}$

This energy difference per time is the power dissipated by the resistor. All this energy is going into heating up the resistor. In symbols:

$$P = V \times I$$

Sometimes it is more useful to use this equation in a slightly different form, e.g.

$P = V \times I$ and $V = I \times R$, so $P = (I \times R) \times I$ or $P = I^2 R$

Similarly, $P = \dfrac{V^2}{R}$

Circuits—Kirchoff's circuit laws

An electric circuit can contain many different devices or **components**. The mathematical relationship $V = IR$ can be applied to any component or group of components in a circuit.

When analysing a circuit it is important to look at the circuit as a whole. The power supply is the device that is providing the energy, but it is the whole circuit that determines what current flows through the circuit.

Two fundamental conservation laws apply when analysing circuits: the conservation of electric charge and the conservation of energy. These laws are collectively known as Kirchoff's circuit laws and can be stated mathematically as:

first law: $\Sigma I = 0$ (junction)

second law: $\Sigma V = 0$ (loop)

The first law states that the total current going into any junction in the circuit must be the same as the current coming out of the junction.

The second law states that around any loop, the total energy per unit charge must sum to zero. Any source of potential difference within the loop must be completely dissipated across the components in the loop.

Resistance

Resistance is the mathematical ratio between potential difference and current. If something has a high resistance, it means that you would need a large potential difference across it to get a current to flow.

Resistance $= \dfrac{\text{potential difference}}{\text{current}}$

In symbols, $R = \dfrac{V}{I}$

A new unit, the ohm, Ω, is defined to be equal to one volt per amp: **1 ohm = 1 V A^{-1}**

Worked example

A 1.2 kW electric kettle is plugged into the 250 V mains supply. Calculate:

a) the current drawn   b) the resistance of the kettle.

a) $I = \dfrac{1200}{250} = 4.8 \text{ A}$

b) $R = \dfrac{250}{4.8} = 52 \ \Omega$

Resistors in series and parallel

Resistors in series

A **series circuit** has components connected one after another in a continuous chain. The current must be the same everywhere in the circuit since charge is conserved. The total potential difference is shared among the components.

Total resistance $= 3\,\Omega + 4\,\Omega + 5\,\Omega = 12\,\Omega$

You can work out what share they take by looking at each component in turn, e.g.

the potential difference across the resistor $= I \times R_1$

the potential difference across the bulb $= I \times R_2$

$R_{total} = R_1 + R_2 + R_3$

This always applies to a series circuit. Note that $V = IR$ correctly calculates the potential difference across each individual component as well as calculating it across the total.

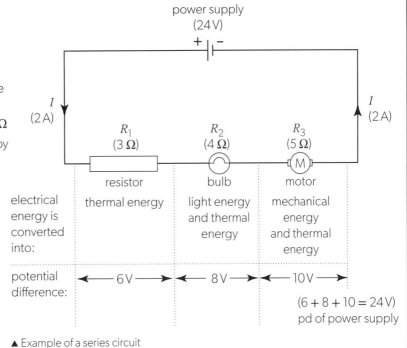

	resistor	bulb	motor
electrical energy is converted into:	thermal energy	light energy and thermal energy	mechanical energy and thermal energy
potential difference:	←— 6 V —→	←— 8 V —→	←— 10 V —→

$(6 + 8 + 10 = 24\,V)$
pd of power supply

▲ Example of a series circuit

Resistors in parallel

A **parallel circuit** branches and allows the charges to take more than one possible route around the circuit.

▲ Example of a parallel circuit

Since the power supply fixes the potential difference, each component has the same potential difference across it.

The total current is the sum of the currents in each branch.

$$I_{total} = I_1 + I_2 + I_3$$

$$= \frac{V}{R_1} + \frac{V}{R_2} + \frac{V}{R_3}$$

$$\frac{1}{R_{total}} = \frac{1}{R_1} + \frac{1}{R_2} + \frac{1}{R_3}$$

$$\frac{1}{R_{total}} = \frac{1}{3} + \frac{1}{4} + \frac{1}{5}\ \Omega^{-1}$$

$$= \frac{20 + 15 + 12}{60}\ \Omega^{-1}$$

$$= \frac{47}{60}\ \Omega^{-1}$$

$$\therefore R_{total} = \frac{60}{47}\ \Omega$$

$$= 1.28\ \Omega$$

Electrical meters

A current-measuring meter is called an **ammeter**. It should be connected in series at the point where the current needs to be measured. A perfect ammeter would have zero resistance. A real ammeter behaves like a perfect ammeter with a small non-negligible resistance in series with it.

A meter that measures potential difference is called a **voltmeter**. It should be placed in parallel with the component or components being considered. A perfect voltmeter has infinite resistance. A real voltmeter behaves like a perfect voltmeter with a large non-infinite resistance in parallel with it.

Potential divider circuits and sensors

Potential divider circuit

The circuit diagram shown in question 1 on page 82 is an example of a circuit involving a **potential divider**. It is so called because the two resistors "divide up" the potential difference of the battery. You can calculate the "share" taken by one resistor from the ratio of the resistances but this approach does not work unless the voltmeter's resistance is considered. An ammeter's internal resistance also needs to be considered. One of the most common mistakes when solving problems involving electrical circuits is to assume that the current or potential difference remains constant after a change to the circuit. After a change, the only way to ensure that your calculations are correct is to start again.

A variable potential divider (a **potentiometer**) is often the best way to produce a variable power supply. When designing the potential divider, the smallest resistor that is going to be connected needs to be taken into account: the potentiometer's resistance should be significantly smaller.

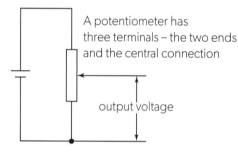

A potentiometer has three terminals – the two ends and the central connection

output voltage

To measure the V–I characteristics of an unknown resistor R, the two circuits (A and B) below are constructed. Both will both provide a range of readings for the potential difference, V, across and current, I, through R. Providing that R is much greater than the resistance of the potentiometer, circuit B is preferred because the range of readings is greater.

- Circuit B allows the potential difference across R (and hence the current through R) to be reduced down to zero. Circuit A will not go below the minimum value achieved when the variable resistor is at its maximum value.

- Circuit B allows the potential difference across R (and hence the current through R) to be increased up to the maximum value V_{supply} that can be delivered by the power supply in regular intervals. The range of values obtainable by Circuit A depends on the maximum resistance of the variable resistor.

Circuit A – variable resistor

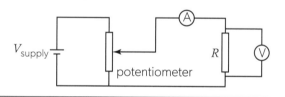

Circuit B – potentiometer

Sensors

A **light-dependent resistor (LDR)**, is a device whose resistance depends on the amount of light shining on its surface. An increase in light causes a decrease in resistance.

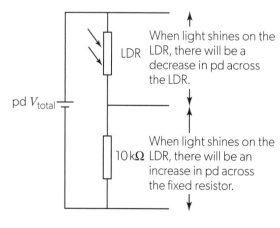

When light shines on the LDR, there will be a decrease in pd across the LDR.

When light shines on the LDR, there will be an increase in pd across the fixed resistor.

A **thermistor** is a resistor whose value of resistance depends on its temperature. Most are semiconducting devices that have a **negative temperature coefficient (NTC)**. This means that an increase in temperature causes a decrease in resistance. Both of these devices can be used in potential divider circuits to create sensor circuits. The output potential difference of a **sensor circuit** depends on an external factor.

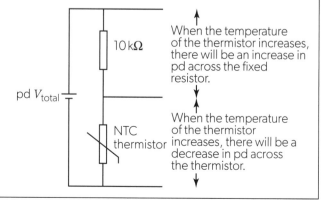

When the temperature of the thermistor increases, there will be an increase in pd across the fixed resistor.

When the temperature of the thermistor increases, there will be a decrease in pd across the thermistor.

Resistivity

Resistivity

The resistivity, ρ, of a material is defined in terms of its resistance, R, its length l and its cross-sectional area A.

$$R = \rho \frac{l}{A}$$

The units of resistivity must be ohm metres (Ω m). Note that this is the ohm multiplied by the metre, not "ohms per metre".

Worked example

The resistivity of copper is $3.3 \times 10^{-7}\,\Omega$ m. Calculate the resistance of a 100 m length of wire of cross-sectional area 1.0 mm²

$$R = 3.3 \times 10^{-7} \times \frac{100}{10^{-4}}$$
$$= 0.33\,\Omega$$

Investigating resistance

The resistivity equation predicts that the resistance R of a substance will be:

- proportional to the length l of the substance
- inversely proportional to the cross-sectional area A of the substance.

These relationships can be predicted by considering resistors in series and in parallel.

- Increasing l is like putting another resistor in series. Doubling l is the same as putting an identical resistor in series. R in series with R has an overall resistance of $2R$. Doubling l means doubling R. So $R \propto l$. A graph of R vs l will be a straight line going through the origin.

- Increasing A is like putting another resistor in parallel. Doubling A is the same as putting an identical resistor in parallel. R in parallel with R has an overall resistance of $\frac{R}{2}$. Doubling A means halving R. So $R \propto \frac{1}{A}$. A graph of R vs $\frac{1}{A}$ will be a straight line going through the origin.

To practically investigate these relationships, you have:

Independent variable	Either l or A
Control variables	A or l (depending on above choice)
	Temperature
	Substance.
Data collection	For each value of independent variable: • a range of values for V and I should be recorded • R can be calculated from the gradient of a V vs I graph.
Data analysis	Values of R and the independent variable are analysed graphically.

Possible sources of error/uncertainty include:

- Temperature variation of the substance (particularly if currents are high). Circuits should not be left connected.

- The cross-sectional area of the wire is calculated by measuring the wire's diameter, d, and using $A = \pi r^2 = \frac{\pi d^2}{4}$. Several sets of measurements should be taken along the length of the wire and the readings in a set should be mutually perpendicular.

- The small value of the diameter of the wire will mean that the uncertainties generated using a ruler will be large. This will be improved using a **vernier caliper** or a **micrometer**.

End of topic questions—B.5 Current and circuits

1. In the circuit below, the voltmeter has a resistance of 20 kΩ. Calculate:

   a. the pd across the 20 kΩ resistor with the switch open (2)

   b. the reading on the voltmeter with the switch closed. (3)

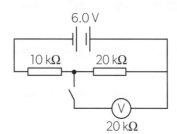

2. A student connects the circuit below to take current and voltage readings to calculate the resistance of R.

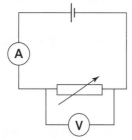

The student records the following data for different values of the variable resistor:

Pd across R/V	Current through R/A
3.1	1.52
2.3	1.15
2.0	0.99
1.5	0.74
1.0	0.49
0.5	0.26

   a. Sketch an appropriate graph to estimate the value of the unknown resistance R. (5)

The student now moves the voltmeter to be across the terminals of the cell and takes another set of data:

Pd across the cell / V	Current through R/A
3.0	1.51
3.6	1.20
4.0	1.00
4.5	0.75
5.0	0.50
5.5	0.26

   b. Sketch an appropriate graph to estimate the emf of the cell.

      i. Estimate the emf of the cell. (3)

      ii. Estimate the internal resistance of the cell. (3)

Another student attempts to repeat the first experiment, **but they accidentally swap the positions of the voltmeter and ammeter** to give the following incorrect circuit:

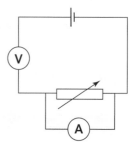

The student notices that the readings on the voltmeter and ammeter do not change for different values of the variable resistor.

   c. Determine the value shown on:

      i. the ammeter (3)

      ii. the voltmeter. (3)

3. A battery is connected to two 2.5 Ω resistors connected in parallel. The total current flowing out of the battery is 5.1 A. The resistors are then connected in series and the total current flowing out of the battery is 2.0 A. Calculate:

   a. the internal resistance of the battery (3)

   b. the emf of the battery (3)

   c. the power dissipated in one of the resistors:

      i. when connected in parallel (3)

      ii. when connected in series. (2)

C.1 Simple harmonic motion

Oscillations

Definitions

Many systems involve vibrations or oscillations; an object continually moves to-and-fro about a fixed average point (the **mean position**) retracing the same path through space taking a fixed time between repeats. Oscillations involve the interchange of energy between kinetic and potential.

	Kinetic energy	Potential energy store
Mass moving between two horizontal springs	Moving mass	Elastic potential energy in the springs
Mass moving on a vertical spring	Moving mass	Elastic potential energy in the springs and gravitational potential energy
Simple pendulum	Moving pendulum bob	Gravitational potential energy of bob
Buoy bouncing up and down in water	Moving buoy	Gravitational PE of buoy and water
An oscillating ruler as a result of one end being displaced while the other is fixed	Moving sections of the ruler	Elastic PE of the bent ruler

	Definition
Displacement, x	The instantaneous distance (SI measurement: m) of the moving object from its mean position (in a specified direction)
Amplitude, A	The maximum displacement (SI measurement: m) from the mean position
Frequency, f	The number of oscillations completed per unit time. The SI measurement is the number of cycles per second or Hertz (Hz).
Period, T	The time taken (SI measurement: s) for one complete oscillation. $T = \dfrac{1}{f}$
Phase difference, ϕ	This is a measure of how "in step" different particles are. If moving together they are **in phase**. ϕ is measured in either degrees (°) or radians (rad). 360° or 2π rad is one complete cycle, so 180° or π rad is completely out of phase by half a cycle. A phase difference of 90° or $\dfrac{\pi}{2}$ rad is a quarter of a cycle.

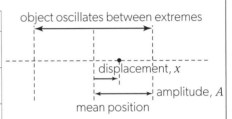

object oscillates between extremes

displacement, x

amplitude, A

mean position

Simple harmonic motion (SHM)

Simple harmonic motion is defined as the motion that takes place when the acceleration, a, of an object is always directed towards, and is proportional to, its displacement from a fixed point. This acceleration is caused by a **restoring force** that must always be pointed towards the mean position and also proportional to the displacement from the mean position.

$$F \propto -x \text{ or } F = -(\text{constant}) \times x$$

Since $F = ma$, $a \propto -x$ or $a = -(\text{constant}) \times x$

The negative sign signifies that the acceleration is always pointing back towards the mean position.

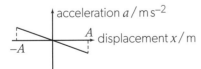

acceleration $a\,/\,\mathrm{m\,s^{-2}}$

A displacement $x\,/\,\mathrm{m}$

$-A$

Points to note about SHM:

- The time period T does not depend on the amplitude A. It is **isochronous**.
- Not all oscillations are SHM, but there are many everyday examples of natural SHM oscillations.

Example of SHM: mass between two springs

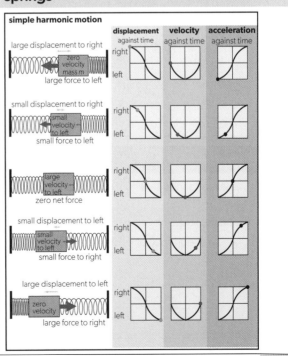

simple harmonic motion

Simple harmonic motion

Simple harmonic motion (SHM) equation

SHM occurs when the forces on an object are such that the resultant acceleration, a, is directed towards, and is proportional to, its displacement, x, from a fixed point.

$$a \propto -x \text{ or } a = -(\text{constant}) \times x$$

The mathematics of SHM is simplified if the constant of proportionality between a and x is identified as the square of another constant ω which is called the angular frequency. Therefore the general form for the equation that defines SHM is:

$$a = -\omega^2 x$$

The solutions for this equation follow below. The angular frequency ω has the units of rad s^{-1} and is related to the time period, T, of the oscillation by the following equation:

$$\omega = \frac{2\pi}{T}$$

Identification of SHM

In order to analyse a situation to decide if SHM is taking place, the following procedure should be followed.

- Identify all the forces acting on an object when it is displaced an arbitrary distance x from its rest position using a free-body diagram.
- Calculate the resultant force using Newton's second law. If this force is proportional to the displacement and always points back towards the mean position (i.e. $F \propto -x$), then the motion of the object must be SHM.

- Once SHM has been identified, the equation of motion must be in the following form:

$$a = -\left(\frac{\text{restoring force per unit displacement, } k}{\text{oscillating mass, } m} \right) \times x$$

- This identifies the angular frequency ω as $\omega^2 = \left(\frac{k}{m} \right)$ or $\omega = \sqrt{\left(\frac{k}{m} \right)}$. Identification of ω allows quantitative equations to be applied.

Two examples of SHM

Two common situations that approximate to SHM are:

1. Mass, m, on a vertical spring

   Provided that:

   - the mass of the spring is negligible compared with the mass of the load
   - friction (air friction) is negligible
   - the spring obeys Hooke's law with spring constant k at all times (i.e. elastic limit is not exceeded)
   - the gravitational field strength g is constant
   - the fixed end of the spring cannot move.

   Then it can be shown that:

   $$\omega^2 = \frac{k}{m}$$

   $$\text{or } T = 2\pi \sqrt{\frac{m}{k}}$$

2. The simple pendulum of length l and mass m

Provided that:

- the mass of the string is negligible compared with the mass of the load
- friction (air friction) is negligible
- the maximum angle of swing is small ($\leq 5°$ or 0.1 rad)
- the gravitational field strength g is constant
- the length of the pendulum is constant.

Then it can be shown that:

$$\omega^2 = \frac{g}{l}$$

$$\text{or } T = 2\pi \sqrt{\frac{l}{g}}$$

Note that the mass of the pendulum bob, m, is not in this equation and so does not affect the time period of the pendulum, T.

Worked example

A 600 g mass is attached to a light spring with spring constant 30 N m^{-1}.

a) Show that the mass moves with SHM.

b) Calculate the frequency of its oscillation.

a) Weight of mass $= mg = 6.0$ N

Additional displacement x down means that resultant force on mass $= kx$ upwards. Since $F \propto -x$, the mass will oscillate with SHM.

b) Since SHM, $T = 2\pi \sqrt{\left(\frac{m}{k} \right)} = 2\pi \sqrt{\left(\frac{0.6}{30} \right)} = 0.889$ s

$$f = \frac{1}{T} = \frac{1}{0.889} = 1.1 \text{ Hz}$$

Graphs of simple harmonic motion

Acceleration, velocity and displacement during SHM

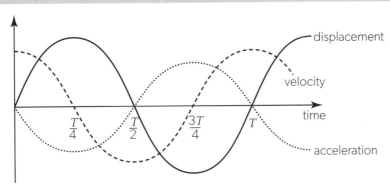

- acceleration leads velocity by 90°
- velocity leads displacement by 90°
- acceleration and displacement are 180° out of phase

- displacement lags velocity by 90°
- velocity lags acceleration by 90°

Energy changes during simple harmonic motion

During SHM, energy is interchanged between KE and PE. Providing there are no resistive forces which dissipate this energy, the total energy must remain constant. The oscillation is said to be **undamped**.

Energy in SHM is proportional to:

- the mass m
- the (amplitude)^2
- the (frequency)^2

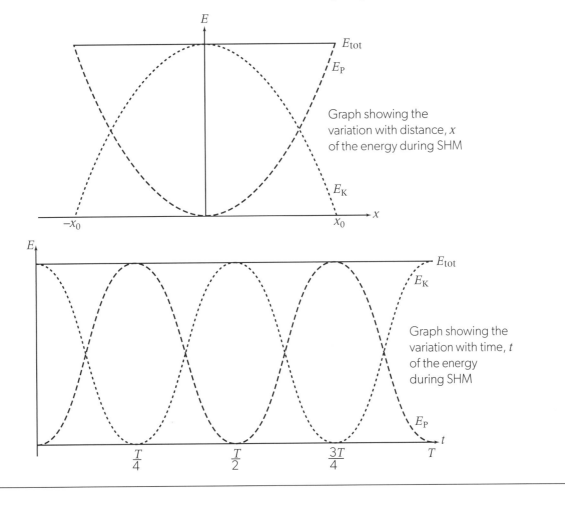

Graph showing the variation with distance, x of the energy during SHM

Graph showing the variation with time, t of the energy during SHM

85

AHL : Phase angle and energy equations

Acceleration, velocity and displacement during SHM

The variation with time of the acceleration, a, velocity, v, and displacement, x, of an object moving with SHM depends on the angular frequency ω.

The precise format of the relationships depends on where the object is when the clock is started (time $t = $ zero). In the table below, the left-hand set of equations correspond to an oscillation when the object is in the mean position when $t = 0$. The right-hand set of equations correspond to an oscillation when the object is at maximum displacement when $t = 0$.

$x = x_0 \sin \omega t$	$x = x_0 \cos \omega t$
$v = \omega x_0 \cos \omega t$	$v = -\omega x_0 \sin \omega t$
$a = -\omega^2 x_0 \sin \omega t$	$a = -\omega^2 x_0 \cos \omega t$

The equations for displacement and velocity can be rearranged to produce the following relationship:

$$v = \pm\omega\sqrt{x_0^2 - x^2}$$

x_0 is the amplitude of the oscillation measured in m

t is the time taken measured in s

ω is the angular frequency measured in rad s^{-1}

ωt is an angle that increases with time measured in radians. A full oscillation is completed when $(\omega t) = 2\pi$ rad.

The angular frequency is related to the time period T by the following equation:

$$T = \frac{2\pi}{\omega} = 2\pi\sqrt{\frac{m}{k}}$$

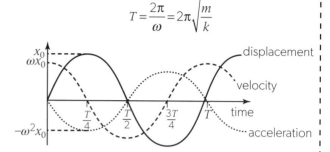

- acceleration leads velocity by $\dfrac{\pi}{2}$ rad
- velocity leads displacement by $\dfrac{\pi}{2}$ rad
- acceleration and displacement are π rad out of phase
- displacement lags velocity by $\dfrac{\pi}{2}$ rad
- velocity lags acceleration by $\dfrac{\pi}{2}$ rad

Phase angle

The equations and graphs have been introduced with the assumption that $t = 0$ corresponds to the instant when the displacement is zero and the velocity is at a maximum. An example of this situation is when an oscillating mass is passing through the mean position.

If the zero of time corresponds to a different instant during the oscillations, then the equations for simple harmonic motion are adapted by using the concept of a phase angle ϕ.

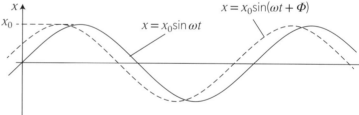

$$x = x_0 \sin(\omega t + \phi)$$
$$v = \omega x_0 \cos(\omega t + \phi)$$

Phase angles are usually measured in radians.

Energy equations

Graphs of the energy changes during SHM are shown on page 85. The mathematical relationships are derived as follows.

The kinetic energy can be calculated from:

$$E_k = \frac{1}{2}mv^2 = \frac{1}{2}m\omega^2\left(x_0 - x^2\right)$$

The potential energy can be calculated from:

$$E_p = \frac{1}{2}m\omega^2 x^2$$

The total energy is:

$$E = E_k + E_p = \frac{1}{2}m\omega^2\left(x_0 - x^2\right) + \frac{1}{2}m\omega^2 x^2 = \frac{1}{2}m\omega^2 x_0$$

Energy in SHM is proportional to:

- the mass m
- the (amplitude)^2
- the (frequency)^2

End of topic questions—C.1 Simple harmonic motion

1. An object of mass M is subject to a varying force F. As a result, the object has a varying displacement from its starting position of x. Outline the necessary conditions for the object to be moving with simple harmonic motion. (4)

2. A body of mass 500 g is hung on the end of a given type of spring. It oscillates with simple harmonic motion with a period of 0.5 s and an amplitude of 1.0 cm.

   a. Calculate:

      i. the frequency of oscillation (2)

      ii. the angular velocity of the oscillation (2)

      iii. the spring constant, k (2)

      iv. the maximum acceleration. (2)

   b. Calculate the time period that would be obtained:

      i. if two springs were used, both identical to the first, connected in parallel (2)

      ii. if two springs were used, both identical to the first, connected in series (2)

      iii. on the Moon, where the gravitational field is one sixth of the gravitational field on the Earth. (3)

   c. The springs are removed, and the mass is now suspended by a string creating a simple pendulum. Calculate:

      i. the length of the pendulum needed for the period of SHM to remain at 0.5 s (3)

      ii. the time period of this pendulum if taken to the Moon. (3)

3. A pendulum is undergoing SHM in a lift (elevator). Suggest what will happen to its time period if:

   i. the lift moves upwards at a steady speed (2)

   ii. the lift accelerates upwards at a constant rate (2)

   iii. the lift cable breaks. (2)

4.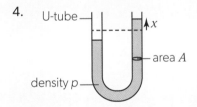

   The diagram above shows a column of liquid inside a U-tube at one instant of time when the liquid in the right-hand column is displaced a distance x from its equilibrium position. The liquid has a total length of l and will oscillate.

   a. Determine an expression for the total mass of the liquid. (2)

   b. Determine an expression for the restoring force when the liquid is displaced as shown. (2)

   c. Determine an expression for the acceleration of the liquid when the liquid is displaced as shown. (2)

   d. Use your answer to (c) to explain why the motion of the liquid is simple harmonic. (2)

5.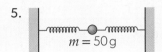

   A mass of 50 g is held by two identical horizontal springs, each of which has a spring constant of $1.0\,\mathrm{N\,m^{-1}}$. The mass is displaced by 0.20 m towards the right-hand spring. Its subsequent motion is simple harmonic. Calculate:

   a. the maximum value of stored elastic potential energy (2)

   b. the maximum speed of the mass (2)

   c. the maximum acceleration of the mass (2)

   d. the frequency of vibration (2)

   e. the displacement when the stored potential energy equals the kinetic energy. (2)

AHL -

6. An object of mass, m, is undergoing simple harmonic motion. The expression for the displacement, x, at any given time, t is:

   $$x = x_0 \sin(\omega t)$$

   a. Determine an expression for the kinetic energy of the mass at any given time, t. (2)

   b. Determine an expression for the potential energy of the mass at any given time, t. (2)

   c. Use your answers to (a) and (b) to determine an expression for the total energy of the mass at any given time, t. (2)

   d. Explain how your answer to (c) shows that the total energy of the mass remains constant. (2)

7. The tip of a tuning fork undergoes SHM at a frequency of 512 Hz and has a maximum speed of $3.5\,\mathrm{m\,s^{-1}}$. Determine the amplitude of its oscillation.

8. A particle undergoes SHM. At any given time, t, its displacement (in cm from its mean position), x, is given by

   $$x = 3.5\sin\left(\omega t + \frac{\pi}{2}\right)$$

   where $\omega = 3\pi\,\mathrm{rad\,s^{-1}}$

   Calculate:

      i. the period of the oscillation (2)

      ii. the maximum speed of the particle (3)

      iii. the maximum acceleration of the particle (3)

      iv. the first time when the instantaneous velocity of the particle is zero after the particle has started to move. (3)

Travelling waves

Introduction—rays and wavefronts

Light, sound and ripples on the surface of a pond are all examples of wave motion.

- They all transfer energy from one place to another.
- They do so without a net motion of the medium through which they travel.
- They all involve oscillations (vibrations) of one sort or another. The oscillations are SHM.

A **continuous wave** involves a succession of individual oscillations. A **wave pulse** involves just one oscillation. Two important categories of wave are **transverse** and **longitudinal**. The table gives some examples.

	Example of energy transfer
Water ripples (transverse)	A floating object gains an "up and down" motion.
Sound waves (longitudinal)	The sound received by the ear makes the eardrum vibrate.
Light wave (transverse)	The back of the eye (the retina) is stimulated when light is received.
Earthquake waves (both transverse and longitudinal)	Buildings collapse during an earthquake.

Transverse waves

Suppose a stone is thrown into a pond. Waves spread out on the surface as shown below.

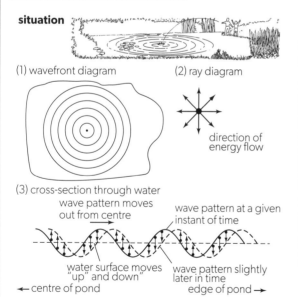

situation

(1) wavefront diagram

(2) ray diagram

direction of energy flow

(3) cross-section through water

wave pattern moves out from centre

wave pattern at a given instant of time

water surface moves "up" and down"

wave pattern slightly later in time

← centre of pond

edge of pond →

The top of the wave is known as the **crest**, whereas the bottom of the wave is known as the **trough**.

These aspects are important to all waves.

- The movement of the wave pattern. The **wavefronts** highlight the parts of the wave that are moving together.

Longitudinal waves

Sound is a longitudinal wave. This is because the oscillations are **parallel** to the direction of energy transfer.

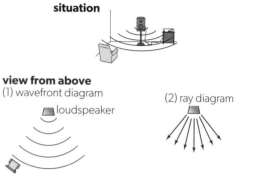

situation

view from above

(1) wavefront diagram

loudspeaker

(2) ray diagram

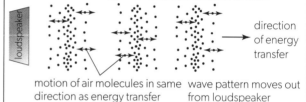

cross-section through wave at one instant of time

loudspeaker

direction of energy transfer

motion of air molecules in same direction as energy transfer

wave pattern moves out from loudspeaker

A point on the wave where everything is "bunched together" (high pressure) is known as a **compression**. A point where everything is "far apart" (low pressure) is known as a **rarefaction**.

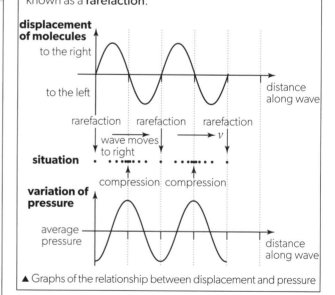

displacement of molecules

to the right

to the left

distance along wave

rarefaction   rarefaction   rarefaction

wave moves to right

v

situation

compression compression

variation of pressure

average pressure

distance along wave

▲ Graphs of the relationship between displacement and pressure

- The direction of energy transfer. The **rays** highlight the direction of energy transfer.
- The oscillations of the medium.

Note that the rays are at right angles to the wavefronts in the above diagrams. This is always the case.

This wave is an example of a transverse wave because the oscillations are at **right angles** to the direction of energy transfer.

Transverse mechanical waves cannot be propagated through fluids (liquids or gases).

Wave characteristics

Definitions

There are some useful terms that need to be defined in order to analyse wave motion in more detail. The table below explains these terms and they are also shown on the graphs.

Because the graphs seem to be identical, you need to look at the axes of the graphs carefully.

- The displacement–time graph (top right) represents the oscillations for one point on the wave. All the other points on the wave will oscillate in a similar manner, but they will not start their oscillations at exactly the same time.

- The displacement–position graph (bottom right) represents a "snapshot" of all the points along the wave at one instant of time. At a later time, the wave will have moved on but it will retain the same shape.

- The graphs can be used to represent longitudinal AND transverse waves because the y-axis records only the value of the displacement. It does NOT specify the direction of this displacement. So, if this displacement were parallel to the direction of the wave energy, the wave would be a longitudinal wave. If this displacement were at right angles to the direction of the wave energy, the wave would be a transverse wave.

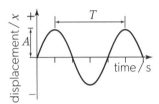

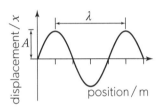

Term	Symbol	Definition
Displacement	x	This measures the change that has taken place as a result of a wave passing a particular point. Zero displacement refers to the mean (or average) position. For mechanical waves the displacement is the distance (in metres) that the particle moves from its undisturbed position.
Amplitude	A	This is the maximum displacement from the mean position. If the wave does not lose any of its energy, then its amplitude is constant.
Period	T	This is the time taken (in seconds) for one complete oscillation. It is the time taken for one complete wave to pass any given point.
Frequency	f	This is the number of oscillations that take place in one second. The unit is the hertz (Hz). A frequency of 50 Hz means that 50 cycles are completed every second.
Wavelength	λ	This is the shortest distance (in metres) along the wave between two points that are **in phase** with one another. "In phase" means that the two points are moving exactly in step with one another. For example, the distance from one crest to the next crest on a water ripple or the distance from one compression to the next one on a sound wave.
Wave speed	v	This is the speed (in m s^{-1}) at which the wavefronts pass a stationary observer.
Intensity	I	The intensity of a wave is the power per unit area that is received by the observer. The unit is W m^{-2}. The intensity of a wave is proportional to the square of its amplitude: $I \propto A^2$.

The period and the frequency of any wave are inversely related. For example, if the frequency of a wave is 100 Hz, then its period must be exactly $\frac{1}{100}$ of a second. In symbols, $T = \frac{1}{f}$.

Wave equation

There is a very simple relationship that links wave speed, wavelength and frequency. It applies to all waves.

The time taken for one complete oscillation is the period of the wave, T.

In this time, the wave pattern will have moved on by one wavelength, λ.

This means that the speed of the wave must be given by:

$$v = \frac{distance}{time} = \frac{\lambda}{T}$$

Since $\frac{1}{T} = f$

$$v = f\lambda$$

In words, **velocity = frequency × wavelength**

Electromagnetic spectrum

Electromagnetic waves

Visible light is one part of a much larger spectrum of similar waves that are all electromagnetic.

Charges that are accelerating generate electromagnetic fields. If an electric charge oscillates, it will produce a varying electric and magnetic field at right angles to each other.

These oscillating fields propagate (move) as a transverse wave through space. Since no physical matter is involved in this propagation, they can travel through a vacuum. The speed of this wave in a vacuum can be calculated from basic electric and magnetic constants and it is the same for all electromagnetic waves, $3.0 \times 10^8 \, \text{m s}^{-1}$.

Although all electromagnetic waves are identical in their nature, they have very different properties. This is because of the huge range of frequencies (and thus energies) involved in the electromagnetic spectrum.

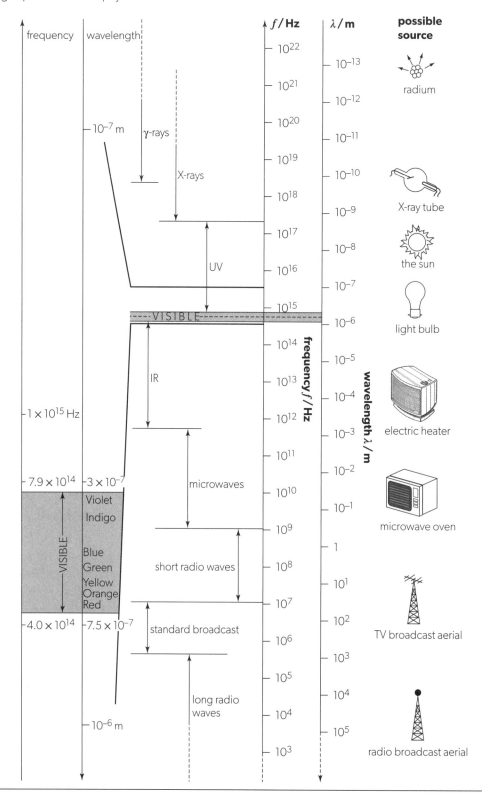

End of topic questions—C.2 Wave model

1. Sound waves travel in air at room temperature at approximately $3.3 \times 10^3 \, \text{m s}^{-1}$ whereas light, which is an electromagnetic wave, travels at $3.0 \times 10^8 \, \text{m s}^{-1}$.

   a. Outline the nature of:

      i.   sound waves (2)

      ii. electromagnetic waves. (2)

   b. In a lightning strike, sound and light are emitted at the same time. The emitted sound and the emitted light contain a mixture of wavelengths and frequencies. Calculate:

      i.   the wavelength of sound waves of frequency 120 Hz (2)

      ii. the frequency of light waves of wavelength 500 nm. (2)

   c. During a thunderstorm, an observer times an interval of 2.5 s between seeing the lightning flash and hearing the thunder. Estimate the distance between the observer and the lightning strike. (2)

2. A stone is thrown onto the surface of still water and creates a wave. A small floating cork 1.0 m away from the impact point has the following displacement–time graph (time is measured from the instant when the stone hits the water).

   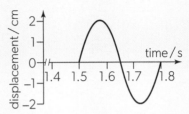

   Find:

   a. the amplitude of the wave (1)

   b. the speed of the wave (2)

   c. the frequency of the wave (2)

   d. the wavelength of the wave. (2)

3. Discuss the similarities and differences between transverse and longitudinal waves. (4)

Wavefronts and reflection (1)

Wavefronts and rays

As introduced on page 88, waves can be described in terms of the motion of a wavefront and/or in terms of rays.

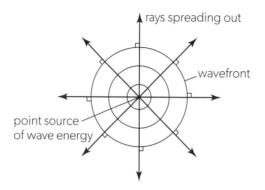

rays spreading out

wavefront

point source of wave energy

A **ray** is the path taken by the wave energy as it travels out from the source.

A **wavefront** is a surface joining neighbouring points where the oscillations are in phase with one another. In two dimensions, the wavefront is a line, and in one dimension, the wavefront is a point. In three dimensions, the wavefront is a sphere with rays spreading out in all directions.

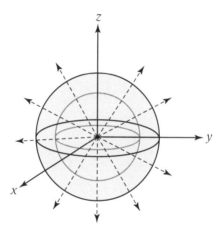

Reflection and transmission

In general, when any wave meets the boundary between two different media it is partially reflected and partially transmitted.

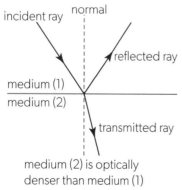

normal

incident ray

reflected ray

medium (1)

medium (2)

transmitted ray

medium (2) is optically denser than medium (1)

Reflection of two-dimensional plane waves

The diagram below shows what happens when plane waves are reflected at a boundary. When working with rays, by convention, you always measure the angles between the rays and the **normal**. The normal is a construction line that is drawn at right angles to the surface.

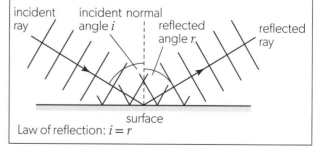

incident ray

incident angle i

normal

reflected angle r

reflected ray

surface

Law of reflection: $i = r$

Wavefronts and reflection (2)

Types of reflection

When a single ray of light strikes a smooth mirror it produces a single reflected ray. This type of "perfect" reflection is very different from the reflection that takes place from an uneven surface such as the walls of a room. In this situation, a single incident ray is generally scattered in all directions. This is an example of a **diffuse** reflection.

You see objects by receiving light that has come from them. Most objects do not give out light by themselves so you cannot see them in the dark. Objects become visible with a source of light (e.g. the Sun or a light bulb) because diffuse reflections have taken place that scatter light from the source towards our eyes.

Our brains are able to work out the location of the object by assuming that rays travel in straight lines.

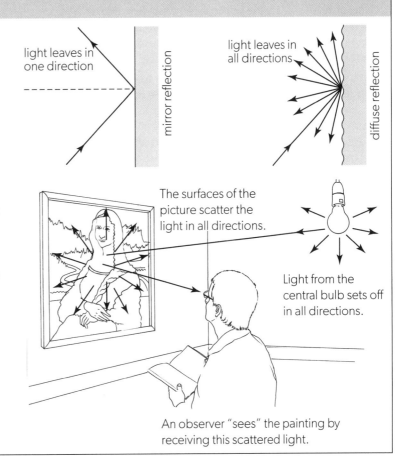

light leaves in one direction

mirror reflection

light leaves in all directions

diffuse reflection

The surfaces of the picture scatter the light in all directions.

Light from the central bulb sets off in all directions.

An observer "sees" the painting by receiving this scattered light.

Law of reflection

The location and nature of optical images can be worked out using **ray diagrams** and the principles of **geometric optics**. A ray

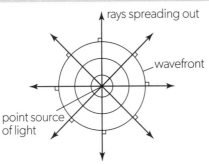

rays spreading out

wavefront

point source of light

is a line showing the direction in which light energy is propagated. The ray must always be at right angles to the wavefront. The study of geometric optics ignores the wave and particle nature of light.

When reflection in a mirror takes place, the direction of the reflected ray can be predicted using the laws of reflection. To specify the ray directions involved, it is usual to measure all angles with respect to an imaginary construction line called the **normal**. For example, the

incident angle is always taken as the angle between the incident ray and the normal. The normal to a surface is the line at right angles to the surface, as shown below.

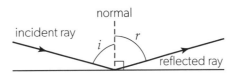

normal

incident ray

i

r

reflected ray

The laws of reflection are that:

- the incident angle is equal to the reflected angle
- the incident ray, the reflected ray and the normal all lie in the same plane (as shown in the diagram).

The second statement is only included in order to be precise and is often omitted. It should be obvious that a ray arriving at a mirror (such as the one represented above) is not suddenly reflected in an odd direction (e.g. out of the plane of the page).

Snell's law and refractive index

Refractive index and Snell's law

Refraction takes place at the boundary between two media. In general, a wave that crosses the boundary will undergo a change of direction. The reason for this change in direction is the change in wave speed that has taken place.

As with reflection, the ray directions are always specified by considering the angles between the ray and **the normal**. If a ray travels into an optically denser medium (e.g. from air into water), then the ray of light is refracted **towards** the normal. If the ray travels into an optically less dense medium, then the ray of light is refracted **away from** the normal.

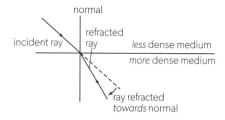

Snell's law allows you to work out the angles involved. When a ray is refracted between two different media,

the ratio $\dfrac{\sin(\text{angle of incidence})}{\sin(\text{angle of refraction})}$ is a constant.

The constant is called the refractive index n between the two media. This ratio is equal to the ratio of the speeds of the waves in the two media.

$$\frac{\sin i}{\sin r} = n$$

If the refractive index for a particular substance is given as a number and the other medium is not mentioned, then you can assume that the other medium is air (or, to be absolutely correct, a vacuum). Another way of expressing this is to say that the refractive index of air can be taken to be 1.0.

For example, the refractive index for a type of glass might be given as

$$n_{\text{glass}} = 1.34$$

This means that a ray entering the glass from air with an incident angle of 40° would have a refracted angle given by

$$\sin r = \frac{\sin 40°}{1.34} = 0.4797$$

$$\therefore r = 28.7°$$

$$n_{\text{glass}} = \frac{n_{\text{glass}}}{n_{\text{air}}} = \frac{\sin \theta_{\text{air}}}{\sin \theta_{\text{glass}}} = \frac{v_{\text{air}}}{v_{\text{glass}}} \quad \begin{array}{l} \leftarrow \text{speed of wave in air} \\ \leftarrow \text{speed of wave in glass} \end{array}$$

(remember that $n_{\text{air}} = 1$)

Example—ray travelling between two media

If a ray goes between two different media, the two individual refractive indices can be used to calculate the overall refraction using the following equation:

$$n_1 \sin \theta_1 = n_2 \sin \theta_2 \quad \text{or} \quad \frac{n_1}{n_2} = \frac{\sin \theta_2}{\sin \theta_1}$$

n_1 refractive index of medium 1

θ_1 angle in medium 1

n_2 refractive index of medium 2

θ_2 angle in medium 2

Suppose a ray of light is shone into a fish tank that contains water. The refraction that takes place is calculated as shown on right.

1st refraction:

$$n_{\text{glass}} = \frac{\sin a}{\sin b}$$

2nd refraction:

$$n_{\text{glass}} \times \sin b = n_{\text{water}} \times \sin c$$

$$\frac{n_{\text{glass}}}{n_{\text{water}}} = \frac{\sin c}{\sin b}$$

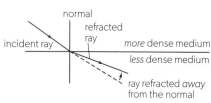

Overall, the refraction is from incident angle a to refracted angle c.

$$\text{i.e. } n_{\text{overall}} = \frac{\sin a}{\sin c} = \frac{\sin a}{\sin b} \times \frac{\sin b}{\sin c}$$

$$= n_{\text{water}}$$

Refraction of plane waves

The reason for the change in direction in refraction is the change in speed of the wave.

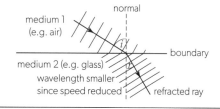

Snell's law (an experimental law of refraction) states that the ratio $\dfrac{\sin i}{\sin r} = $ constant, for a given frequency.

The ratio is equal to the ratio of the speeds in the different media

$$\frac{n_1}{n_2} = \frac{\sin \theta_2}{\sin \theta_1} = \frac{v_2}{v_1} \quad \begin{array}{l} \leftarrow \text{speed of wave in medium 2} \\ \leftarrow \text{speed of wave in medium 1} \end{array}$$

Refraction and critical angle

Total internal reflection and critical angle

In general, both reflection and refraction can happen at the boundary between two media.

It is, under certain circumstances, possible to guarantee complete (total) reflection with no transmission at all. This can happen when a ray meets the boundary and it is travelling in the denser medium.

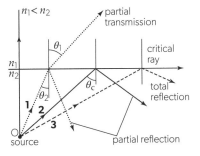

Ray 1 This ray is partially reflected and partially refracted.

Ray 2 This ray has a refracted angle of 90°. It is called the **critical ray**. The **critical angle** is the angle of incidence θ_c for the critical ray.

Ray 3 This ray has an angle of incidence **greater** than the critical angle. Refraction cannot occur so the ray must be totally reflected at the boundary and stay inside medium 2. The ray is said to be **totally internally reflected**.

The critical angle can be worked out as follows. For the critical ray,

$$n_1 \sin \theta_1 = n_2 \sin \theta_2$$
$$\theta_1 = 90°$$
$$\theta_2 = \theta_c$$
$$\therefore \sin \theta_c = \frac{1}{n_2} \text{ if the less dense medium is air.}$$

Methods for determining refractive index experimentally

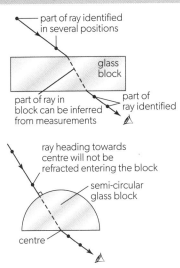

1. Locate paths taken by different rays either by sending a ray through a solid and measuring its position or aligning objects by eye. Uncertainties in angle measurement are dependent on protractor measurements. (See diagrams above.)

2. Use a travelling microscope to measure real and apparent depth and apply the following formula:

$$n = \frac{\text{real depth of object}}{\text{apparent depth of object}}$$

3. Very accurate measurements of angles of refraction can be achieved using a prism of the substance and a custom piece of equipment call a **spectrometer**.

Examples

1. What a fish sees under water

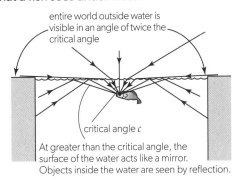

At greater than the critical angle, the surface of the water acts like a mirror. Objects inside the water are seen by reflection.

2. Prismatic reflectors

A prism can be used in place of a mirror. If the light strikes the surface of the prism at greater than the critical angle, it must be totally internally reflected.

Prisms are used in many optical devices, for example:

- periscopes—the double reflection allows the user to see over a crowd

- binoculars—the double reflection means that the binoculars do not have to be too long

- SLR cameras—the view through the lens is reflected up to the eyepiece.

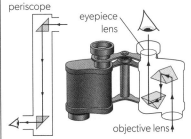

binoculars
The prism arrangement delivers the image to the eyepiece the right way up. By sending the light along the instrument three times, it also allows the binoculars to be shorter.

Diffraction

Diffraction

When waves pass through apertures they tend to spread out. Waves also spread around obstacles. This wave property is called **diffraction**. The wave energy is received in the geometric shadow region.

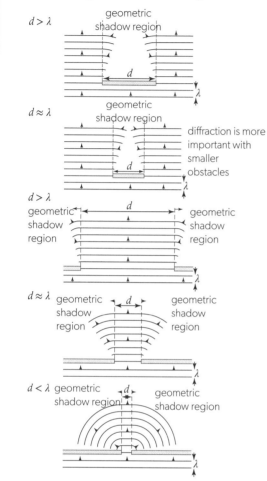

d = width of obstacle/gap

- Diffraction becomes relatively more important when the wavelength is large in comparison to the size of the aperture (or the object).
- The wavelength needs to be of the same order of magnitude as the aperture for diffraction to be noticeable.

Basic observations

Diffraction is a wave effect. The objects involved (slits, apertures, etc.) have a size that is of the same order of magnitude as the wavelength. The diagram shows diffraction at a single slit.

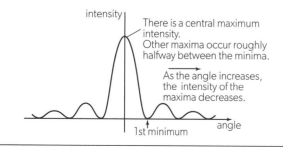

There is a central maximum intensity.
Other maxima occur roughly halfway between the minima.

As the angle increases, the intensity of the maxima decreases.

Practical significance of diffraction

Whenever an observer receives information from a source of electromagnetic waves, diffraction causes the energy to spread out. This spreading takes place as a result of any obstacle in the way and the width of the device receiving the electromagnetic radiation. Two sources of electromagnetic waves that are angularly close will both spread out and interfere with one another. This can affect whether or not they can be resolved.

Diffraction effects mean that it is impossible ever to see atoms because they are smaller than the wavelength of visible light, which means that light will diffract around the atoms. It is, however, possible to image atoms using smaller wavelengths. Practical devices where diffraction needs to be considered include:

- CDs and DVDs—the maximum amount of information that can be stored depends on the size and the method used for recording information.
- The electron microscope—resolves items that cannot be resolved using a light microscope. The electrons have an effective wavelength that is much smaller than the wavelength of visible light.
- Radio telescopes—the size of the dish limits the maximum resolution possible. Several radio telescopes can be linked together in an array to create a virtual radio telescope with a greater diameter and with a greater ability to resolve astronomical objects.

Examples of diffraction

Diffraction provides the reason why you can hear something even if you cannot see it. Sound wave will diffract around everyday objects, whereas light waves will not. This is because the wavelength of sound is much larger than the wavelength of light.

If you look at a distant street light at night and then squint your eyes, the light spreads sideways—this is as a result of diffraction taking place around your eyelashes! (Needless to say, this explanation is a simplification.)

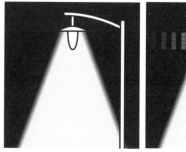

Superposition

Interference of waves

When two waves of the same type meet, they **interfere** and you can work out the resulting wave using the principle of superposition. The overall disturbance at any point and at any time where the waves meet is the vector sum of the disturbances that would have been produced by each of the individual waves. This is shown below.

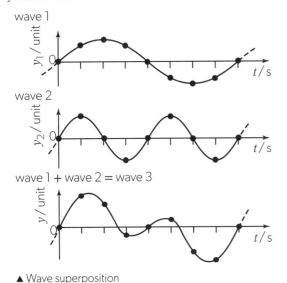

▲ Wave superposition

If the waves have the same amplitude and the same frequency, then the interference **at a particular point** can be **constructive** or **destructive**.

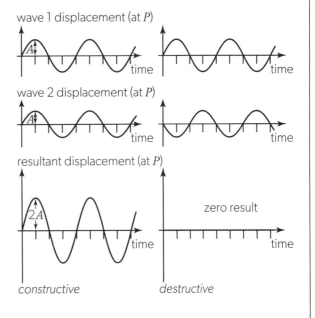

Technical language

Constructive interference takes place when the two waves are "in step" with one another—they are said to be **in phase**. There is a zero **phase difference** between them. Destructive interference takes place when the waves are exactly "out of step"—they are said to be **out of phase**. There are several different ways of saying this. One could say that the phase difference is equal to "half a cycle" or "180 degrees" or "π radians".

Interference can take place if there are two possible routes for a ray to travel from source to observer.

If the path difference between the two rays is a whole number of wavelengths, then constructive interference will take place.

path difference $= n\lambda \rightarrow$ constructive

path difference $= \left(n+\dfrac{1}{2}\right)\lambda \rightarrow$ destructive

$n = 0, 1, 2, 3 \ldots$

For constructive or destructive interference to take place, the sources of the waves must be phase linked or **coherent**.

Superposition of wave pulses

Whenever wave pulses meet, the principle of superposition applies: at any instant in time, the net displacement that results from different waves meeting at the same point in space is just the vector sum of the displacements that would have been produced by each individual wave. $y_{\text{overall}} = y_1 + y_2 + y_3 \ldots$

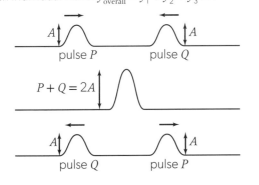

Examples of interference

Water waves
A ripple tank can be used to view the interference of water waves. Regions of large-amplitude waves are constructive interference. Regions of still water are destructive interference.

Sound
It is possible to analyse any noise in terms of the component frequencies that make it up and generate the same frequencies but of a different phase. This "antisound" will interfere with the original sound and cancel the original noise. This is the principle behind noise-cancelling headphones.

Light
The colours seen on the surface of a soap bubble are a result of constructive and destructive interference of two light rays. One ray is reflected off the outer surface of the bubble whereas the other is reflected off the inner surface.

Two-source interference of waves

Principles of the two-source interference pattern

Two-source interference is simply another application of the principle of superposition, for two coherent sources having roughly the same amplitude.

Two sources are coherent if:

- they have the same frequency
- there is a constant phase relationship between the two sources.

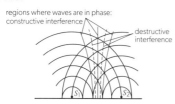

Two dippers in water moving together are coherent sources. This forms regions of water ripples and other regions with no waves.

Two loudspeakers both connected to the same signal generator are coherent sources. This forms regions of loud and soft sound.

A set-up for viewing two-source interference with light is shown on the right. It is known as **Young's double slit** experiment. A **monochromatic** source of light is one that gives out only one frequency. Light from the twin slits (the sources) interferes and patterns of light and dark regions, called **fringes**, can be seen on the screen.

Set-up 1

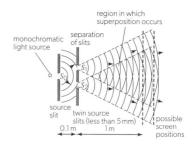

Set-up 2

The use of a laser makes the set-up easier.

The experiment results in a regular pattern of light and dark strips across the screen, as represented below.

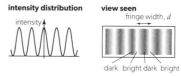

Mathematics

The location of the light and dark fringes can be mathematically derived in two ways. The derivations do not need to be recalled.

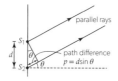

Method 1

The simplest way is to consider two parallel rays setting off from the slits as shown.

If these two rays result in a bright patch, then the two rays must arrive in phase. The two rays of light started out in phase but the light from source 2 travels an extra distance. This extra distance is called the **path difference**. Constructive interference can only happen if the path difference is a whole number of wavelengths.

Path difference $= n\lambda$

(where n is an integer, e.g. 1, 2, 3 . . .)

From the geometry of the situation,

path difference $= d\sin\theta$

so $n\lambda = d\sin\theta$

Method 2

If a screen is used to make the fringes visible, then the rays from the two slits cannot be absolutely parallel, but the physical set-up means that this is effectively true.

$$\sin\theta = \frac{p}{s}$$

$$\tan\theta = \frac{X}{D}$$

If θ is small, $\sin\theta = \tan\theta$

so $\dfrac{p}{s} = \dfrac{X}{D}$

$$\therefore p = \frac{Xs}{D}$$

For constructive interference:

$$p = n\lambda$$

$$\therefore n\lambda = \frac{X_n s}{D} \therefore X_n = \frac{n\lambda D}{s}$$

Fringe separation $d = X_{n+1} - X_n = \dfrac{\lambda D}{s}$

$$\therefore s = \frac{\lambda D}{d}$$

This equation only applies when the angle is small.

Worked example

Laser light of wavelength 450 nm is shone on two slits that are 0.1 mm apart. How far apart are the fringes on a screen placed 5.0 m away?

$$d = \frac{\lambda D}{s} = \frac{4.5\times10^{-7}\times5}{1.0\times10^{-4}} = 0.0225\,\text{m} = 2.25\,\text{cm}$$

AHL | Mathematics of diffraction

Basic observations

Diffraction is a wave effect. The objects involved (slits, apertures, etc.) have a size that is of the same order of magnitude as the wavelength of visible light.

Nature of obstacle	Geometrical shadow	Diffraction pattern
straight edge		
single long slit $b \sim 3\lambda$		
circular aperture		
single long slit $b \sim 5\lambda$		

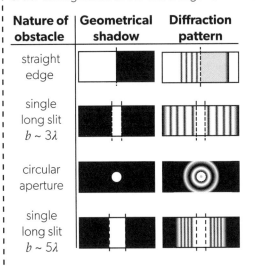

The intensity plot for a single slit is:

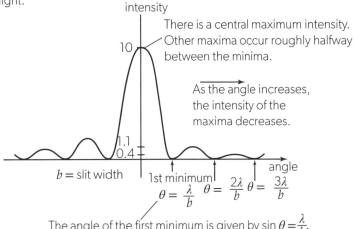

There is a central maximum intensity. Other maxima occur roughly halfway between the minima.

As the angle increases, the intensity of the maxima decreases.

b = slit width

1st minimum $\theta = \frac{\lambda}{b}$ $\theta = \frac{2\lambda}{b}$ $\theta = \frac{3\lambda}{b}$

The angle of the first minimum is given by $\sin \theta = \frac{\lambda}{b}$.
For small angles, this can be simplified to $\theta = \frac{\lambda}{b}$.

Explanation

The shape of the relative intensity versus angle plot can be derived by applying an idea called **Huygens' principle**. You can treat the slit as a series of secondary wave sources. In the forward direction (θ = zero), these are all in phase so they add up to give a maximum intensity. At any other angle, there is a path difference between the rays that depends on the angle.

The overall result is the addition of all the sources. The condition for the first minimum is that the angle must make all of the sources across the slit cancel out.

The condition for the first maximum out from the centre is when the path difference across the whole slit is $\frac{3\lambda}{2}$.

At this angle the slit can be analysed as being three equivalent sections each having a path difference of $\frac{\lambda}{2}$ across its length. Together, two of these sections will destructively interfere leaving the resulting amplitude to be $\frac{1}{3}$ of the maximum. Since intensity $\propto$ (amplitude)^2, the first maximum intensity out from the centre will be $\frac{1}{9}$

of the central maximum intensity. By a similar argument, the second maximum intensity out from the centre will have $\frac{1}{5}$ of the maximum amplitude and thus be $\frac{1}{25}$ of the central maximum intensity.

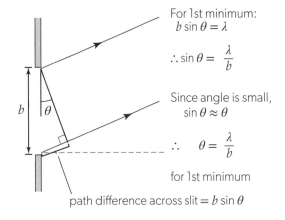

For 1st minimum:
$b \sin \theta = \lambda$

$\therefore \sin \theta = \frac{\lambda}{b}$

Since angle is small,
$\sin \theta \approx \theta$

$\therefore \quad \theta = \frac{\lambda}{b}$

for 1st minimum

path difference across slit $= b \sin \theta$

Single-slit diffraction with white light

When a single slit is illuminated with white light, each component colour has a specific wavelength and so the associated maxima and minima for each wavelength will be located at a different angle. For a given slit width, colours with longer wavelengths (red, orange, etc.) will diffract more than colours with short wavelengths (blue, violet, etc.). The maxima for the resulting diffraction pattern will show all the colours of the rainbow with blue and violet nearer to the central position and red appearing at greater angles.

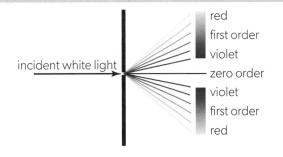

red
first order
violet
zero order
violet
first order
red

incident white light

AHL Young's double slit experiment

Double-slit interference

The double-slit interference pattern shown on page 98 was derived assuming that each slit was behaving like a perfect point source. This can only take place if the slits are infinitely small. In practice, they have a finite width. The diffraction pattern of each slit needs to be taken into account when working out the overall double slit interference pattern, as shown below.

Decreasing the slit width will mean that the observed pattern becomes more and more "idealized". Unfortunately, it will also mean that the total intensity of the light will be decreased. The interference pattern will become harder to observe.

(a) **Young's fringes for infinitely narrow slits**

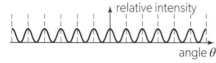

(b) **diffraction pattern for a finite-width slit**

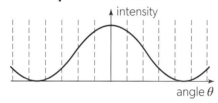

(c) **Young's fringes for slits of finite width**

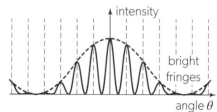

$s = \frac{\lambda D}{d}$ still applies, but different fringes will have different intensities and some fringes may possibly be missing.

Investigating Young's double-slit experimentally

Possible set-ups for the double-slit experiment are shown on page 98.

Set-up 1

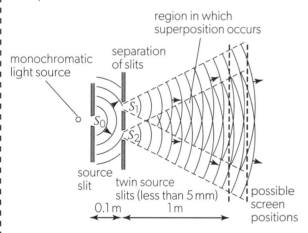

In the original set-up (set-up 1) light from the monochromatic source is diffracted at S_0 to ensure that S_1 and S_2 are receiving coherent light. Diffraction takes place providing S_1 and S_2 are narrow enough. The slit separations need to be approximately 1 mm (or less), so the slit widths are of the order of 0.1 mm (or less). This will provide fringes that are separated by approximately

0.5 mm on a screen (semi-transparent or translucent) situated 1 m away. The laboratory will need to be darkened to allow the fringes to be visible. They can be viewed using a microscope.

The most accurate measurements for slit separation and fringe width are achieved using a **travelling microscope**. This is a microscope that is mounted on a frame so that it can be moved perpendicular to the direction in which it is pointing. The microscope is moved across ten or more fringes and the distance moved by the microscope can be read off from the scale. The precision of this measurement is often improved by utilizing a vernier scale.

In the simplified version (set-up 2) of the experiment, fringes can still be bright enough to be viewed several metres away from the slits, so they can be projected onto an opaque screen (it is dangerous to look into a laser beam). Their separation can be then be directly measured with a ruler.

Set-up 2

AHL Multiple-slit diffraction

The diffraction grating

The diffraction that takes place at an individual slit affects the overall appearance of the fringes in Young's double-slit experiment (see page 100 for more details). This section considers the effect on the final interference pattern of adding further slits. A series of parallel slits (at a regular separation) is called a **diffraction grating**.

Additional slits at the same separation will not affect the condition for constructive interference. In other words, the angle at which the light from slits adds constructively will be unaffected by the number of slits. The situation is shown below.

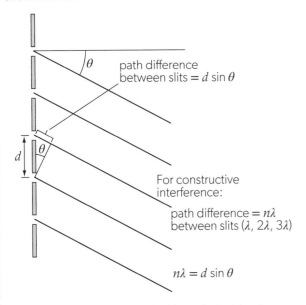

path difference
between slits = $d \sin \theta$

For constructive interference:

path difference = $n\lambda$
between slits (λ, 2λ, 3λ)

$$n\lambda = d \sin \theta$$

This formula also applies to the Young's double-slit arrangement. The difference between the patterns is most noticeable at the angles where perfect constructive interference does not take place. If there are only two slits, the maxima will have a significant angular width. Two sources that are just out of phase interfere to give a resultant that is nearly the same amplitude as two sources that are exactly in phase.

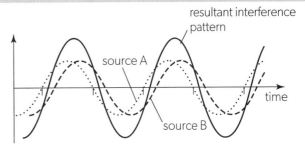

resultant interference pattern

source A

source B

time

The addition of more slits will mean that each new slit is just out of phase with its neighbour. The overall interference pattern will be totally destructive.

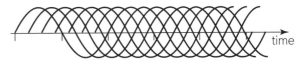

overall interference pattern is totally destructive

time

The addition of further slits at the same slit separation has the following effects:

- the principal maxima maintain the same separation
- the principal maxima become much sharper
- the overall amount of light being let through is increased, so the pattern increases in intensity.

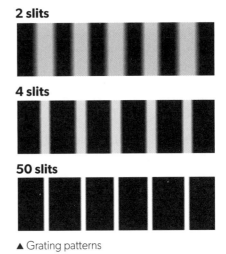

2 slits

4 slits

50 slits

▲ Grating patterns

Uses

One of the main uses of a diffraction grating is the accurate experimental measurement of the different wavelengths of light contained in a given spectrum. If white light is incident on a diffraction grating, the angle at which constructive interference takes place depends on wavelength. Different wavelengths can be observed at different angles. The accurate measurement of the angle provides the experimenter with an accurate measurement of the exact wavelength (and thus frequency) of the colour of light that is being considered. The apparatus that is used to achieve this accurate measurement is called a **spectrometer**.

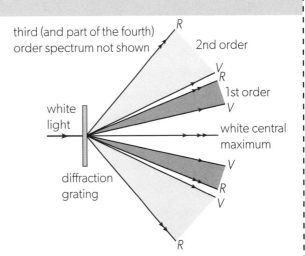

third (and part of the fourth) order spectrum not shown

2nd order

1st order

white light

white central maximum

diffraction grating

1. Calculate the wavelength for electromagnetic radiation of frequency 5.0×10^{14} Hz:

   a. in air (1)

   b. in glass of refractive index 1.5. (2)

AHL

2. A diffraction grating is just able to give a fourth-order spectrum for sodium light of wavelength 589 nm that is incident normally on the grating. Estimate the largest grating spacing that this diffraction grating could have. (3)

3. Red light of wavelength 700 nm is incident normally on a diffraction grating. The first-order maximum is at a deviation of effectively 90°.

   a. Estimate the grating spacing. (2)

   b. Blue light has a wavelength of 400 nm. Calculate the angle taken up by the whole first order of the visible spectrum when it is incident on this diffraction grating. (2)

   c. Infrared radiation of wavelength 750 nm replaces the red light. Determine how this will change the diffraction pattern detected. (2)

4. The image shows light from a laser that has passed through a single slit of width 0.080 mm and then projected onto a ruler 2.0 m away from the slit. The image shows the central maximum of the light projected onto the ruler.

   Calculate the wavelength of the laser light. (3)

5. A diffraction grating has 20 lines per mm and has light of wavelength 500 nm incident normally on the grating.

   a. Calculate the angular separation of the fringes. (2)

   b. The slits are not infinitely narrow but of width 2.5×10^{-5} m.

      i. Sketch a graph to show the variation, with angle, of the relative intensity of the resulting diffraction pattern **from one slit**. (3)

      ii. Suggest whether a fifth-order fringe would be observable for this set-up. (3)

C.4 Standing waves and resonance

Nature and production of standing (stationary) waves

Standing waves

A special case of interference occurs when two waves meet that are:

- of the same amplitude
- of the same frequency
- travelling in opposite directions.

In these conditions a **standing wave** will be formed.

The conditions needed to form standing waves seem quite specific, but standing waves are, in fact, quite common. They often occur when a wave reflects back from a boundary along the route on which it came. Since the reflected wave and the incident wave are of (nearly) equal amplitude, these two waves can interfere and produce a standing wave.

Perhaps the simplest way of picturing a standing wave would be to consider two transverse waves travelling in opposite directions along a stretched rope. The series of diagrams below shows what happens.

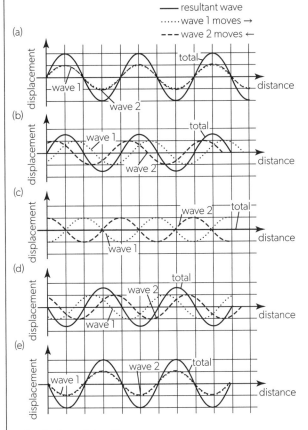

▲ Production of standing waves

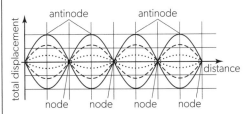

▲ A standing wave—the pattern remains fixed

There are some points on the rope that are always at rest. These are called the **nodes**. The points where the maximum movement takes place are called **antinodes**. The resulting standing wave is so called because the wave pattern remains fixed in space—it is its amplitude that changes over time. A comparison with a normal (travelling) wave is given below.

	Stationary wave	Normal (travelling) wave
Amplitude	All points on the wave have different amplitudes. The maximum amplitude is 2A at the antinodes. It is zero at the nodes.	All points on the wave have the same amplitude.
Frequency	All points oscillate with the same frequency.	All points oscillate with the same frequency.
Wavelength	This is **twice** the distance from one node (or antinode) to the next node (or antinode).	This is the shortest distance (in metres) along the wave between two points that are in phase with one another.
Phase	All points between one node and the next node are moving in phase.	All points along a wavelength have different phases.
Energy	Energy is not transmitted by the wave, but it does have an energy associated with it.	Energy is transmitted by the wave.

Although the example on the left involved transverse waves on a rope, a standing wave can also be created using sound or light waves. All musical instruments involve the creation of a standing sound wave inside the instrument. The production of laser light involves a standing light wave. Even electrons in hydrogen atoms can be explained in terms of standing waves.

A standing longitudinal wave can be particularly hard to imagine. The diagram below attempts to represent one example—a standing sound wave.

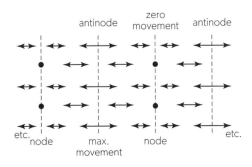

▲ A longitudinal standing wave

103

Boundary conditions

Boundary conditions

The boundary conditions of the system specify the conditions that must be met at the edges (the boundaries) of the system when standing waves are taking place. Any standing wave that meets these boundary conditions will be a possible resonant mode of the system.

1. Transverse waves on a string

If the string is fixed at each end, the ends of the string cannot oscillate. Both ends of the string would reflect a travelling wave and thus a standing wave is possible. The only standing waves that fit these boundary conditions are ones that have nodes at each end. The diagrams below show the possible resonant modes.

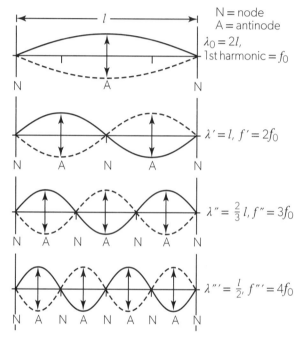

N = node
A = antinode
$\lambda_0 = 2l$,
1st harmonic = f_0

$\lambda' = l, f' = 2f_0$

$\lambda'' = \frac{2}{3}l, f'' = 3f_0$

$\lambda''' = \frac{l}{2}, f''' = 4f_0$

▲ Harmonic modes for a string

The resonant mode that has the lowest frequency is called the fundamental or the **first harmonic**. Higher resonant modes are called **harmonics**. Many musical instruments (e.g. piano, violin, guitar) involve similar oscillations of metal "strings".

2. Longitudinal sound waves in a pipe

A longitudinal standing wave can be set up in the column of air enclosed in a pipe. As above, this results from the reflections that take place at both ends.

As before, the boundary conditions determine the standing waves that can exist in the tube. A closed end must be a displacement node. An open end must be an antinode. Possible standing waves are shown for a pipe open at both ends and a pipe closed at one end.

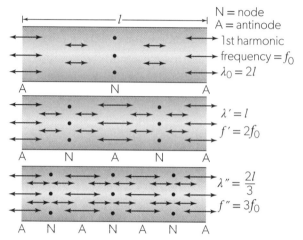

N = node
A = antinode
1st harmonic
frequency = f_0
$\lambda_0 = 2l$

$\lambda' = l$
$f' = 2f_0$

$\lambda'' = \frac{2l}{3}$
$f'' = 3f_0$

▲ Harmonic modes for a pipe open at both ends

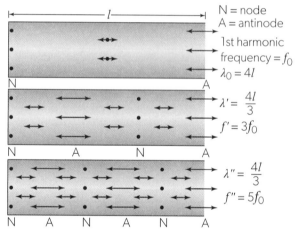

N = node
A = antinode
1st harmonic
frequency = f_0
$\lambda_0 = 4l$

$\lambda' = \frac{4l}{3}$
$f' = 3f_0$

$\lambda'' = \frac{4l}{3}$
$f'' = 5f_0$

▲ Harmonic modes for a pipe closed at one end

Musical instruments that involve a standing wave in a column of air include the flute, the trumpet, the recorder and organ pipes.

The accurate location of the antinode at the open end of a pipe is slightly beyond the end of the pipe. This **end correction** can often be ignored.

Worked example

An organ pipe (open at one end) is 1.2 m long.
Calculate its fundamental frequency.
The speed of sound is 330 m s⁻¹.

$l = 1.2\,\text{m}$ $\quad \therefore \frac{\lambda}{4} = 1.2\,\text{m (first harmonic)}$

$\therefore \lambda = 4.8\,\text{m}$

$v = f\lambda$

$f = \frac{330}{4.8} \approx 69\,\text{Hz}$

Resonance tube

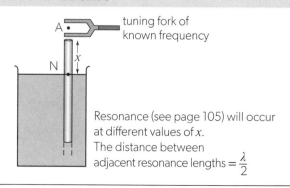

tuning fork of known frequency

Resonance (see page 105) will occur at different values of x.
The distance between adjacent resonance lengths $= \frac{\lambda}{2}$

Forced oscillations and resonance (1)

Damping

Damping involves a frictional force that is always in the opposite direction to the direction of motion of an oscillating particle. As the particle oscillates, it does work against this resistive (or dissipative) force and so the particle loses energy. As the total energy of the particle is proportional to the (amplitude)^2 of the SHM, the amplitude decreases exponentially with time.

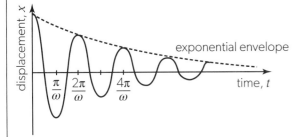

The above example shows the effect of **light damping** (the system is said to be **underdamped**) where the resistive force is small so a small fraction of the total energy is removed each cycle. The time period of the oscillations is not affected and the oscillations continue for a significant number of cycles. The time taken for the oscillations to "die out" can be long.

Heavy damping or **overdamping** involves large resistive forces (e.g. the SHM taking place in a viscous liquid)

and can completely prevent the oscillations from taking place. The time taken for the particle to return to zero displacement can again be long.

Critical damping involves an intermediate value for resistive force such that the time taken for the particle to return to zero displacement is a minimum. Effectively, there is no "overshoot". Examples of critically damped systems include electric meters with moving pointers and door closing mechanisms.

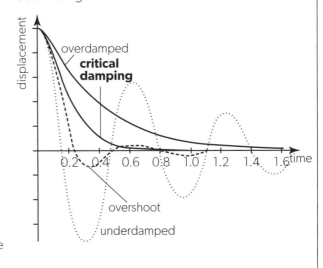

Natural frequency and resonance

If a system is temporarily displaced from its equilibrium position, the system will oscillate as a result. This oscillation will be at the **natural frequency of vibration** of the system. For example, if you tap the rim of a glass with a knife, it will oscillate and you can hear a note for a short while. Complex systems tend to have many possible modes of vibration each with its own natural frequency.

It is also possible to force a system to oscillate at any frequency that you choose by subjecting it to a changing force that varies with the chosen frequency. This periodic driving force must be provided from outside the system. When this **driving frequency** is first applied, a combination of natural and forced oscillations take place which produces complex **transient** oscillations. Once the amplitude of the transient oscillations "die down", a steady condition is achieved with the following properties.

- The system oscillates at the driving frequency.
- The amplitude of the forced oscillations is fixed. Each cycle energy is dissipated as a result of damping and the driving force does work on the system. The overall result is that the energy of the system remains constant.

- The amplitude of the forced oscillations depends on:
  - o the comparative values of the natural frequency and the driving frequency
  - o the amount of damping present in the system.

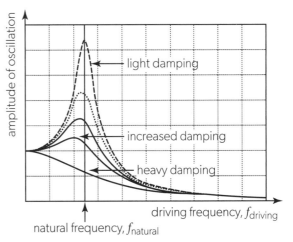

Resonance occurs when a system is subject to an oscillating force at exactly the same frequency as the natural frequency of oscillation of the system.

Resonance (2)

Phase of forced oscillations

After transient oscillations have died down, the frequency of the forced oscillations equals the driving frequency. The phase relationship between these two oscillations is complex and depends on how close the driven system is to resonance.

Examples of resonance

Vibrations in machinery	When in operation, the moving parts of machinery provide regular driving forces on the other sections of the machinery. If the driving frequency is equal to the natural frequency, the amplitude of a particular vibration may have dangerous implications, e.g. at a particular engine speed, a truck's rear view mirror can be seen to vibrate.
Quartz oscillators	A quartz crystal feels a force if placed in an electric field. When the field is removed, the crystal will oscillate. Appropriate electronics are added to generate an oscillating voltage from the mechanical movements of the crystal and this is used to drive the crystal at its own natural frequency. These devices provide accurate clocks for microprocessor systems.
Microwave generator	Microwave ovens produce electromagnetic waves at a known frequency. The changing electric field is a driving force that causes all charges to oscillate. The driving frequency of the microwaves provides energy, which means that water molecules, in particular, are provided with kinetic energy—i.e. the temperature is increased.
Radio receivers	Electrical circuits can be designed (using capacitors, resistors and inductors) that have their own natural frequency of electrical oscillations. The free charges (electrons) in an aerial will feel a driving force as a result of the frequency of the radio waves that it receives. Adjusting the components of the connected circuit allows its natural frequency to be adjusted to equal the driving frequency provided by a particular radio station. When the driving frequency equals the circuit's natural frequency, the electrical oscillations will increase in amplitude and the chosen radio station's signal will dominate the other stations.
Musical instruments	Many musical instruments produce their sounds by arranging for a column of air or a string to be driven at its natural frequency which causes the amplitude of the oscillations to increase.
Greenhouse effect	The natural frequency of oscillation of the molecules of greenhouse gases is in the infra-red region. Radiation emitted from the Earth can be readily absorbed by the greenhouse gases in the atmosphere. See page 61 for more details.
Buildings and bridges	Buildings and bridges can resonate if one of their natural frequencies of vibration is stimulated by an external oscillation (e.g. an earthquake, people walking in step on a bridge, or high winds). Historically, some structures have collapsed due to resonance. As a result, modern buildings are designed to withstand such situations.
Opera singer breaking a glass	If the rim of a glass is hit, it will oscillate at its resonant frequency. If sound of this exact frequency is received by the glass, the amplitude of its oscillation will grow, and it is possible for the glass to break as a result.

End of topic questions—C.4 Standing waves and resonance

1. An oscillator with a frequency of 50 Hz sends transverse waves at a speed of 60 m s^{-1} along a stretched spring.
   a. Calculate the length of string that would allow a standing wave pattern with **three** displacement antinodes. (3)
   b. The time $t = 0$ corresponds to a maximum displacement. Sketch diagrams to show the string at the following times:
      i. $t = 0$ (2)
      ii. $t = 5.0$ ms (2)
      iii. $t = 10.0$ ms (2)

2. The length of the air column in a glass tube that is closed at one end can be adjusted to be between 0.50 m and 2.00 m. The speed of sound in air is 340 m s^{-1}. Determine the length of the air column when there would be resonance for a tuning fork of frequency 280 Hz. (3)

3. The third harmonics of an open pipe, A, and a closed pipe B have the same frequency. Calculate the ratio:
   a. $\dfrac{\text{length of pipe A}}{\text{length of pipe B}}$ (4)
   b. $\dfrac{\text{1st harmonic frequency of pipe A}}{\text{1st harmonic frequency of pipe B}}$ (4)

4. The following data is obtained using a resonance tube of varying length that is closed at one end. The value of the shortest resonance length, l, was measured for tuning forks of different frequencies, f.

f / Hz	l / mm
200	423
250	342
300	281
400	209
500	170

   a. Sketch an appropriate straight-line graph to show the relationship between f and l. (4)
   b. Use your graph to calculate a value for the speed of sound. (3)

The Doppler effect

The Doppler effect

The Doppler effect is the name given to the change of frequency of a wave as a result of the movement of the source or the movement of the observer.

When a source of sound is moving:

- Sound waves are emitted at a particular frequency from the source.
- The speed of the sound wave in air does not change, but the motion of the source means that the wave fronts are "bunched up" ahead of the source.
- This means that the stationary observer receives sound waves of reduced wavelength.
- A reduced wavelength corresponds to an increased frequency of sound.

The overall effect is that the observer will hear sound at a higher frequency than it was emitted by the source. This applies when the source is moving towards the observer. A similar analysis shows that if the source is moving away from the observer, then sound of a lower frequency will be received. A change of frequency can also be detected if the source is stationary, but the observer is moving.

- When a police car or ambulance passes you on the road, you can hear the pitch of the sound change from high to low frequency. It is high when it is approaching and low when it is going away.
- Radar detectors can be used to measure the speed of a moving object. They do this by measuring the change in the frequency of the reflected wave.
- For the Doppler effect to be noticeable with light waves, the source (or the observer) needs to be moving at high speed. If a source of light of a particular frequency is moving away from an observer, the observer will receive light of a lower frequency. Since the red part of the spectrum has a lower frequency than all the other colours, this is called a **redshift**.
- If the source of light is moving towards the observer, there will be a **blueshift**.

See the following page for examples in more detail.

Motion of galaxies

It is a surprising observational fact that the vast majority of galaxies are moving away from us. The general trend is that the more distant galaxies are moving away at a greater speed as the Universe expands. This does not, however, mean that you are at the centre of the Universe—this would be observed wherever you are located in the Universe.

A good way to imagine this expansion is to think of space itself expanding. It is the expansion of space (as opposed to the motion of the galaxies through space) that results in the galaxies' relative velocities. In this model, the redshift of light can be thought of as the expansion of the wavelength due to the "stretching" of space.

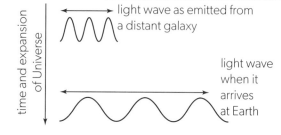

Mathematics

If a star or a galaxy moves away from us, then the wavelength of the light will be altered as predicted by the Doppler effect. If a galaxy is going away from the Earth, the speed of the galaxy with respect to an observer on the Earth can be calculated from the fractional change in the frequency or wavelength of the light. As long as the velocity is small when compared with the velocity of light, ($v \ll c$) the following equation can be used:

$$\frac{\Delta f}{f} = \frac{\Delta \lambda}{\lambda} \approx \frac{v}{c}$$

Δf = change in frequency of observed light (positive if frequency is increased)

f = frequency of light emitted

$\Delta \lambda$ = change in wavelength of observed light (positive if wavelength is increased)

λ = wavelength of light emitted

v = relative velocity of source of light

c = speed of light

Worked example

A characteristic absorption line often seen in stars is due to ionized helium. It occurs at 468.6 nm. If the spectrum of a star has this line at a measured wavelength of 499.3 nm, what is the recession speed of the star?

$$v \approx \frac{\Delta \lambda}{\lambda} c = \frac{499.3 - 468.6}{468.6} \times 3.00 \times 10^8$$

$$= 1.97 \times 10^7 \, \text{m s}^{-1}$$

Examples and applications of the Doppler effect

Examples and applications of the Doppler effect

1. Train going through a station

   The sound emitted by the whistle of a moving train is of constant frequency, but the sound received by a passenger standing on the platform will change. At any instant of time, it is the resolved component of the train's velocity towards the passenger that is used to calculate the frequency received.

   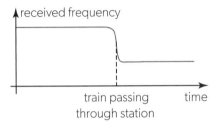

   train passing through station

2. Radar—speed measurement

   In many countries, the police use radar to measure the speed of vehicles to see if they are breaking the speed limit.

   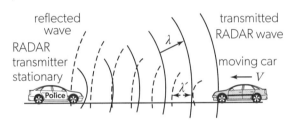

   - A pulse of microwave radiation of known frequency is emitted.
   - The pulse is reflected off moving car and is received back at the source.
   - The difference in emitted and received frequencies is used to calculate speed of car.
   - Double Doppler effect takes place:
     o The moving receives a frequency that is higher than that emitted as it is a moving observer.
     o The moving car acts as a moving source when sending the signal back.

3. Medical physics—blood flow measurements

   Doctors can use a pulse of ultrasound to measure the speed of red blood cells in way that is analogous to how a pulse of microwaves is used to measure the speed of a moving car (above).

   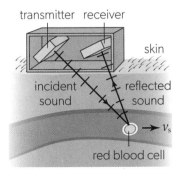

4. Receding galaxies—redshift

   - The relative intensities of the different wavelengths of light received from the stars in distant galaxies can be analysed.
   - The light shows a characteristic absorption spectrum.
   - The measured wavelengths are not the same as those associated with particular elements as measured in the laboratory.
   - For the vast majority of stars in distant galaxies, all the received frequencies have been shifted towards the red end of the visible spectrum (i.e. to lower frequencies). The light shows a **redshift** (see page 108).
   - The magnitude of the redshift is used to calculate the recessional velocity and provides evidence for the Big Bang model of the creation of the Universe.

5. Rotating object

   The rotation of luminous objects (e.g. the Sun) can be measured by looking for a different Doppler shift on one side of the object compared with the other.

   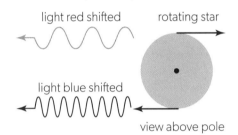

   view above pole

6. Broadening of spectral lines

   - Absorption and emission spectra provide evidence for discrete atomic energy levels (see page 138).
   - Precise measurements show that each individual level is actually equivalent to a small but defined wavelength range.
   - The gas molecules are moving, so light from the molecules will be subjected to Doppler shift.
   - Different molecules have a range of speeds, so there will be a general **Doppler broadening** of the discrete wavelengths.
   - A higher temperature means a wider distribution of kinetic energies and hence more broadening of the spectral line.

AHL Mathematics of the Doppler effect

Moving source

The source moves from A to D with velocity, u_s. The speed of waves is v.

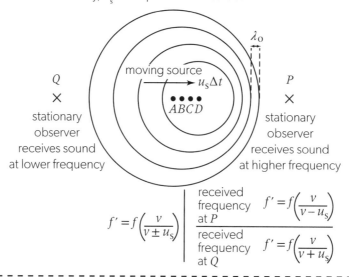

$$f' = f\left(\frac{v}{v \pm u_s}\right)$$

received frequency at P $f' = f\left(\frac{v}{v - u_s}\right)$

received frequency at Q $f' = f\left(\frac{v}{v + u_s}\right)$

Moving observer

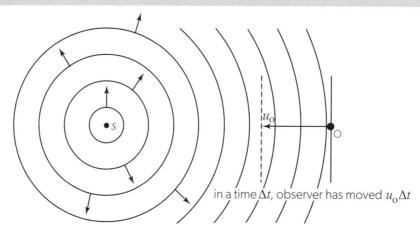

in a time Δt, observer has moved $u_o\Delta t$

$$f' = f\left(\frac{v \pm u_o}{v}\right)$$

If observer is moving away from source:
$$f' = f\left(\frac{v - u_o}{v}\right)$$

If observer is moving towards source:
$$f' = f\left(\frac{v + u_o}{v}\right)$$

Worked example

The frequency of a car's horn is measured by a stationary observer as 200 Hz when the car is at rest. What frequency will be heard if the car is approaching the observer at 30 m s^{-1}? (Speed of sound in air is 330 m s^{-1}.)

$f = 200$ Hz

$f' = ?$

$u_s = 30$ m s^{-1}

$v = 330$ m s^{-1}

$$f' = 200\left(\frac{330}{330-30}\right)$$
$$= 200 \times 1.1$$
$$= 220\,\text{Hz}$$

1. The Pinwheel Galaxy is a spiral galaxy about 21 million light-years away from the Earth. It is moving away from the Earth at approximately $450\,\text{km s}^{-1}$. Light from the galaxy is analysed and contains the hydrogen emission spectrum. The hydrogen emission spectrum as measured in the laboratory contains four wavelengths in the visible portion of the electromagnetic spectrum. The wavelengths are $410.173\,\text{nm}$, $434.047\,\text{nm}$, $486.135\,\text{nm}$ and $656.279\,\text{nm}$. Calculate the wavelengths that will be observed from the Pinwheel galaxy. (4)

2. The Sun is rotating on its own axis. Light from the Sun is analysed and the presences of an absorption spectrum demonstrates the presence of hydrogen. In the laboratory, the hydrogen absorption spectrum contains a wavelength of $434.0472\,\text{nm}$ but light from the **left-hand side** of the Sun shows an absorption line corresponding to a wavelength of $434.0501\,\text{nm}$. Light from the **right-hand side** of the Sun shows an absorption line corresponding to a wavelength of $434.0443\,\text{nm}$.

   a. Explain what is meant by:
      i. redshift (2)
      ii. blueshift. (2)

   b. Suggest why light from different parts of the Sun are showing a redshift and a blueshift. (3)

   c. The radius of the Sun is $6.96 \times 10^5\,\text{km}$. Calculate the time taken for one complete rotation of the Sun. (3)

AHL

3. A train is moving through a station sounding its horn. An observer on the station platform hears the frequency vary from $280\,\text{Hz}$ to $240\,\text{Hz}$.

   a. Sketch a graph to show the variation, with time, of the frequency heard by the observer. (3)

   b. The speed of sound is $330\,\text{m s}^{-1}$. Calculate the speed of the train. (3)

4. Car A is moving at $40\,\text{m s}^{-1}$ towards a stationary car, B. Sound travels at a speed of $330\,\text{m s}^{-1}$.

   a. The driver of car B sounds the horn which emits sound of frequency $100\,\text{Hz}$.
      i. State the frequency of the sound heard by the driver of car B. (1)
      ii. Calculate the frequency of the sound heard by the driver of car A. (2)

   b. As a result of the warning sound, the driver of car A manages to avoid a collision by swerving around car B and then continues at the same speed. The driver of car A now sounds an identical horn. Calculate the frequency of the sound heard by the driver of car B. (2)

D.1 Gravitational fields

Kepler's laws and Newton's law of gravitation

Kepler's three laws of orbital motion

In 1543, Nicolaus Copernicus suggested that the Sun was the centre of the Solar System (and not the Earth). In the 1590s, Tycho Brahe made many years of accurate observations of the motion of the planets. In 1618, Johannes Kepler was able to summarize Brahe's observations into three laws—**Kepler's Laws**. Kepler's laws were originally about the planets orbiting the Sun, but they apply to all objects orbiting a much more massive object as a result of a gravitational force. These three experimental laws remained unexplained for more than 250 years until Isaac Newton suggested a hypothesis to explain them—now known as **Newton's universal law of gravitation**.

Kepler's three laws are:

1. The planets orbit the sun in an ellipse (a flattened circle) with the Sun at on focus of the ellipse.

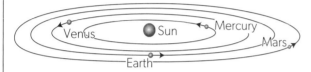

2. The area swept out in a given time by the line joining the Sun to the planet is always the same:

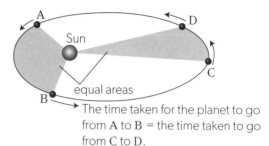

The time taken for the planet to go from A to B = the time taken to go from C to D.

3. The following ratio is always the same:

$$\frac{\left(\text{orbital period}\right)^2}{\left(\text{semimajor axis}\right)^3}$$

For circular orbits of radius, r, with an orbit time, T, this is expressed mathematically as:

$$\frac{T^2}{r^3} = \text{constant}$$

Newton's law of universal gravitation

If you trip over, you will fall down towards the ground.

Newton's theory of **universal gravitation** explains what is going on. It is called "universal" gravitation because at the core of this theory is the statement that every mass in the Universe attracts all the other masses in the Universe. The value of the attraction between two **point** masses is given by the equation below.

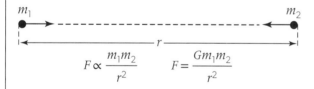

$$F \propto \frac{m_1 m_2}{r^2} \qquad F = \frac{Gm_1 m_2}{r^2}$$

The universal gravitational constant is
$G = 6.67 \times 10^{-11} \, \text{N} \, \text{m}^2 \, \text{kg}^{-2}$

The following points should be noted:

- The law only deals with point masses.

- There is a force acting on each of the masses. These forces are EQUAL and opposite (even if the masses are not equal).

- The forces are always attractive.

- Gravitational forces act between ALL objects in the Universe. The forces only become significant if one (or both) of the objects involved are massive, but they are there nonetheless.

The interaction between two spherical masses turns out to be the same as if the masses were concentrated at the centres of the spheres.

For calculations involving Newton's law of universal gravitation, as applied to orbital motion, it is often appropriate to assume that the orbits are circular (as opposed to elliptical).

Gravitational field strength

Gravitational field strength

An equation for the gravitational force was given on page 14 when defining the weight of an object. Compare it with the equation below.

	Gravitational field strength
Symbol	g
Caused by...	masses
Affects...	masses
Simple force rule:	all masses attract

The gravitational field strength is defined as the force per unit mass: $g = \dfrac{F}{m}$

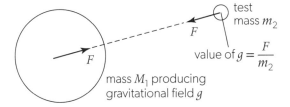

test mass m_2

value of $g = \dfrac{F}{m_2}$

mass M_1 producing gravitational field g

The SI units for g are $N\,kg^{-1}$. These are the same as $m\,s^{-2}$. Field strength is a vector quantity and can be represented using field lines.

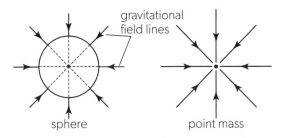

gravitational field lines

sphere   point mass

▲ Field strength around masses (sphere and point)

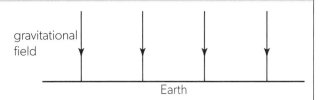

gravitational field

Earth

▲ Gravitational field near surface of the Earth

For a point mass and a sphere, the numerical value for the gravitational field can be calculated using Newton's law:

$$F = \frac{GMm}{r^2} \qquad g = \frac{GM}{r^2}$$

The gravitational field strength at the surface of a planet must be the same as the acceleration due to gravity on the surface.

Field strength is defined to be $\dfrac{\text{force}}{\text{mass}}$

$\text{Acceleration} = \dfrac{\text{force}}{\text{mass}}$ (from $F = ma$)

For the Earth

$$M = 6.0 \times 10^{24}\,kg$$
$$r = 6.4 \times 10^6\,m$$
$$g = \frac{6.67 \times 10^{11} \times 6.0 \times 10^{24}}{\left(6.4 \times 10^6\right)^2} = 9.8\,m\,s^{-2}$$

As shown in the diagrams on the left, the gravitational field of a spherical mass away from the mass behaves the same as a point mass concentrated at it's centre. The further away from any extended body, the more the gravitational field will be like that of a point mass centred at the extended body's centre of gravity.

Example

To calculate the overall gravitational field strength at any point you must use vector addition. The overall gravitational field strength at any point between the Earth and the Moon must be a result of both pulls.

There will be a single point somewhere between the Earth and the Moon where the total gravitational field due to these two masses is zero. Up to this point, the overall pull is back to the Earth; after this point, the overall pull is towards the Moon.

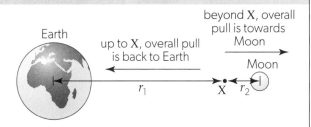

Earth

up to X, overall pull is back to Earth

beyond X, overall pull is towards Moon

Moon

r_1 X r_2

distance between Earth and Moon $= \left(r_1 + r_2\right)$

If resultant gravitational field at X = zero,

$$\frac{GM_{Earth}}{r_1^{\,2}} = \frac{GM_{Moon}}{r_2^{\,2}}$$

Kepler's three laws derived from Newton's law of gravitation

Kepler's third law

There are hundreds of artificial satellites in orbit around the Earth. These satellites do not rely on any engines to keep them in orbit—the gravitational force from the Earth provides the centripetal force required.

Gravitational attraction = centripetal force

$$= \frac{GMm}{r^2}$$

Centripetal force $= \frac{mv^2}{r}$

Therefore $\frac{GMm}{r^2} = \frac{mv^2}{r}$ where r = radius of orbit

$$Gm = v^2 r \qquad (1)$$

$$v = \sqrt{\frac{GM}{r}} \qquad (2)$$

Do not confuse v (velocity of orbit) with v (escape speed).

Since the satellite does one orbit (one circumference in time T,

Speed $v = \dfrac{\text{circumference}}{T} = \dfrac{2\pi r}{T}$

This can be substituted into equation (1) to give:

$$GM = \left(\frac{2\pi r}{T}\right)^2 r = \frac{4\pi^2 r^3}{T^2}$$

G, M and $(4\pi^2)$ are all constants, so $\dfrac{T^2}{r^3}$ = constant

This is an important relationship. It is known as Kepler's third law. Although we derive it for artificial satellites in circular orbits around the Earth, it actually applies to any closed orbit.

Weightlessness

One way of defining the weight of a person is to say that it is the value of the force recorded on a supporting scale.

If the scales were set up in a lift, they would record different values depending on the **acceleration** of the lift.

An extreme version of these situations occurs if the lift cable breaks and the lift (along with the passenger) accelerates down at $9.8\,\text{m s}^{-2}$.

accelerating down at 9.8 m s⁻²

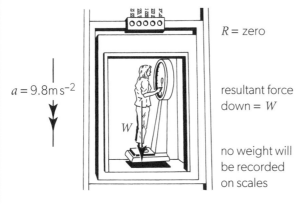

$a = 9.8\,\text{m s}^{-2}$

R = zero

resultant force down = W

no weight will be recorded on scales

The person would appear to be weightless for the duration of the fall. Given the possible ambiguity of

the term "weight", it is better to call this situation the **apparent weightlessness** of objects in free-fall together.

An astronaut in an orbiting space station would also appear weightless. The space station and the astronaut are in free-fall together.

In the space station, the gravitational pull on the astronaut provides the centripetal force needed to stay in the orbit. This resultant force causes the centripetal acceleration. The same is true for the gravitational pull on the satellite and the satellite's acceleration. There is no contact force between the satellite and the astronaut so, once again, you have apparent weightlessness.

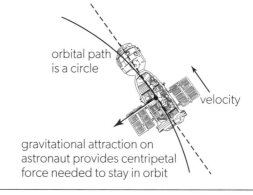

orbital path is a circle

velocity

gravitational attraction on astronaut provides centripetal force needed to stay in orbit

AHL : Gravitational potential energy and potential

Gravitational potential energy

It is easy to work out the difference in gravitational energy when a mass moves between two different heights near the Earth's surface.

$$\text{The difference in energies} = mg(h_2 - h_1)$$

There are two important points to note:

- This derivation has assumed that the gravitational field strength g is constant. However, Newton's theory of universal gravitation states that the field MUST CHANGE with distance. **This equation can only be used if the vertical distance moved is not very large**.

- The equation assumes that the gravitational potential energy gives zero PE at the surface of the Earth. This works for everyday situations but it is not fundamental.

The true zero of gravitational potential energy is taken as infinity.

If the potential energy of the mass, m, was zero at infinity, and it lost potential energy moving in towards mass M, the potential energy must be negative at a given point, P.

The value of gravitational potential energy of a mass at any point in space is defined as the work done in moving it from infinity to that point. The mathematics needed to work this out is not trivial since the force changes with distance.

It turns out that the gravitational potential energy of mass m due to mass M is:

$$E_p = -\frac{GMm}{r}$$

This is a scalar quantity (measured in joules) and is independent of the path taken from infinity.

The gravitational potential energy, E_p, of a system is the work done to assemble the system from infinite separation of the components of the system.

potential energy decreases as gravitational force does work

zero of potential energy taken to be at infinity

M — F_4 m ——— F_3 m ——— F_2 m — F_1 m

as m moves towards M, the force on m increases

Gravitational potential

You can define the **gravitational potential** V_g that measures the energy per unit test mass.

$$V_g = \frac{W}{m} = \frac{(\text{work done})}{(\text{test mass})}$$

The SI units of gravitational potential are $J\,kg^{-1}$. It is a scalar quantity.

Using Newton's law of universal gravitation, you can work out the gravitational potential at a distance r from any point mass.

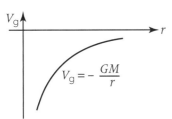

$$V_g = -\frac{GM}{r}$$

This formula and the graph also works for spherical masses (planets etc.). The gravitational potential as a

result of lots of masses is just the sum of the individual potentials. This is an easy addition since potential is a scalar quantity.

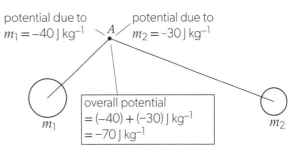

potential due to $m_1 = -40\,J\,kg^{-1}$

potential due to $m_2 = -30\,J\,kg^{-1}$

overall potential $= (-40) + (-30)\,J\,kg^{-1}$ $= -70\,J\,kg^{-1}$

Once you have the potential at one point and the potential at another, the difference between them is the energy you need to move a unit mass between the two points. It is independent of the path taken.

Work done in moving mass m in a gravitational field is given by $W = m\Delta V_g$

Conservative fields

Gravitational fields are an example of **conservative** fields. The work done in moving between two points in a gravitational field is independent of the path taken. Electric and magnetic fields are similarly conservative. This is consistent with the law of conservation of energy. Non-conservative forces are forces which cause a loss of mechanical energy from the system which is dependent on the path taken between two points. An example of a non-conservative force is friction.

AHL Gravitational potential gradient and equipotentials

Equipotential surfaces

The best way of representing how the electric potential varies around a charged object is to identify the regions where the potential is the same. These are called **equipotential** surfaces. In two dimensions they would be represented as lines of equipotential. A good way of visualizing these lines is to start with the contour lines on a map.

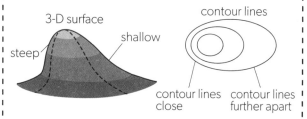

The contour diagram on the right represents the changing heights of the landscape on the left. Each line joins up points that are at the same height. Points that are high up represent a high value of gravitational potential and points that are low down represent a low gravitational potential. Contour lines are lines of equipotential in a gravitational field.

Relationship to field lines

There is a simple relationship between gravitational field lines and lines of equipotential—they are always at right angles to one another. Imagine the contour lines. If you move along a contour line, you stay at the same height in the gravitational field. This does not require work because you are moving at right angles to the gravitational force. Whenever you move along a gravitational equipotential line, you are moving between points that have the same gravitational potential—in other words, no work is being done. Moving at right angles to the gravitational field is the only way to avoid doing work in an gravitational field. Thus equipotential lines must be at right angles to field lines, as shown below.

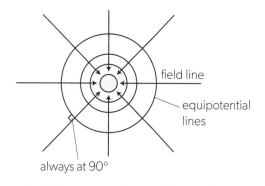

always at 90°

▲ Field lines and equipotentials are at right angles

Escape speed

The escape speed of a rocket is the speed needed to be able to escape the gravitational attraction of the planet. This means getting to an infinite distance away. You know that gravitational potential at the surface of a planet $= -\dfrac{GM}{R_\text{p}}$.

(where R_p is the radius of the planet)

This means that, for a rocket of mass m, the difference between its energy at the surface and at infinity $= \dfrac{GMm}{R_\text{p}}$

Therefore the minimum kinetic energy needed $= \dfrac{GMm}{R_\text{p}}$
In other words,

$$\frac{1}{2}m\left(v_\text{esc}\right)^2 = \frac{GMm}{R_\text{p}}$$

so

$$v_\text{esc} = \sqrt{\left(\frac{2GM}{R_\text{p}}\right)}$$

This derivation assumes that the planet is isolated.

Gravitational potential gradient

In the diagram below, a point test mass m moves in a gravitational field from point A to point B.
The difference in gravitational potential,

$$\Delta V_\text{g} = \frac{\text{average force} \times \text{distance moved}}{m} = -g \times \Delta r$$

The negative sign is because g is directed towards M, but the force doing the work is directed away from M and thus is in the opposite direction from g. Since the gravitational force is attractive, work has to be done in going from A to B, so the potential at A < potential at B.

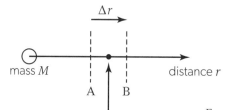

average field between A and B, $g = \dfrac{F_\text{average}}{m}$
(towards M)

$$\Delta V_\text{g} = -g \times \Delta r$$
$$g = -\frac{\Delta V}{\Delta r}$$

$\dfrac{\Delta V}{\Delta r}$ is called the potential gradient. It has units of

$J\,kg^{-1}\,m^{-1}$ (which are the same as $N\,kg^{-1}$ or $m\,s^{-2}$).
The gravitational field strength is equal to minus the potential gradient. An equivalent relationship also applies for electric fields (see page 123).

AHL Energy of an orbiting satellite

Energy of an orbiting satellite

You already know that the gravitational energy $= -\dfrac{GMm}{r}$

The kinetic energy $= \dfrac{1}{2}mv^2$ but $v = \sqrt{\left(\dfrac{GM}{r}\right)}$

(circular motion)

$\therefore$ kinetic energy $= \dfrac{1}{2}m\dfrac{GM}{r} = \dfrac{1}{2}\dfrac{GMm}{r}$

So total energy $=$ KE $+$ PE

$$= \dfrac{1}{2}\dfrac{GMm}{r} - \dfrac{GMm}{r} = -\dfrac{1}{2}\dfrac{GMm}{r}$$

Note that:

- In the orbit, the magnitude of the KE $= \dfrac{1}{2}$ magnitude of the PE.

- The overall energy of the satellite is negative. (A satellite must have a total energy less than zero otherwise it would have enough energy to escape the Earth's gravitational field.)

- To move from a small radius orbit to a large radius orbit, the total energy must increase. To be precise, an increase in orbital radius makes the total energy go from a large negative number to a smaller negative number—this is an increase.

This can be summarized in graphical form.

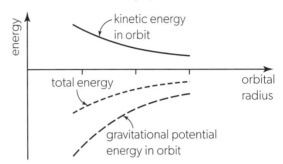

Effect of drag force

The consequences of the energy situation outlined above give rise to a surprising conclusion if the satellite is subjected to a small viscous drag due to the atmosphere. Most people feel confident suggesting that a frictional force must slow the satellite down, but an analysis of the energy situation shows that, in this situation, a friction force must result in an increase in the satellite's speed!

- As one goes further away from the Earth, the atmosphere becomes less dense but it extends out for a significant distance, which means that the satellite is subject to a small viscous drag force.

- The drag force opposes the motion of the satellite.

- The satellite does work against the drag force as it moves forward.

- The total energy of the satellite must **decrease** as a result of doing work against the drag force.

- A decrease in total energy of the satellite means that its total energy must become more negative

- Looking at the graph above, a decrease in total energy means moving to the left of the graph—i.e. the orbital radius must get smaller.

- A smaller orbital radius means that the kinetic energy must increase.

- Increased kinetic energy means that the satellite must be moving faster.

- Thus, overall, the friction force results in an increase in the satellite's speed.

End of topic questions—D.1 Gravitational fields

1. The weight of a person on the surface of the Earth is 700 N. Calculate their weight on another planet that has:

   a. half the radius of the Earth but the same density as the Earth (2)

   b. half the radius of the Earth but the same mass as the Earth. (2)

2. The radius of the Earth's orbit around the Sun is approximately 1.5×10^{14} m.

   The mass of the Earth is 6.0×10^{24} kg and the mass of the Sun is 2.0×10^{30} kg.

   a. Calculate the size of the force of gravitational attraction between the Earth and the Sun. (2)

   b. According to Newton's first law of motion, a non-zero force should cause an object to accelerate. Explain whether the force you calculated in (a) causes the Earth to accelerate. (3)

3. This question is about Kepler's laws of planetary motion.

   a. State three laws of planetary motion. (3)

   b. The table below shows the mean orbital period T and the mean distance r from the Sun of some of the planets of our Solar System.

Planet	T/Earth years	$R/10^{11}$ m
Mercury	0.24	0.58
Venus	0.63	1.1
Earth	1.0	1.5

   Sketch a graph to test whether this data is consistent with Kepler's third law

   Use information from the graph to estimate the mass of the Sun. (3)

4. This question is about gravitational field lines.

   a. Explain how gravitational field lines are used to represent:

   i. the direction of the gravitational field around an object (2)

   ii. the magnitude of the gravitational field around an object. (2)

   b. Draw two field-line diagrams to represent:

   i. the local gravitational field above the surface of the Earth to an approximate height of 50 m above the surface of the Earth (2)

   ii. the gravitational field around the whole Earth to an approximate height of three times the radius of the Earth. (2)

5. Estimate the gravitational force of attraction between two people sitting next to one another. (2)

6. A satellite of mass 4.0×10^3 kg moves around the Earth in a circular orbit of radius 7.5×10^6 m. The mass of the Earth is 6.0×10^{24} kg. (2)

   a. Calculate the kinetic energy of the satellite. (2)

   b. Calculate the potential energy of the satellite. (2)

   c. Calculate the total energy of the satellite. (1)

   d. Discuss the effect that a small viscous drag force acting on the satellite would have on your answers to (a), (b) and (c). (3)

7. This question is about a meteorite striking the Earth's surface.

   a. A meteorite originates from rest at a distance d away from the centre of the Earth. The mass of the Earth is M and the radius of the Earth is R_E. The gravitational constant is G. Determine an expression for the speed v at which the satellite would strike the Earth's surface, in terms of M, G, d and R_E. (3)

   b. Calculate a value for v for a meteorite originating with negligible kinetic energy at a great distance from the Earth. The Earth's mass is 6.0×10^{24} kg and the Earth's radius is 6.4×10^6 m. (3)

   c. Calculate a value for the escape speed from the Earth's surface. (2)

   d. Explain why you might expect your answers to (b) and (c) to be numerically equal. (2)

8. This question is about escape speed from the Earth.

   a. The radius of Earth, $R_E = 6.37 \times 10^6$ m and the mass of the Earth, $M_E = 5.98 \times 10^{24}$ kg. Show that the escape speed from an isolated planet such as Earth is approximately 11 km s^{-1}. (3)

   b. Without considering air resistance, explain why a satellite launched from the Earth at 11 km s^{-1} would fail to leave the Solar System. (2)

   c. The vast majority of rockets are launched from Earth with speeds less than 11 km s^{-1}. Suggest a reason for this. (2)

Electric charge and Coulomb's law

Conservation of charge

Two types of charge exist—positive and negative. Equal amounts of positive and negative charge cancel each other. Matter that contains no charge, or matter that contains equal amounts of positive and negative charge, is said to be electrically **neutral**.

Charges are known to exist because of the forces that exist between all charges, called the **electrostatic force**: like charges repel, unlike charges attract.

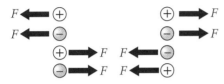

A very important experimental observation is that charge is always conserved.

Charged objects can be created by friction. In this process, electrons are physically moved from one object to another. For the charge to remain on the object, it normally needs to be an insulator.

The total charge before any process must be equal to the total charge afterwards. It is impossible to create a positive charge without an equal negative charge. This is the law of conservation of charge.

before

neutral comb · neutral hair

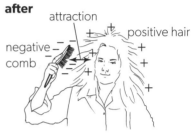

after · attraction

negative comb · positive hair

electrons have been transferred from the hair to the comb

Conductors and insulators

A material that allows the flow of charge through it is called an electrical **conductor**. If charge cannot flow through a material it is called an electrical **insulator**. In solid conductors the flow of charge is always as a result of the flow of electrons from atom to atom.

Electrical conductors	Electrical insulators

all metals
  e.g. copper, aluminium, brass
	plastics
	  e.g. polythene, nylon, acetate

graphite	dry wood
	glass
	ceramics

Coulomb's law

The diagram shows the force between two point charges that are far away from the influence of any other charges.

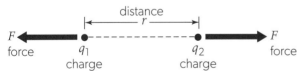

The directions of the forces are along the line joining the charges. If they are like charges, the forces are away from each other—they repel. If they are unlike charges, the forces are towards each other—they attract.

Each charge must feel a force of the same size as the force on the other one.

Experimentally, the force is proportional to the size of both charges and inversely proportional to the square of the distance between the charges.

$$F = \frac{kq_1q_2}{r^2} = k\frac{q_1q_2}{r^2}$$

This is known as Coulomb's law and the constant k is called the Coulomb constant. In fact, the law is often quoted in a slightly different form using a different constant called the permittivity of free space, ε_0:

$$k = \frac{1}{4\pi\varepsilon_0} \quad \text{so} \quad F = \frac{q_1q_2}{4\pi\varepsilon_0 r^2}$$

If there is a material between the charges, the constant k and the permittivity ε will be different.

If there are two or more charges near another charge, the overall force can be worked out using vector addition.

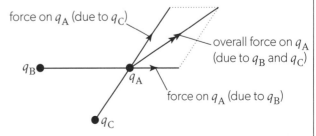

▲ Vector addition of electrostatic forces

Electric fields

Electric fields—definition

A charge, or combination of charges, is said to produce an **electric field** around it. If you place a **test charge** at any point in the field, the value of the force that it feels at any point will depend on the value of the test charge only.

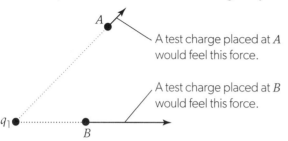

A test charge placed at A would feel this force.

A test charge placed at B would feel this force.

A test charge would feel a different force at different points around a charge q_1.

In practical situations, the test charge needs to be small so that it doesn't disturb the charge or charges that are being considered.

The definition of electric field, E, is

$$E = \frac{F}{q_2} = \text{force per unit positive point test charge}$$

From this definition, the units of electric field are $N\,C^{-1}$. Alternative equivalent units are $V\,m^{-1}$.

Coulomb's law can be used to relate the electric field around a point charge to the charge producing the field.

$$E = \frac{q_1}{4\pi\varepsilon_0 r^2}$$

When using these equations you have to be very careful:

- not to muddle up the charge producing the field and the charge sitting in the field (and thus feeling a force)
- not to use the mathematical equation for the field around a point charge for other situations (e.g. parallel plates).

Representation of electric fields

This is done using field lines.

At any point in a field:

- the direction of the field is represented by the direction of the field lines closest to that point
- the magnitude of the field is represented by the number of field lines passing near that point.

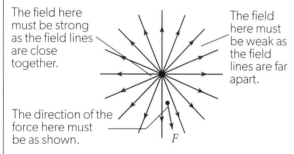

The field here must be strong as the field lines are close together.

The field here must be weak as the field lines are far apart.

The direction of the force here must be as shown.

F

▲ Field around a positive point charge

The resultant electric field at any position due to two point charges is shown to the right.

The parallel field lines between two plates mean that the electric field is uniform.

Electric field lines:

- begin on positive charges and end on negative charges
- never cross
- are close together when the field is strong.

The value of the uniform electric field strength, E, between the parallel plates can be calculated from the potential difference across the plates, V, and the separation of the plates, d.

The relationship (see page 125 for derivation) is:

$$E = \frac{V}{d}$$

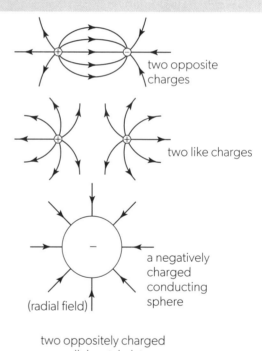

two opposite charges

two like charges

a negatively charged conducting sphere

(radial field)

two oppositely charged parallel metal plates

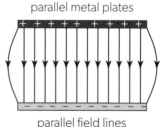

parallel field lines in the centre

▲ Patterns of electric fields

e.g. the electric field between two parallel plates 1 mm apart that have a pd of 300 V across them is:

$$E = \frac{300}{1 \times 10^{-3}} = 3 \times 10^5\,V\,m^{-1}$$

Millikan's experiment—quantization of electric charge

Overview

The motion of charged oil drops falling under gravity is affected by a vertical electric field. Millikan made careful observations of the oil drops:

1. Before: when falling freely in the absence of an electric field
2. After: in an electric field and when charged (either by friction or, in the original experiment, by a burst of X-rays)

Observations 1 and 2 were done on the same drop which allowed Millikan to calculate the charge on each oil drop he observed. The procedure was repeated many times. Analysing the results showed that the charge

on the oil drops did not just have any value but was calculated to always be whole multiples of one particular value, e. For example, he might have found charges with the following values (but nothing in between):

$$-3.2 \times 10^{-19}\,C \quad +6.4 \times 10^{-19}\,C \quad +1.6 \times 10^{-19}\,C$$
$$-4.8 \times 10^{-19}\,C \quad -1.6 \times 10^{-19}\,C$$

In other words, electric charge is quantized with e as the smallest possible amount of charge (the quantum of charge). No fraction of e has ever been observed. The value of $e = -1.6 \times 10^{-19}\,C$. This is the charge on one electron.

Apparatus

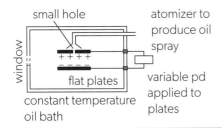

small hole

atomizer to produce oil spray

window

++++

flat plates

variable pd applied to plates

constant temperature oil bath

Procedure

- Observe a falling given oil drop falling under gravity and measure its downward terminal velocity, V_d.
- Charge the drop with a burst of X-rays and apply an electric field so that it experiences an electric force as well.
- Adjust the electric field so that the same drop acquires a new **upwards** terminal velocity, V_u.

Calculation

The forces acting on the drop are as follows:

U is buoyancy force: see page 11 $(F_b = \frac{4}{3}\pi r^3 \rho_{air} g)$

F_d is viscous drag: see page 11 $(F_d = 6\pi\eta r v_d)$

W is weight $(W = \frac{4}{3}\pi r^3 \rho_{oil} g)$

F_E is electric force $(F_E = EQ = \frac{VQ}{d})$

with the following variables:

r is radius of drop

ρ_{air} is density of air

η is viscosity of air

v_d is initial terminal velocity (down)

v_u is final terminal velocity (up)

ρ_{oil} is density of oil

E is electric field strength

V is pd between the plates

d is separation of the plates

Q is charge on drop (to be calculated)

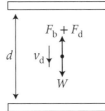

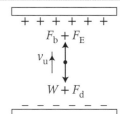

(1) Before applying electric field (drop moving down)

(2) After applying electric field (drop moving up)

Before charging, the drop is falling at terminal velocity so the forces on it are balanced.

$$F_b + F_d = W$$

After charging, the drop is moving **upwards** at a new terminal velocity so the forces on it are again balanced.

$$F_b + F_E = W + F_d$$

(If the drop if moving downwards at terminal velocity, the equation would be $F_b + F_E + F_d = W$)

For the situation before charging, Millikan knew the values of ρ_{air}, η, ρ_{oil} and measured v_d so he could calculate r.

For the situation after charging, Millikan knew the value of d and measured V and v_u so he could calculate Q.

Possible simplifications

- In principle, a charged oil drop could be held stationary between the charged plates. In this situation, you would not need to include the drag force F_d in the analysis.
- In practice, without the use of the X-rays, the drops will become charged anyway. This is a result of

electrons being transferred to or from the drop through collisions with air molecules in the tube or with the wall in the tube. Millikan used X-rays to **change** the charge on the drop by ionizing the air.

- The buoyancy force is typically much smaller than the weight of the drop and can be ignored in the analysis.

Magnetic force and fields

Magnetic field lines

There are many similarities between the magnetic force and the electrostatic force. In fact, both forces have been shown to be two aspects of one force—the electromagnetic interaction (see page 36).

Page 120 introduced the idea of electric fields. A similar concept is used for magnetic fields. A table of the comparisons between these two fields is shown below.

	Electric field	Magnetic field
Symbol	E	B
Caused by ...	Charges	Magnets (or electric currents)
Affects ...	Charges	Magnets (or electric currents)
Two types of ...	Charge: positive and negative	Pole: north and south
Simple force rule:	Like charges repel, unlike charges attract	Like poles repel, unlike poles attract

To help to visualize a magnetic field you, once again, use the concept of field lines. This time the field lines are lines of magnetic field—also called **flux** lines. If a "test" magnetic North pole is placed in a magnetic field, it will feel a force.

- The direction of the force is shown by the direction of the field lines.
- The strength of the force is shown by how close the lines are to one another.

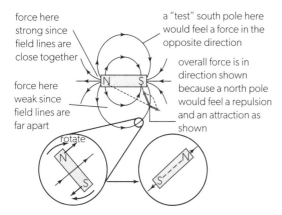

force here strong since field lines are close together

force here weak since field lines are far apart

a "test" south pole here would feel a force in the opposite direction

overall force is in direction shown because a north pole would feel a repulsion and an attraction as shown

rotate

▲ Field pattern of an isolated bar magnet

A small magnet placed in the field would rotate until lined up with the field lines. This is how a compass works. Small pieces of iron (iron filings) will also line up with the field lines—they will be induced to become little magnets.

However, there are differences between electric fields and magnetic fields:

- A magnet does not feel a force when placed in an electric field.
- A positive charge does not feel a force when placed stationary in a magnetic field.
- Isolated charges exist whereas isolated poles do not.
- The Earth itself has a magnetic field that is similar to that of a bar magnet with a magnetic south pole near the geographic North Pole.

A magnet free to move in all directions would line up pointing along the field lines. A compass is normally only free to move horizontally, so it ends up pointing along the horizontal component of the field. The magnetic north pole of the compass points towards the geographic North pole; hence its name.

geographic North Pole

Earth

geographic South Pole

An electric current can also cause a magnetic field. The mathematical value of the magnetic field produced in this way is given on page 128. The field patterns due to different currents can be seen in the diagrams below.

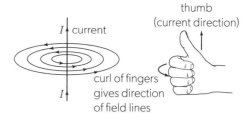

I current

thumb (current direction)

curl of fingers gives direction of field lines

I

▲ Field pattern of a straight wire carrying a current

The field lines are circular around the current. The direction of the field lines can be remembered with the right-hand grip rule. If the thumb of the right hand is arranged to point along the direction of a current, the way the fingers of the right hand naturally curl will give the direction of the field lines.

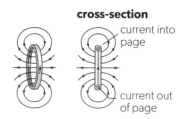

cross-section

current into page

current out of page

▲ Field pattern of a flat circular coil

A long current-carrying coil is called a solenoid. The field pattern for a solenoid is the same as for a bar magnet.

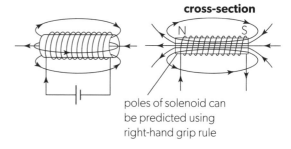

cross-section

poles of solenoid can be predicted using right-hand grip rule

▲ Field pattern for a solenoid

Electric potential energy and potential

Potential and potential difference

The concept of electrical potential difference between two points was introduced on page 120. As the name implies, potential difference is just the difference between the potential at one point and the potential at another. Potential is simply a measure of the total electrical energy per unit charge at a given point in space. The definition is very similar to that of gravitational potential.

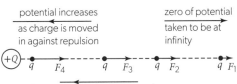

potential increases as charge is moved in against repulsion

zero of potential taken to be at infinity

As *q* comes in, the force on *q* increases.

If the total work done in bringing a positive test charge *q* from infinity to a point in an electric field is W, then the electric potential at that point, V, is defined to be:

$$V = \frac{W}{q}$$

The units for potential are the same as the units for potential difference: JC^{-1} or volts. Potential and potential difference are scalar quantities.

$$V = \frac{Q}{4\pi\varepsilon_0 r}$$

This equation only applies to a single point charge.

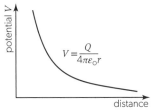

$$V = \frac{Q}{4\pi\varepsilon_0 r}$$

Potential due to more than one charge

If several charges all contribute to the total potential at a point, it can be calculated by adding up the individual potentials due to the individual charges.

The electric potential at any point outside a charged conducting sphere is exactly the same as if all the charge had been concentrated at its centre.

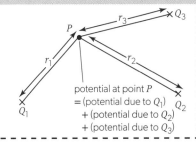

potential at point P
= (potential due to Q_1)
+ (potential due to Q_2)
+ (potential due to Q_3)

Potential inside a charged conducting sphere

Charge will distribute itself uniformly on the outside of a conducting sphere.

- **Outside the sphere**, the field lines and equipotential surfaces are the same as if all the charge was concentrated at a point at the centre of the sphere.

- **Inside the sphere**, there is no net contribution from the charges outside the sphere and the electric field is zero. The potential gradient is thus also zero meaning that every point inside the sphere is at the same potential—the potential at the sphere's surface.

The graphs below show how field and potential vary for a sphere of radius *a*.

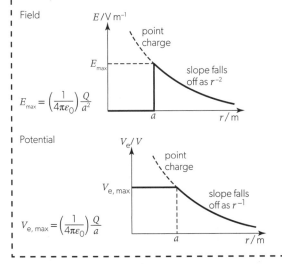

Field

$$E_{max} = \left(\frac{1}{4\pi\varepsilon_0}\right)\frac{Q}{a^2}$$

slope falls off as r^{-2}

Potential

$$V_{e,\,max} = \left(\frac{1}{4\pi\varepsilon_0}\right)\frac{Q}{a}$$

slope falls off as r^{-1}

Potential and field strength

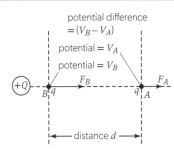

potential difference
$= (V_B - V_A)$
potential $= V_A$
potential $= V_B$

distance d

Bringing a positive charge from A to B means work needs to be done against the electrostatic force.

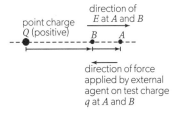

direction of E at A and B

point charge Q (positive)

direction of force applied by external agent on test charge q at A and B

The work done $\delta W = -Eq\delta x$ [the negative sign is because the direction of the force needed to do the work is opposite to the direction of E]

Therefore, $E = -\frac{1}{q}\frac{\delta W}{\delta x} = -\frac{\delta V}{\delta x}$ (since $\delta V = \frac{\delta W}{q}$)

In words, electric field = −potential gradient

Units $= Vm^{-1}$ or NC^{-1}

AHL Electric and gravitational potentials compared

Describing fields: g and e

The concept of field lines can be used to visually represent:

- the gravitational field, g, around a mass (or collection of masses)
- the electric field, E, around a charge (or collection of charges).

Magnetic fields can also be represented using field lines (see page 122). In all cases, the field is the force per unit test point object placed at a particular point in the field with:

- gravitational field = force per unit test point mass (units: $N\,kg^{-1}$)
- electric field = force per unit test point positive charge (units: $N\,C^{-1}$)

Forces are vectors and field lines represent both the magnitude and the direction of the force that would be felt by a test object.

- The **magnitude** of the force is represented by how close the field lines are to one another (for an

example of a more precise definition, see definition of magnetic flux on page 128).

- The **direction** of the force is represented by the direction of the field lines.

This means that, for both gravitational and electric fields, as a test object is moved:

- **along** a field line, work will be done (force and distance moved are in the same direction)
- **at right angles** to a field line, no work will be done (force and distance moved are perpendicular).

An alternative method of mapping the fields around an object is to consider the energy needed to move between points in the field. This defines the new concepts of electric potential and gravitational potential (see below).

In both gravitational and electric fields, equipotential surfaces and field lines are perpendicular to one another.

Potential, V (gravitational or electric)

The *field* (gravitational or electric) is defined as the force per unit test point object placed at a particular point in the field. In an analogous definition, the *potential* (gravitational, V_g, or electric, V_e) is defined as the energy per unit test point object that it has as a result of the field. The full mathematical relationships are shown on page 113.

Gravitational potential, $V_g = \dfrac{energy}{mass}$

Units of $V_g = J\,kg^{-1}$

Electric potential, $V_e = \dfrac{energy}{charge}$

Units of $V_e = J\,C^{-1}$ (or volts)

Potential difference ΔV (electric and gravitational)

Potential is the energy per unit test object. In general, moving a mass between two points, A and B, in a gravitational field (or moving a charge between two points, A and B, in an electric field) means that work is done. When work is done, the potential at A and the potential at B will be different. Between the points A and B, there will be a potential difference, ΔV.

- If positive work is done *on* a test object as it moves between two points, then the potential between the two points must increase.
- If work is done *by* the test object as it moves between the two points, then the potential between the two points must decrease.

Gravitational potential difference between two points:

$$\Delta V_g = \frac{\text{work done moving a test mass}}{\text{test mass}}$$

Units of $\Delta V_g = J\,kg^{-1}$

Electric potential difference between two points:

$$\Delta V_e = \frac{\text{work done moving a test charge}}{\text{test charge}}$$

Units of $\Delta V_e = J\,C^{-1}$ or V (volts)

Thus to calculate the work done, W, in moving a charge q or a mass m between two points in a field:

$$W = q\Delta V_e \quad \text{or} \quad W = m\Delta V_g$$

The SI unit of work is the joule.

When working at the atomic scale, the joule is far too big to use for a unit for energy. The everyday unit used by physicists for this situation is the electronvolt. As could be guessed from its name, the electronvolt is the energy gained by an electron moving through a potential difference of 1 volt.

$$1 \text{ electronvolt} = 1 \text{ volt} \times 1.6 \times 10^{-19}\,C = 1.6 \times 10^{-19}\,J$$

The normal SI prefixes also apply, so you can measure energies in kiloelectronvolts (keV) or megaelectronvolts (MeV). The latter unit is very common in particle physics.

AHL : Electric and gravitational fields compared

Comparison between electric and gravitational field

Electrostatics	Gravitational
Force can be attractive or repulsive	Force always attractive
Coulomb's law—for point charges	Newton's law—for point masses
$F_E = \dfrac{q_1 q_2}{4\pi\varepsilon_0 r^2} = k\dfrac{q_1 q_2}{r^2}$	$F = G\dfrac{m_1 m_2}{r^2}$
Electric field	Gravitational field
$E = \dfrac{F}{q_2} = \dfrac{q_1}{4\pi\varepsilon_0 r^2} = k\dfrac{q_1}{r^2}$	$g = \dfrac{F}{m_2} = \dfrac{Gm_1}{r^2}$
Electric potential due to a point charge	Gravitational potential due to a point mass, m_1
$V_e = \dfrac{q_1}{4\pi\varepsilon_0 r} = k\dfrac{q_1}{r}$	$V_g = -\dfrac{Gm_1}{r}$
Electric potential gradient	Gravitational potential gradient
$E = -\dfrac{\Delta V_e}{\Delta r}$	$g = -\dfrac{\Delta V_g}{\Delta r}$
Electric potential energy	Gravitational potential energy
$E_p = qV_e = \dfrac{q_1 q_2}{4\pi\varepsilon_0 r} = k\dfrac{q_1 q_2}{r}$	$E_p = mV_g = -\dfrac{GMm}{r}$

Uniform fields

Field strength is equal to minus the potential gradient.

A constant field thus means that:

- a constant potential gradient, i.e. a given increase in distance will equate to a fixed change in potential
- in 3D, this means that equipotential surfaces will be flat planes that are equally spaced apart; in 2D, equipotential lines will be equally spaced
- field lines (perpendicular to equipotential surfaces) will be equally spaced parallel lines.

1. Constant gravitational field

   The gravitational field near the surface of a planet is effectively constant. At the surface of the Earth, the field lines will be perpendicular to the Earth's surface. Since $g = 9.81\ \mathrm{m\,s^{-2}}$, the potential gradient must also be $9.81\ \mathrm{J\,kg^{-1}\,m^{-1}}$. Equipotential surfaces that are 1 000 m apart represent changes of potential approximately equal to $10\ \mathrm{kJ\,kg^{-1}}$.

PE using PE $= mgh$ PE from 1st principles
zero at surface   zero at infinity

30 000 J ———— height = 3 km ———— -6.2575×10^7 J

20 000 J ———— height = 2 km ———— -6.2584×10^7 J

10 000 J ———— height = 1 km ———— -6.2593×10^7 J

PE difference, ΔPE $= 10\,000$ J $= 0.001$ times 10^7 J

0 J ————————————— -6.2603×10^7 J
surface of Earth

2. Constant electrical field

   The electric field in between charged parallel plates is effectively constant in the middle section.

   In the diagram below, the potential difference across the plates is V and the separation of the plates is d. Thus the electric potential gradient is $\dfrac{V}{d}$ and the constant field in the centre of the plates, $E = \dfrac{V}{d}$. The units $\mathrm{V\,m^{-1}}$ and $\mathrm{N\,C^{-1}}$ are equivalent and can both be used for E.

   Strictly, the electric field between two charged parallel plates cannot remain uniform throughout the plates and there will be an edge effect. It is straightforward to show that, at the edge, the field must have dropped to half the value in the centre, but modelling the field as constant everywhere between the parallel plates with the edge effects occurring beyond the limits of the plates can be acceptable.

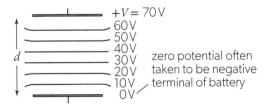

▲ Equipotential lines between charged parallel plates.

1. Two small identical conducting spheres are suspended from a single point by fine insulating threads and are initially in contact. Both spheres are given an electrical charge which they share, and as a result they move apart, as shown below.

The weight of each sphere is 4.0×10^{-3} N and the length of each insulating thread is 1.0 m. The spheres come to rest with a separation of 2.0×10^{-2} m. Calculate the size of the charge that they shared. (4)

2. Two identical point charges repel each other with a force of 1.0×10^{-4} N. They are moved 5.0 mm further apart and the repulsive force is reduced to 2.5×10^{-5} N.

   a. Determine how far apart the point charges were originally. (2)

   b. Calculate the size of the charges. (2)

3. An oil drop of weight 2.0×10^{-14} N has a negative charge as a result of having two extra electrons. Calculate the pd that should be applied between a pair of horizontal parallel metal plates 10 mm apart in order to hold it in equilibrium. (3)

4. In a Millikan experiment an oil drop is observed between two horizontal parallel metal plates.

   a. The oil drop has one extra electron and is held stationary between the plates when the electric field is 3.0×10^5 V m^{-1}.

      i. Estimate the radius of the drop. The density of oil is $\rho_0 = 874$ kg m^{-3}. (3)

      ii. State any approximations or assumptions that you have made. (1)

   b. The same drop suddenly starts to fall at a measured terminal speed of 2.0×10^{-4} m s^{-1}. This speed remains the same and is independent of the value of the pd applied between the plates.

      i. Suggest what change must have occurred to make the drop start to fall. (2)

      ii. Estimate the viscosity of the air. (4)

   c. What would be the terminal velocity of this drop if it acquired three excess electrons?

5. This question is about electric fields.

   a. Sketch the variation in electric field between:

      i. two identical positive point charges

      ii. two identical oppositely charged parallel plates. (4)

   b. By referring to your answers for (a), explain how the field strength varies between:

      i. two identical positive point charges

      ii. two identical oppositely charged parallel plates. (4)

AHL

6. Two point charges +0.90 nC and +0.10 nC are placed 100 mm apart. There is a point (called the *neutral point*) between the two charges where the electric field is zero.

   a. Calculate the location of the neutral point. (3)

   b. Calculate the value of the electric potential at the neutral point. (3)

7. Calculate the speed of an electron accelerated in a vacuum by a pd of 1 000 V (energy = 1 KeV). (3)

Motion of a charged particle in an electric field

Motion of a charged particle in an electric field

A charged particle will experience a force in an electric field. If the charged particle is positive, then the force will be in the same direction as the field lines. If the charged particle is negative, then the force will be antiparallel to the field lines.

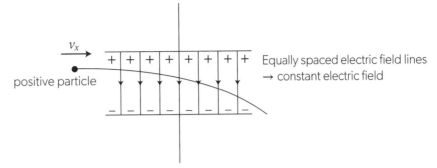

Equally spaced electric field lines → constant electric field

▲ Motion of a charged particle in a constant electric field

If the electric field is constant, then the charged particle will feel a constant force and undergo constant acceleration. The constant acceleration equations can be used. The motion of a charged particle in a constant electric field is similar to the motion of a mass in a constant gravitational field. A positively charged particle "falls" along the electric field lines in the same way as a mass falls along the gravitational field lines.

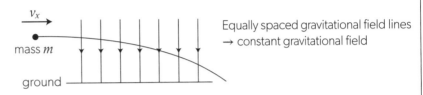

Equally spaced gravitational field lines → constant gravitational field

▲ Motion of a mass in a constant gravitational field

1. Charged particle starting from rest

   The field between two oppositely charged parallel plates is constant. In this situation, a positively charged particle will "fall" towards the negative plate and a negatively charged particle will "fall" towards the positive plate.

2. Moving perpendicularly to the electric field

   The path of both objects is parabolic just like the motion of a mass in a gravitational field when initially moving horizontally (see page 5).

   Horizontally: constant velocity

   Vertically: constant acceleration

Magnetic forces

Magnetic force on a current

When a current-carrying wire is placed in a magnetic field the magnetic interaction between the two results in a force. This is known as the **motor effect**. The direction of this force is at right angles to the plane that contains the field and the current, as shown below.

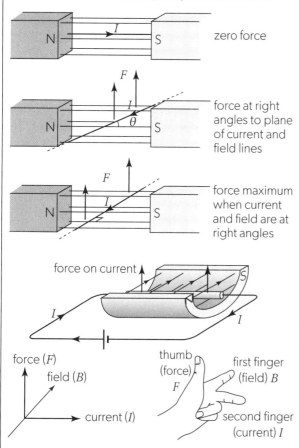

zero force

force at right angles to plane of current and field lines

force maximum when current and field are at right angles

force on current

▲ Fleming's left-hand rule

Experiments show that the force is proportional to:

- the magnitude of the magnetic field, B
- the magnitude of the current, I
- the length of the current, L, that is in the magnetic field
- the sine of the angle, θ, between the field and current.

The magnetic field strength, B is defined as follows:

$$F = BIL \sin \theta \qquad \text{or} \qquad B = \frac{F}{IL \sin \theta}$$

The unit for the magnetic field strength is the tesla. $1\,\text{T}$ is defined to be equal to $1\,\text{N}\,\text{A}^{-1}\,\text{m}^{-1}$. Another possible unit for magnetic field strength is $\text{Wb}\,\text{m}^{-2}$. Another term for magnetic field strength is magnetic flux density.

Magnetic force on a moving charge

A single charge moving through a magnetic field also feels a force in exactly the same way as a current feels a force.

In this case, the force on a moving charge is proportional to:

- the magnitude of the magnetic field, B
- the magnitude of the charge, q
- the velocity of the charge, v
- the sine of the angle, θ, between the velocity of the charge and the field.

You can use these relationships to give an alternative definition of the magnetic field strength, B. This definition is exactly equivalent to the previous definition.

$$F = Bqv \sin \theta \qquad \text{or} \qquad B = \frac{F}{qv \sin \theta}$$

Since the force on a moving charge is always at right angles to the velocity of the charge, the resultant motion can be circular. An example of this would be when an electron enters a region where the magnetic field is at right angles to its velocity, as shown below.

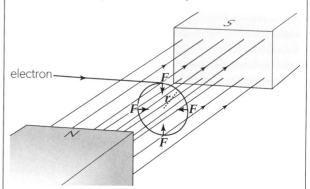

▲ An electron moving at right angles to a magnetic field

Note that as the force is always perpendicular to the velocity, the kinetic energy of the charged particle stays constant in a magnetic field.

When moving in a circular path, the magnetic force provides the centripetal force required.

$$\frac{m_e v^2}{r} = Bev$$

m_e is mass of the electron

B is magnetic field strength

r is radius of circular path

e is charge on an electron

Investigation into the path of the electron would allow the charge to mass ratio $\frac{e}{m_e}$ to be determined.

Motion of a charged particle in perpendicularly oriented uniform electric and magnetic fields

Overview

In a famous experiment in 1897, J J Thomson used perpendicularly oriented electric and magnetic fields to alter the path of moving electrons. At the time of the experiment, he was working on what seemed to be an unknown type of radiation called cathode rays at a time when nobody knew what cathode rays were. He was able to show that these rays were moving charged objects (now called electrons). He was not able to measure independently the charge, e, or the mass m_e, of these unknown particles, but he could measure their charge to mass ratio, $\frac{e}{m_e}$, (called the **specific charge**).

Experiment set-up for deflection

With no electric and no magnetic field, the electrons move in a straight path at a speed v through the vacuum and their arrival on a fluorescent screen can be observed from a spot of light on the screen.

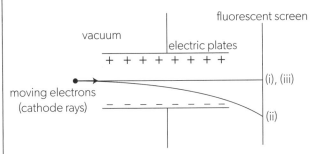

The magnetic field and the electric field are perpendicular to one another.

The electrons can be deviated by a uniform electric field, E. In the above set-up, E is down the page from top plate to bottom plate. When E is switched on, the electrons are accelerated towards the top plate.

The electrons can be deviated by a uniform magnetic field, B. In the above set-up, B is directed into the page,

which means that it will follow a section of a circular path whenever it is in the magnetic field (see page 128). Using the left-hand rule, the magnetic force will be down.

(i) With the electric field and magnetic field both zero, the arrival position of the electrons is noted.

(ii) The magnetic field is then applied which causes the arrival position to change.

(iii) The electric field is then applied in addition to the magnetic field. By adjusting the value of E, the arrival position can be returned to the original (undeflected) position.

The electron beam is undeflected because the magnetic force (down the page) is balanced by the electric force (up the page).

$$Bev = eE \qquad \text{so} \qquad v = \frac{E}{B}$$

The value of speed, v, can then be substituted into the equations of motion for the section of circular motion when the magnetic field was applied alone:

$$Bev = \frac{m_e v^2}{r} \qquad \frac{e}{m_e} = \frac{v}{Br}$$

Examples of the magnetic field due to currents (1)

Straight wire

The field pattern around a long straight wire shows that as you move away from the wire, the strength of the field gets weaker. Experimentally, the field is proportional to:

- the value of the current, I
- the inverse of the distance away from the wire, r; if the distance away is doubled, the magnetic field will halve.

The field also depends on the medium around the wire. These factors are summarized in the equation:

$$B = \frac{\mu I}{2\pi r}$$

The constant μ is called the permeability and changes if the medium around the wire changes. Most of the time you consider the field around a wire when there is nothing there—so you use the value for the permeability of a vacuum, μ_0. There is almost no difference between the permeability of air and the permeability of a vacuum. There are many possible units for this constant, but it is common to use $N A^{-2}$ or $T m A^{-1}$.

Permeability and permittivity are related constants. In other words, if you know one constant you can calculate the other. In the SI system of units, the permeability of a vacuum is defined to have a value of exactly $4\pi \times 10^{-7} N A^{-2}$. See the definition of the ampere (page 130) for more details.

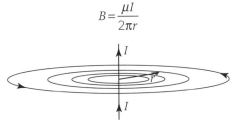

▲ Magnetic field of a straight current

Examples of the magnetic field due to currents (2)

Magnetic field in a solenoid

The magnetic field of a solenoid is very similar to the magnetic field of a bar magnet. As shown by the parallel field lines, the magnetic field inside the solenoid is constant. It might seem surprising that the field does not vary at all inside the solenoid, but this can be experimentally verified near the centre of a long solenoid. It tends to decrease near the ends of the solenoid, as shown in the graph below.

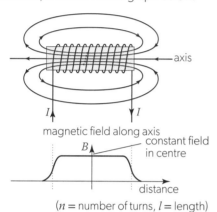

magnetic field along axis

(n = number of turns, l = length)

▲ Variation of magnetic field in a solenoid

The mathematical equation for this constant field at the centre of a long solenoid is:

$$B = \mu\left(\frac{n}{l}\right)I$$

Therefore the field depends on only:

- the current, I
- the number of turns per unit length, $\frac{n}{l}$
- the nature of the solenoid core, μ.

It is independent of the cross-sectional area of the solenoid.

Two parallel wires—definition of the ampere

Two parallel current-carrying wires provide a good example of the concepts of magnetic field and magnetic force. Because there is a current flowing down the wire, each wire is producing a magnetic field. The other wire is in this field so it feels a force. The forces on the wires are an example of a Newton's third law pair of forces.

Magnitude of force per unit length on

either wire $= \dfrac{\mu I_1 I_2}{2\pi r}$

This equation is experimentally used to define the ampere. The coulomb is then defined to be one ampere second. If you imagine two infinitely long wires carrying a current of one amp separated by a distance of one metre, the equation would predict the force per unit length to be 2×10^{-7} N. Although it is not possible to have infinitely long wires, an experimental set-up can be arranged with very long wires. This allows the forces to be measured and ammeters to be properly calibrated.

The IB Physics course does not require the study of rms values in detail. It is sufficient to know that ac currents and voltages can use the same format equations for energy and power as are used for dc currents and voltages.

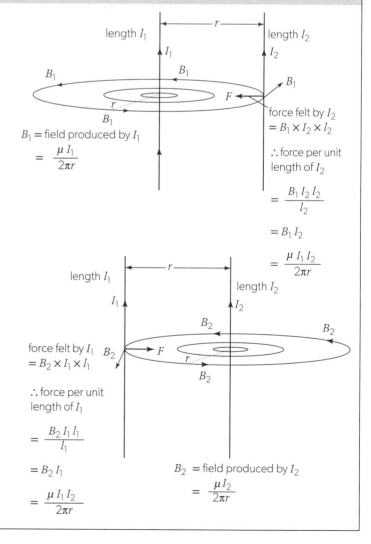

B_1 = field produced by I_1

$\quad = \dfrac{\mu I_1}{2\pi r}$

force felt by I_2
$= B_1 \times I_2 \times l_2$

∴ force per unit length of I_2

$\quad = \dfrac{B_1 I_2 l_2}{l_2}$

$\quad = B_1 I_2$

$\quad = \dfrac{\mu I_1 I_2}{2\pi r}$

force felt by I_1 $\quad = B_2 \times I_1 \times l_1$

∴ force per unit length of I_1

$\quad = \dfrac{B_2 I_1 l_1}{l_1}$

$\quad = B_2 I_1$

$\quad = \dfrac{\mu I_1 I_2}{2\pi r}$

B_2 = field produced by I_2

$\quad = \dfrac{\mu I_2}{2\pi r}$

1. A proton with kinetic energy 4.0×10^{-12} J moves at right angles to a magnetic field of 0.25 T in a vacuum. Calculate the radius of the circular path that it follows. (4)

2. The horizontal component of the Earth's magnetic field near the equator is $30\,\mu T$. A cosmic-ray proton arrives into the field with a vertical velocity $2.8 \times 10^8\,m\,s^{-1}$.

   Calculate the ratio $\dfrac{\text{magnetic force on the proton}}{\text{gravitational force on the proton}}$ (4)

3. A straight wire of length 50 mm carries a current of 1.5 A and experiences a force of 4.5 mN when placed in a uniform magnetic field of 90 mT. Calculate the angle between the direction of the magnetic field and that of the conductor. (3)

4. A flat, square coil of wire is placed in a uniform magnetic field of magnitude 0.40 T. Two sides of the coil of wire are at right angles to the magnetic field and the coil is initially horizontal. The length of each side of the coil is 5.0 cm and the coil has 50 turns.

   a. Calculate the force that one side of the coil experiences when a current of 0.15 A flows through the coil. (4)

   b. Predict the motion of the coil. (2)

5. Two long straight conductors are placed 90 mm apart. They carry currents of 2.0 A and 4.0 A in the same direction.

   a. Explain whether or not one wire experiences a greater force than the other. (2)

   b. Determine the force exerted on a 0.20 m section of the wire carrying 2.0 A. (2)

   c. Determine the locations where the resultant magnetic field is zero. (3)

D.4 Induction

AHL : Induced electromotive force (emf)

Induced emf

When a conductor moves through a magnetic field, an emf is induced. The emf induced depends on:

- the speed of the wire
- the strength of the magnetic field
- the length of the wire in the magnetic field.

The atoms of the moving wire contain fixed positive nuclei and negative electrons that are free to move. In the diagram below, the protons moving down feel a force towards the end labelled as the positive end, but they are not free to move. The electrons feel a force towards the end labelled negative. They are free to move and set up a potential difference across the wire. Equilibrium is reached when the electric force on an electron in the centre of the wire (due to the potential difference) balances the magnetic force on that electron. You can calculate the magnitude of the induced emf by considering an electron in equilibrium in the middle of the wire. The induced electric force and the magnetic force are balanced.

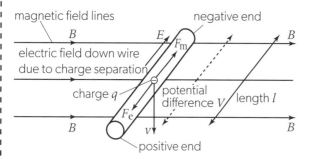

The electrical force due to emf: $F_e = E \times q = \left(\dfrac{V}{l}\right) \times q$

Magnetic force due to movement: $F_m = Bqv$

So $Bqv = \left(\dfrac{V}{l}\right)q$

$$V = Blv$$

As no current is flowing, the emf ε = potential difference

$$\varepsilon = Blv$$

If the wire is part of a complete circuit (outside the magnetic field), the emf induced causes a current to flow.

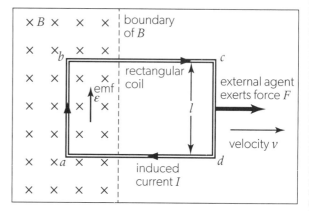

If this situation is repeated with a rectangular coil with N turns, each section ab generates an emf equal to Bvl. The total emf generated will thus be:

$$\varepsilon = BvlN$$

Note that, in the situation above, a current only flows when one side of the coil (ab) is moving through the magnetic field and the other side (cd) is outside the field. If the whole coil was inside the magnetic field, each side would generate an emf. The two emfs would oppose one another and no current would flow.

Production of induced emf by relative motion

An emf is induced in a conductor whenever lines of magnetic flux are cut. But flux is more than just a way of picturing the situation; it has a mathematical definition.

If the magnetic field is perpendicular to the surface, the magnetic flux $\Delta\phi$ passing through the area ΔA is defined in terms of the magnetic field strength B as follows.

$\Delta\phi = B\Delta A$, so $B = \dfrac{\Delta\phi}{\Delta A}$

In a uniform field, $B = \dfrac{\phi}{A}$

An alternative name for "magnetic field strength" is **flux density**.

If the area is not perpendicular, but at an angle θ to the field lines, the equation becomes:

$\phi = BA\cos\theta$ (units: T m²)

θ is the angle between B and the normal to the surface.

Flux can also be measured in webers (Wb), where $1\,\text{Wb} = 1\,\text{T m}^2$

These relationships allow you to calculate the induced emf ε in a moving wave in terms of flux.

in a time Δt:

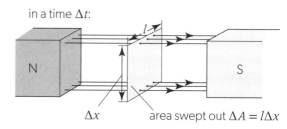

area swept out $\Delta A = l\Delta x$

$\varepsilon = Blv$ since $v = \dfrac{\Delta x}{\Delta t}$ so $\varepsilon = \dfrac{Bl\Delta x}{\Delta t}$

But $l\Delta x = \Delta A$, the area "swept out" by the conductor in a time Δt so $\varepsilon = \dfrac{B\Delta A}{\Delta t}$

Also, $B\Delta A = \Delta\phi$ so $\varepsilon = \dfrac{\Delta\phi}{\Delta t}$

In words, "the emf induced is equal to the rate of cutting of flux". The same effect is produced if the conductor is kept stationary and the magnets are moved.

AHL : Lenz's law and Faraday's law

Lenz's law

Lenz's law states that

"The direction of the induced emf is such that if an induced current were able to flow, it would oppose the change which caused it."

Lenz's law can be explained in terms of the conservation of energy. The electrical energy generated within any system must result from work being done on the system. When a conductor is moved through a magnetic field and an induced current flows, an external force is needed to keep the conductor moving (the external force balances the opposing force that Lenz's law predicts). The external force does work and this provides the energy for the current to flow.

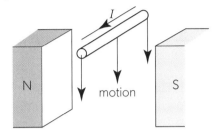

If current is induced in this direction; the force will be upwards (left-hand rule)
∴ original motion will be opposed.

If current is induced this way, the induced field will repel the magnet and so oppose motion.

Put another way, if the direction of an induced current did not oppose the change that caused it, then it would be acting to support the change. If this was the case, then a force would be generated that further accelerated the moving object which would generate an even greater emf—electrical energy would be generated without work being done.

Application of Faraday's law to moving and rotating coils

There are many situations involving magnetic fields with moving or rotating coils. To decide whether or not an emf is generated and, if it is, to calculate its value, the following procedure can be used:

- Choose the period of time, Δt, over which the motion of the coil is to be considered.

- At the beginning of the period, work out the flux passing through one turn of the coil, $\phi_{initial}$. Note that the shape of the coil is not relevant; just the cross-sectional area.

$$\phi = BA \cos \theta$$

- At the end of the period, work out the flux passing through one turn of the coil ϕ_{final} using the equation

above. Note that the sense of the magnetic field is important. If the magnitude of the field is the same but it is passing through the coil in the opposite direction, then:

$$\phi_{final} = -\phi_{initial}$$

- Determine the change in flux, $\Delta\phi$:

$$\Delta\phi = \phi_{final} - \phi_{initial}$$

- If there is no overall change of flux then, overall, no emf will be induced. If there is a change in flux, then the emf induced in a coil of N turns will be:

$$\varepsilon = -N\frac{\Delta\phi}{\Delta t}$$

Transformer-induced emf

An emf is also produced in a wire if the magnetic field changes with time.

If the amount of flux passing through one turn of a coil is ϕ, then the total **flux linkage** with all N turns of the coil is given by

flux linkage $= N\phi$

The universal rule that applies to all situations involving induced emf can now be stated as

"The magnitude of an induced emf is proportional to the rate of change of flux linkage."

This is known as **Faraday's law** $\varepsilon = N\frac{\Delta\phi}{\Delta t}$

Faraday's law and Lenz's law can be combined together in the following mathematical statement for the emf, ε, generated in a coil of N turns with a rate of change of flux through the coil of $\frac{\Delta\phi}{\Delta t}$:

$$\varepsilon = -N\frac{\Delta\phi}{\Delta t}$$

The dependence on the rate of change of flux and the number of turns is Faraday's law and the negative sign (opposing the change) is Lenz's law.

AHL Using induction (1)

Coil rotating in a magnetic field—ac generator

The structure of a typical ac generator is shown below.

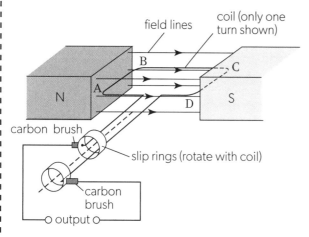

▲ ac generator

The coil of wire rotates in the magnetic field due to an external force. As it rotates, the flux linkage of the coil changes with time and induces an emf (Faraday's law) causing a current to flow. The sides **AB** and **CD** of the coil experience a force opposing the motion (Lenz's law). The work done rotating the coil generates electrical energy.

A coil rotating at constant speed will produce a sinusoidal induced emf. Increasing the speed of rotation will reduce the time period of the oscillation *and* increase the amplitude of the induced emf (as the rate of change of flux linkage is increased).

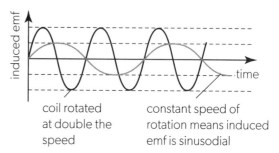

coil rotated at double the speed

constant speed of rotation means induced emf is sinusodial

rms values

If the output of an ac generator is connected to a resistor an alternating current will flow. A sinusoidal potential difference means a sinusoidal current.

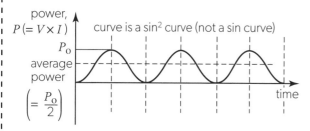

The graph shows that the average power dissipation is half of the peak power dissipation for a sinusoidal current.

Average power $\overline{P} = \dfrac{I_0^2 R}{2} = \left(\dfrac{I_0}{\sqrt{2}}\right)^2 R$

Thus the effective current through the resistor is $\sqrt{}$ (mean value of I^2) and it is called the root mean square current or rms current, I_{rms}:

$$I_{rms} = \frac{I_0}{\sqrt{2}} \text{ (for sinusoidal currents)}$$

When ac values for voltage or current are quoted, it is the root mean square value that is being used. In Europe this value is 230 V, whereas in the USA it is 120 V.

$$V_{rms} = \frac{V_0}{\sqrt{2}}$$

$$\overline{P} = V_{rms} I_{rms} = \frac{1}{2} I_0 V_0$$

$$P_{max} = I_0 V_0$$

$$R = \frac{V}{I} = \frac{V_0}{I_0} = \frac{V_{rms}}{I_{rms}}$$

AHL Using induction (2)

Self-induction

When a potential difference is connected across a **coil of wire**, a current will be established. The final value of steady current that flows is calculated from the coil's electrical resistance: $I = \dfrac{V}{R}$

It turns out that the current does not instantly jump from zero to this value when the potential difference is connected but it takes time to build up to the final value.

The reason for this delay in the build-up of current is that the coil's magnetic field needs to be established. When there was no current in

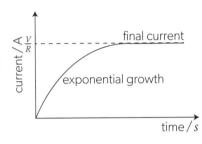

the coil, there was no magnetic flux in the coil. When a current is established, there will be magnetic flux in the coil. While the current is being established, there will be a change of flux and this change of flux induces an emf **in the coil itself**. This is an example of **self-inductance**.

The emf is induced according to Faraday's law and Lenz's law and the direction of the induced emf opposes the change. As the current is building up, the emf acts to oppose the build-up of current. For this reason, the

emf is sometimes called a **back emf**. As the current is building up, at any given instant of time:

$$I_{instantaneous} = \frac{\left(\text{external pd} - \text{back emf}\right)}{R}$$

The quantitative analysis of the growth of current in a circuit involving a coil and a resistor is not part of the IB Physics course but it turns out to be another example of exponential growth—like the growth of a stable daughter product in radioactive decay (see page 153).

If the external potential difference is switched off, then, as the magnetic field collapses, an emf will again be induced. This time, to oppose the change, the emf would be induced such as to try to maintain the current. The collapse of the magnetic field can happen very quickly, which means that the rate of change of flux is large and the induced emf can also be large.

In fact, the induced emf can be larger than the external potential difference and can be large enough to cause a spark (electric field needed for a spark is approximately $10^4\,\text{V}\,\text{cm}^{-1}$). This effect is used in petrol engines. A rapidly collapsing magnetic field in a coil generates the sparks needed in the spark plugs to ignite the petrol in the cylinders of the petrol engine—the heated expansion of the air/petrol mixture drives the engine around. From an energy perspective, energy is stored whenever a magnetic field is established, and this energy can be recovered and cause the spark. The process of building up a magnetic field and then collapsing it happens many times a second in a petrol engine.

1. An aeroplane flies at 200 m s^{-1}. Estimate the maximum pd that can be generated across its wings.

   Vertical component of Earth's magnetic field = 10^{-5} T

   Length across wings = 30 m   (4)

2. A physicist holds her hand so that the magnetic field of the Earth (50 μT) passes through a ring on her hand.

$B = 5 \times 10^{-5}$ T

   In 0.1 s, she quickly turns her hand through 90° so that the magnetic field of the Earth no longer goes through the ring. Estimate the emf generated in the ring.

   Estimate of cross-sectional area of ring:
   $A \approx 1$ cm$^2 = 10^{-4}$ m^2 (4)

3. In a simple generator, a coil of wire of cross-sectional area, A, is rotated in a uniform magnetic field, B, as shown in the diagram below. When time $t = 0$, $\theta = 0$.

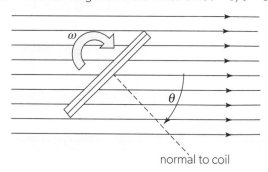

normal to coil

   a.
      i. State an expression for the value for the flux linked with each turn of the coil in terms of B, A and θ.   (2)
      ii. The angular velocity of the rotation of the coil is ω. State an expression for the value for the flux linked with each turn of the coil in terms of B, A, ω and t.   (2)
      iii. The coil has N turns. Suggest an expression for the instantaneous value of the induced emf, ε. (4)

   b. The coil is rotated 50 times a second. The induced emf is sinusoidal with an amplitude of 2.0 V.
      i. Sketch a graph to show the variation, with time, of the induced emf, ε.   (4)

   ii. Using the same axes, sketch a graph to show the output you would expect if the magnitude of the magnetic field was doubled.   (2)
   iii. Sketch a graph to show the output you would expect if the angular velocity was doubled.   (3)
   iv. Sketch a graph to show the output you would expect if the angular velocity was halved.   (3)

4. A small bar magnet fits inside a long vertical coil of wire. The ends of the coil are connected to a sensitive voltmeter and the magnet is held above the coil with its north pole pointing towards the coil. The magnet is released and falls down, passing through the coil.

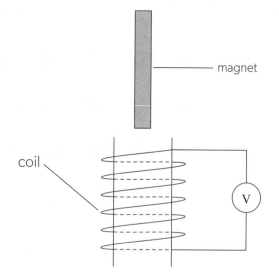

magnet

coil

   a. When the magnet is falling towards the coil, an emf is induced in the coil.
      i. Explain how Lenz's law applies to this situation.   (2)
      ii. Show how Lenz's law is consistent with the law of conservation of energy in this situation.   (2)

   b. When the magnet is inside the coil, explain whether or not an emf continues to be induced in the coil.   (3)

   c. When the magnet exits the coil, it is moving at a faster speed than when it entered the coil.
      i. Explain how the magnitude of the induced emf when the magnet is exiting the coil compares with the magnitude of the induced emf when the magnet is entering the coil.   (3)
      ii. Explain how the direction of the induced emf when the magnet is exiting the coil compares with the direction of the induced emf when the magnet is entering the coil.   (3)

   d. Sketch a graph to show the variation, with time t, of the induced emf in the coil as a result of the magnet falling through the coil.   (4)

E.1 Structure of the atom

Structure of matter

Introduction

All matter that surrounds us, living or otherwise, is made up of different combinations of atoms. There are only a hundred, or so, different types of atoms present in nature. Atoms of a single type form an element. Each of these elements has a name and a chemical symbol; e.g. hydrogen, the simplest of all the elements, has the chemical symbol H. Oxygen has the chemical symbol O. The combination of two hydrogen atoms with one oxygen atom is called a water molecule—H_2O. The full list of elements is shown in a periodic table. Atoms consist of a combination of three things: protons, neutrons and electrons.

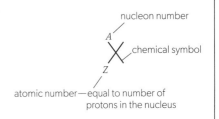

In the basic atomic model, you are made up of protons, neutrons, and electrons—nothing more.

Atomic model

The basic atomic model, known as the nuclear model, was developed during the twentieth century and describes a very small central nucleus surrounded by electrons arranged in different energy levels. The nucleus itself contains protons and neutrons (collectively called **nucleons**). All of the positive charge and almost all of the mass of the atom is in the nucleus. The electrons provide only a tiny bit of the mass but all of the negative charge. Overall, an atom is neutral. The vast majority of the volume is nothing at all—a vacuum. The nuclear model of the atom seems so strange that there must be good evidence to support it.

This simple model has limitations. Accelerated charges are known to radiate energy so orbital electrons should constantly lose energy (the changing direction means that the electrons are accelerating).

	Protons	Neutrons	Electrons
Relative mass	1	1	Negligible
Charge	+1	Neutral	−1

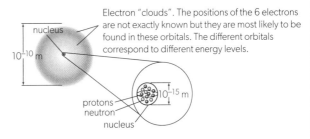

Electron "clouds". The positions of the 6 electrons are not exactly known but they are most likely to be found in these orbitals. The different orbitals correspond to different energy levels.

▲ Atomic model of carbon

Evidence

One of the most convincing pieces of evidence for the nuclear model of the atom comes from the Rutherford–Geiger–Marsden experiment. Positive alpha particles were "fired" at a thin gold leaf. The relative size and velocity of the alpha particles meant that most of them were expected to travel straight through the gold leaf. The idea behind this experiment was to see if there was any detectable structure within the gold atoms. The amazing discovery was that some of the alpha particles were deflected through huge angles. The mathematics of the experiment showed that the numbers being deflected at any given angle agreed with an inverse square law of repulsion from the nucleus. Evidence for electron energy levels comes from emission and absorption spectra (see page 138). The existence of isotopes (see page 147) provides evidence for neutrons.

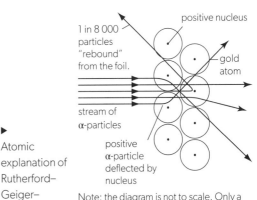

▲ Rutherford–Geiger–Marsden experiment

► Atomic explanation of Rutherford–Geiger–Marsden experiment

Note: the diagram is not to scale. Only a minute percentage of α-particles are scattered or rebound.

Emission and absorption spectra

Emission spectra and absorption spectra

When an element is given enough energy it emits light. This light can be analysed by splitting it into its various colours (or frequencies) using a prism or a diffraction grating. If all possible frequencies of light were present, this would be called a **continuous spectrum**. The light an element emits, its **emission spectrum**, is not continuous, but contains only a few characteristic colours. The frequencies emitted are particular to the element in question. For example, the yellow-orange light from a street lamp is often a sign that the element sodium is present in the lamp. Exactly the same particular frequencies are **absent** if a continuous spectrum of light is shone through an element when it is in gaseous form. This is called an **absorption** spectrum.

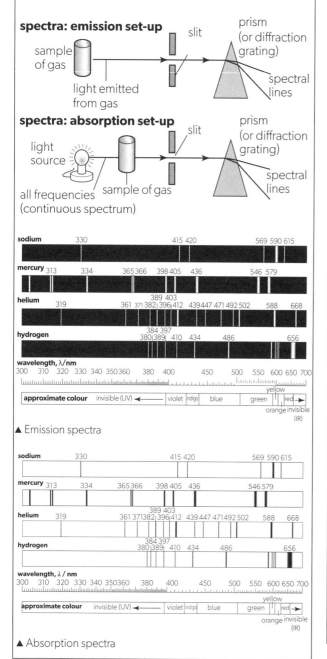

▲ Emission spectra

▲ Absorption spectra

Explanation of atomic spectra

In an atom, electrons are bound to the nucleus. This means that they cannot "escape" without the input of energy. If enough energy is put in, an electron can leave the atom. If this happens, the atom is now positive overall and is said to be ionized. Electrons can only occupy given energy levels—the energy of the electron is said to be **quantized**. These energy levels are fixed for particular elements and correspond to "allowed" orbitals. The reason why only these energies are "allowed" forms a significant part of quantum theory.

When an electron moves between energy levels it must emit or absorb energy. The energy emitted or absorbed corresponds to the difference between the two allowed energy levels. This energy is emitted or absorbed as "packets" of light called photons. A higher energy photon corresponds to a higher frequency (shorter wavelength) of light.

Given that $c = f\lambda$ and $\lambda = \dfrac{hc}{E}$, where $h = 6.63 \times 10^{-34}$ J s is Plank's constant, the energy of a photon is:

$$E = hf$$

Thus the frequency of the light, emitted or absorbed, is fixed by the energy difference between the levels. Since the energy levels are unique to a given element, this means that the emission (and the absorption) spectrum will also be unique.

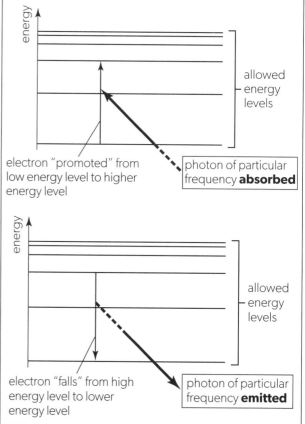

electron "promoted" from low energy level to higher energy level

photon of particular frequency **absorbed**

electron "falls" from high energy level to lower energy level

photon of particular frequency **emitted**

AHL | The nucleus

Nuclear radii and nuclear densities

Not surprisingly, more massive nuclei have larger radii. Detailed analysis of the data implies that the nuclei have a spherical distribution of positive charge with an essentially constant density. The results are consistent with a model in which the protons and neutrons can be imagined to be hard spheres that are bonded tightly together in a sphere of constant density. A nucleus that is twice the size of a smaller nucleus will have roughly $8 (= 2^3)$ times the mass.

The nuclear radius R of an element with atomic mass number A can be modelled by the relationship:

$$R = R_0 A^{\frac{1}{3}}$$

where R_0 is a constant roughly equal to 10^{-15} m (or 1 fm). $R_0 = 1.2 \times 10^{-15}$ m $= 1.2$ fm.

e.g. the radius of a uranium-238 nucleus is predicted to be

$$R = 1.2 \times 10^{-15} \times (238)^{\frac{1}{3}} \text{ m} = 7.4 \text{ fm}$$

The volume of a nucleus, V, of radius, R is given by:

$$V = \frac{4}{3}\pi R^3 = \frac{4}{3}\pi A R_0^3$$

where the mass number A is equal to the number of nucleons.

The number of nucleons per unit volume $= \dfrac{A}{V} = \dfrac{3A}{4\pi A R_0^3}$

$$= \frac{3}{4\pi R_0^3}$$

The mass of a nucleon is m ($\approx 1.7 \times 10^{-27}$ kg), so the nuclear density ρ is:

$$\rho = \frac{3m}{4\pi R_0^3} = \frac{3 \times 1.7 \times 10^{-27}}{4\pi \left(1.2 \times 10^{-15}\right)^3} = 2 \times 10^{17} \text{ kg m}^{-3}$$

This is a vast density (a teaspoon of matter of this density has a mass $\approx 10^{12}$ kg). The only macroscopic objects with the same density as nuclei are neutron stars (see page 162).

The nucleus—size

In the example below, alpha particles are allowed to bombard gold atoms.

As they approach the gold nucleus, they feel a force of repulsion. If an alpha particle is heading directly for the nucleus, it will be reflected straight back along the same path.

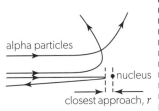

alpha particles

nucleus

closest approach, r

It will have got as close as it can. Note that none of the alpha particles actually collides with the nucleus—they do not have enough energy.

Alpha particles are emitted from their source with a known energy. As they come in they gain electrostatic potential energy and lose kinetic energy (they slow down). At the closest approach, the alpha particle is temporarily stationary and all its energy is potential.

Since electrostatic energy $= \dfrac{q_1 q_2}{4\pi\varepsilon_0 r}$, and you know q_1, the charge on an alpha particle, and q_2, the charge on the gold nucleus, you can calculate r.

Worked example

If the α particles ($Z = 2$) have an energy of 4.2 MeV, the closest approach to the gold nucleus ($Z = 79$) is given by

$$\frac{\left(2 \times 1.6 \times 10^{-19}\right)\left(79 \times 1.6 \times 10^{-19}\right)}{4 \times \pi \times 8.85 \times 10^{-12} \times r}$$

$$= 4.2 \times 10^6 \times 1.6 \times 10^{-19}$$

$$\therefore r = \frac{2 \times 1.6 \times 10^{-19} \times 79}{4 \times \pi \times 8.85 \times 10^{-12} \times 4.2 \times 10^6}$$

$$= 5.4 \times 10^{-14} \text{ m}$$

Deviations from Rutherford scattering in high energy experiments

Rutherford scattering is modelled in terms of the Coulomb repulsion between the alpha particle and the target nucleus. At relatively low energies, detailed analysis of this model accurately predicts the relative intensity of scattered alpha particles at given angles of scattering. At high energies, however, the scattered intensity departs from predictions.

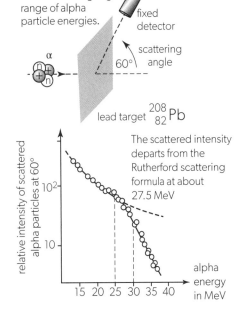

Fixed scattering angle, range of alpha particle energies.

fixed detector

scattering angle

$60°$

α

lead target $^{208}_{82}$Pb

The scattered intensity departs from the Rutherford scattering formula at about 27.5 MeV

relative intensity of scattered alpha particles at 60°

10^2

10

alpha energy in MeV

15 20 25 30 35 40

▲ Eisberg, R. M. and Porter, C. E., Rev. Mod. Phys. 33, 190 (1961)

At these high energies, the alpha particles are beginning to get close enough to the target nucleus for the strong nuclear force (see page 150) to begin to have an effect. To investigate the size of the nucleus in more detail, high energy electrons can be used.

> **AHL** # Atomic spectra and atomic energy states

Introduction

As you have already seen, atomic spectra (emission and absorption) provide evidence for the quantization of the electron energy levels. See page 138 for the laboratory set-up. Different atomic models have attempted to explain these energy levels. The first quantum model of matter was the Bohr model for hydrogen: modern models describe the electrons by using wavefunctions (see page 144).

Hydrogen spectrum

The emission spectrum of atomic hydrogen consists of particular wavelengths. In 1885, a Swiss schoolteacher called Johann Jakob Balmer found that the visible wavelengths fitted a mathematical formula.

These wavelengths, known as the **Balmer series**, were later shown to be just one of several similar series of possible wavelengths that all had similar formulas. These can be expressed in one overall formula called the **Rydberg formula**.

$$\frac{1}{\lambda} = R_H \left(\frac{1}{n^2} - \frac{1}{m^2} \right)$$

λ is the wavelength

m is a whole number larger than 2, i.e. 3, 4, 5 etc.

For the **Lyman series** of lines (in the ultra-violet range) $n = 1$. For the **Balmer series** $n = 2$. The other series are the **Paschen** ($n = 3$), **Brackett** ($n = 4$) and the **Pfund** ($n = 5$) series. In each case, the constant R_H, called the **Rydberg constant**, has the one unique value, $1.097 \times 10^7 \, \text{m}^{-1}$.

Worked example

The diagram below represents some of the electron energy levels in the hydrogen atom. Calculate the wavelength of the photon emitted when an electron falls from $n = 3$ to $n = 2$.

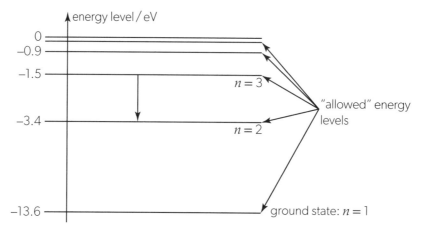

Energy difference in levels = $3.4 - 1.5 = 1.9 \, \text{eV} = 1.9 \times 1.6 \times 10^{-19} \, \text{J} = 3.04 \times 10^{-19} \, \text{J}$

Frequency of photon $f = \dfrac{E}{h} = \dfrac{3.04 \times 10^{-19}}{6.63 \times 10^{-34}} = 4.59 \times 10^{14} \, \text{Hz}$

Wavelength of photon $\lambda = \dfrac{c}{f} = \dfrac{3.00 \times 10^8}{4.59 \times 10^{14}} = 6.54 \times 10^{-7} \, \text{m} = 654 \, \text{nm}$

This is in the visible part of the electromagnetic spectrum and one wavelength in the Balmer series.

Note that the value for the discrete energy levels used in the above example come from the Bohr model of the hydrogen atom (see page 141). This model predicts that the discrete energy levels are given by:

$$E = -\frac{13.6}{n^2} \, \text{eV}$$

Substituting $n = 1, 2, 3$ etc, gives the energy levels shown in the above diagram ($-13.6 \, \text{eV}, -3.4 \, \text{eV}, -1.9 \, \text{eV}, -0.9 \, \text{eV}$ etc.)

The transitions between these levels accurately predict the actual wavelengths observed in the hydrogen spectrum as summarized by the Rydberg formula.

Bohr model of the atom

Bohr model

Niels Bohr took the standard "planetary" model of the hydrogen atom and filled in the mathematical details. Unlike planetary orbits, there are only a limited number of "allowed" orbits for the electron. Bohr suggested that these orbits had fixed multiples of angular momentum. The orbits were quantized in terms of angular momentum. The energy levels predicted by this quantization were in exact agreement with the discrete wavelengths of the hydrogen spectrum. Although this agreement with experiment is impressive, the model has some problems associated with it.

Bohr postulated that:

- An electron does not radiate energy when in a stable orbit. The only stable orbits possible for the electron are ones where the **angular momentum** of the orbit is an integral multiple of $\dfrac{h}{2\pi}$ where h is a fixed number (6.6×10^{-34} J s) called Planck's constant. Mathematically:

$$m_e v r = \frac{nh}{2\pi}$$

(angular momentum is equal to $m_e v r$)

- When electrons move between stable orbits they radiate (or absorb) energy.

$$F_{\text{electrostatic}} = \text{centripetal force}$$

$$\therefore \frac{e^2}{4\pi\varepsilon_0 r^2} = \frac{m_e v^2}{r}$$

but $v = \dfrac{nh}{2\pi m_e r}$ (from 1st postulate)

$$\therefore r = \frac{\varepsilon_0 n^2 h^2}{\pi m_e e^2} \text{ (by substitution)}$$

Total energy of electron = KE + PE

where KE $= \dfrac{1}{2} m_e v^2 = \dfrac{1}{2} \dfrac{e^2}{(4\pi\varepsilon_0 r)}$

and PE $= -\dfrac{e^2}{4\pi\varepsilon_0 r}$ (electrostatic PE)

so total energy $E_n = -\dfrac{1}{2} \dfrac{e^2}{4\pi\varepsilon_0 r} = -\dfrac{m_e e^4}{8\varepsilon_0^2 n^2 h^2}$

This final equation shows that:

- the electron is bound to (= "trapped by") the proton because overall it has negative energy.
- the energy of an orbit is proportional to $-\dfrac{1}{n^2}$. In electronvolts

$$E_n = -\frac{13.6}{n^2}$$

The second postulate can be used (with the full equation) to predict the wavelength of radiation emitted when an electron makes a transition between stable orbits.

$$hf = E_2 - E_1$$

$$= \frac{m_e e^4}{8\varepsilon_0^2 h^2}\left(\frac{1}{n_1^2} - \frac{1}{n_2^2}\right)$$

but $f = \dfrac{c}{\lambda}$

$$\therefore \frac{1}{\lambda} = \frac{m_e e^4}{8\varepsilon_0^2 c h^2}\left(\frac{1}{n_1^2} - \frac{1}{n_2^2}\right)$$

Note that:

- This equation is of the same form as the Rydberg formula (see page 140).
- The values predicted by this equation are in very good agreement with experimental measurement.
- The Rydberg constant can be calculated from other (known) constants. Again, the agreement with experimental data is good.

The limitations to this model are:

- If the same approach is used to predict the emission spectra of other elements, it fails to predict the correct values for atoms or ions with more than one electron.
- The first postulate (about angular momentum) has no theoretical justification.
- Theory predicts that electrons should, in fact, not be stable in circular orbits around a nucleus. Any accelerated electron should radiate energy. An electron in a circular orbit is accelerating so it should radiate energy and thus spiral in to the nucleus.
- It is unable to account for relative intensity of the different lines.
- It is unable to account for the fine structure of the spectral lines.

End of topic questions—E.1 Structure of the atom

1. The diagram below represents the lowest four energy levels in the Bohr model of the hydrogen atom.

increasing electron energy

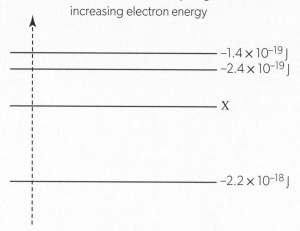

—————————————— -1.4×10^{-19} J
—————————————— -2.4×10^{-19} J

—————————————— X

—————————————— -2.2×10^{-18} J

a. Explain the significance of the negative values of these energy levels. (3)

b. Calculate the longest and shortest wavelengths that will be produced by transitions between these four states. (3)

c. Determine the number of different spectral lines that can be produced by transitions between these four states. (2)

d. Show that the energy level labelled X in the above diagram is approximately -5.5×10^{-19} J. (2)

2. When light from a distant star is analysed, an absorption spectrum can be identified.

a. Explain how an absorption spectrum arises in the light from a star. (3)

b. Outline the information that can be deduced from the observed absorption spectrum. (3)

3. Nuclear notation has the general form $^A_Z X$.

a. Discuss which two symbols from A, Z and X effectively provide the same information. (2)

b. Explain which symbol will be the largest number. (2)

c. The chemical symbol for the element uranium is U. A nucleus of one form of uranium contains 92 protons and 143 neutrons. State the nuclear notation for this form. (1)

AHL

4. Show that the plank constant h has the same units as angular momentum. (3)

5. In a Geiger–Marsden–Rutherford experiment, α-particles of mass 6.7×10^{-27} kg are moving at a speed of 2.0×10^6 m s^{-1}. Calculate how close these α-particles could get to the nucleus of a gold atom. The atomic number for gold is 79. (3)

E.2 Quantum physics

Photoelectric effect

Photoelectric effect

Under certain conditions, when light (ultra-violet) is shone onto a metal surface (such as zinc), electrons are emitted from the surface. More detailed experiments (see below) showed that:

- below a certain **threshold frequency**, f_0, no photoelectrons are emitted, no matter how long one waits

- above the threshold frequency, the maximum kinetic energy of these electrons depends on the frequency of the incident light

- the number of electrons emitted depends on the intensity of the light and does not depend on the frequency

- there is no noticeable delay between the arrival of the light and the emission of electrons.

These observations cannot be reconciled with the view that light is a wave. A wave of any frequency should eventually bring enough energy to the metal plate.

Einstein model

Einstein introduced the idea of light being made up of particles and explained this as follows.

- Electrons at the surface need a certain minimum energy in order to escape from the surface. This minimum energy is called the **work function** of the metal and given the symbol ϕ.

- The UV light energy arrives in lots of little packets of energy called photons.

- The energy in each packet is fixed by the frequency of UV light that is being used, whereas the number of packets arriving per second is fixed by the intensity of the source.

- The energy carried by a photon is given by $E = hf$

- Different electrons absorb different photons. If the energy of the photon is sufficient, it gives the electron enough energy to leave the metal surface.

- Any "extra" energy would be retained by the electron as kinetic energy.

- If the energy of the photon is too small, the electron will still gain this amount of energy but it will soon share it with other electrons.

Above the threshold frequency, incoming energy of photons = energy needed to leave the surface + kinetic energy.

In symbols, $E_{max} = hf - \phi$

$$hf = \phi + E_{max} \text{ or } hf = \phi + V_s e$$

Therefore a graph of frequency against stopping potential should be a straight line with gradient $\dfrac{e}{h}$.

Stopping potential experiment

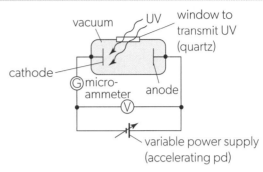

In the apparatus above, photoelectrons are emitted by the cathode. They are then accelerated across to the anode by the potential difference.

The potential between cathode and anode can also be reversed. In this situation, the electrons are decelerated. At a certain value of potential, the stopping potential, V_s, no more photocurrent is observed. The photoelectrons have been brought to rest before arriving at the anode.

The stopping potential depends on the frequency of UV light in the linear way shown in the graph below.

The stopping potential is a measure of the maximum kinetic energy of the electrons.

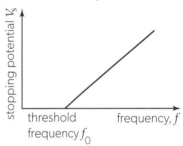

Max KE of electrons $= V_s e$

(since pd $= \dfrac{\text{energy}}{\text{charge}}$ and $e =$ charge on an electron)

$$\therefore \frac{1}{2}mv^2 = V_s e \quad \therefore v = \sqrt{\frac{2V_s e}{m}}$$

Worked example

What is the maximum velocity of electrons emitted from a zinc surface ($\phi = 4.2\,\text{eV}$) when illuminated by electromagnetic radiation of wavelength 200 nm?

$$\phi = 4.2\,\text{eV} = 4.2 \times 1.6 \times 10^{-19}\,\text{J} = 6.72 \times 10^{-19}\,\text{J}$$

$$\text{Energy of photon} = h\frac{c}{\lambda} = \frac{6.63 \times 10^{-34} \times 3 \times 10^8}{2 \times 10^{-7}}$$

$$= 9.945 \times 10^{-19}\,\text{J}$$

$$\therefore \text{KE of electron} = (9.945 - 6.72) \times 10^{-19}\,\text{J}$$

$$= 3.225 \times 10^{-19}\,\text{J}$$

$$\therefore v = \sqrt{\frac{2E_k}{m}} = \sqrt{\frac{2 \times 3.225 \times 10^{-19}}{9.1 \times 10^{-31}}} = 8.4 \times 10^5\,\text{m s}^{-1}$$

AHL Matter waves

Wave–particle duality

The photoelectric effect of light waves clearly demonstrates that light can behave like particles, but its wave nature can also be demonstrated—it reflects, refracts, diffracts and interferes just like all waves. So what exactly is it? It seems reasonable to ask two questions.

1. *Is light a wave or is it a particle?*

The correct answer to this question is "yes"! At the most fundamental and even philosophical level, light is just light. Physics tries to understand and explain what it is. You do this by imagining models of its behaviour. Sometimes it helps to think of it as a wave and sometimes

it helps to think of it as a particle, but neither model is complete. Light is just light. This dual nature of light is called **wave–particle duality**.

2. *If light waves can show particle properties, can particles such as electrons show wave properties?*

Again the correct answer is "yes". Most people imagine moving electrons as little particles having a definite size, shape, position and speed. This model does not explain why electrons can be diffracted through small gaps. In order to diffract, they must have a wave nature. Once again they have a dual nature. See the experiment below.

de Broglie hypothesis

If matter can have wave properties and waves can have matter properties, there should be a link between the two models. The de Broglie hypothesis is that all moving particles have a "matter wave" associated with them. This matter wave can be thought of as a probability function associated with the moving particle. The (amplitude)^2 of the wave at any given point is a measure of the probability of finding the particle at that point. The wavelength of this matter wave is given by the de Broglie equation:

$$\lambda = \frac{hc}{pc} = \frac{hc}{E} \text{ for photons}$$

λ is the wavelength in m

h is Plank's constant $= 6.63 \times 10^{-34}$ J s

c is the speed of light $= 3.0 \times 10^8$ m s^{-1}

p is the momentum of the particle

The higher the energy, the lower the de Broglie wavelength. This equation was introduced on page 143 as the method of calculating a photon's wavelength from its energy, E. For the wave nature of particles to be observable in experiments, the particles often have very high velocities. In these situations, the proper calculations are relativistic but simplifications are possible.

1. At very high energies, $pc = E$

In these situations, the rest energy of the particles can be negligible compared with their energy of motion.

For example, the rest energy of an electron (0.511 MeV) is negligible if it has been accelerated through an effective potential difference of 420 MV to have kinetic energy of 420 MeV. In these circumstances, the total energy of an electron is effectively 420 MeV. The de Broglie wavelength of 420 MeV electrons is:

$$\lambda = \frac{6.6 \times 10^{-34} \times 3.0 \times 10^8}{420 \times 10^6 \times 1.6 \times 10^{-19}} = 2.9 \times 10^{-15} \text{ m}$$

2. At low energies

In these situations, the relationship can be restated in terms of the momentum p of the particle measured in kg m s^{-1}
(in non-relativistic mechanics, $p =$ mass $\times$ velocity):

$$\lambda = \frac{h}{p}$$

For example, electrons accelerated through 1 kV would gain a KE of 1.6×10^{-16} J. Since KE and non-relativistic momentum are related by $E_k = \frac{p^2}{2m}$, this gives $p = 1.7 \times 10^{-23}$ kg m s^{-1}

$$\lambda = \frac{6.6 \times 10^{-34}}{1.7 \times 10^{-23}} = 3.9 \times 10^{-11} \text{ m}$$

Electron diffraction experiment

In order to show diffraction, an electron "wave" must travel through a gap of the same order as its wavelength. The atomic spacing in crystal atoms provides such gaps. If a beam of electrons impinges upon powdered carbon, then the electrons will be diffracted according to the wavelength.

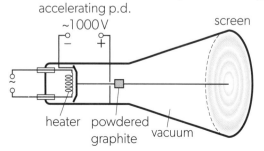

accelerating p.d.

~1000 V

screen

heater powdered graphite vacuum

The circles correspond to the angles where constructive interference takes place. They are circles because the powdered carbon provides every possible orientation of gap. A higher accelerating potential for the electrons would result in a higher momentum for each electron. According to the de Broglie relationship, the wavelength of the electrons would thus decrease. This would mean that the size of the gaps is now proportionally bigger than the wavelength, so there would be less diffraction. The circles would move in to smaller angles. The predicted angles of constructive interference are accurately verified experimentally.

AHL : **The Compton effect**

The Compton effect

The Compton effect provides further evidence of the particle nature of light. In the experiment, high energy X-rays or γ-rays of a known wavelength are scattered by a target substance (e.g. graphite). The scattered radiation contains two different wavelengths. One has the same wavelength as that of the incident radiation. The other has an increased wavelength (decreased frequency) when compared with the incident radiation.

The scattered X-rays that have a higher wavelength than the incident X-rays are the result of an elastic collision with an outer/free electron target. This free electron gains kinetic energy, so the scattered photon is of a lower energy (higher wavelength). The shift in wavelength is dependent on the angle of scattering and is in agreement with predictions from conservation of energy and momentum. The scattered photon is behaving like a particle with energy and momentum.

Set-up

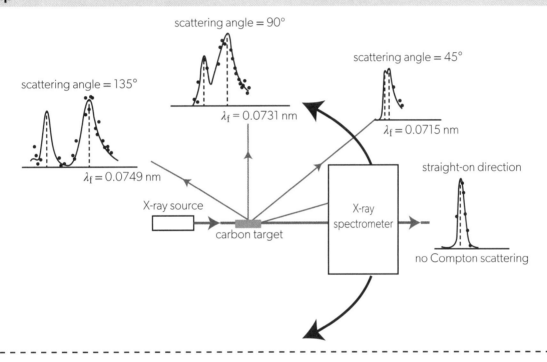

scattering angle = 90°

scattering angle = 135°

scattering angle = 45°

$\lambda_f = 0.0731$ nm

$\lambda_f = 0.0715$ nm

$\lambda_f = 0.0749$ nm

straight-on direction

X-ray source

carbon target

X-ray spectrometer

no Compton scattering

Explanation in terms of photons

Application of conservation of energy and momentum to this elastic collision between an incident photon and an electron gives:

$$\lambda_f - \lambda_i = \Delta\lambda = \frac{h}{m_e c}(1 - \cos\theta)$$

The maximum increase in wavelength happens when $(1 - \cos\theta)$ has its maximum value (= 2), when $\cos\theta = -1$ i.e. $\theta = 180°$.

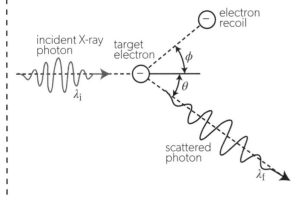

electron recoil

incident X-ray photon

target electron

ϕ

θ

λ_i

scattered photon

λ_f

Worked example

An X-ray of wavelength 7.1000×10^{-11} m is incident on a calcite target. Find the wavelength of the X-ray scattered at a 30° angle.

$$\Delta\lambda = \frac{h}{m_e c}(1 - \cos\theta) = \frac{6.63 \times 10^{-34}}{9.11 \times 10^{-31} \times 3 \times 10^8}(1 - \cos 30°)$$

$$= 3.25 \times 10^{-13} \text{ m}$$

$$\lambda_f = \lambda_i + \Delta\lambda = (71.000 + 0.325) \times 10^{-12} = 71.325 \times 10^{-12} \text{ m}$$

$$= 71.325 \text{ pm}$$

End of topic questions—E.2 Quantum physics

1. This question is about the photoelectric effect.
   a. Describe what is meant by the *photoelectric effect*. (2)

   b. An experiment into the photoelectric effect using a piece of metal obtains the following data.

Frequency of light / 10^{14} Hz	Stopping potential / V
6.0	0.6
7.0	1.0
8.0	1.4
9.0	1.8
10.0	2.2

   i. Explain what is meant by *stopping potential*. (2)

   ii. Sketch an appropriate graph in order to deduce the threshold frequency for the piece of metal. (2)

   iii. Use your graph to calculate a value for Plank's constant. (3)

2. This question is about wave–particle duality.
   a. Outline what is meant by the phrase *wave-particle duality*. (2)

   b. *Compton scattering* of light by electrons provides evidence for the particular nature of light.
   i. Outline what is meant by the *Compton scattering* of light. (2)

   ii. Discuss how the particular nature of light can explain Compton scattering. (4)

3. This question is about the de Broglie wavelength.
   a. Estimate:
   i. the de Broglie wavelength of electrons moving in a vacuum at half the speed of light, $0.5c$ (2)

   ii. the de Broglie wavelength for alpha particles moving at 2×10^7 m s^{-1} (2)

   iii. the de Broglie wavelength of a person with a mass of 70 kg walking at 1 m s^{-1}. (2)

   b. For each of objects (i)–(iii), discuss whether it would be possible to experimentally observe the object's wave nature. (2,2,2)

4. a. Calculate the momentum of a visible light photon of wavelength 550 nm. (2)

   b. The radiation pressure received at the surface of the Earth as a result of photons from the Sun is approximately 1 μPa. Estimate the number of photons of wavelength 550 nm that would have to arrive every second on 1 m^2 of the Earth's surface. (4)

   c. Outline any assumptions that you have made in order to make the estimate in (b). (2)

5. A photon of wavelength 6.00×10^{-12} m collides with a stationary electron. After the collision, the photon's wavelength is **changed** by exactly 2.43×10^{-12} m.
   a. Calculate the wavelength of the photon after the collision. (2)

   b. Deduce the angle through which the photon has been deflected in this collision. (3)

   c. Explain whether the angle between the original direction of the photon and the final direction of the electron is greater, smaller or equal to your answer (b). (3)

   d. Determine the kinetic energy of the electron after the collision. (3)

E.3 Radioactive decay

Nuclear stability

Isotopes

When a chemical reaction takes place, it involves the outer electrons of the atoms concerned. Different elements have different chemical properties because the arrangement of outer electrons varies from element to element. The chemical properties of a particular element are fixed by the amount of positive charge that exists in the nucleus—in other words, the number of protons. In general, different nuclear structures will imply different chemical properties. A **nuclide** is the name given to a particular species of atom (one whose nucleus contains a specified number of protons and a specified number of neutrons). Some nuclides are the same element—they have the same chemical properties and contain the same number of protons. These nuclides are called **isotopes**—they contain the same number of protons but different numbers of neutrons.

Notation

atomic number – equal to number of protons in the nucleus

mass number – equal to number of nucleons

$$_Z^A X$$

chemical symbol

▲ Nuclide notation

Examples

	Notation	Description	Comment
1	$_6^{12}C$	carbon-12	isotope of 2
2	$_6^{13}C$	carbon-13	isotope of 1
3	$_{92}^{238}U$	uranium-238	
4	$_{78}^{198}Pt$	platinum-198	same mass number as 5
5	$_{80}^{198}Hg$	mercury-198	same mass number as 4

Each element has a unique chemical symbol and its own atomic number. $_6^{12}C$ and $_6^{13}C$ are examples of two isotopes, whereas $_{78}^{198}Pt$ and $_{80}^{198}Hg$ are not.

In general, when physicists use this notation they are concerned with the nucleus rather than the whole atom. Chemists use the same notation but tend to include the overall charge on the atom. So $_6^{12}C$ can represent the carbon nucleus to a physicist or the carbon atom to a chemist depending on the context. If the charge is present the situation becomes unambiguous. $_{17}^{35}Cl^-$ must refer to a chlorine ion—an atom that has gained one extra electron.

Nuclear reactions (1)

Unified mass units

The individual masses involved in nuclear reactions are tiny. To compare atomic masses physicists often use unified mass units, u. These are defined in terms of the most common isotope of carbon, carbon-12. There are 12 nucleons in the carbon-12 atom (6 protons and 6 neutrons) and one unified mass unit is defined as exactly one twelfth of the mass of a carbon-12 atom. Essentially, the mass of a proton and the mass of a neutron are both approximately 1 u, as shown on the right.

$$1\,u = \frac{1}{12}\ \text{mass of a (carbon-12) atom} = 1.66 \times 10^{-27}\,kg$$

rest mass of 1 proton $= 1.007\,276\,u$

rest mass of 1 neutron $= 1.008\,665\,u$

rest mass of 1 electron $= 0.000\,549\,u$

A mass of $1\,MeV\,c^{-2}$ is equivalent to $1.8 \times 10^{-30}\,kg$, which is roughly the mass of two stationary electrons.

Mass defect and binding energy

The masses of neutrons and protons are shown above. If you add together the masses of 6 protons, 6 neutrons and 6 electrons you will get a number bigger than 12 u, the mass of a carbon-12 atom. What has gone wrong? The answer becomes clear when you investigate what keeps the nucleus bound together.

The difference between the mass of a nucleus and the masses of its component nucleons is called the **mass defect**. If one imagined assembling a nucleus, the protons and neutrons would initially need to be brought together. Doing this takes work because the protons repel one another. Creating the bonds between the protons and neutrons releases a greater amount of energy than

the work done in bringing them together. This energy released must come from somewhere. The answer lies in Einstein's famous mass–energy equivalence relationship.

$$\Delta E = \Delta mc^2$$

In Einstein's equation, mass is another form of energy and it is possible to convert mass directly into energy and vice versa. The **binding energy** is the amount of energy that is released when a nucleus is assembled from its component nucleons. It comes from a decrease in mass. The binding energy would also be the energy that needs to be added in order to separate a nucleus into its individual nucleons. The mass defect is thus a measure of the binding energy.

Nuclear reactions (2)

Units

Using Einstein's equation, 1 kg of mass is equivalent to 9×10^{16} J of energy. This is a huge amount of energy. At the atomic scale other units of energy tend to be more useful. The electronvolt (see page 124), or more usually, the megaelectronvolt is often used.

$$1\,\text{eV} = 1.6 \times 10^{-19}\,\text{J}$$
$$1\,\text{MeV} = 1.6 \times 10^{-13}\,\text{J}$$

1 u of mass converts into 931.5 MeV

Since mass and energy are equivalent, it is sometimes useful to work in units that avoid having to do repeated multiplications by the (speed of light)^2. A new possible unit for mass is thus $\text{MeV}\,c^{-2}$. It works like this:

If $1\,\text{MeV}\,c^{-2}$ worth of mass is converted you get 1 MeV worth of energy.

Worked example

How much energy would be released if 14 g of carbon-14 decayed as shown in the equation below?

$$^{14}_{6}\text{C} \rightarrow\, ^{14}_{7}\text{N} + \,^{0}_{-1}\beta + \bar{\nu}$$

Information given

atomic mass of carbon-14 = 14.003242 u;
atomic mass of nitrogen-14 = 14.003074 u;
mass of electron = 0.000549 u

$$\text{mass of left-hand side} = \text{nuclear mass of}\, ^{14}_{6}\text{C}$$
$$= 14.003242 - 6(0.000549)\,\text{u}$$
$$= 13.999948\,\text{u}$$
$$\text{nuclear mass of}\, ^{14}_{7}\text{N} = 14.003074 - 7(0.000549)\,\text{u}$$
$$= 13.999231\,\text{u}$$
$$\text{mass of right-hand side} = 13.999231 + 0.000549\,\text{u}$$
$$= 13.999780\,\text{u}$$

$$\text{mass difference} = \text{LHS} - \text{RHS}$$
$$= 0.000168\,\text{u}$$
$$\text{energy released per decay} = 0.000168 \times 931.5\,\text{MeV}$$
$$= 0.156492\,\text{MeV}$$

14 g of C-14 is 1 mol

1 mole contains 6.022×10^{23} atoms (Avogadro's number (N_A)

$\therefore$ total number of decays $= N_A = 6.022 \times 10^{23}$

$\therefore$ total energy release $= 6.022 \times 10^{23} \times 0.156492\,\text{MeV}$
$$= 9.424 \times 10^{22}\,\text{MeV}$$
$$= 9.424 \times 10^{22} \times 1.6 \times 10^{-13}\,\text{J}$$
$$= 1.51 \times 10^{10}\,\text{J}$$
$$\approx 15\,\text{GJ}$$

Many calculations avoid the need to consider the masses of the electrons by providing you with the *nuclear mass* as opposed to the *atomic mass*.

Artificial transmutations

There is nothing that you can do to change the likelihood of a certain radioactive decay happening, but under certain conditions you can make nuclear reactions happen. This can be done by bombarding a nucleus with a nucleon, an alpha particle or another small nucleus. Such reactions are called **artificial transmutations**. In general, the target nucleus first "captures" the incoming object and then an emission takes place. The first ever artificial transmutation was carried out by Rutherford in 1919. Nitrogen was bombarded by alpha particles and the presence of oxygen was detected spectroscopically.

$$^{4}_{2}\text{He}^{2+} + \,^{14}_{7}\text{N} = \,^{17}_{8}\text{O} + \,^{1}_{1}\text{p}$$

The mass numbers $(4 + 14 = 17 + 1)$ and the atomic numbers $(2 + 7 = 8 + 1)$ on both sides of the equation must balance.

Fission and fusion

Binding energy per nucleon

Whenever a nuclear reaction (fission or fusion) releases energy, the products of the reaction are in a lower energy state than the reactants. Mass loss must be the source of this energy. To compare the energy states of different nuclei, physicists calculate the binding energy per nucleon. This is the total binding energy for the

nucleus divided by the total number of nucleons. One of the nuclei with the largest binding energy per nucleon is iron-56, $^{56}_{26}$Fe.

A reaction is energetically feasible if the products of the reaction have a greater binding energy per nucleon when compared with the reactants.

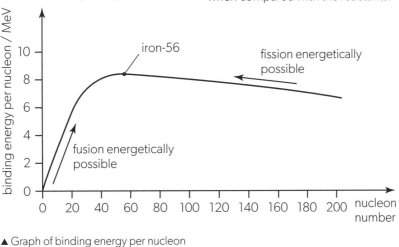

▲ Graph of binding energy per nucleon

Fission

Fission is the name given to the nuclear reaction whereby large nuclei are induced to break up into smaller nuclei and release energy in the process. It is the reaction that is used in nuclear reactors and atomic bombs. A typical single reaction might involve bombarding a uranium nucleus with a neutron. This can cause the uranium nucleus to break up into two smaller nuclei. A typical reaction might be:

$$^{1}_{0}n + ^{235}_{92}U \rightarrow ^{141}_{56}Ba + ^{92}_{36}Kr + 3\,^{1}_{0}n + energy$$

Since the one original neutron causing the reaction has resulted in the production of three neutrons, there is the possibility of a **chain reaction** occurring. It is technically quite difficult to get the neutrons to lose enough energy to go on and initiate further reactions, but it is achievable.

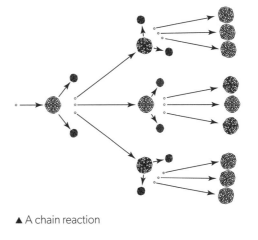

▲ A chain reaction

▲ A fission reaction

Fusion

Fusion is the name given to the nuclear reaction whereby small nuclei are induced to join together into larger nuclei and release energy in the process. It is the reaction that "fuels" all stars including the Sun. A typical reaction that is taking place in the Sun is the fusion of two different isotopes of hydrogen to produce helium.

$$^{2}_{1}H + ^{3}_{1}H \rightarrow ^{4}_{2}He + ^{1}_{0}n + energy$$

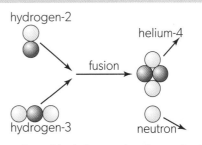

▲ One of the fusion reactions happening in the Sun

Fundamental forces

Strong nuclear force

The protons in a nucleus are all positive. Since like charges repel, they must be repelling one another all the time. This means there must be another force keeping the nucleus together. Without it the nucleus would "fly apart". A few things are known about this force:

- It must be strong. If the proton repulsions are calculated it is clear that the gravitational attraction between the nucleons is far too small to be able to keep the nucleus together.

- It must be very short ranged as you do not observe this force anywhere other than inside the nucleus.

- It is likely to involve the neutrons as well. Small nuclei tend to have equal numbers of protons and neutrons. Large nuclei need proportionately more neutrons in order to keep the nucleus together.

The name given to this force is the **strong nuclear force**.

Weak nuclear force

The strong nuclear force (see box above) explains why nuclei do not fly apart and thus why they are stable. Most nuclei, however, are unstable. Mechanisms to explain alpha and gamma emission (see page 151) can be identified but another nuclear force must be involved if you wish to be able to explain all aspects of the nucleus, including beta emission. A few things are known about this force:

- It must be weak. Many nuclei are stable and beta emission does not always occur.

- It must be very short ranged as you do not observe this force anywhere other than inside the nucleus.

- Unlike the strong nuclear force, it involves the lighter particles (e.g. electrons, positrons and neutrinos) as well as the heavier ones (e.g. protons and neutrons).

The name given to this force is the **weak nuclear force**. The weak nuclear force is only included here for completeness, but it is not considered in this course so will not be tested in examination questions.

Other fundamental forces/interactions

The standard model of particle physics is based around the forces that you observe on a daily basis along with the two "new" forces that have been identified as being involved in nuclear stability (above). As a result, in the standard model, there are only four fundament forces (or **interactions**) that are known to exist. These are Gravity, Electromagnetic, Strong and Weak. The strong and weak forces are described above. Some information about the two "everyday" interactions is listed below.

Gravity

- Gravity is the force of attraction between all objects that have mass.

- Gravity is always attractive—masses are pulled together.

- The range of the gravity force is infinite.

- Despite the above, the gravity force is relatively quite weak. At least one of the masses involved needs to be large for the effects to be noticeable. For example, the gravitational force of attraction between you and this book is negligible, but the force between this book and the Earth can be demonstrated easily (drop it).

- Newton's law of gravitation describes the mathematics governing this force.

Electromagnetic

- This single force includes all the forces that you normally categorize as either electrostatic or magnetic.

- Electromagnetic forces involve charged matter.

- Electromagnetic forces can be attractive or repulsive.

- The range of the electromagnetic force is infinite.

- The electromagnetic force is relatively strong—tiny imbalances of charges on an atomic level give rise to significant forces on the laboratory scale.

- At the end of the 19th century, Maxwell showed that the electrostatic force and the magnetic force were just two different aspects of the more fundamental electromagnetic force.

- The mathematics of the electromagnetic force is described by Maxwell's equations.

- Friction (and many other "everyday" forces) is simply the result of the force between atoms and this is governed by the electromagnetic interaction.

The electromagnetic force and the weak nuclear force are now considered to be aspects of the single electroweak force.

Radioactivity (1)

Ionizing properties

Many atomic nuclei are unstable. The process by which they decay is called **radioactive decay**. Every decay involves the emission of one of three different possible radiations from the nucleus: alpha (α), beta (β) or gamma (γ).

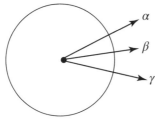

▲ Alpha, beta and gamma all come from the nucleus

All three radiations are ionizing. This means that as they go through a substance, collisions occur which cause electrons to be removed from atoms. Atoms that have lost or gained electrons are called ions. This ionizing property allows the radiations to be detected. It also explains their dangerous nature. When ionizations occur in biologically important molecules, such as DNA, their function can be affected.

Radiation safety

There is no such thing as a safe dose of ionizing radiation. At the molecular level, an ionization could cause damage directly to a biologically important molecule such as DNA or RNA.

As well as molecular damage, potentially causing the cell to die, an ionization could affect the process of cell division and multiplication. It can even cause the transformation of the cell into a malignant form—a cancer.

There are three main ways of protecting yourself from too large a dose.

- **Run away!**
  The simplest method of reducing the dose received is to increase the distance between you and the source. Only electromagnetic radiation can travel large distances and this follows an inverse square relationship with distance.

- **Don't waste time!**
  If you have to receive a dose, then it is important to keep the time of this exposure to a minimum.

- **If you can't run away, hide behind something!**
  Shielding can always be used to reduce the dose received. Lead-lined aprons can also be used to limit the exposure for both patient and operator.

Random decay

Radioactive decay is a **random** process and is not affected by external conditions. For example, increasing the temperature of a sample of radioactive material does not affect the rate of decay. This means that is there no way of knowing whether or not a particular nucleus is going to decay within a certain period of time. All you know is the *chance* of a decay happening in that time.

Although the process is random, the large numbers of atoms involved allows you to make some accurate predictions. If you start with a given number of atoms, then you can expect a certain number to decay in the next minute. If there were more atoms in the sample, you would expect the number decaying to be larger. On average, the rate of decay of a sample is proportional to the number of atoms in the sample. This proportionality means that radioactive decay is an **exponential** process. The number of atoms of a certain element, N, decreases exponentially over time. Mathematically this is expressed as:

$$\frac{dN}{dt} \propto -N$$

Nature of alpha, beta and gamma decay

When a nucleus decays the mass numbers and the atomic numbers must balance on each side of the nuclear equation.

- Alpha particles are helium nuclei, $^4_2\alpha$ or $^4_2\text{He}^{2+}$. In alpha decay, a "chunk" of the nucleus is emitted. The portion that remains will be a different nuclide.

$$^A_Z X \rightarrow {}^{(A-4)}_{(Z-2)} Y + {}^4_2\alpha$$

e.g. $^{241}_{95}\text{Am} \rightarrow {}^{237}_{93}\text{Np} + {}^4_2\alpha$

The atomic numbers and the mass numbers balance on each side of the equation.

($95 = 93 + 2$ and $241 = 237 + 4$)

- Beta particles are electrons, $^0_{-1}\beta$ or $^0_{-1}e^-$, emitted **from the nucleus**. These electrons are formed when a neutron decays. At the same time, another particle, called an antineutrino, is emitted.

$$^1_0 n \rightarrow {}^1_1 p + {}^0_{-1}\beta + \bar{v}$$

Since an antineutrino has no charge and virtually no mass it does not affect the equation.

$$^A_Z X \rightarrow {}^A_{(Z+1)} Y + {}^0_{-1}\beta + \bar{v}$$

e.g. $^{90}_{38}\text{Sr} \rightarrow {}^{90}_{39}Y + {}^0_{-1}\beta + \bar{v}$

- Gamma rays are unlike the other two radiations as they are part of the electromagnetic spectrum. After their emission, the nucleus has less energy, but its mass number and its atomic number have not changed. It is said to have changed from an **excited state** to a lower energy state.

$$^A_Z X^* \rightarrow {}^A_Z X + {}^0_0\gamma$$

Radioactivity (2)

Antimatter

The nuclear model given on page 137 is somewhat simplified. One important thing that is not mentioned there is the existence of antimatter. Every form of matter has its equivalent form of antimatter. If matter and antimatter came together they would annihilate each other. Not surprisingly, antimatter is rare but it does exist. For example, another form of radioactive decay that can take place is beta plus or positron decay. In this decay a proton decays into a neutron, and the antimatter version of an electron, a positron, is emitted.

$$_{1}^{1}p \rightarrow {}_{0}^{1}n + {}_{+1}^{0}\beta^{+} + \nu$$

$$\text{e.g. } _{10}^{19}Ne \rightarrow {}_{9}^{19}F + {}_{+1}^{0}\beta^{+} + \nu$$

The positron, β^{+}, emission is accompanied by a neutrino. The antineutrino is the antimatter form of the neutrino.

Properties of alpha, beta and gamma radiations

Property	Alpha, α	Beta, β	Gamma, γ
Effect on photographic film	Yes	Yes	Yes
Approximate number of ion pairs produced in air	10^4 per mm travelled	10^2 per mm travelled	1 per mm travelled
Typical material needed to absorb it	10^{-2} mm aluminium; piece of paper	A few mm aluminium	10 cm lead
Penetration ability	Low	Medium	High
Typical path length in air	A few cm	Less than one m	Effectively infinite
Deflection by E and B fields	Behaves like a positive charge	Behaves like a negative charge	Not deflected
Speed	About 10^7 m s^{-1}	About 10^8 m s^{-1}, very variable	3×10^8 m s^{-1}

Background radiation

Radioactive decay is a natural phenomenon and is going on around you all the time. The activity of any given source is measured in terms of the number of individual nuclear decays that take place in a unit of time. This information is quoted in **becquerels** (Bq) with 1 Bq = 1 nuclear decay per second.

Experimentally, this would be measured using a **Geiger counter**, which detects and counts the number of ionizations taking place inside a Geiger–Müller tube (**GM tube**). A working Geiger counter will always detect some radioactive ionizations taking place even when there is no identified radioactive source: there is a **background count** as a result of the **background radiation**. A reading of 30 counts per minute, which corresponds to the detector registering 30 ionizing events, would not be unusual for a normal safe level of background radiation.

To analyse the activity of a given radioactive source, it is necessary to correct for the background radiation taking place. The background count without the radioactive source present should be recorded and this value can then be subtracted from all readings with the source present.

Some cosmic gamma rays will be responsible, but there will also be α, β and γ radiation received as a result of radioactive decays that are taking place in the surrounding materials. The pie chart below identifies typical sources of radiation, but the actual value varies from country to country and from place to place.

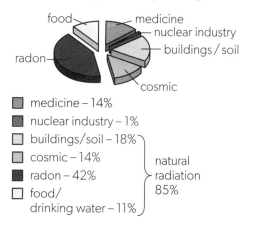

- medicine – 14%
- nuclear industry – 1%
- buildings/soil – 18%
- cosmic – 14%
- radon – 42%
- food/drinking water – 11%

natural radiation 85%

Half-life

Half-life

There is a temptation to think that every quantity that decreases with time is an exponential decrease, but exponential curves have a particular mathematical property. In the graph shown below, the time taken for half of the number of nuclides to decay is always the same, whatever starting value you choose. This allows you to express the chances of decay happening in a property called the **half-life**, $T_{\frac{1}{2}}$. The half-life of a nuclide is the time taken for half of the number of nuclides present in a sample to decay. An equivalent statement is that the half-life is the time taken for the rate of decay (or activity) of a particular sample of nuclides to halve. A substance with a large half-life takes a long time to decay. A substance with a short half-life will decay quickly. Half-lives can vary from fractions of a second to millions of years.

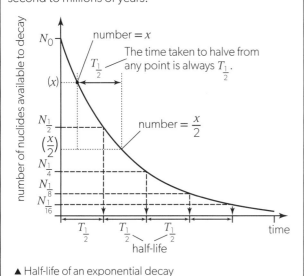

▲ Half-life of an exponential decay

Investigating half-life experimentally

When measuring the activity of a source, the background rate should be subtracted.

- If the half-life is short, then readings can be taken of activity against time.
  - A simple graph of activity against time would produce the normal exponential shape. Several values of half-life could be read from the graph and then averaged. This method is simple and quick but not the most accurate.
  - A graph of ln (activity) against time could be produced. This should give a straight line and the decay constant can be calculated from the gradient (see page 188).
- If the half-life is long, then the activity will effectively be constant over a period of time. In this case, you need to find a way to calculate the number of nuclei present, N, and then use:

$$\frac{\mathrm{d}N}{\mathrm{d}t} = -\lambda N$$

Example

In simple situations, working out how much radioactive material remains is a matter of applying the half-life property several times. A common mistake is to think that if the half-life of a radioactive material is 3 days then it will all decay in six days. In fact, after six days (two half-lives) a "half of a half" will remain, i.e. a quarter.

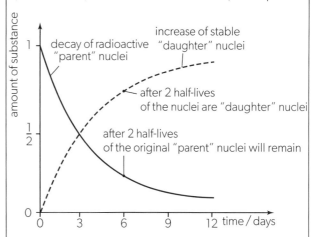

▲ The decay of parent into daughter.

e.g. The half-life of $^{12}_{6}C$ is 5 570 years.
Approximately how much time will pass before less than 1% of a sample of $^{14}_{6}C$ remains?

Time	Percentage left
1 $T_{\frac{1}{2}}$	50%
2 $T_{\frac{1}{2}}$	25%
3 $T_{\frac{1}{2}}$	12.5%
4 $T_{\frac{1}{2}}$	~6.3%
5 $T_{\frac{1}{2}}$	~3.1%
6 $T_{\frac{1}{2}}$	~1.6%
7 $T_{\frac{1}{2}}$	~0.8%
6 half lives	= 33 420 years
7 half lives	= 38 990 years

∴ approximately 37 000 years needed

Simulation

The result of the throw of dice is a random process and can be used to simulate radioactive decay. The dice represent nuclei available to decay. Each throw represents a unit of time. Every six represents a nucleus decaying, which means these dice is are longer available.

Uses of radioactivity

Uses of radioactivity

The specific choice of which radioactive isotope to use in any given situation depends on:

- the penetration ability of the decay particle
- the half-life of the isotope
- the chemical properties of the element being used (is it safe for humans?)
- the state of the element (solid, liquid or gas).

Medical use

a) Tracers

Radioactive tracers can be used as "tags". If they are introduced into the body, their progress around the body can be monitored from outside (as long as they are gamma emitters). This can give information about how a specific organ is functioning, as well as being used to analyse a whole body system (e.g. the circulation of blood around the body). The factors that affect the choice of radioisotope include:

- the radioisotope should be able to be "taken up" by the organ in question in its usual way. In other words, it needs to have specific chemical properties.
- the quantity of the radioisotope needs to be as small as possible to minimise the harmful ionizing radiation received by the body.
- the lifetime of the tracer needs to be matched to the timescale of the process being studied.

b) Radiotherapy

Ionizing radiation can be used for treatment of cancer. The aim of radiotherapy is to target malignant cells in preference to normal healthy cells.

The dose that is used is critical. Too high a dose and too many healthy cells are killed. Too low a dose and the cancer is not destroyed. The dose needs to be as high as possible in the region of the cancer and as low as possible elsewhere. This can be achieved by one of two techniques:

- A radioactive source can be placed in the tumour itself. This can be done chemically or physically.
- Overlapping beams of radiation can be used. Where they overlap the dose will be high; elsewhere the dose will be lower.

The source of the ionizing radiation can be a radioactive element, but it is also common to use high-energy X-rays or gamma rays from particle accelerators. High-energy protons can also be used directly.

c) Sterilisation of surgical instruments

Surgical instruments can be exposed to a high doses of gamma radiation to kill any microbes on the surface of the instrument. Given the high dose, this exposure needs to take place in a well-shielded area to as to avoid harm to any users. One of the factors in the choice of radioisotope would be a reasonably long half-life so that the gamma source does not need to be replaced too frequently.

Leaks in underground pipes

In the same way as tracers can be used to track flow around the body, a gamma source can be introduced into an underground pipe which has a suspected leak. The isotope will build up at the location of the leak—allowing it to be detected from the surface. Obviously, gamma is used, as alpha and beta would be blocked by material surrounding the pipe. A risk assessment means that the half-life should be short so that the leaked isotope does not build up in the environment.

Thickness of materials

Many manufacturing processes involve passing material through a set of rollers to achieve a certain desired thickness (e.g. making paper, cardboard, metal).

The radioactive source is chosen so that it penetrates the material but is still affected by thickness (e.g. beta for paper and cardboard, gamma for metal sheets). It should have a long half-life so that the emission rate is reasonably constant. The detector measures the amount of radiation that has penetrated the material. Too high a reading means the material is too thin and the controller reduces the pressure on the rollers. Too low a reading and the pressure on the rollers in increased.

Radioactive dating

a) Archaeological specimens (carbon dating)

The vast majority of naturally occurring carbon is either C-12 (98.9%) or C-13 (1.1%). Both of these isotopes are stable. A tiny fraction (about 10^{-10} %) is the radioactive isotope C-14 which has a half-life of 5 700 years. The proportion of C-14 to C-12 in the air is relatively constant and this proportion would be the same in all living objects (e.g. trees). When the living thing dies or the tree is cut down, the C-14 trapped in the material will radioactively decay whereas the C-12 trapped in the material remains stable. The ratio of C-14 to C-12 decreases over time and can be used to date the object. Obviously, this only works for materials that used to be part of something living. Samples from objects of known age can be used to calibrate any long-term variations of C-14 to C-12 in the air (e.g. samples from old trees where the age of a particular sample can be deduced by counting the tree "rings"—each year the tree is alive, it adds another ring of growth.)

b) Rocks

Rock samples can be dated by looking at the relative proportions of some known radioactive isotopes. Commonly used isotopes are:

- the decay chain of uranium-235 to stable lead-297 (half-life = 700 million years)
- the decay chain of uranium-238 to stable lead-206 (half-life = 4.5 billion years)
- the decay chain of potassium-40 to stable argon-40 (half-life = 1.3 billion years). The argon needs to be trapped in the rock.

AHL : Evidence for the strong nuclear force

Evidence for the strong nuclear force

The evidence for the existence of a stable nucleus within atoms comes from the Geiger–Marsden–Rutherford experiment (see page 137). The identification of protons and neutrons as components of the nucleus implies the existence of a strong nuclear force (see page 150). High energy deviations from the Geiger–Marsden–Rutherford experiment provide evidence for the existence of the strong nuclear force.

Nuclear stability

Many atomic nuclei are unstable. The process by which they decay is called radioactive decay (see page 151). It involves emission of alpha (α), beta (β) or gamma (γ) radiation. The stability of a particular nuclide depends greatly on the numbers of neutrons present. The graph (right) shows the stable nuclides that exist.

- For small nuclei, the number of neutrons tends to be equal to the number of protons.

- For large nuclei, there are more neutrons than protons.

- Nuclides above the band of stability have "too many neutrons" and will tend to decay with either alpha or beta decay.

- Nuclides below the band of stability have "too few neutrons" and will tend to emit positrons (see page 152).

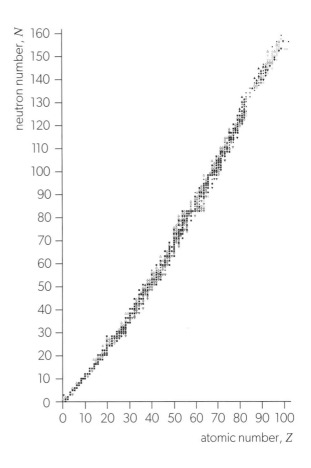

   Key

   N number of neutrons

   Z number of protons

   ■ naturally occurring stable nuclide

   ● naturally occurring α-emitting nuclide

   ○ artificially produced α-emitting nuclide

   ▲ naturally occurring β^--emitting nuclide

   △ artificially produced β^+-emitting nuclide

   ▽ artificially produced β^--emitting nuclide

   ▼ artificially produced electron-capturing nuclide

   ▼ artificial nuclide decaying by spontaneous fission

Binding energy for high nucleon numbers

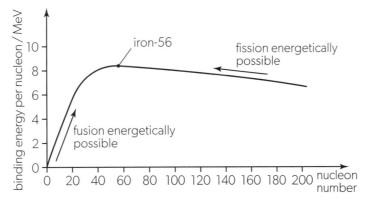

The binding energy curve (see page 149) is approximately constant for nuclei with a nucleon number above 60. Therefore the binding energy **per nucleon** for strontium-90, $^{90}_{38}$Sr, is approximately the same as tungsten-180, $^{180}_{74}$W. Since the nucleon number for tungsten-180 is twice the nucleon number for strontium-90, the **total** binding energy for the tungsten nucleus is twice that of the strontium nucleus.

AHL : Nuclear energy levels and radioactive decay

Energy levels

When an alpha particle or a gamma photon is emitted from the nucleus, only discrete energies are observed. These energies correspond to the difference between two **nuclear energy levels** in the same way that the photon energies correspond to the difference between two **atomic energy levels**.

Beta particles are, however, observed to have a continuous spectrum of energies. There is another particle (the antineutrino in the case of beta minus decay) that shares the energy. The amount of energy released in the decay is fixed by the difference between the nuclear energy levels involved. The beta particle and the antineutrino can take varying proportions of the energy available. The antineutrino, however, is very difficult to observe.

Neutrinos and antineutrinos

Understanding beta decay requires accepting the existence of a virtually undetectable particle, the neutrino. It is needed to account for the "missing" energy and (angular) momentum when analysing the decay mathematically. Calculations involving mass difference mean that you know how much energy is available in beta decay. For example, an isotope of hydrogen, tritium, decays as follows:

$$^3_1H \rightarrow {}^3_2He + {}^0_{-1}\beta$$

The mass difference for the decay is 19.5 keV c^{-2}. This means that the beta particles should have 19.5 keV of kinetic energy. In fact, a few beta particles are emitted with this energy, but all the others have less than this. The average energy is about half of this and there is no accompanying gamma photon. All beta decays seem to follow a similar pattern.

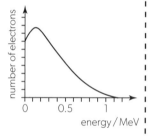

▲ The energy distribution of the electrons emitted in the beta decay of bismuth-210.

The neutrino (and antineutrino) must be electrically neutral. Its mass would have to be very small, or even zero. It carries away the excess energy but it is very hard to detect. One of the triumphs of the particle physics of the last century was to be able to design experiments that confirmed its existence. The full equation for the decay of tritium is:

$$^3_1H \rightarrow {}^3_2He + {}^0_{-1}\beta + \bar{\nu} \quad \text{where } \bar{\nu} \text{ is an antineutrino.}$$

Positron decay can also take place. In this decay, a proton within the nucleus decays into a neutron and the antimatter version of an electron, a positron, which is emitted.

$$^1_1p \rightarrow {}^1_0n + {}^0_{+1}\beta^+ + \nu$$

In this case, the positron, β^+, is accompanied by a neutrino.

The antineutrino is the antimatter form of the neutrino.

e.g. $^{19}_{10}Ne \rightarrow {}^{19}_9F + {}^0_{+1}\beta^+ + \nu$

$$^{12}_6C \rightarrow {}^{14}_7F + {}^0_{-1}\beta + \bar{\nu}$$

Mathematics of exponential decay

The relationship that defines exponential decay as a random process is $\dfrac{dN}{dt} \propto -N$

The constant of proportionality between the rate of decay and the number of nuclei available to decay is called the decay constant and given the symbol λ. Its units are time^{-1}, i.e. s^{-1} or yr^{-1}: $\dfrac{dN}{dt} = -\lambda N$

The solution of this equation is $N = N_0 e^{-\lambda t}$

The activity of a source is $A = -\dfrac{dN}{dt}$

$$A = A_0 e^{-\lambda t} = \lambda N_0 e^{-\lambda t}$$

It is useful to take natural logarithms:

$$\ln(N) = \ln\left(N_0 e^{-\lambda t}\right) = \ln(N_0) + \ln\left(e^{-\lambda t}\right) = \ln(N_0) - \lambda t \ln(e)$$

$$\therefore \ln(N) = \ln(N_0) - \lambda t \quad (\text{since } \ln(e) = 1)$$

This is of the form $y = c + mx$ so a graph of ln N vs t will give a straight line.

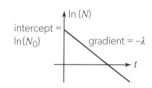

If $t = T_{\frac{1}{2}}$, $N = \dfrac{N_0}{2}$

So $\dfrac{N_0}{2} = N_0 e^{-\lambda T_{\frac{1}{2}}} \Rightarrow \dfrac{1}{2} = e^{-\lambda T_{\frac{1}{2}}} \Rightarrow \ln\dfrac{1}{2} = -\lambda T_{\frac{1}{2}}$

$$\therefore \lambda T_{\frac{1}{2}} = -\ln\dfrac{1}{2} = \ln 2 \therefore T_{\frac{1}{2}} = \dfrac{\ln 2}{\lambda}$$

The decay constant, λ, is related to the probability, P, that a given unstable nucleus decays in a small time interval Δt (which must be much smaller than the half-life of the nuclide): $P = \lambda \Delta t$

Worked example

The half-life of a radioactive isotope is 10 days. Calculate the fraction of the sample that remains after 25 days.

$$T_{\frac{1}{2}} = 10 \text{ days} \quad \lambda = \dfrac{\ln 2}{T_{\frac{1}{2}}} = 6.93 \times 10^{-2} \text{ day}^{-1}$$

$$N = N_0 e^{-\lambda t} \qquad \dfrac{N}{N_0} = e^{-\left(6.93 \times 10^{-2} \times 25\right)} = 0.177$$

Fraction remaining = 17.7%

End of topic questions—E.3 Radioactive decay

1. The count rate near a radioactive source was initially measured to be 82 counts s^{-1}.

   After 210 seconds the count rate had dropped to 19 counts s^{-1}.

   When the radioactive source was removed, the average background count was 10 counts s^{-1}.

   Calculate the half-life of the radioactive source. (3)

AHL

2. This question is about half-life.

   a. Radium-226 has a half-life of 5.1×10^{13} s. Calculate the decay constant of radium-226. (2)

   b. A substance has a decay constant of $6.9 \times 10^{-4}\,s^{-1}$.

      i. Calculate the half-life of the substance. (2)

      ii. Calculate the percentage of the substance that remains after 1 hour. (2)

3. A sample of uranium-238 has a mass of 1.00 mg. Uranium-238 has a half-life of 1.42×10^{17} s.

   a. Calculate the number of atoms in the sample. (2)

   b. Calculate the decay constant of uranium-238. (2)

   c. Calculate the activity of the sample. (3)

   d. Discuss how the activity of the sample will change over a period of:

      i. 10 years (2)

      ii. 10^6 years. (2)

E.4 Fission

Nuclear power—process

Principles of energy production

Many nuclear power stations use uranium-235 as the "fuel". This fuel is not burned—the release of energy is achieved using a fission reaction. An overview of this process is described on page 149. In each individual reaction, an incoming neutron causes a uranium nucleus to split apart. The fragments are moving fast. In other words, the temperature is very high. Among the fragments are more neutrons. If these neutrons go on to initiate further reactions then a chain reaction is created.

The design of a nuclear reactor needs to ensure that, on average, only one neutron from each reaction goes on to start a further reaction. If more reactions took place, then the number of reactions would increase all the time and the chain reaction would run out of control.

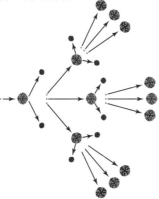

If fewer reactions took place, then the number of reactions would be decreasing and the fission process would soon stop.

The chance that a given neutron goes on to cause a fission reaction depends on several factors. Two important ones are:

- the number of potential nuclei "in the way"
- the speed (or the energy) of the neutrons.

As a general trend, as the size of a block of fuel increases so does the chance of a neutron causing a further reaction (before it is lost from the surface of the block). As the fuel is assembled together, a stage is reached when a chain reaction can occur. This happens when a so-called critical mass of fuel has been assembled. The exact value of the critical mass depends on the exact nature of the fuel being used and the shape of the assembly.

There are particular neutron energies that make them more likely to cause nuclear fission. In general, the neutrons created by the fission process are moving too fast to make reactions likely. Before they can cause further reactions the neutrons have to be slowed down.

Moderator, control rods and heat exchanger

Three important components in the design of all nuclear reactors are the **moderator**, the **control rods** and the **heat exchanger**.

- Collisions between the neutrons and the nuclei of the moderator slow them down and allow further reactions to take place.

- The control rods are movable rods that readily absorb neutrons. They can be introduced or removed from the reaction chamber in order to control the chain reaction.

- The heat exchanger allows the nuclear reactions to occur in a place that is sealed off from the rest of the environment. The reactions increase the temperature in the core. This thermal energy is transferred to heat water and the steam that is produced turns the turbines.

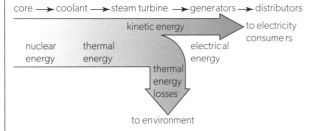

A general design for one type of nuclear reactor (PWR or pressurized water reactor) is shown here. It uses water as the moderator and as a coolant.

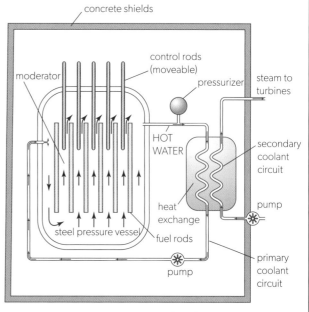

▲ Pressurized water nuclear reactor (PWR)

Advantages and disadvantages

Advantages

- Extremely high "specific energy"—a great deal of energy is released from a very small mass of uranium.
- Reserves of uranium are large compared with oil.

Disadvantages

- Process produces radioactive nuclear waste that is currently just stored.
- High possible risk if anything should go wrong.
- Non-renewable (but should last a long time).

Nuclear power—safety and risks

Enrichment and reprocessing

Naturally occurring uranium contains less than 1% of uranium-235. Enrichment is the process by which this percentage composition is increased to make nuclear fission more likely.

In addition to uranium-235, plutonium-239 is also capable of sustaining fission reactions. This nuclide is formed as a by-product of a conventional nuclear reactor. A uranium-238 nucleus can capture fast-moving neutrons to form uranium-239. This undergoes β-decay to neptunium-239 which undergoes further β-decay to plutonium-239:

$$^{238}_{92}U + ^{1}_{0}n \rightarrow ^{239}_{92}U$$

$$^{239}_{92}U \rightarrow ^{239}_{93}Np + ^{0}_{-1}\beta + \bar{\nu}$$

$$^{239}_{93}Np \rightarrow ^{239}_{94}Pu + ^{0}_{-1}\beta + \bar{\nu}$$

Reprocessing involves treating used fuel waste from nuclear reactors to recover uranium and plutonium and to deal with other waste products. A fast breeder reactor is one design that utilizes plutonium-239.

Health, safety and risks

Issues associated with the use of nuclear power stations for generation of electrical energy include the following.

- If the control rods were all removed, the reaction would rapidly increase its rate of production. Completely uncontrolled nuclear fission would cause an explosion and **thermal meltdown** of the core. The radioactive material in the reactor could be distributed around the surrounding area causing many fatalities. Some argue that the terrible scale of such a disaster means that the use of nuclear energy is a risk not worth taking. Nuclear power stations could be targets for terrorist attacks.

- The reaction produces radioactive nuclear waste. While much of this waste is of a low level risk and will radioactively decay within decades, a significant amount of material is produced that will remain dangerously radioactive for millions of years. The current solution is to bury this waste in geologically secure sites.

- The uranium fuel is mined from underground and any mining operation involves significant risk. The ore is also radioactive so extra precautions are necessary to protect the workers involved in uranium mines.

- The transportation of the uranium from the mine to a power station and of the waste from the nuclear power station to the reprocessing plant needs to be secure and safe.

- By-products of the civilian use of nuclear power can be used to produce nuclear weapons.

Nuclear weapons

A nuclear power station involves controlled nuclear fission whereas an uncontrolled nuclear fission produces the huge amount of energy released in nuclear weapons. Weapons have been designed using both uranium and plutonium as the fuel. Issues associated with nuclear weapons include:

- Moral issues associated with any weapon of aggression that is associated with warfare. Nuclear weapons have such destructive capability that since the Second World War the threat of their deployment has been used as a deterrent to prevent non-nuclear aggressive acts against the possessors of nuclear capability.

- The unimaginable consequences of a nuclear war have forced many countries to agree to non-proliferation treaties, which attempt to limit nuclear power technologies to a small number of nations.

- A by-product of the peaceful use of uranium for energy production is the creation of plutonium-239 which could be used for the production of nuclear weapons. Is it right for the small number of countries that already have nuclear capability to prevent other countries from acquiring that knowledge?

Fusion reactors

Fusion reactors offer the theoretical potential of significant power generation without many of the problems associated with current nuclear fission reactors. The fuel used, hydrogen, is in plentiful supply and the reaction (if it could be sustained) would not produce significant amounts of radioactive waste.

The reaction is the same as takes place in the Sun (as outlined on page 149) and requires creating temperatures high enough to ionize atomic hydrogen into a plasma state (this is the "fourth state of matter", in which electrons and protons are not bound in atoms but move independently). Currently, the principal design challenges are associated with maintaining and confining the plasma at a sufficiently high temperature and density for fusion to take place.

End of topic questions—E.4 Fission

1. This question is about the operation of a nuclear power plant.

   a. By referring to the concept of binding energy per nucleon, explain why energy is released in the neutron-induced fission of uranium-235. (3)

   b. Explain the concept of a chain reaction in the operation of a nuclear power plant. (3)

   c. Outline the role of the following features of a nuclear power plant.

   i. Fuel rods (2)

   ii. Control rods (2)

   iii. Moderators (2)

   iv. Heat exchangers (2)

   v. Shielding (2)

   d. Some of the products of nuclear fission will remain dangerously radioactive for many hundreds of years. Discuss the potential impact of the long-term storage of this type of nuclear waste. (4)

2. Typical nuclear fission reactions, A and B, that take place in the core of a nuclear reactor include:

$$A: {}^1_0n + {}^{235}_{92}U \rightarrow {}^{141}_{56}Ba + {}^{92}_{36}Kr + 3{}^1_0n$$

$$B: {}^1_0n + {}^{235}_{92}U \rightarrow {}^{138}_{55}Cs + {}^{96}_{37}Rb + 2{}^1_0n$$

The following data is available for the masses of various isotopes.

Nuclide	Isotopic mass / u
${}^{235}_{92}U$ Uranium-235	235.04393
${}^{141}_{56}Ba$ Barium-141	140.91440
${}^{92}_{36}Kr$ Krypton-92	91.92616
${}^{138}_{55}Cs$ Caesium-138	137.91102
${}^{96}_{37}Rb$ Rubidium-96	95.93427

a. The isotopic mass data (see table) records the mass of the neutral atoms. This is equal to the mass of the nucleus plus the mass of the electrons.

Calculate the mass of the uranium-235 **nucleus**. (3)

b. Determine which reaction, A or B, will release the most energy. (4)

c. State the form in which the energy is released in these reactions. (1)

d. Explain why the mass of uranium must be above a certain minimum amount to ensure that a chain reaction is maintained. (3)

e. Calculate the energy released in reaction A. (3)

f. The total energy released in the nuclear reactor is 2 400 MW. Assume that all this power comes as a result of the reaction that you used in part (e).

   i. Estimate the number of fission reactions taking place per second. (3)

   ii. Deduce the mass of U-235 that undergoes fission in one year. (3)

E.5 Fusion and stars

The nature of stars

Equilibrium

The Sun has been radiating energy for the past 4.5 billion years. It might be imagined that the powerful reactions in the core should have forced away the outer layers of the Sun a long time ago. Like other stars, the Sun is stable because there is an **equilibrium** between this outward pressure and the inward gravitational force.

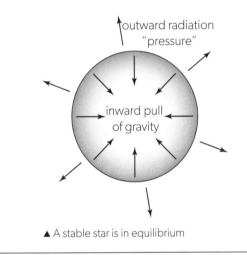

▲ A stable star is in equilibrium

Energy flow for stars

The stars are emitting a great deal of energy. The source for all this energy is the fusion of hydrogen into helium. See page 149. Sometimes this is referred to as "hydrogen burning" but it this is not a precise term. The reaction is a nuclear reaction, not a chemical one (such as combustion). Overall the reaction is

$$4{}^1_1p \rightarrow {}^4_2He + 2{}^0_1e^+ + 2\nu$$

The mass of the products is less than the mass of the reactants. Using $\Delta E = \Delta mc^2$ you can work out that the Sun is losing mass at a rate of $4 \times 10^9 \text{ kg s}^{-1}$. This takes place in the core of a star. Eventually, all this energy is radiated from the surface—approximately 10^{26} J every second. You do not need to know the structure inside a star in detail.

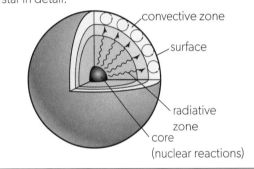

Main sequence stars

The general name for the creation of nuclei of different elements as a result of fission reactions is **nucleosynthesis**.

One process is known as the **proton–proton** cycle or **p–p cycle**.

For any of these reactions to take place, two positively charged particles (hydrogen or helium nuclei) need to come close enough for interactions to take place. Obviously, they will repel one another.

This means that they must be at a high temperature.

If a large cloud of hydrogen is hot enough, then these nuclear reactions can take place spontaneously. The power radiated by the star is balanced by the power released in these reactions—the temperature is effectively constant.

The star remains a stable size because the outward pressure of the radiation is balanced by the inward gravitational pull.

But how did the cloud of gas get to be at a high temperature in the first place? As the cloud comes together, the loss of gravitational potential energy must mean an increase in kinetic energy and hence temperature. In simple terms, the gas molecules speed up as they fall in towards the centre to form a proto-star.

Once ignition has taken place, the star can remain stable for billions of years. See page 164 for more details.

step 1 ${}^1_1H + {}^1_1H \rightarrow {}^2_1H + {}^0_1e^+ + {}^0_0\nu$

step 2 ${}^2_1H + {}^1_1H \rightarrow {}^3_2He + {}^0_0\gamma$

step 3 ${}^3_2He + {}^3_2He \rightarrow {}^4_2He + 2{}^1_1p$

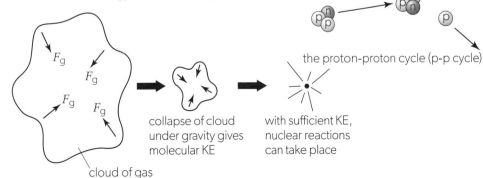

the proton-proton cycle (p-p cycle)

cloud of gas

collapse of cloud under gravity gives molecular KE

with sufficient KE, nuclear reactions can take place

Nuclear fusion

The Jeans criterion

As seen on page 161, stars form out of interstellar clouds of hydrogen, helium and other materials. Such clouds can exist in stable equilibrium for many years until an external event (e.g. a collision with another cloud or the influence of another incident such as a supernova) starts the collapse. At any given point in time, the total energy associated with the gas cloud can be thought of as a combination of:

- the negative gravitational potential energy, E_p, which the cloud possesses as a result of its mass and how it is distributed in space; important factors are thus the mass and the density of the cloud.

- the positive random kinetic energy, E_k, that the particles in the cloud possess; an important factor is thus the temperature of the cloud.

The cloud will remain gravitationally bound together if $E_p + E_k <$ zero. Using this information allows you to predict that the collapse of an interstellar cloud may begin if its mass is greater than a certain critical mass, M_J. This is the **Jeans criterion**. For a given cloud of gas, M_J is dependent on the cloud's density and temperature. A cloud is more likely to collapse if it has:

- large mass
- small size
- low temperature.

In symbols, the Jeans criterion is that collapse can start if $M > M_J$

Nuclear fusion

A star on the main sequence is fusing hydrogen nuclei to produce helium nuclei. One process by which this is achieved is the proton–proton chain as outlined on page 161. This is the predominant method for nuclear fusion to take place in small mass stars (up to just above the mass of our Sun). An alternative process, called the CNO (carbon–nitrogen–oxygen) process takes place at higher temperatures in larger mass stars. In this reaction, carbon, nitrogen and oxygen are used as catalysts to aid the fusion of protons into helium nuclei. One possible cycle is shown.

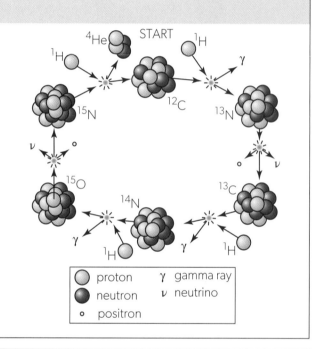

○ proton	γ gamma ray
● neutron	ν neutrino
○ positron	

Stellar types and black holes

The source of energy for our Sun is the fusion of hydrogen into helium. This is also true for many other stars.

There are, however, other types of object that are known to exist in the Universe. See the following pages.

Type of object	Description
Red giant stars	As the name suggests, these stars are large in size and red in colour. Since they are red, they are comparatively cool. They turn out to be one of the later possible stages for a star. The source of energy is the fusion of some elements other than hydrogen. **Red supergiants** are even larger.
White dwarf stars	As the name suggests, these stars are small in size and white in colour. Since they are white, they are comparatively hot. They turn out to be one of the final stages for some smaller mass stars. Fusion is no longer taking place, and a white dwarf is just a hot remnant that is cooling down. Eventually it will cease to give out light when it becomes sufficiently cold. It is then known as a **brown dwarf**.
Neutron stars	Neutron stars are the post-supernova remnants of some larger mass stars. The gravitational pressure has forced a total collapse and the mass of a neutron star is not composed of atoms—it is essentially composed of neutrons. The density of a neutron star is enormous. Rotating neutron stars have been identified as **pulsars**.
Black holes	Black holes are the post-supernova remnant of larger mass stars. There is no known mechanism to stop the gravitational collapse. The result is an object whose escape velocity is greater than the speed of light. See page 165.

Red giant stars

After the main sequence

A star cannot continue in its main sequence state forever. It is fusing hydrogen into helium and at some point hydrogen in the core will become rare. The fusion reactions will happen less often. This means that the star is no longer in equilibrium and the gravitational force will, once again, cause the core to collapse.

This collapse increases the temperature of the core still further and helium fusion is now possible. The net result is that the star increases massively in size—this expansion means that the outer layers are cooler. It becomes a red giant star.

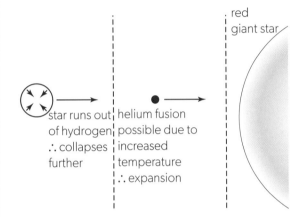

If it has sufficient mass, a red giant can continue to fuse higher and higher elements and the process of nucleosynthesis can continue.

newly formed red giant star

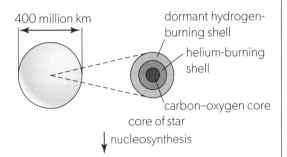

old, high-mass red giant star

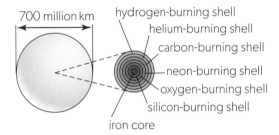

This process of fusion as a source of energy must come to an end with the nucleosynthesis of iron. The iron nucleus has one of the greatest binding energies per nucleon of all nuclei. In other words, the fusion of iron to form a higher mass nucleus would need to take in energy rather than release energy. The star cannot continue to shine. What happens next is outlined on page 165.

The Hertzsprung–Russell diagram

H–R diagram

The point of classifying the various types of stars is to see if any patterns exist. A useful way of making this comparison is the **Hertzsprung–Russell** diagram. Each dot on the diagram represents a different star. The following axes are used to position the dot.

- The vertical axis is the luminosity of the star as compared with the luminosity of the Sun. It should be noted that the scale is logarithmic.

- The horizontal axis a scale of **decreasing** temperature. Once again, the scale is not a linear one. (Astronomers sometimes label this axis by something called the spectral class of the star—these are categories used to classify different stares represented by the letters: OBAFGKM.)

The result of such a plot is shown below.

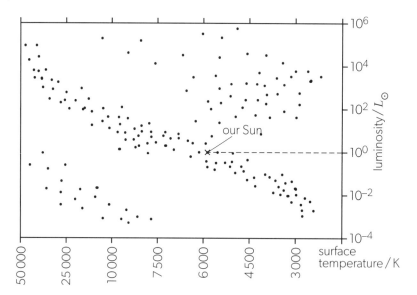

A large number of stars fall on a line that (roughly) goes from top left to bottom right. This line is known as the **main sequence** and stars that are on it are known as main sequence stars. Our Sun is a main sequence star. These stars are "normal" stable stars—the only difference between them is their mass. They are fusing hydrogen to helium. The stars that are not on the main sequence can also be broadly put into categories.

In addition to the broad regions, lines of constant radius can be added to show the size of stars in comparison with our Sun's radius. These are lines going from top left to bottom right.

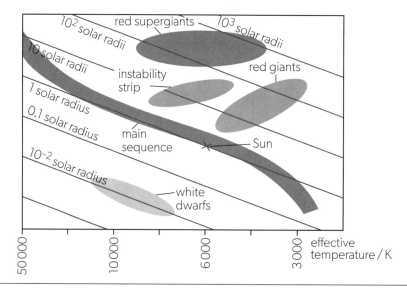

Stellar evolution

Possible fates for a star (after red giant phases)

Page 163 showed that the red giant phase for a star must eventually come to an end. There are essentially two possible routes with different final states. The route that is followed depends on the initial mass of the star and thus the mass of the remnant that the red giant star leaves behind: with no further nuclear reactions taking place, gravitational forces continue the collapse of the remnant. An important "critical" mass is called the **Chandrasekhar limit** and it is equal to approximately 1.4 times the mass of our Sun. Below this limit a process called **electron degeneracy pressure** prevents the further collapse of the remnant.

If a star has a mass less than 4 solar masses, its remnant will be less than 1.4 solar masses and so it is below the Chandrasekhar limit. In this case, the red giant forms a **planetary nebula** and becomes a **white dwarf** which ultimately becomes invisible. The name "planetary nebula" is term that can cause confusion. The ejected material would not be planets in the same sense as the planets in our Solar System.

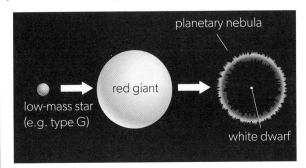

If a star is greater than 4 solar masses, its remnant will have a mass greater than 1.4 solar masses. It is above the Chandrasekhar limit and electron degeneracy pressure is not sufficient to prevent collapse. In this case, the red supergiant experiences a **supernova**. It then becomes a **neutron star** or collapses to a **black hole**. The final state again depends on mass.

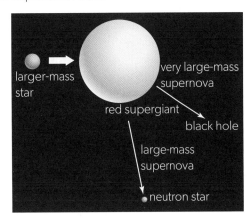

A neutron star is stable due to neutron degeneracy pressure. It should be emphasized that white dwarfs and neutron stars do not have a source of energy to fuel their radiation. They must be losing temperature all the time. The fact that these stars can still exist for many millions of years shows that the temperatures and masses involved are enormous. The largest mass a neutron star can have is called the **Oppenheimer–Volkoff limit** and is 2–3 solar masses. Remnants above this limit will form black holes.

H–R diagram interpretation

All of the possible evolutionary paths for stars that have been described here can be represented on a H–R diagram. A common mistake in examinations is for candidates to imply that a star somehow moves along the line that represents the main sequence. It does not. Once formed it stays at a stable luminosity and spectral class—i.e. it is represented by one fixed point in the H–R diagram.

evolution of a low-mass star

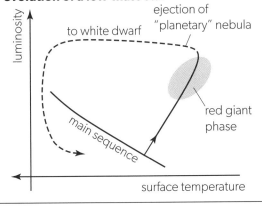

evolution of a high-mass star

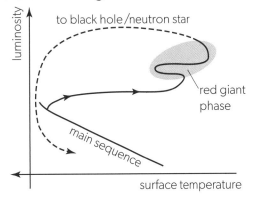

Stellar parallax

Principles of measurement

As you move from one position to another, objects change their relative positions. As far as you are concerned, near objects appear to move when compared with far objects. Objects that are very far away do not appear to move at all. You can demonstrate this effect by closing one eye and moving your head from side to side. An object that is near to you (for example, the tip of your finger) will appear to move when compared with objects that are far away (for example, a distant building).

This apparent movement is known as **parallax** and the effect can used to measure the distance to some of the stars in our galaxy. All stars appear to move over the period of a night, but some stars appear to move in relation to other stars over the period of a year.

The reason for this apparent movement is that the Earth has moved over the period of a year. This change in observing position has

If carefully observed, over the period of a year some stars can appear to move between two extremes.

meant that a close star will have an apparent movement when compared with a more distant set of stars. The closer a star is to the Earth, the greater will be the parallax shift.

Since all stars are very distant, this effect is a very small one and the parallax angle will be very small. It is usual to quote parallax angles not in degrees, but in seconds. An angle of 1 second of arc (") is equal to one sixtieth of 1 minute of arc (') and 1 minute of arc is equal to one sixtieth of a degree: $3600" = 1°$: $360° = 1$ full circle.

Determining stellar radii

- The measured intensity of light received from a start and a knowledge of its distance from Earth means the luminosity, L, of the star can be calculated.

- Analysis of the light emitted by a star will mean the wavelength with the peak intensity is known. Wien's displacement law can be used to calculate the surface temperature, T.

- The luminosity/temperature relationship can be used to calculate the surface area, A of the star.

- The equation for the surface area of a sphere $A = 4\pi r^2$, can be used to calculate the radius.

Mathematics—units

The situation that gives rise to a change in apparent position for close stars is shown below.

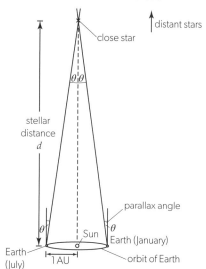

The parallax angle, θ, can be measured by observing the changes in a star's position over the period of a year. From trigonometry, if you know the distance from the Earth to the Sun, you can work out the distance from the Earth to the star using

$$\tan\theta = \frac{\left(\text{distance from Earth to Sun}\right)}{\left(\text{distance from Sun to star}\right)}$$

Since θ is a very small angle, $\tan\theta \approx \sin\theta \approx \theta$ (in radians)

This means that $\theta \propto \dfrac{1}{\left(\text{distance from Earth to star}\right)}$

In other words, parallax angle and distance away are inversely proportional. If you use the right units, you can end up with a very simple relationship. The units are defined as follows.

The distance from the Sun to the Earth is defined to be one **astronomical unit (AU)**. It is 1.5×10^{11} m. Calculations show that a star with a parallax angle of exactly one second of arc must be 3.08×10^{16} m away (3.26 light years). This distance is defined to be one **parsec (pc)**. The name "parsec" represents "**par**allax angle of one **sec**ond".

If distance $= 1$ pc, $\theta = 1$ second

If distance $= 2$ pc, $\theta = 0.5$ second etc.

Or, distance in pc $= \dfrac{1}{\left(\text{parallax angle in seconds}\right)}$

$$d = \frac{1}{p}$$

The parallax method can be used to measure stellar distances that are less than **about 100 parsecs**. The parallax angle for stars that are at greater distances becomes too small to measure accurately. It is common, however, to continue to use the unit. The standard SI prefixes can also be used even though this is not strictly an SI unit.

1000 parsecs $= 1$ kpc

10^6 parsecs $= 1$ Mpc etc.

1. The star alpha Eridani (Achemar) is 1.32×10^{18} m away. Calculate its parallax angle. (3)

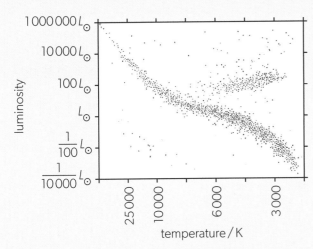

2. a. On the Hertzsprung–Russell diagram above, sketch the following features:

   i. the main sequence (2)

   ii. red giant stars (1)

   iii. supergiants (1)

   iv. white dwarfs (1)

   v. the instability strip (2)

   vi. the approximate location of some lines of constant radius. (2)

   b. The table below gives some data about some stars.

Star	Surface temperature / K	Luminosity / L⊙
Aldebaran	4700	200
Betelgeuse	3000	20000
Regulus	14000	200
Rigel	13000	20000
Sirius B	20000	0.002

   For each of the stars listed above,

   i. annotate the star's approximate location on the HR diagram (6)

   ii. determine the stellar type. (6)

3. When released from its container, a hot gas surrounded by a vacuum would be expected to expand to fill the space available. Explain why stars remain fixed in size despite being surrounded by the vacuum of space. (4)

4. The very early universe (before any stars evolved) only contained the elements hydrogen and helium. Your body, however, contains many elements including oxygen-16, ^{16}O, and small amounts of iron-56, ^{56}Fe, and iodine-127, ^{127}I. Outline the process that created these three elements. (4, 2, 4)

5. a. State the name of the process that is the source of energy in stars. (1)

   b. Outline the conditions necessary for the process that you have identified in (a) to spontaneously take place for a cloud of hydrogen in space, in terms of:

   i. the density of the hydrogen (2)

   ii. the temperature of the hydrogen. (2)

   c. Outline the processes by which the conditions identified in part (b) take place. (3)

6. The following data is available about a star and the Sun.

   Data about the star

   Luminosity $= 10^6 \times$ luminosity of the Sun

   Brightness $= 7.0 \times 10^{-8}\,W\,m^{-2}$

   Peak wavelength of its emitted radiation $= 500\,nm$

   Data about the Sun

   Brightness $= 1.4 \times 10^3\,W\,m^{-2}$

   Average distance of the Sun from the Earth $= 1.0\,AU$

   Radius $= 6.96 \times 10^8\,m$

   a. Calculate the luminosity of the Sun. (3)

   b. Calculate the distance of the star from Earth. (4)

   c. Explain why the distance of the star cannot be determined using stellar parallax. (2)

   d. Calculate the radius of the star. (3)

Safety and measuring variables (1)

Safety concerns

When planning any experimental work, making sure that everybody is safe and protecting the environment are the most important considerations. Before getting started it should always be routine to do a risk assessment to identify relevant **safety**, **ethical** or **environmental** issues.

Luckily, it is rare for physics experiments to introduce ethical or environmental issues, but the use of human volunteers and/or the disposal of waste chemicals could be causes for concern.

Most experiments undertaken in the physics laboratory tend to be safe, but accidents may occur. For example:

* A trailing power cable might be a trip hazard.
* Low voltage electrical circuits can overheat and cause injury if not properly controlled.

* Use of high voltage power sources can be dangerous.
* Any heating experiment or the use of an open flame could be hazardous.
* Radioactive sources have many safety issues that need to be kept in mind.

When planning an investigation, it is not necessary to invent possible difficulties to demonstrate that you are thinking about the safety. The simple statement "*The procedure does not raise any specific issues of safety*" is sufficient to show the reader that you are keeping safety issues in mind.

Mass

Mass is measured using an electric top pan balance or scales. Technically, the balance measures the pull of gravity on the object (the weight in newtons) and converts this to give a reading of mass in kg. The assumption is, of course, that you are using the balance on the surface of the Earth, so the value of g is known.

A top pan balance has a greater **precision** if the answer it gives has a greater number of significant figures. For example, a reading of 56.629 g is a more precise reading that 57 g. This is not the same as being more accurate (see page 195). Typically, the uncertainty in measurement of mass can be taken as ± (smallest

recorded digit).

The balance should be on a level surface, and it needs to be zeroed before each reading. When measuring very small masses it is better to measure the total mass of a known number of identical objects rather than just one: for example, it is better to measure the total mass of 100 sheets of paper rather than attempt to measure the mass of only one sheet:

Suppose 100 sheets of paper have a mass of 541 g and the implied uncertainty in this reading is ± 1 g.

The mass of one sheet of paper is thus 5.41 ± 0.01 g

Time

A stopwatch (either digital or analogue) is often used to record the time taken in physics experiments. Human reaction time (typically 0.2 s) can affect the precision and/or accuracy of a reading but it is also possible to anticipate events to minimize this effect. Very short time intervals can be recorded using sensors/light gates that can be controlled automatically by a data logger and/or computer.

The analysis of a video recording can also be used to record the passage of time by knowing how many different individual "frames" are recorded in one second. Similarly, a flashing light or stroboscope can be used to capture a moving object after known intervals of time. A ticker-timer allows the distance travelled by a moving object to be recorded regularly (typically, 50 times a second).

Measuring variables (2)

Length

The metre rule is the most common piece of equipment used to measure everyday objects. This easily records lengths to the nearest mm and possibly to ±0.5 mm if used carefully. A vernier scale eliminates the guesswork when estimating the value between the scale divisions. An example is vernier calipers.

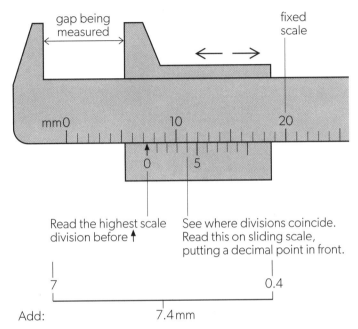

Read the highest scale division before ↑

See where divisions coincide. Read this on sliding scale, putting a decimal point in front.

7   0.4

Add: 7.4 mm

Even greater precision comes from the use of a micrometer screw gauge.

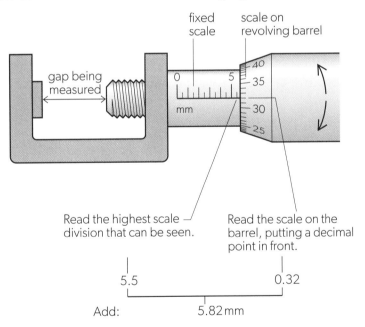

Read the highest scale division that can be seen.

Read the scale on the barrel, putting a decimal point in front.

5.5   0.32

Add: 5.82 mm

Vernier calipers and micrometer screw gauges need to be carefully checked to see if there is a zero error (see page 182) that needs to be taken into consideration.

Volume

The volumes of many types of regular objects can be calculated from length measurements. For example, a measurement of the diameter of a sphere, d, allows the volume to be calculated from $V = \frac{\pi d^3}{6}$. The volume of irregular shapes can often be found by submerging the object in water and noting how much water is displaced. The volume of displaced water = volume of the object.

You need to take care when converting between different units of volume. For example,

$1\,m^3 = 10^6\,cm^3 = 10^9\,mm^3$.

Measuring variables (3)

Electric current

Electric current at any point in a circuit is measured by an ammeter. An ideal ammeter would have zero resistance, but practical ammeters have a non-zero resistance, which means that they can slightly alter the circuit when added in. It is important to check for any zero error. In simple circuits, the electric current flowing into an electronic device must always equal the electric current flowing out of the device. Ammeters are added in **series** with any device being investigated.

▲ An ammeter measures the current coming out of a resistor

Temperature

Temperature is measured using a thermometer, but many different types exist. All thermometers work by using a physical change that happens with a change in temperature. The thermometer is then calibrated using defined fixed points on a given temperature scale.

For example, a standard mercury in glass thermometer is based on the relative expansion of mercury compared with the expansion of glass. Approximate fixed points that could be used for calibration could be the freezing point of pure water (0 °C) and the boiling point of pure water (100 °C).

The most appropriate thermometer will depend on the context but could include a measurement of resistance (platinum resistance thermometer), a measurement of emf of two wires of non-identical metals (thermocouple) or the analysis of specific EM radiation emitted by a hot body (radiation pyrometer).

Electronic versions that give a direct reading of temperature are also available.

Force

A spring is a simple device that can be used to measure the force applied by measuring the extension of the spring and using Hooke's law (see page 14).

Electronic force sensors are also available that can be connected to data loggers to record the changing force during a collision.

Electric potential difference

Electric potential difference between two different points is measured by a voltmeter. An ideal voltmeter would have infinite resistance, but practical voltmeters have a non-infinite resistance, which means that they can slightly alter the circuit when connected. A voltmeter is connected between two different points in a circuit. Voltmeters are connected in **parallel** with any device being investigated. It is important to check for any zero error.

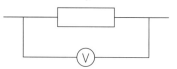

▲ A voltmeter measures the potential difference across a resistor

Rapidly changing potential differences can be measured using a **cathode ray oscilloscope**. This is a sophisticated piece of equipment. Its output is effectively a graph of voltage against time. Both the time and the voltage axes can be scaled appropriately by changing the sensitivity settings.

Angle

The protractor is the simplest direct instrument for measuring angles. The alternative is to use trigonometry (see page 173) to calculate the angle in a given situation.

Sound and light intensity

The fundamental definition of intensity (of sound or light) is the amount of energy that the wave brings to a unit area every second. The units of intensity are $W\,m^{-2}$. The intensity depends on the amplitude of the wave. For all waves:

$$intensity \propto (amplitude)^2$$

1. Sound intensity

Sound intensity sensors are available that can provide direct readings of intensity. Readings are often given on the decibel scale. This is a logarithmic scale that compares the measured sound intensity with a threshold value (just able to be heard) of $10^{-12}\,W\,m^{-2}$.

2. Light intensity

The measurement of light intensity is complex as the human eye responds differently to different frequencies of light. Light meters are available that make a comparison between different sources with the light falling on a particular surface. They often give readings in **lux**.

Applying technology to collect and process data

Sensors

A sensor is any device that measures a physical quantity. Sensors can be standalone devices (such as a light meter used by a photographer) or they can be connected to a **data logger** (or computer) in order to record the variations of the physical quantity that is being measured. Sensors can be classified as either **analogue** or **digital**. An analogue sensor has a continuous range of values to represent the data and information (such as a meter with a moving pointer or a light dependent resistor). Digital sensors use discrete values to represent the data and information (such as a meter with an electronic display or a pressure sensor connected to a data logger).

Most sensors are constructed around electrical circuits and are thus also called **input transducers**. For example, the conversion of an audible sound wave into a varying electrical potential difference takes place in a microphone. Sensors are available for all common physical quantities that are normally measured in the Physics laboratory. These include the measurement of temperature, light, pressure, force, displacement, and so on. The conversion is always from some physical quantity into an electrical signal.

The combination of sensors and a data logger allows much more sophisticated data to be collected than would be possible for one person to be able to gather when working alone. The data collected can be:

- **More detailed** as many, very precise, physical quantities can be simultaneously gathered at any given time. Data loggers allow for millions of readings to be recorded in one second.

- **Measured remotely** meaning that physical quantities can be recorded in very difficult locations or circumstances and even in dangerous locations.

- **Measured automatically** meaning that physical quantities can be recorded over very short or very long periods of time.

Spreadsheets, and computer modelling

Spreadsheets on computers or graphics calculators allow a large number of calculations to be performed in a very short time. A powerful tool is to use an **iterative technique**, in which the results of one calculation are fed into the next calculation, and so on, by following a simple rule.

For example, predicting the time taken for an object to free-fall a known distance (e.g. 10 m) under gravity involves a straightforward application of the uniform acceleration equations. This prediction assumes that, throughout the fall, air resistance can be taken as negligible.

Initial velocity $u = 0$
Final velocity $v = ?$
Acceleration $a = 9.81\,\mathrm{m\,s^{-2}}$
Time taken $t = ?$
Final displacement $s = 10\,\mathrm{m}$

$$t = \sqrt{\frac{2s}{a}} = \sqrt{\frac{2 \times 10}{9.81}} = 1.43\,\mathrm{s}$$

Databases

The scientific community often shares data internationally via the use of open data bases. These can be available online and many can be searched for specific types of data. This allows new investigations to be created and new hypotheses to be tested. For example, a stellar database records a huge amount of information on many different stars, which means that research can be undertaken without having to return to first principles for the collection of data. It is important to understand the uncertainty limits on any data gathered from a database.

Models and simulations

Technology can be used to gather data from a mathematical model or a simulation. The process of comparing the predicted results of the model or simulation with a real-world situation brings insights into the factors that are important in the observed outcomes. This allows models to be refined and developed over time.

Image and video analysis

Complex situations can be photographed or videoed and then technology can be used to undertake detailed analysis. The frame capture rate of a video allows changes over small time intervals to be recorded.

This situation can be modelled using the iterative technique by breaking down the motion into small sections of time, Δt. The starting conditions are used to calculate the velocity after Δt.

- The initial and final velocities over Δt can be used to calculate an average velocity.

- The average velocity over Δt can be used to calculate the distance travelled.

The final velocity now becomes the new starting condition for the previous calculations to be repeated. The sum of all the small distances travelled will be the total distance travelled.

The smaller the choice for Δt, the more accurate the achieved result will be. A smaller Δt means that the number of calculations that need to be done is greater, and hence the use of a computer is required.

If, however, the air resistance has a significant effect, the problem is much harder to solve mathematically. Air resistance acts to oppose the motion through the air. At any given instant in time this results in a reduction of the object's acceleration.

Under these circumstances, the iterative technique can still be used. Instead of using a fixed acceleration due to gravity, the acceleration is reduced by an amount calculated from the velocity at the start of Δt and a friction constant. This will predict that the falling object reaches a **terminal velocity**.

Algebra, trigonometry, rates of change and averages (1)

Basic arithmetic and algebra—areas and volumes

The use, and manipulation, of mathematical relationships using symbols to represent quantities is a basic tool in physics. Ideally you need to become comfortable in rearranging any formula to calculate the quantity that you wish to find.

Here are some mathematical formulas for the areas and volumes of some common shapes that you may need to use in calculations.

Area of a triangle
$$A = \frac{1}{2}(bh)$$

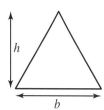

Area of a circle
$$A = \pi h^2$$

Circumference of a circle
$$C = 2\pi r$$

Volume of a cuboid
$$V = lwh$$

Volume of a prism
$$V = Ah$$

Volume of a cylinder
$$V = \pi r^2 h$$

Area of the curved surface of a cylinder
$$A = 2\pi r h$$

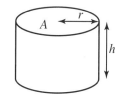

Volume of a sphere
$$V = \frac{4}{3}\pi r^3$$

Algebra, trigonometry, rates of change and averages (2)

Trigonometry

Trigonometry is the mathematics used when dealing with angles. The fundamental relationships are defined in terms of a right-angled triangle.

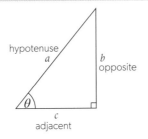

$$\sin\theta = \frac{\text{opposite}}{\text{hypotenuse}}; \quad \cos\theta = \frac{\text{adjacent}}{\text{hypotenuse}}; \quad \tan\theta = \frac{\text{opposite}}{\text{adjacent}}$$

As θ varies from $0°$ to $360°$ (0 to 2π radians), $\sin\theta$ and $\cos\theta$ are always between -1 and $+1$, whereas $\tan\theta$ varies from $-\infty$ to $+\infty$.

$\sin\theta$, $\cos\theta$ and $\tan\theta$ are all positive numbers if θ is between $0°$ and $90°$ ($\frac{\pi}{2}$ radians).

Some useful relationships include:

$$\sin(90-\theta) = \cos\theta \qquad \tan\theta = \frac{\sin\theta}{\cos\theta}$$

$$\cos(90-\theta) = \sin\theta \qquad \sin^2\theta + \cos^2\theta = 1$$

$$\tan(90-\theta) = \frac{1}{\tan\theta}$$

Rates of change

If a quantity N varies with time, t, then the average rate of change between t_1 and t_2 is:

$$\text{average rate of change} = \frac{\Delta N}{\Delta t} = \frac{N_{\text{at time } t=t_2} - N_{\text{at time } t=t_1}}{t_2 - t_1}$$

The instantaneous rate of change is equal to the average rate of change if Δt is very small. See page 186 for information about graphical interpretation.

$$\text{Instantaneous rate of change} = \frac{dN}{dt}$$

Logs—base ten and base e

Mathematically,

If $a = 10^b$, then $\log(a) = b$

(to be precise, $\log_{10}(a) = b$)

Most calculators have a "log" button. You don't have to use 10 as the base—you can use any number that you like. For example, you could use 2.0, 563.2, 17.5, 42 or even 2.718 281 828 459 045 235 360 287 471 4. For complex reasons this last number is the most useful number to use! It is given the symbol e and logarithms to this base are called natural logarithms. The symbol for natural logarithms is $\ln(x)$. This is also on most calculators.

If $p = e^q$, then $\ln(p) = q$

Here are some useful rules of logarithms:

$$\ln(c \times d) = \ln(c) + \ln(d)$$
$$\ln(c \div d) = \ln(c) - \ln(d)$$
$$\ln(c^n) = n\ln(c)$$
$$\ln\left(\frac{1}{c}\right) = -\ln(c)$$

These rules have been expressed for natural logarithms, but they work for all logarithms whatever the base.

Logarithms can be used to express some relationships (particularly power laws and exponentials) in straight-line form. This means that you will plot graphs with logarithmic scales.

A normal scale increases by the same amount each time.

1 2 3 4 5 6 7 8 9 10 11

A logarithmic scale increases by the same ratio all the time.

10^0 10^1 10^2 10^3

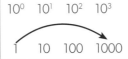

1 10 100 1000

Mean and range

The **range** is the difference between the minimum value and the maximum value in a data set of readings of a quantity.

Mathematicians use three different averages: the **mean**, the **mode** and the **median**.

Mean—this is commonly called the average value. Add all the values together and divide by the number of readings.

Mode—this is the value that occurs the most in the set.

Median—when you arrange a set of values from smallest to largest, the *median* is the one in the middle.

An analysis in a physics experiment hardly ever uses the median or mode.

Estimations, variables, relationships and scale diagrams (1)

Orders of magnitude

It is important to develop a "feeling" for some of the numbers that you use. When using a calculator, it is very easy to make a simple mistake (e.g. by entering the data incorrectly). A good way of checking the answer is to first make an estimate before entering the numbers into the calculator.

Approximate values for each of the fundamental SI units are given below.

1 kg	A packet of sugar, 1 litre of water. A person would be about 50 kg or more
1 m	Distance between a person's hands with their arms outstretched
1 s	Duration of a heartbeat (when resting—it can easily halve with exercise)
1 A	Current flowing from the mains electricity when a computer is connected. The maximum current to a domestic device would be about 10 A
1 K	1 kelvin is a very low temperature. Water freezes at 273 K and boils at 373 K. Room temperature is about 300 K
1 mol	12 g of carbon-12. About the number of atoms of carbon in the "lead" of a pencil

Here are some approximate values using some of the derived units.

$1\,m\,s^{-1}$	Walking speed. A car moving at $30\,m\,s^{-1}$ would be fast
$1\,m\,s^{-2}$	Quite a slow acceleration. The acceleration due to gravity is $10\,m\,s^{-2}$
1 N	A small force—about the weight of an apple
1 V	Batteries generally range from a few volts up to 20 V, the mains is several hundred volts
1 Pa	A very small pressure. Atmospheric pressure is about $10^5\,Pa$
1 J	A very small amount of energy—the work done lifting an apple off the ground

Possible reasonable assumptions

Everyday situations are very complex. Physicists often simplify a problem by making some assumptions. Even if you know that these assumptions are not absolutely true, they allow you to gain an understanding of what is going on. At the end of the calculation, it is often possible to go back and work out what would happen if the assumption turned out not to be true.

The table below lists some common assumptions. Be careful not to assume too much! Additionally, you often have to assume that some quantity is constant even if you know that in reality it is varying slightly all the time.

Assumption	Example
Object treated as point particle	Mechanics: linear motion and translational equilibrium
Friction is negligible	Many mechanics situations—but you need to be very careful
No thermal energy ("heat") loss	Almost all thermal situations
Mass of connecting string, etc. is negligible	Many mechanics situations
Resistance of ammeter is zero	Circuits
Resistance of voltmeter is infinite	Circuits
Internal resistance of battery is zero	Circuits
Material obeys Ohm's law	Circuits
Machine 100% efficient	Many situations
Gas is ideal	Thermodynamics
Collision is elastic	Only gas molecules have perfectly elastic collisions
Object radiates as a perfect black body	Thermal equilibrium, e.g. planets

Scientific notation

Numbers that are too big or too small for decimals are often written in **scientific notation**:

$$a \times 10^b$$

where $1 \leq a < 10$ and b is an integer.
e.g. $153.2 = 1.532 \times 10^2$; $0.00872 = 8.72 \times 10^{-3}$

Continuous and discrete variables

Quantitative variables are variables that can be measured using numbers. They can be **discrete** or **continuous**. A discrete variable represents a count (e.g. the number of electrons in a neutral atom). Continuous variables represent measurable amounts that can take any number (e.g. mass, length or time taken).

Estimations, variables, relationships and scale diagrams (2)

Relationships

The words describing the relationship between two variables have precisely defined meanings. The table below describes a number of possible relationships in terms of two variables, P and Q. See page 194 for how the following relationships can be deduced from the shape of graphs.

(Directly) proportional	P is **proportional** to Q if P doubles when Q doubles, so that they vary in proportion to one another. P would also treble when Q trebles etc. Proportional and directly proportional mean the same thing.
	The general mathematical form for this relationship is:
	$P = k \times Q$ where k is a constant
	The addition of another constant c to the equation means that P and Q are no longer directly proportional to one another.
	$P = k \times Q + c$ where k and c are constants is a *linear relationship*.
Inversely proportional	P is inversely proportional to Q if P doubles when Q halves, so that they vary **in inverse proportion** to one another.
	The general mathematical form for this relationship is:
	$P = \dfrac{k}{Q}$ where k is a constant.
Positive relationship/positive correlation	P has a positive correlation with Q if P gets bigger when Q gets bigger, and if P gets smaller when Q gets smaller.
Negative relationship/negative correlation	P has a negative correlation with Q if P gets bigger when Q gets smaller, and if P gets smaller when Q gets bigger.

Percentages

A percentage is a convenient way of representing a ratio. For example, this might be a percentage uncertainty or a percentage change:

$$\frac{\Delta p}{P}$$

This ratio is expressed in terms of fractions of one hundred:

$$\frac{\Delta p}{P} \times 100\%$$

$0\% = 0$; $100\% = 1$; $56\% = 0.56$ etc.

Scale diagrams

Scale diagrams are often a useful technique for helping solve problems that involved vector addition or subtraction (see page 176). Typical problems include displacements, forces, velocities or accelerations. An arrow can be drawn **to scale** with its length representing the magnitude of the vector and its direction representing the direction of the vector. Care should be taken to identify the location of the vector. It is good practice to explicitly record the scale used in the diagram.

In the diagram below, 1 cm represents a force of 5 N and the resultant force is 30 N.

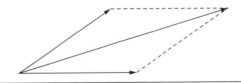

Vectors and scalars

Difference between vectors and scalars

If you measure any quantity, it must have a number AND a unit. Together they express the **magnitude** of the quantity. Some quantities also have a direction associated with them. A quantity that has magnitude and direction is called a **vector** quantity whereas one that has only magnitude is called a **scalar** quantity. For example, all forces are vectors.

The table lists some common quantities. The first two quantities in each list are linked to one another by their definitions (see page 1). All the others are in no particular order.

Vectors	Scalars
Displacement ←——————→	Distance
Velocity ←——————→	Speed
Acceleration	Mass
Force	Energy (all forms)
Momentum	Temperature
Electric field strength	Potential or potential difference
Magnetic field strength	Density
Gravitational field strength	Area

Although the vectors used in many of the given examples are forces, the techniques can be applied to all vectors.

Components of vectors

It is also possible to "split" one vector into two (or more) vectors. This process is called resolving and the vectors that we get are called the components of the original vector. This can be a very useful way of analysing a situation if you choose to resolve all the vectors into two directions that are at right angles to one another.

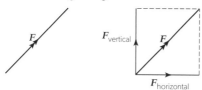

▲ Splitting a vector into components

These "mutually perpendicular" directions are totally independent of each other and can be analysed

separately. If appropriate, both directions can then be combined at the end to work out the final resultant vector.

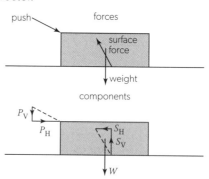

▲ Pushing a block along a rough surface

Representing vectors

In most books a bold letter is used to represent a vector whereas a normal letter represents a scalar. For example $\mathbf{F}$ would be used to represent a force in magnitude AND direction. The list below shows some other recognized notation.

$$\vec{F}, \overline{F} \text{ or } \underline{F}$$

Vectors are best shown in diagrams using arrows:

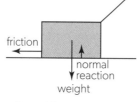

- the relative magnitudes of the vectors involved are shown by the relative length of the arrows
- the direction of the vectors is shown by the direction of the arrows.

In free-body diagrams (see page 8), the length of the arrow represents the force. In some situations, it is important to show the point of application of the forces. In other situations, it may be appropriate to show the forces acting on the centre of mass.

Addition/subtraction of vectors

If you have a 3 N and a 4 N force, the overall force (resultant force) can be anything between 1 N and 7 N depending on the directions involved.

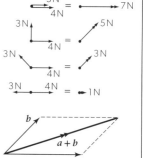

The way to take the directions into account is to construct a scale diagram and use the parallelogram law of vectors. This process is the same as adding vectors in turn—the "tail" of one vector is drawn starting from the head of the previous vector.

▲ Parallelogram of vectors

When you multiply a vector by a scalar, the direction remains unchanged, but the magnitude is multiplied.

Trigonometry

Vector problems can always be solved using scale diagrams, but it may be easier to resolve the vectors into two perpendicular components using sine and cosine. The diagram shows how to calculate the values of these components.

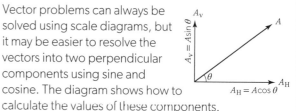

Range of magnitudes of quantities in our universe

Orders of magnitude—including their ratios

Physics seeks to explain nothing less than the Universe itself. In attempting to do this, the range of the magnitudes of various quantities will be huge.

If the numbers involved are going to mean anything, it is important to get some feel for their relative sizes. To avoid "getting lost" among the numbers it is helpful to state them to the nearest **order of magnitude** or power of ten. The numbers are just rounded up or down as appropriate.

Comparisons can then be made easily because working out the ratio between two powers of ten is just a matter of adding or subtracting whole numbers. The diameter of an atom, 10^{-10} m, does not sound that much larger than the diameter of a proton in

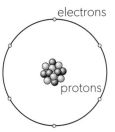
electrons
protons
Carbon atom

railway station
Earth

its nucleus, 10^{-15} m, but the ratio between them is 10^5 or 100 000 times bigger. This is the same ratio as between the size of a railway station (order of magnitude 10^2 m) and the diameter of the Earth (order of magnitude 10^7 m).

For example, you would probably feel very pleased with yourself if you designed a new, environmentally friendly source of energy that could produce 2.03×10^3 J from 0.72 kg of natural produce. But the meaning of these numbers is not clear—is this a lot or is it a little? In terms of orders of magnitudes, this new source produces 10^3 joules per kilogram of produce. This does not compare very well with the 10^5 joules provided by a slice of bread or the 10^8 joules released per kilogram of petrol.

You do NOT need to memorize all of the values shown in the tables, but you should try to develop a familiarity with them.

Range of masses

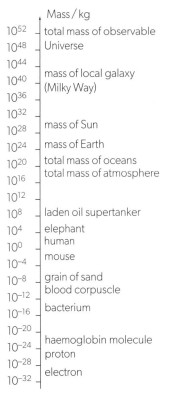

Mass / kg	
10^{52}	total mass of observable
10^{48}	Universe
10^{44}	
10^{40}	mass of local galaxy
10^{36}	(Milky Way)
10^{32}	
10^{28}	mass of Sun
10^{24}	mass of Earth
10^{20}	total mass of oceans
10^{16}	total mass of atmosphere
10^{12}	
10^{8}	laden oil supertanker
10^{4}	elephant
10^{0}	human
	mouse
10^{-4}	
10^{-8}	grain of sand
	blood corpuscle
10^{-12}	
10^{-16}	bacterium
10^{-20}	
10^{-24}	haemoglobin molecule
	proton
10^{-28}	electron
10^{-32}	

Range of times

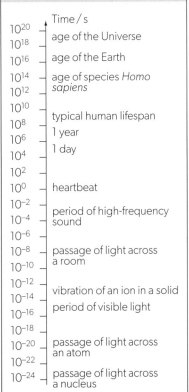

Time / s	
10^{20}	
10^{18}	age of the Universe
10^{16}	age of the Earth
10^{14}	age of species *Homo*
10^{12}	*sapiens*
10^{10}	
10^{8}	typical human lifespan
10^{6}	1 year
10^{4}	1 day
10^{2}	
10^{0}	heartbeat
10^{-2}	period of high-frequency
10^{-4}	sound
10^{-6}	
10^{-8}	passage of light across
10^{-10}	a room
10^{-12}	vibration of an ion in a solid
10^{-14}	period of visible light
10^{-16}	
10^{-18}	
10^{-20}	passage of light across
10^{-22}	an atom
10^{-24}	passage of light across a nucleus

Range of lengths

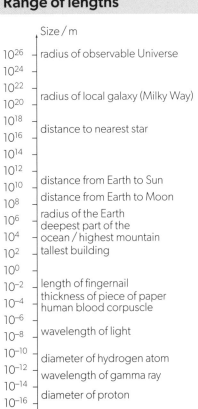

Size / m	
10^{26}	radius of observable Universe
10^{24}	
10^{22}	radius of local galaxy (Milky Way)
10^{20}	
10^{18}	distance to nearest star
10^{16}	
10^{14}	
10^{12}	
10^{10}	distance from Earth to Sun
10^{8}	distance from Earth to Moon
10^{6}	radius of the Earth
	deepest part of the
10^{4}	ocean / highest mountain
10^{2}	tallest building
10^{0}	
10^{-2}	length of fingernail
	thickness of piece of paper
10^{-4}	human blood corpuscle
10^{-6}	
10^{-8}	wavelength of light
10^{-10}	diameter of hydrogen atom
10^{-12}	wavelength of gamma ray
10^{-14}	diameter of proton
10^{-16}	

Range of energies

Energy / J	
10^{42}	energy released in a supernova
10^{38}	
10^{34}	
10^{30}	
10^{26}	energy radiated by Sun in 1 second
10^{22}	energy released in an earthquake
10^{18}	
	energy released by annihilation of
10^{14}	1 kg of matter
10^{10}	energy in a lightning discharge
10^{6}	energy needed to charge a car
	battery
10^{2}	kinetic energy of a tennis ball
10^{-2}	during game
	energy in the beat of a fly's wing
10^{-6}	
10^{-10}	
10^{-14}	
10^{-18}	energy needed to remove electron
	from the surface of a metal
10^{-22}	

The SI system of fundamental and derived units

Fundamental units

Any measurement and every quantity can be thought of as being made up of two important parts:

1. the number
2. the units.

Without **both** parts, the measurement does not make sense. For example, a person's age might be quoted as "seventeen" but without the "years" the situation is not clear. Are they 17 minutes, 17 months or 17 years old? In this case, you would know if you saw them, but a statement like:

"length = 4.2"

actually says nothing. Having said this, it is surprising how many candidates forget to include the units in their answers to examination questions.

In order for the units to be understood, they need to be defined. There are many possible systems of

measurement that have been developed. In science, the International System of units (SI) is used. In SI, the **fundamental** or **base** units are as follows.

Quantity	SI unit	SI symbol
Mass	kilogram	kg
Length	metre	m
Time	second	s
Electric current	ampere	A
Amount of substance	mole	mol
Temperature	kelvin	K
Luminous intensity	candela	cd

You do not need to know the precise definitions of any of these units in order to use them properly.

Derived units

Having fixed the fundamental units, all other measurements can be expressed as different combinations of the fundamental units. In other words, all the other units are **derived units**. For example, the fundamental list of units does not contain a unit for the measurement of speed. The definition of speed can be used to work out the derived unit.

$$\text{speed} = \frac{\text{distance}}{\text{time}}$$

$$\text{Units of speed} = \frac{\text{units of distance}}{\text{units of time}}$$

$$= \frac{\text{metres}}{\text{seconds}} \text{ (pronounced "metres per second")}$$

$$= \frac{\text{m}}{\text{s}} = \text{m s}^{-1}$$

Of all the ways of writing this unit, the last way (m s^{-1}) is the best.

Sometimes particular combinations of fundamental units are so common that they are given a new derived name. For example, the unit of force is a derived unit—it turns out to be kg m s^{-2}. This unit is given a new name the newton (N) so that $1\,\text{N} = 1\,\text{kg m s}^{-2}$.

The great thing about SI is that, as long as the numbers that are substituted into an equation are in SI units, then the answer will also come out in SI units. You can always "play safe" by converting all the numbers into proper SI units. Sometimes, however, this would be a waste of time.

There are some situations where the use of SI becomes awkward. In astronomy, for example, the distances

involved are so large that the SI unit (the metre) always involves large orders of magnitudes. In these cases, the use of a different (but non SI) unit is very common. Astronomers can use the astronomical unit (AU), the light-year (ly) or the parsec (pc), as appropriate. Whatever the unit, the conversion to SI units is simple arithmetic.

$$1\,\text{AU} = 1.5 \times 10^{11}\,\text{m}$$
$$1\,\text{ly} = 9.5 \times 10^{15}\,\text{m}$$
$$1\,\text{pc} = 3.1 \times 10^{16}\,\text{m}$$

There are also some units (for example, the hour) which are so common that they are often used even though they are not SI. Once again, before these numbers are substituted into equations they need to be converted. Some common unit conversions are given on page 4 of the IB Physics data booklet.

The table below lists the SI derived units that you will meet.

SI derived unit	SI base unit	Alternative SI unit
newton (N)	kg m s^{-2}	—
pascal (Pa)	$\text{kg m}^{-1}\text{s}^{-2}$	N m^{-2}
hertz (Hz)	s^{-1}	—
joule (J)	$\text{kg m}^2\text{s}^{-2}$	N m
watt (W)	$\text{kg m}^2\text{s}^{-3}$	J s^{-1}
coulomb (C)	A s	—
volt (V)	$\text{kg m}^2\text{s}^{-3}\text{A}^{-1}$	W A^{-1}
ohm (Ω)	$\text{kg m}^2\text{s}^{-3}\text{A}^{-2}$	V A^{-1}
weber (Wb)	$\text{kg m}^2\text{s}^{-2}\text{A}^{-1}$	V s
tesla (T)	$\text{kg s}^{-2}\text{A}^{-1}$	Wb m^{-2}
becquerel (Bq)	s^{-1}	—

Prefixes

To avoid the repeated use of scientific notation, an alternative is to use one of the list of agreed prefixes given on page 4 in the IB Physics data booklet. These can be very useful but they can also lead to errors in

calculations. It is very easy to forget to include the conversion factor.

For example, $1\,\text{kW} = 1000\,\text{W}$. $1\,\text{mW} = 10^{-3}\,\text{W}$

(in other words, $1\,\text{mW} = \frac{1\,\text{W}}{1000}$)

SI units (1)

Table of SI base units

The following table lists the base units of quantities used in the course. SI units are given for important constants in the IB Physics data booklet and these can be converted to base units as required.

Quantity	Symbol	Value	Common SI unit	SI base unit	Alternative unit
Area	A	length $\times$ width	–	m^2	–
Volume	V	length $\times$ width $\times$ height	–	m^3	–
Density	ρ	$\dfrac{mass}{volume}$	–	$kg\,m^{-3}$	–
Velocity	v, u	$\dfrac{displacement}{time}$	–	$m\,s^{-1}$	–
Acceleration	a	$\dfrac{change\ of\ velocity}{time}$	–	$m\,s^{-2}$	–
Momentum	p	mass $\times$ velocity	–	$kg\,m\,s^{-1}$	$N\,s$
Impulse	J	force $\times$ time (change in momentum)	$N\,m$	$kg\,m\,s^{-1}$	–
Force	F	mass $\times$ acceleration	newton (N)	$kg\,m\,s^{-2}$	–
Coefficient of friction	μ	ratio of friction force to normal force	(ratio)	–	–
Viscosity	η	constant in Stoke's law: $F_D = 6\pi\eta rv$	$Pa\,s$	$kg\,m^{-1}\,s^{-1}$	$N\,s\,m^{-2}$
Pressure	P	$\dfrac{force}{area}$	pascal (Pa)	$kg\,m^{-1}\,s^{-2}$	$N\,m^{-2}$
Angular velocity	Ω	$\dfrac{angle}{time}$	–	s^{-1}	–
Angular acceleration	α	rate of change of angular velocity	–	s^{-2}	$rad\,s^{-2}$
Energy (work)	Q, W, E	force $\times$ distance	joule (J)	$kg\,m^2\,s^{-2}$	$N\,m$
Power	P	rate of doing work	watt (W)	$kg\,m^2\,s^{-3}$	$J\,s^{-1}$
Efficiency	η	$\dfrac{energy\ output}{energy\ input}$	(ratio)	–	–
Torque	τ	force $\times$ perpendicular distance	$N\,m$	$kg\,m^2\,s^{-2}$	–
Moment of inertia	I	sum of mass $\times$ radius^2	–	$kg\,m^2$	–
Angular momentum	L	moment of inertia $\times$ angular velocity	–	$kg\,m^2\,s^{-1}$	–
Relativistic constant	γ	$\gamma = \dfrac{1}{\sqrt{1-\dfrac{v^2}{c^2}}}$	(ratio)	–	–
Specific heat capacity	c	$\dfrac{energy\ transfer}{mass \times temperature\ change}$	$J\,kg^{-1}\,K^{-1}$	$m^2\,s^{-2}\,K^{-1}$	–
Luminosity	L	power radiated	W	$kg\,m^2\,s^{-3}$	–
Brightness	B	power received per unit area	$W\,m^{-2}$	$kg\,s^{-3}$	–
Intensity	I	$\dfrac{power\ received}{area}$	$W\,m^{-2}$	$kg\,s^{-3}$	–
Emissivity	e	$\dfrac{power\ emitted}{power\ emitted\ by\ a\ black\ body}$	(ratio)	–	–
Albedo	a	$\dfrac{total\ scattered\ power}{total\ incident\ power}$	(ratio)	–	–
Entropy	S	$\dfrac{change\ in\ energy}{temperature}$	$J\,K^{-1}$	$kg\,m^2\,s^{-2}\,K^{-1}$	–
Charge	Q	current $\times$ time	coulomb (C)	$A\,s$	–
Potential difference	V	$\dfrac{energy}{charge}$	volt (V)	$kg\,m^2\,s^{-3}\,A^{-1}$	$W\,A^{-1}$ $J\,C^{-1}$

SI units (2)

Table of SI base units

Quantity	Symbol	Value	Common SI unit	SI base unit	Alternative unit
Resistance	R	$\dfrac{\text{potential difference}}{\text{current}}$	ohm (Ω)	$\text{kg m}^2\,\text{s}^{-3}\,\text{A}^{-2}$	V A^{-1}
Resistivity	ρ	$\dfrac{\text{resistance} \times \text{area}}{\text{length}}$	$\Omega\,\text{m}$	$\text{kg m}^3\,\text{s}^{-3}\,\text{A}^{-2}$	—
Frequency	f	$\dfrac{\text{number of cycles}}{\text{time}}$	hertz (Hz)	s^{-1}	—
Thermal conductivity	k	$\dfrac{\text{rate of energy transfer}}{\text{area of material} \times \text{temperature gradient}}$	$\text{W m}^{-1}\,\text{K}^{-1}$	$\text{kg m s}^{-3}\,\text{K}^{-1}$	—
Gravitational field strength	g	force per unit test mass	N kg^{-1}	m s^{-2}	—
Gravitational potential	V_g	energy per unit test mass	J kg^{-1}	$\text{m}^2\,\text{s}^{-2}$	—
Electric field strength	E	$\dfrac{\text{force}}{\text{unit charge}}$	V m^{-1}	$\text{kg m s}^{-3}\,\text{A}^{-1}$	N C^{-1}
Magnetic flux	ϕ	emf $\times$ time	weber (Wb)	$\text{kg m}^2\,\text{s}^{-2}\,\text{A}^{-1}$	V s
Magnetic flux density	B	$\dfrac{\text{force}}{\text{current} \times \text{length}}$	tesla (T)	$\text{kg s}^{-2}\,\text{A}^{-1}$	Wb m^{-2}
Activity	A	$\dfrac{\text{number of decays}}{\text{time}}$	becquerel (Bq)	s^{-1}	—

Dimensional analysis and significant figures

Dimensional analysis

As well as agreeing in terms of the numbers, all equations in physics also have to balance in terms of the units that are used. It is always possible to check an expression using a **dimensional analysis** of the units involved. Some textbooks use the phrase *dimensional analysis* to refer to a formal process which can be used to derive the format of relationships. This involves looking at the dependence of all quantities on some fundamental physics concepts e.g. mass $[M]$, length $[L]$, time $[T]$, charge $[Q]$, temperature $[\theta]$ etc. This formal process in not studied in the IB DP course, but a simple check can be done using SI base units.

Example 1

One of the constant acceleration formulae is:

$$s = ut + \frac{1}{2}at^2$$

A dimensional analysis of the unit of each of these terms should show them to be the same.

SI units of s = m

SI units of ut = $\mathrm{m\,s^{-1} \times s}$ = m

SI units of $\frac{1}{2}at^2$ = $\mathrm{m\,s^{-2} \times s^2}$ = m

Note: $\frac{1}{2}$ does not have a unit so does not affect the unit of that term.

The units of the LHS of the equation are the same as the units of each term on the RHS, so the expression possible.

Example 2

The PE of a falling object is converted into KE as it accelerates.

$$mg\Delta h = \frac{1}{2}mv^2$$

SI units of LHS = $\mathrm{kg \times m\,s^{-2} \times m = kg\,m^2\,s^{-2}}$
SI units of RHS = $\mathrm{kg \times (m\,s^{-1})^2 = kg\,m^2\,s^{-2}}$

The units of the LHS of the equation are the same as the units of each term on the RHS so the expression possible.

The analysis of the units in any formulae cannot not help you with the value any pure numbers—e.g. the units would also balance in the following equation: $mg\Delta h = 3mv^2$ but the equation is **incorrect**.

Example 3

It is suggested that the formula for the time period the oscillation of a mass on the end of spring is given by:

$$T = 2\pi\sqrt{\frac{m}{k^2}}$$

where k is the Hooke's law spring constant (= force per unit extension)

SI units of k = $\mathrm{kg\,m\,s^{-2} \div m = kg\,s^{-2}}$

SI units of LHS = s

SI units of RHS = $\mathrm{(kg \div (kg\,s^{-2})^2)^{0.5} = (kg \div (kg^2\,s^{-4}))^{0.5}}$
$\qquad\qquad = \mathrm{(kg^{-1}\,s^4)^{0.5} = kg^{-0.5}\,s^2}$

The SI units are not equal so the equation above **cannot** be correct. The correct equation is

$$T = 2\pi\sqrt{\frac{m}{k}}$$

This does balance in terms of units (= s on both sides)

Significant figures

Any experimental measurement should be quoted with its uncertainty. This indicates the possible range of values for the quantity being measured. At the same time, the number of **significant figures** used will act as a guide to the amount of uncertainty. For example, a measurement of mass which is quoted as 23.456 g implies an uncertainty of ± 0.001 g (it has five significant figures),

whereas one of 23.5 g implies an uncertainty of ± 0.1 g (it has three significant figures).

A simple rule for calculations (multiplication or division) is to quote the answer to the same number of significant digits as the LEAST precise value that is used.

For a more complete analysis of how to deal with uncertainties in calculated results, see page 182.

Uncertainties and error in experimental measurement

Errors—random and systematic (precision and accuracy)

An experimental error just means that there is a difference between the recorded value and the "perfect" or "correct" value. Errors can be categorized as **random** or **systematic**.

Repeating readings does not reduce systematic errors.

Sources of random errors include:

- the readability of the instrument
- the observer being less than perfect
- the effects of a change in the surroundings.

Sources of systematic errors include:

- an instrument with **zero error**; to correct for zero error the value should be subtracted from every reading
- an instrument being wrongly **calibrated**
- the observer being less than perfect in the same way for every measurement.

An **accurate** experiment is one that has a small systematic error, whereas a **precise** experiment is one that has a small random error.

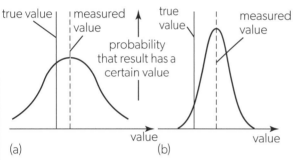

(a)   (b)

▲ Two examples illustrating the nature of experimental results:
(a) an accurate experiment of low precision
(b) a less accurate but more precise experiment

Systematic and random errors can often be recognized from a graph of the results.

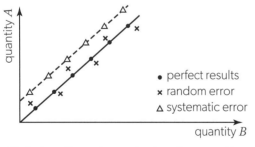

- perfect results
- × random error
- △ systematic error

▲ Perfect results, random and systematic errors of two proportional quantities

Significant figures in uncertainties

Final uncertainty values should be rounded to one or two significant figures: e.g. a calculation that finds the value of a force to be 4.264 N with an uncertainty of ± 0.362 N can be quoted as 4.3 ± 0.4 N or 4.26 ± 0.36 N.

Graphical representation of uncertainty

In many situations, the best method of presenting and analysing data is to use a graph. If this is the case, a neat way of representing the uncertainties is to use **error bars**. The graphs below explain their use.

Since the error bar represents the uncertainty range, the "best-fit" line of the graph should pass through ALL of the rectangles created by the error bars.

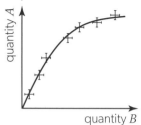

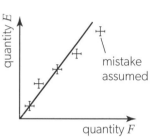

mistake assumed

Estimating the uncertainty range

An **uncertainty range** applies to any experimental value. Instead of giving just one value that implies perfection, you give the likely range for the measurement.

1. Estimating from first principles

All measurement involves a readability error: e.g. if you use a measuring cylinder to find the volume of a liquid, you might think that the best estimate is 73 cm³, but you know that it is not exactly this value (73.000 000 000 00 cm³).

Uncertainty range is ± 5 cm³. You say volume = 73 ± 5 cm³.

The uncertainty range due to readability is estimated as shown below.

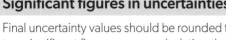

Device	Example	Uncertainty
Analogue scale	Rulers, meters with moving pointers	± (half the smallest scale division)
Digital scale	Top-pan balances, digital meters	± (the smallest scale division)

2. Estimating uncertainty range from several repeated measurements

If the time taken for a trolley to go down a slope is measured five times, the readings in seconds might be 2.01, 1.82, 1.97, 2.16 and 1.94. The average of these five readings is 1.98 s. The deviation of the largest and smallest readings can be calculated (2.16 – 1.98 = 0.18; 1.98 – 1.82 = 0.16). The largest value is taken as the uncertainty range. In this example, the time is 1.98 s ± 0.18 s. It would also be appropriate to quote this as 2.0 ± 0.2 s.

Uncertainties in calculated results

Mathematical representation of uncertainties

If the mass of a block is measured as 10 ± 1 g and the volume is measured as 5.0 ± 0.2 cm^3, then the full calculations for the density would be as follows.

$$\text{Best value for density} = \frac{\text{mass}}{\text{volume}} = \frac{10}{5} = 2.0 \, \text{g cm}^{-3}$$

The largest possible value of density $= \frac{11}{4.8} = 2.292 \, \text{g cm}^{-3}$

The smallest possible value of density $= \frac{9}{5.2} = 1.731 \, \text{g cm}^{-3}$

Rounding these values gives density $= 2.0 \pm 0.3 \, \text{g cm}^{-3}$

We can express this uncertainty in one of three ways—using **absolute**, **fractional** or **percentage** uncertainties.

If a quantity P is measured, then the absolute uncertainty would be expressed as $\pm \Delta P$.

Then the fractional uncertainty becomes $\pm \dfrac{\Delta P}{P}$,

which makes the percentage uncertainty $\pm \dfrac{\Delta P}{P} \times 100\%$.

In the example above, the fractional uncertainty of the density is ± 0.15 or $\pm 15\%$.

Equivalent ways of expressing this error are

density $= 2.0 \pm 0.3 \, \text{g cm}^{-3}$

OR density $= 2.0 \, \text{g cm}^{-3} \pm 15\%$

Working out the uncertainty range is very time consuming. There are some mathematical "short-cuts" that can be used. These are introduced in the boxes below.

Multiplication, division or powers

Whenever two or more quantities are multiplied or divided and they each have uncertainties, the overall uncertainty is approximately equal to the **sum** of the **percentage** (fractional) uncertainties.

Using the same numbers from above,

$$\Delta m = \pm 1 \, \text{g and } \frac{\Delta m}{m} = \pm \left(\frac{1 \, \text{g}}{10 \, \text{g}} \right) = \pm 0.1 = \pm 10\%$$

$$\Delta V = \pm 0.2 \, \text{cm}^3 \text{ and } \frac{\Delta V}{V} = \pm \left(\frac{0.2 \, \text{cm}^3}{5 \, \text{cm}^3} \right) = \pm 0.04 = \pm 4\%$$

$$\text{The total \% uncertainty in the result} = \pm (10 + 4)\%$$
$$= \pm 14\%$$

14% of $2.0 \, \text{g cm}^{-3} = 0.28 \, \text{g cm}^{-3} \approx 0.3 \, \text{g cm}^{-3}$

So density $= 2.0 \pm 0.3 \, \text{g cm}^{-3}$ as before.

In symbols, if $y = \dfrac{ab}{c}$

then $\dfrac{\Delta y}{y} = \dfrac{\Delta a}{a} + \dfrac{\Delta b}{b} + \dfrac{\Delta c}{c}$ (note: this is ALWAYS added)

Power relationships are just a special case of this law.

If $y = a^n$

then $\dfrac{\Delta y}{y} = \left| n \dfrac{\Delta a}{a} \right|$ (always positive)

For example, if a cube is measured to be 4.0 ± 0.1 cm in length along each side, then

% uncertainty in length $= \pm \dfrac{0.1}{4.0} = \pm 2.5\%$

Volume $= (\text{length})^3 = (4.0)^3 = 64 \, \text{cm}^3$

% uncertainty in (volume) $= $ % uncertainty in $[(\text{length})^3]$
$$= 3 \times (\text{\% uncertainty in length})$$
$$= 3 \times (\pm 2.5\%)$$
$$= \pm 7.5\%$$

Absolute uncertainty $= 7.5\%$ of $64 \, \text{cm}^3$
$$= 4.8 \, \text{cm}^3 \approx 5 \, \text{cm}^3$$

So, volume of cube $= 64 \pm 5 \, \text{cm}^3$

Other mathematical operations

If the calculation involves mathematical operations other than multiplication, division or raising to a power, then you have to find the highest and lowest possible values.

Addition or subtraction

Whenever two or more quantities are added or subtracted and they each have uncertainties, the overall uncertainty is equal to the **sum** of the **absolute** uncertainties.

In symbols, if $y = a \pm b$ $\Delta y = \Delta a + \Delta b$

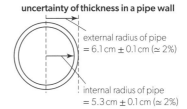

uncertainty of thickness in a pipe wall

external radius of pipe $= 6.1 \, \text{cm} \pm 0.1 \, \text{cm} \, (\approx 2\%)$

internal radius of pipe $= 5.3 \, \text{cm} \pm 0.1 \, \text{cm} \, (\approx 2\%)$

thickness of pipe wall $= 6.1 - 5.3 \, \text{cm} = 0.8 \, \text{cm}$

uncertainty in thickness $= \pm (0.1 + 0.1) \, \text{cm} = \pm 0.2 \, \text{cm}$
$$= \pm 25\%$$

Other functions

There are no "short-cuts" possible. Find the highest and lowest values: e.g. uncertainty of $\sin \theta$ if $\theta = 60° \pm 5°$

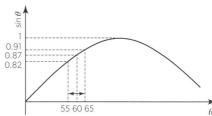

best value of $\sin \theta = 0.87$

maximum value of $\sin \theta = 0.91$

minimum value of $\sin \theta = 0.82$

∴ $\sin \theta = 0.87 \pm 0.05$ ← worst value used

Tables and graphs (1)

Tables

Quantitative raw data is often recorded in a table. Important things to remember are:

1. The title of any column should make clear the precise quantity that is being measured: e.g. a complete column title might be "Time taken for 10 complete swings of the pendulum" rather than just "Time".

2. The unit that the quantity is being measured in, e.g. "seconds" or "/s".

3. The uncertainty of the measurements being recorded, e.g. ±0.01 s.

4. The numbers being recorded need to match the declared uncertainty.

5. Processed data is often added to the table but it is good practice to keep processed data and raw data separate.

6. Each separate reading should be recorded. An average value of repeated readings is processed data.

An experiment to measure the pd across a bulb and the current going through it might be set out as follows.

Potential difference across bulb, V/V ± 0.1 V	Current through bulb I/A ± 0.01 A
0.0	0.00
2.0	1.03
4.0	2.08
6.0	3.12
8.0	4.13
10.0	5.25

In physics, the majority of graphs involve one quantity plotted on the x-axis and another quantity plotted on the y-axis, to produce a **scatter graph** of the values. This presents the data visually and allows trends to be identified—typically using straight lines or curves. There are also other ways to visually represent data (see below).

Bar charts

In a bar chart the vertical height of the bar (or the horizontal length of the bar) is proportional to the value assigned to different categoric variables according to the label on the horizontal axis. More complex bar charts break down the total value of a particular bar into different proportions. Here is an example.

▶ World coal consumption, 1990–2030

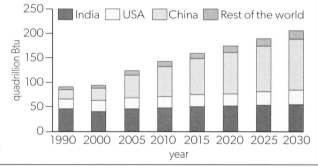

Pie charts

A pie chart compares the relative values of different quantities to allow numerical comparison by ratio. The area of each slice is proportional to the quantity it represents, with the full circle representing 100% of the quantity. The quantity represented is also proportional to either the arc length of the sector or the sector angle.

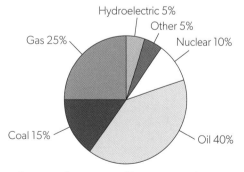

▲ Sources of energy used in a power station

Histograms

A histogram is a visual representation of how continuous numerical data is distributed. In the simplest version, the whole range of data is divided into different equal intervals or "bins". The number of data values in each interval are counted. A bar is then drawn with its height representing the number of data values in each bin—i.e. the frequency.

Another type of histogram can be drawn with bars of unequal width, as shown below.

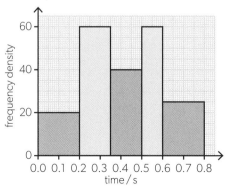

▲ Detection time of background radiation

Tables and graphs (2)

Differences between bar charts and histograms

Comparison	Bar chart	Histogram
Aim	To compare different categories	To display a variable's distribution
Variable type	Categorical	Numerical
Link to data	Each data point is a separate bar	Data points are grouped into different "bins"
Space between bars	Possible	Not possible
Order of bars	Can be changed	Cannot be changed

A more sophisticated type of histogram, as shown on page 184, can be constructed with "bins" of unequal size. In this type of histogram, each bar an **area** proportional to the frequency. The vertical axis shows the **frequency density** which is the frequency divided by the width of the interval.

An example of how this approach can be used is the energy density distribution for black body radiation (see page 55) at different temperatures.

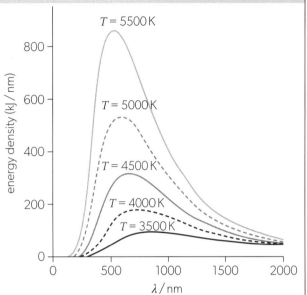

The **area** under any of the curves between any two chosen wavelengths is proportional to the energy radiated from the black body in that wavelength range.

Scatter graphs

A scatter graph is the name given to a plot that records matching values of two measured variables using coordinates. A dot is placed in the position where one variable determines the value on the x-axis and the other variable determines the matching value on the y-axis. A trend line can be added to emphasize the relationship between the two variables and outlying points can be identified and discussed. Trend lines can be straight lines or smooth curves that do not "join the dots" but emphasize the general trend.

As well as identifying trends, trend lines can be used to identify the maximum and minimum values of a variable.

Each axis needs to be properly scaled so that the same length along the axis represents the same incremental value. Axes can be linear or logarithmic (see page 188).

Line graphs

Line graphs are used to show how measured variables vary with time when the time variation is essentially categoric (a different measurement at a regular time interval, e.g. every day or every year). Points can be joined to show how the measured variables changed over time, which thus allows a comparison to be made.

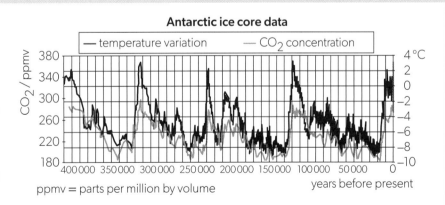

Antarctic ice core data

ppmv = parts per million by volume

One piece of evidence that links global warming to increased levels of greenhouse gases comes from ice core data. The ice cores have been drilled in the Russian Antarctic base at Vostok. Each year's new snowfall adds another layer to the ice.

Isotopic analysis allows the temperature to be estimated, and air bubbles trapped in the ice cores can be used to measure the atmospheric concentrations of greenhouse gases. The record provides data from over 400 000 years ago to the present. The variations of temperature and carbon dioxide are very closely correlated.

Graphs

Plotting graphs—axes and best fit

Plotting a graph allows you to identify trends. It gives a visual way of representing the variation of one quantity with respect to another.

- A graph should have a title. Sometimes they also need a key.

- The scales of the axes should be suitable—there should not be any sudden or uneven "jumps" in the numbers on the axes.

- You need to decide whether or not to include the origin. Most graphs should have the origin included. If in doubt include it. You can draw a second graph without it if necessary.

- The final graph should, if possible, cover more than half of the paper in either direction.

- The axes should be labelled with both the quantity (e.g. current) AND the units (e.g. amps).

- All points must be clear and be plotted correctly. Vertical and horizontal lines to make crosses are better than 45° crosses or dots.

- Error bars should be included, if appropriate.

- A best-fit trend line should be added. This line NEVER just "joins the dots"—it is there to show the overall trend.

- If the best-fit line is a curve, this needs to be drawn as a single smooth line. If the best-fit line is a straight line, this should be drawn with a ruler.

- As a general rule, there should be roughly the same number of points above the line as below the line and should be randomly above and below it. Sometimes people try to fit a best-fit straight line to points that should be represented by a gentle curve. If you do this, then points below the line will be at the beginning of the curve and all the points above the line will be at the end, or vice versa.

- Any points that do not agree with the best-fit line should be been identified.

Measuring intercept, gradient and area under the graph

Useful features of graphs are the **intercept**, the **gradient** and the **area under the graph**.

1. Intercept

In general, a graph can intercept (cut) either axis any number of times. A straight-line graph can only cut each axis once and often it is the y-intercept (often simply called "the intercept") that has particular importance. If a graph has an intercept of zero, then it goes through the origin. Note that two quantities are **proportional** if the graph is a straight line that passes through the origin.

Sometimes a graph has to be "continued on" (outside the range of the readings) so that the intercept can be found. This process is known as **extrapolation**. The process of assuming that the trend line applies between two points is known as **interpolation**.

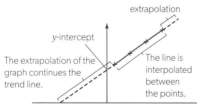

2. Gradient

The gradient of a straight-line graph is the increase in the y-axis value divided by the increase in the x-axis value.

- A straight-line graph has a constant gradient.

- The triangle used to calculate the gradient should be as large as possible.

- The gradient has units. They are the units on the y-axis divided by the units on the x-axis.

- Only if the x-axis is a measurement of time does the gradient represent the RATE at which the quantity on the y-axis increases.

The gradient of a curve at any particular point is the gradient of the tangent to the curve at that point.

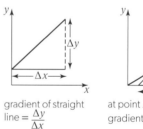

gradient of straight line $= \dfrac{\Delta y}{\Delta x}$

at point P on the curve, gradient $= \dfrac{\Delta y}{\Delta x}$

3. Area under a graph

The area under a straight-line graph is the product of multiplying the average quantity on the y-axis by the quantity on the x-axis. This does not always represent a useful physical quantity. When working out the area under the graph:

- If the graph consists of straight-line sections, the area can be worked out by dividing the shape up into simple shapes.

- If the graph is a curve, the area can be calculated by "counting the squares" and working out what one square represents.

- The units for the area under the graph are the units on the y-axis multiplied by the units on the x-axis.

- If the mathematical equation of the line is known, the area under the graph can be calculated using a process called **integration**.

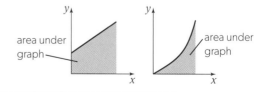

Graphical analysis and determination of relationships

Equation of a straight-line graph

All straight-line graphs can be described using one general equation: $y = mx + c$

x and y are the two variables (to match with the x-axis and the y-axis).

m and c are both constants—they have fixed values.

- c represents the intercept on the y-axis (the value y takes when $x = 0$)

- m is the gradient of the graph.

For example, a simple experiment might measure the velocity of a trolley as it rolls down a slope. The equation that describes the motion is $v = u + at$, where u is the initial velocity of the object. In this situation, v and t are the variables; a and u are the constants.

The physics equation has exactly the same form as the mathematical equation. The order has been changed below to emphasize the link.

$$v = u + at \qquad y = c + mx$$

If you plot the velocity on the y-axis and the time on the x-axis, you will get a straight-line graph.

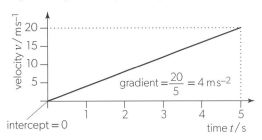

The comparison also works for the constants.

- c (the y-intercept) must be equal to the initial velocity u

- m (the gradient) must be equal to the acceleration a.

In this example, the graph tells you that the trolley must have started from rest (intercept zero) and it had a constant acceleration of $4.0\,\mathrm{m\,s^{-2}}$.

Choosing what to plot to get a straight line

With a little rearrangement, you can often end up with the physics equation in the same form as the mathematical equation of a straight line.

- Identify which symbols represent variables and which symbols represent constants.

- The symbols that correspond to x and y must be variables and the symbols that correspond to m and c must be constants.

- If you take a variable reading and square it (or cube, square root, reciprocal etc.)—the result is still a variable and you could choose to plot this on one of the axes.

- You can plot any mathematical combination of your original readings on one axis—this is still a variable.

- Sometimes the physical quantities involved use the symbols m (e.g. mass) or c (e.g. speed of light). Be careful not to confuse these with the symbols for gradient or intercept.

Example 1

The gravitational force F that acts on an object at a distance r away from the centre of a planet is given by the equation

$$F = \frac{GMm}{r^2}$$ where M is the mass of the planet and m is the mass of the object.

If you plot force against distance you get a curve (graph 1). You can restate the equation as $F = \frac{GMm}{r^2} + 0$ and if you plot F on the y-axis and $\frac{1}{r^2}$ on the x-axis you will get a straight-line (graph 2).

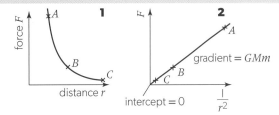

Example 2

If an object is placed in front of a lens you get an image. The image distance v is related to the object distance u and the focal length of the lens f by the following equation.

$$\frac{1}{u} + \frac{1}{v} = \frac{1}{f}$$

There are many possible ways to rearrange this in order to get it into straight-line form. You should check that all of these are algebraically the same.

$$v + u = \frac{uv}{f} \quad \text{or} \quad \frac{v}{u} = \frac{v}{f} - 1 \quad \text{or} \quad \frac{1}{u} = \frac{1}{f} - \frac{1}{v}$$

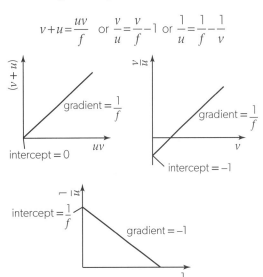

Graphical analysis—logarithmic functions

Exponentials and logs

Natural logarithms (logs) are very important because many natural processes are exponential. Radioactive decay is an important example. In this case, the taking of logarithms allows the equation to be compared with the equation for a straight line.

For example, the count rate R at any given time t is given by the equation

$$R = R_0 e^{-\lambda t}$$

where R_0 and λ are constants.

If you take logs, you get

$$\ln(R) = \ln\left(R_0 e^{-\lambda t}\right)$$

$$\ln(R) = \ln(R_0) + \ln\left(e^{-\lambda t}\right)$$

$$\ln(R) = \ln(R_0) - \lambda t \ln(e)$$

$$\ln(R) = \ln(R_0) - \lambda t \quad [\ln(e) = 1]$$

This can be compared with the equation for a straight-line graph

$$y = c + mx$$

If you plot $\ln(R)$ on the y-axis and t on the x-axis, you will get a straight line.

Gradient $= -\lambda$

Intercept $= \ln(R_0)$

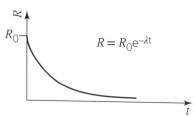

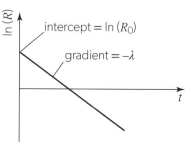

Power laws and logs

When an experimental situation involves a power law, it is often only possible to transform it into straight-line form by taking logs: for example, the time period of a simple pendulum, T, is related to its length, l, by the following equation.

$$T = kl^p$$

where k and p are constants.

A plot of the variables will give a curve, but it is not clear from this curve what the values of k and P work out to be. Also, if you do not know what the value of P is, you cannot calculate the values to plot a straight-line graph.

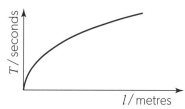

▲ Time period versus length for a simple pendulum

The trick is to take logs of both sides of the equation. The equations below use natural logarithms, but the technique would work for all logarithms, whatever the base.

$$\ln(T) = \ln\left(kl^p\right)$$

$$\ln(T) = \ln(k) + \ln\left(l^p\right)$$

$$\ln(T) = \ln(k) + p\ln(l)$$

This is now in the same form as the equation for a straight line: $y = c + mx$

So, if you plot $\ln(T)$ on the y-axis and $\ln(l)$ on the x-axis you will get a straight-line graph.

The gradient will be equal to p.

The intercept will be equal to $\ln(k)$ (so $k = e^{(\text{intercept})}$)

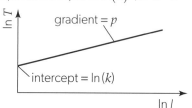

▲ A plot of ln (time period) versus ln (length) gives a straight-line graph

Both the gravitational force and the electrostatic force are inverse-square relationships. This means that force $\propto$ (distance apart)$^{-2}$. The same technique can be used to generate a straight-line graph.

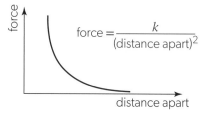

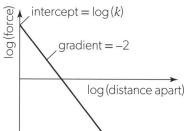

▲ Inverse square relationship—direct plot and log–log plot

Uncertainties in graphs

Error bars

Plotting a graph allows you to visualize all the readings at one time. Ideally, all of the points should be plotted with their error bars. In principle, the size of the error bar could well be different for every single point and so they should be individually worked out.

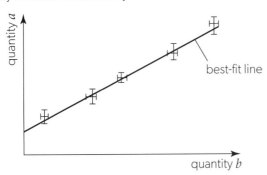

A full analysis to determine the uncertainties in the gradient of a best straight-line graph should **always make use of the error bars for all of the data points**.

In practice, it would often take too much time to add all the correct error bars, so some (or all) of the following short-cuts could be considered.

- Rather than working out error bars for each point—use the worst value and assume that all of the other error bars are the same.

- Only plot the error bar for the "worst" point, i.e. the point that is furthest from the line of best fit. If the line of best fit is within the limits of this error bar, then it will probably be within the limits of all the error bars.

- Only plot the error bars for the first and the last points. These are often the most important points when considering the uncertainty ranges calculated for the gradient or the intercept (see right).

- Only include the error bars for the axis that has the worst uncertainty.

Uncertainty in slopes

If the gradient of the graph has been used to calculate a quantity, then the uncertainties of the points will give rise to an uncertainty in the gradient. Using the steepest and the shallowest lines possible (i.e. the lines that are still consistent with the error bars) the uncertainty range for the gradient is obtained. This process is represented below.

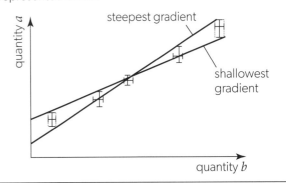

Uncertainty in intercepts

If the intercept of the graph has been used to calculate a quantity, then the uncertainties of the points will give rise to an uncertainty in the intercept. Using the steepest and the shallowest lines possible (i.e. the lines that are still consistent with the error bars) you can obtain the uncertainty in the result. This process is represented below.

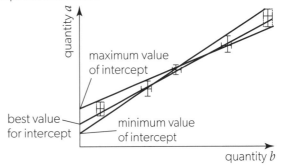

Exploring and designing (1)

Exploring

The process of inquiry involves being curious about the universe. This means being prepared to take the initiative to explore specific aspects in detail rather than always waiting to be told what to do. Being an independent thinker is the best way to build your own understanding of physics. Key aspects of a successful and valid investigation are highlighted in the following pages, but an additional essential key ingredient is the initiative that you bring to the process.

The following approaches are often demonstrated by students who have "taken charge" of their own education:

- They bring independent thinking to a problem and use initiative and insight to try to understand the situation.

- In researching possible understandings and solutions, they consult a variety of sources (books, internet sites, people etc.)

- As a result of this research, they select sufficient and relevant sources of information.

- When thinking about a problem, they can formulate their own research questions and/or hypotheses to test.

- They are able to come up with predictions based on scientific understanding that can be stated with precision and explained to others.

- They can bring their own creativity to the design, implementation and presentation (if appropriate) of an investigation.

Types of investigation

Physics is an experimental science that attempts to understand the universe in which we live. New understandings are often developed from experimental investigations in the laboratory, but these are not the only types of investigation that can be successful. Broadly, there are three different approaches that investigations can involve.

- Laboratory experiments—where a controlled set-up is created involving the manipulation and measurement of different variables.

- Databases—where available data is interrogated and manipulated to produce new knowledge and understanding.

- Simulations and/or modelling—where models are created and variables are controlled virtually by controlling different parameters within the model or simulation.

It is also possible to do any combination of these.

Variables

All experiments must involve observations. Usually, the observations will be quantitative measurements of a given property, such as mass, length, volume or time. In any experiment the value of the measured property depends on several variables. For example, the pressure of a sample of gas depends on at least four different variables:

- the volume of the gas

- the temperature of the gas

- the mass of the gas

- the particular gas used.

It is no use changing each of these variables at random and hoping that some pattern will be obvious from the results. You need to discover how each one affects the pressure. For the experiment to be a **fair test**, it needs to be designed so that you can vary only one at a time.

The variable that you choose to control (the one that is manipulated) is called the **independent variable**: for example, the volume of the gas.

The variable that you measure is called the **dependent variable**: for example, the pressure of the gas.

The variables that are held constant throughout the experiment (so that only one thing is affecting the

dependent variable) are called the **control variables:** for example, the temperature of the gas, its mass and the particular gas used.

Your experimental report needs to identify explicitly the dependent variable (measured), the independent variable (manipulated) and the control variables (constants).

Usually, the raw data from an experiment must include four things:

- corresponding values for the independent and dependent variables

- a wide range of values for the independent variable

- repeated readings where possible

- readings of all the control variables, when possible, to check that they have been kept constant during the experiment.

When designing an investigation, it is good practice to draw up a table that identifies the choice of dependent, independent and control variables. This same table can be used later when evaluating the chosen methodology (see page 195).

Exploring and designing (2)

Methodologies

The **methodology** is the chosen procedure for the investigation. Having identified all the variables, the experimenter needs to identify how the variables are going to be measured. The variables can be measured directly, or other measurements can be taken to allow them to be calculated.

The chosen methodology needs to allow:

- the independent variable to be measured **and** changed
- the dependent variable to be measured.

In addition, the methodology must effectively control those variables that need to be controlled—it is good practice to measure them to check that the procedures are effectively doing this. For example, if the temperature of the laboratory needs to be constant, then the temperature should be recorded several times during the experiment.

Decisions also need to be taken as to the **range** and **quantity** of measurements (while keeping safety in mind at all times, of course). These decisions need to take many factors into account including:

- the time needed to set up the apparatus (and to take it down)
- the time needed to take each pair of readings and whether there needs to be a wait between readings

- how easy it is to repeat readings
- the precision of the readings
- how many readings it is sensible to take.

Before fixing the procedure, it is good practice to do a **trial** set of readings to check that the process works and gives reasonable results. A simple test would be to set up the apparatus with the smallest and the largest proposed value of the independent variable in a **pilot** version of the final methodology. This sets the proposed range and allows the experimenter to check that the dependent variable does show a reasonable variation that can be recorded. This approach also allows the experimenter to change the methodology in light of experience.

The number of readings also depends on the above factors. There is no fixed rule as to the number that need to be taken for an experiment to be valid, but it is helpful to think of any graph that these readings might produce. As a bare minimum, a graph of five points would just about allow the experimenter to identify a point that was anomalous (eight would be better). Ideally, readings should be repeated and doing each reading at least three times allows mis-readings to be identified. Taken together, this means that a minimum of 15 readings should be taken, but, ideally, there should be many more.

Controlling variables

Calibration

Calibration is the process of checking the readings provided by a measuring device with another device that is known to be accurate. The same word is often also used to describe any modifications that one makes in order to make the measuring device more accurate (e.g. accounting for zero error—see page 182). Often the specific combination of a given data logger and a sensor will need to be calibrated each time they are used together. In a typical physics laboratory, a very simple check is to repeat a measurement after swapping a suspect measuring device with an identical replacement. In an ideal world, the reading would remain the same.

Possible reasons for suspecting that calibration may be necessary include if:

- an instrument is providing readings that do not seem right
- an instrument might have been damaged or has been repaired
- an instrument has been modified
- an instrument has been moved
- a significant time has passed since the last calibration
- there has been a recent change in environmental conditions.

Reducing problems

During an investigation, the aim is to measure the effect that one variable has on another. In an ideal world, all other variables would be kept constant and nothing else would happen that might affect the outcomes. In real experiments, however, this is not always possible. It is important to think about how such problems can be minimized. A good start is to try to ensure that all environmental conditions (temperature, presence of wind etc.) are maintained in a constant way. Any significant changes should be recorded in case they have an effect.

Thermal energy
In all thermal energy investigations, as far as it is practically possible, one should try to insulate against heat loss or heat gain. Heat flow to or from the surrounding will affect the results. If temperature changes can be kept small, then heat loss to the surrounding may be minimized. It may also be worth considering compensating by starting the investigation at a temperature **below** room temperature and ending when the material under consideration is the same temperature difference **above** room temperature. This helps to compensate for any unwanted heat flow, as it could be assumed that heat gained when below room temperature = heat lost when above room temperature.

Kinematics
The motion of all moving objects will be affected by friction so there are many circumstances when it is important to reduce friction as much as possible (using trolleys with free-running wheels or using an **air track**).

If all objects are moving in a straight line, it is also possible to compensate for friction using a downward facing slope. If a trolley is given a push forward on a horizontal surface, it will slowly decelerate as a result of friction (friction in axles or wheels + air friction). On a steep slope, gravity will cause the trolley to accelerate down the slope. On a gentle downwards slope, at

exactly the correct angle, once given a push forward, the trolley would move at a constant velocity.

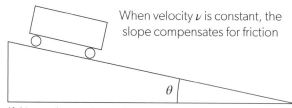

When velocity v is constant, the slope compensates for friction

If θ is too large, the trolley accelerates.
If θ is too small, the trolley decelerates.

Electrical circuits
In electrical circuits, the assumption is often that the connecting wires and ammeters are perfect conductors. In reality, there will be a small, non-zero, resistance. Similarly, the power source used will have an internal resistance. The combination of all these unwanted resistances may affect the results and it may be necessary to explore ways to reduce the resistance in the circuit. Note that a voltmeter is added to an electrical circuit in parallel (see page 79), which means that the resistance of perfect voltmeter would be infinite. This is one resistance that does not benefit from being reduced.

A second issue concerns temperature. Often it is assumed that the temperature of all components in a circuit is constant, but a flowing current has a heating effect. It is important to monitor whether the heating effect is significant.

Measurements of radioactivity
It is important to take background radiation into account when recording the activity of a radioactive source (see page 152). Unless there is significant shielding of the apparatus, naturally occurring background radiation will be added to the radiation emitted from the radioactive source being studied.

1.2 Calculating and processing data

Collecting and processing data

Recording data

Accurately and precisely recording data in a way that is not ambiguous is a practical skill at the core of any inquiry. Data can be both **qualitative** and **quantitative**.

Recording **qualitative** data involves identifying physical changes that might be relevant when considering the reliability of individual data points.

- If the appearance changes (e.g. a change of colour), then this might signal that a reaction is taking place.
- If a falling object is blown off target by a breeze, it may not be appropriate to include that piece of data when calculating averages.

It is important to both **identify** the observation and to **record** it and, if appropriate, modify the procedure to address any issues that arise.

Quantitative data involves measurements of a physical quantity, which means recording:

- the value
- the units
- the direction (if the physical quantity is a vector)
- every piece of raw, unprocessed data that is observed—anomalous readings can be identified when the data is processed and when you try to interpret the data, but **all** readings need to be recorded; this is often best presented in a **table of readings**.
- a sufficient number of pieces of raw data to allow conclusions to be drawn.

Processing data

Processing raw data involves using the raw data in calculations that, often with the aid of graphs and charts, help to identify and explain patterns, trends and relationships. Calculating the average of repeated readings (see above) is perhaps, the simplest processing technique, but often more complicated data processing is undertaken. In this context, the processing needs to be:

- relevant—any calculations undertaken should be appropriate to the aim of the investigation; a clear research question to ensure that the data processing that is being done helps to answer the question

- accurate—any calculations need to be done with precision; a calculation that gives rise to a result that looks anomalous needs to be checked
- able to be understood—for somebody else to be able to follow the data processing that has been done, it is important to give the reader enough information to be able to check the data processing themselves. This does not mean that every calculation needs to be fully written out. It is often sufficient to record a sample calculation and then record the results of the data processing in **a table of results**. (Readings = raw data; results = calculated values.)

Interpreting results (1)

Dealing with outliers

As shown on page 182, the trend line for any graph needs to pass through the error bars associated with **every** data point. There are, however, occasions when a graph contains **outliers**—these are points that do not agree with the trend shown by the other data points. There are circumstances when it might be appropriate to assume that one such data point is the result of a mistake rather than being reliable.

The simplest check is to repeat the measurements that gave rise to the outlier. If repetition provides a point that is more in line with the trend, then it would be acceptable to assume that a mistake had been made. If, however, repetition provides a point that remains away from the trend, then this suggests that the point should be included. This probably means that the observed relationship is more complex than previously thought. The following two steps need to be taken with outliers.

1. They need to be **identified**.
2. Their removal or inclusion needs to be **justified**.

When interpreting any results, it is important to assess the following.

- Accuracy—how close are the results to a "true" or "accepted" value? Accuracy in readings can be affected by systematic errors (see page 182).
- Precision—how close are readings of the same value to one another? To what significant figure can the readings be quoted? Precision can be affected by poor experimental technique (see page 182).
- Reliability—if the experiment were to be repeated would it produce the same results? Reliability can be affected by random errors (see page 182).
- Validity—is the methodology of the experiment appropriate and does it address the inquiry question? Validity can be affected by failing to keep the control variables constant (see page 190).

Interpreting results (2)

Looking for trends

The aim of any inquiry is to interpret the results. In physics, this often involves interpreting graphs in order to identify, describe and explain:

- patterns
- trends
- relationships.

An important skill is to be able to describe the relationship implied from the shape of a graph.

Each of the graphs A to H represents a common mathematical relationship that occurs in physics between a dependent and an independent variable.

- Graph **A**: This graph shows two variables that are directly **proportional**, because the line is straight and goes through the origin.
- Graph **B**: This graph shows a **linear** relationship between two variables.
- Graph **C**: This graph shows two variables that are **inversely related**: as one increases, the other decreases.
- Graph **D**: This graph shows two variables that are inversely proportional: as one doubles, the other one halves.
- Graph **E**: In this graph the y-value is proportional to the square of the x-value.
- Graph **F**: The graph hits the y-axis but does not cross the x-axis. This is an **exponential decrease**.
- Graph **G**: In this graph the y-value is proportional to the square root of the x-value.
- Graph **H**: The graph hits the y-axis and the slope continues to increase as x increases. This is an **exponential increase**.

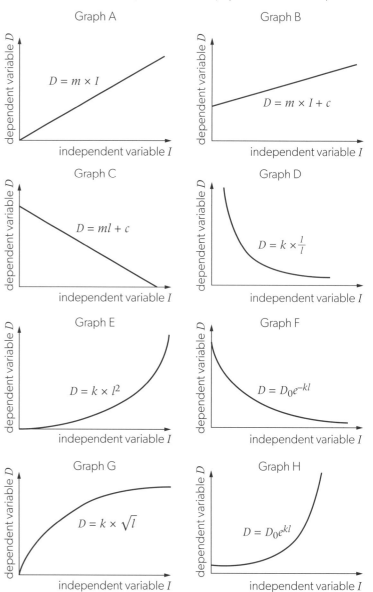

Choosing what to plot to get a straight line

It is useful to plot an appropriate straight-line graph if possible. For example, the time t taken for an object to fall, from rest, a distance s as a result of gravity is given by the equation $s = \frac{1}{2}gt^2$, where g is the acceleration due to gravity. Readings can be taken of the time taken to fall and the distance fallen.

A plot with s on the y-axis and t on the x-axis would look like graph E. It would be more useful to plot s on the y-axis and t^2 on the x-axis. A comparison with the general formula for a straight-line graph shows that this plot would be a straight line, with gradient equal to $\frac{1}{2}g$.

Concluding and evaluating

Concluding

The purpose of most physics investigations is either to measure a physical quantity or to investigate the relationship between two (or more) variables. A good overall conclusion of an experiment does the following.

- It summarizes the findings of the experiment and discusses these findings in the context of the assessed uncertainty limits.

- It relates the findings of the experiment to the stated research question or hypothesis.

- In light of what has been discovered, it critically analyses the outcome of the investigation in the accepted scientific context.

The first element of a detailed conclusion is a statement of any trends or patterns that have been identified by your experiment. As all measurements are subject to uncertainties, it is important to consider all sources of uncertainties in detail. Are your results reliable and/or repeatable? See page 182 for ways to assess uncertainties. You should look critically at the data to see whether an alternative interpretation is possible within the uncertainties that have been acknowledged.

It is worth taking the time to consider the possible sources of error associated with each variable that was measured. It is helpful to assess the relative impacts of any identified weakness on the data collected. Remember to keep an open mind about possible sources of systematic error.

Having identified the trend, this can be discussed in relation to the stated research question or hypothesis. Try to think critically about what the data is telling you and whether there might be another just as likely interpretation.

Finally, the conclusion needs to be considered in terms of accepted scientific models. Sometimes the result of an investigation will be a statement of the value of a known physical quantity (with uncertainty limits). Your value should be compared with accepted literature values. The range of these two values should overlap. If they don't, there are only two options. You have either made a mistake (perhaps you have underestimated possible errors in measurement) or you have discovered new physics.

This sounds straightforward but it is all too easy to state the conclusion that you are expecting to see rather than a conclusion that matches the data that the inquiry has generated. For example:

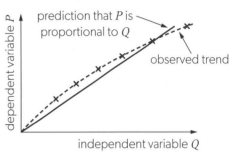

In the graph above, a best fit straight line through the origin has been fitted to some observed data. On closer inspection, the actual observed trend is more like a curve rather than the straight line. It is always important to look critically at the data.

Impact of errors

A well-planned investigation outlines the choice of dependent, independent and control variables. This information can usefully be summarized in a table when the methodology is being explained. The same table can be used later to methodically consider every appropriate variable. This allows an analysis to assess the extent to which uncertainties have affected the readings. Specifically, the impacts of both random and systematic errors (see page 182) could be identified from the data.

This evaluation, if carried out systematically, will help to identify improvements that can sensibly be made to the methodology and priorities for future work.

Methodological weaknesses

You need to critically evaluate the experimental methodology (procedure) that was followed and look for weaknesses in the approach that you took and/or possible sources of uncertainty. In addition, you can consider whether you had the right equipment for the investigation and/or whether you made good use of the time available. An important reflection is whether the method was based on assumptions that are, if fact, not valid. For example, electrical resistance experiments often assume that the temperature is kept constant but electrical currents heat the wires through which they flow so the temperature probably changes. Ideally the relative significance of any identified weakness should be considered.

Possible improvements

A good critical evaluation of the methodology of the investigation should lead directly to some suggestions for improvements. Ideally any such suggestions need to be linked to an identified methodological weakness and be both practical and sensible. Remember to focus on the most significant sources of uncertainty rather than the easiest to improve. For example, it is pointless suggesting replacing a stopwatch with an electronic timer if the biggest source of experimental uncertainty was not in the measurement of time.

End of topic questions—Tools and inquiry process

1. You are told that a gold bar is pure gold. Using a metre ruler, the bar measures $1.0\,cm \times 4.0\,cm \times 12.0\,cm$. The uncertainty in each measurement of length is $\pm 0.1\,cm$. Using a top pan balance, the block has a mass of $811\,g \pm 1\,g$.

   a. Show that the density of the gold bar is approximately $17\,g\,cm^{-3}$. (2)

   b. Calculate the absolute uncertainty in the density calculated in (a). (2)

   c. According to a data booklet, the density of pure gold is $(1.93 \pm 0.01) \times 10^4\,kg\,m{-3}$. Discuss if the bar could be pure gold. (2)

   d. Discuss how to make this measurement of density more accurate. (2)

2. Two students are measuring the time period, T, of a simple pendulum using a stopwatch that records times to the nearest $0.01\,s$. T is approximately $1.0\,s$.

   Student A takes 30 individual readings of T and then averages all 30 readings to get their final answer.

   Student B takes 1 reading of $30T$. The student then divides by 30 to get an answer to get their final answer.

   a. The stopwatch has been properly calibrated. Suggest the source of any uncertainties in the measurement of T. (1)

   b. Suggest an appropriate value for the uncertainty of the time measurements taken by the students. (2)

   c. Explain which student's method produces a final value with the lowest uncertainty. (2)

3. Two students are each doing an experiment to measure the acceleration due to gravity g, in the same room.

   a. Student A drops a $100\,g$ mass from rest and times how long it takes to reach the ground. The experiment is repeated 10 times. The student records the following data:

Height of drop / m	1.63 ± 0.01
Time of drop / s	0.575, 0.542, 0.491, 0.619, 0.589, 0.598, 0.567, 0.535, 0.604, 0.550

   i. Calculate the acceleration due to gravity according to student A. (4)

   ii. Explain why the data suggests that the uncertainty in the measurement of the time of drop is not just due to the readability of the stopwatch. (2)

   iii. Suggest an appropriate value for the % uncertainty of the measurement of time. (3)

   iv. Calculate the overall % uncertainty in student A's measurement of g. (4)

   v. State student A's value for g with its overall absolute uncertainty to the appropriate number of significant figures. (3)

   b. Student B uses a simple pendulum. They record the time taken for 10 complete swings of the pendulum. Theory predicts that the time period of the pendulum, T, and the length pendulum, l, are related to the acceleration due to gravity, g, by the following relationship:

   $$T = 2\pi\sqrt{\frac{l}{g}}$$

   Student B records the following data:

$10T$	$18.6\,s \pm 0.1\,s$
l	$85.0\,cm \pm 0.5\,cm$

   i. Calculate the acceleration due to gravity according to student B. (4)

   ii. Calculate the overall percentage uncertainty in student B's measurement of g. (4)

   iii. State student B's value for g with its overall absolute uncertainty to the appropriate number of significant figures. (3)

   c. Explain whether the students' experiments agree with one another. (2)

4. a. Outline the difference between a random error and a systematic error. (2)

   b. Explain a procedure to minimize the random errors in an experiment. (2)

   c. Outline the difference between improving the *accuracy* of an experimental measurement and improving the *precision* of an experimental measurement. (2)

   d. Explain the difference between the following categories of variables in an experimental investigation:

   i. the *independent* variable (2)

   ii. the *dependent* variable (2)

   iii. the control variables. (2)

5. A convex lens of focal length, f, (such as a camera lens) forms an image of an object at a certain point in space. Theory predicts that the object distance, u, is related to the image distance, v, by the following relationship:

   $$\frac{1}{u} + \frac{1}{v} = \frac{1}{f}$$

   a. The base units of u and v are m. State the units of f. (1)

   A student measures u and v for a given lens. The following data is available:

Object distance, u / cm $\pm 0.1\,cm$	Image distance, v / cm $\pm 0.1\,cm$
20.0	5.4
15.0	5.9
10.0	7.2
8.0	9.0
6.0	14.1
5.0	26.0

   i. Suggest what graph you should plot to determine whether this data is in agreement with the predicted relationship. (2)

   ii. Explain how to determine f using your plot. (2)

   iii. Sketch an accurate graph to determine f. (4)

Answers

A.1—Kinematics

1. **a.** $t=\sqrt{\dfrac{2h}{10}}$ **b.** $x=u_{H}\sqrt{\dfrac{2h}{10}}$ **c.** $\sqrt{20h}$

2. **a.** $7.5\,\mathrm{m\,s^{-1}}$ **b.** The pupil is "stationary" for the duration they are at school, so the average speed of the entire day is lower than $7.5\,\mathrm{m\,s^{-1}}$. **c.** $-2.5\,\mathrm{m\,s^{-1}}$ (taking the direction from their home to their school as positive)

3. **a.** $660\,\mathrm{m\,s^{-1}}$ **b.** $24\,000\,\mathrm{m}$ **c. i.** $73\,\mathrm{s}$ **ii.** $147\,\mathrm{s}$
   d. i. 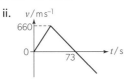 **ii.**

4. **a. i.** $344\,\mathrm{m\,s^{-1}}$ **ii.** $161\,\mathrm{m\,s^{-1}}$ **iii.** $33\,\mathrm{s}$ **iv.** $11\,\mathrm{km}$

   b. i. The minimum value of u occurs when $\theta=45°$.
   $$u_{min}=330\,\mathrm{m\,s^{-1}}$$
   ii. $u_{H}=u\cos\theta \quad u_{V}=u\sin\theta$
   $$t=\frac{2u_{V}}{g}$$
   $$R=u_{H}t=u_{H}\times\frac{2u_{V}}{g}$$
   $$=u\cos\theta\times\frac{2u\sin\theta}{g}=\frac{2u^{2}}{g}\sin\theta\cos\theta$$

   c. Non-negligible air resistance would mean a resistive force on the projectile in the opposite direction to its motion. This resistive force is dependent on the velocity of the projectile. The net effect is that the projectile would not reach as great a **maximum height,** and the **time of flight** and the **range** would be reduced.

5. **a.** $0.14\,\mathrm{m}$ **b.** $0.55\,\mathrm{s}$ **c.** The bullets will reach the ground at the same time. The vertical motion is independent of the horizontal motion, and the vertical components of the motion of the bullets are the same. **d. i.** $45.9\,\mathrm{km}$ **ii.** Assume that the acceleration due to gravity is constant over this distance. **iii.** $61\,\mathrm{s}$

6. **a.** This situation is possible if the magnitude of the velocity remains constant, but the direction of the object varies. For example, an object undergoing horizontal circular motion at constant speed.
   b. This situation is **not** possible. If the speed changes then the magnitude of the velocity changes, so the velocity is not constant. **c.** This is possible.
   For example, an object thrown vertically into the air has a constant downwards acceleration due to gravity. When it reaches the maximum height, the velocity is instantaneously zero. At that instant, it is still accelerating but going from positive (upwards) velocity to negative (downwards) velocity.
   d. This situation is **not** possible as acceleration is a vector quantity. Constant acceleration means the velocity much be changing—either the direction or the magnitude of the velocity must be changing (or both). The magnitude of the velocity will only be instantaneously constant if the acceleration is at right angles to the velocity. An object undergoing horizontal circular motion at constant speed has a changing acceleration—the direction of acceleration is always towards the centre of the circle.

7. **a.** $0.86\,\mathrm{s}$ **b.** $9.88\,\mathrm{m}$ from the bottom of the cliff.

A.2—Forces and momentum

1. **a.** $0.5\,\mathrm{m}$ **b.** $9.5\,\mathrm{m}$ 2. **a.** $0.41\,\mathrm{N}$ **b.** $0.63\,\mathrm{m}$

3. **a.**
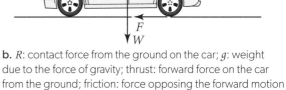

   b. R: contact force from the ground on the car; g: weight due to the force of gravity; thrust: forward force on the car from the ground; friction: force opposing the forward motion between the tyres and the ground **c.** $2.5\,\mathrm{s}$
   d. $2.4\times10^{4}\,\mathrm{kg\,m\,s^{-1}}$ **e.** The centripetal force during the turn is from the friction between the tyres and the ground.
   f.
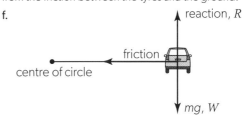

   g. $10\,500\,\mathrm{N}$ **h.** 0.89

4. **a.** Inelastic **b.** $1.2\,\mathrm{m\,s^{-1}}$ **c.** $1440\,\mathrm{Ns}$ **d.** $2160\,\mathrm{J}$

5. **a.** $11.3\,\mathrm{N}$ **b.** Frictional forces will also oppose the motion of the conveyor belt.

6. **a.**
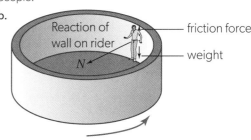

   b. $\mu_{s}=\tan\theta$ **c.** When it starts to move, the kinematic friction acting must be less than the static friction which just prevented it from moving. The coefficient of static friction is greater than the coefficient of kinematic friction. Therefore, there is a resultant force down the slope so the block will initially accelerate.

7. $36\,\mu\mathrm{m}$

8. **a.** The horizontal force acting on the people is the centripetal force provided by the reaction force of the wall on the people.
   b.

   c. 0.30

9. **a.** The $6\,\mathrm{kg}$ mass accelerates down at $1.96\,\mathrm{m\,s^{-2}}$ and the $4\,\mathrm{kg}$ mass accelerates up at $1.96\,\mathrm{m\,s^{-2}}$. **b.** $47\,\mathrm{N}$

10. **a.** $\sqrt{rg}$ **b.** $\sqrt{5rg}$

A.3—Work, energy and power

1. **a.** $39\,\mathrm{N}$ **b.** $54\,\mathrm{N}$ **c.** At constant velocity, the horizontal

component of the force does work against the frictional force. As a result, the surface and block must gain thermal energy—their temperatures increase. Work done by the force = increase in thermal energy. **d.** When the force direction changes to be horizontal, there is now a resultant force forwards so the block must accelerate. The friction force from the surface is (approximately) independent of the velocity of the block. As it accelerates, however, air resistance will increase and eventually the block will have a new constant velocity when F = frictional force from surface + air resistance.

2. **a. i.** 7.7 m s⁻¹ **ii.** 6.6 m s⁻¹ **iii.** 0.40 J **b.** The energy lost by the tennis ball has been converted into other forms, including sound and the energy lost when the tennis ball deforms as it hits the floor.

3. **a. i.** 5 N **ii.** 0.1 J **iii.** 0.63 m s⁻¹ **b. i.** 3.9 cm **ii.** 0.096 J **c. i.** 7.9 cm **ii.** 0.39 J **iii.** 0.20 J **iv.** 0.096 J **v.** 0.63 m s⁻¹ **d.** These two answers are equal to one another. In both the horizontal and the vertical set-ups, the resultant restoring force towards equilibrium is the same for any given displacement.

4. **a.** 540 N **b.** Assume the friction between the tyres and the road is negligible, and all the work done by the engine goes into resisting the frictional force from the air.

5. **a.** 11 110 MJ **b.** $\dfrac{11{,}110}{31{,}000} \times 100 = 35.8\%$

c.

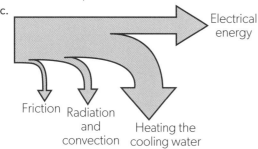

d. 1 kWh = (1,000 J s⁻¹)h⁻¹ = 1,000 × 60 × 60 J = 3.6 MJ
e. 9.1 × 10⁸ kg **f.** 5.0 kg

A.4—Rigid body mechanics

1. Conservation of energy: $\Delta E = mgh = \dfrac{1}{2}mv^2 + \dfrac{1}{2}I\omega^2$.
   $I = \dfrac{2}{5}mr^2$ and $\omega = \dfrac{v}{r}$ as the ball is rolling without slipping.
   Substitute these into the equation:
   $mgh = \dfrac{1}{2}mv^2 + \dfrac{1}{5}mv^2$
   $gh = \dfrac{7}{10}v^2$, and making v the subject we arrive at the equation.

2. **a.** 0.95 N m **b.** 25 J **c.** Use $\omega^2 = \omega 0^2 + 2\alpha\Delta\theta$ (where $\Delta\theta = 4\pi$) to find the angular deceleration to be 2.7 rad s⁻². $F \times r = I\alpha$ so $F = 13$ N.

3. **a.** 20 rad s⁻² **b.** 3640 rad s

4. **a.** $\dfrac{31}{0.35} = 89$ rad s⁻¹ **b.** At the point where the wheel touches the ground, the motion of the wheel is in the opposite direction to that of the car. Since the wheel rolls without slipping, these velocities exactly cancel to zero. On the opposite side of the wheel, the velocities add, giving 62 m s⁻¹. The velocity of any point along the circumference could be given by $v(\theta) = v_{car}(1 - \cos(\theta))$, where the point $\theta = 0$ is the top of the wheel.

c.

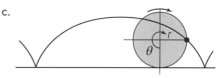

d. Use $\omega^2 = \omega_0^2 + 2\alpha\Delta\theta$ (where $\Delta\theta = 40 \times 2\pi$) to find the angular deceleration to be 16 rad s⁻².
e. $40 \times 2\pi r = 88$ m

5. **a.** 170 s **b.** 17 000 rad

6. 62.5 Nm

7. **a.** 8.5 kJ **b.** 1.7 kW

8. 8×10^{-5} kg m²

9. **a.** 0.05 rads⁻² **b.** 5.2 m s⁻²

10. **a.** The lagging moon provides a gravitational force on the tidal bulges. A component of that force acts as a torque, slowing the rotation of Earth and therefore reducing its angular momentum. **b.** The total angular momentum of the Earth–Moon system is constant since no external torque acts on it. **c.** By conservation of angular momentum, the Moon's orbital angular momentum increases by sapping the rotational angular momentum of Earth. **d.** The moon recesses from Earth to more distant orbits with higher angular momentum.

A.5—Galilean and special relativity

1. Two events A and B occur at times t_A and t_B, and at locations x_A and x_B respectively, where $t_A = t_B$. Demanding that another observer sees the events happen at the same time in their reference frame ($t'_A = t'_B$), the Lorentz transformations demand that $x_A = x_B$. Events that are simultaneous in one reference frame are only simultaneous in another moving reference frame if the events happen at the same position in space.

2. **a.** The spacetime interval Δs^2 is a value that can be obtained from the spacetime coordinates of two events (for example, an event and the origin). The spacetime interval between two events has the same value when calculated in any reference frame or coordinate system. It has the form: $\Delta s^2 = c^2\Delta t^2 - \Delta x^2 - \Delta y^2 - \Delta z^2$. **b.** $\Delta s^2 = 9$, $\Delta s = \pm 3$ **c.** $\Delta s^2 = c^2\Delta t^2 - \Delta x^2 = 9 = c^2\Delta t'^2 - \Delta x'^2$. $\Delta x'^2 = 0$ so $\Delta t' = 3$ ly c⁻¹ **d.** Time passes differently between observers in motion relative to each other. In a reference frame that is perceived to be stationary (such as S), an event may take 5 years to transpire. In a reference frame perceived to be in motion (such as S'), the same event takes place in a smaller amount of time (3 years). **e.** Using either Lorentz transformation of x' or ct' in terms of x and ct, find $v = \dfrac{4}{5}c = 2.4 \times 10^{10}$ m s⁻¹.

3. **a.** $t = 2$ ly c⁻¹ **b.** $t = 4$ ly c⁻¹ **c.** $x = 5$ ly
   d. $v = \dfrac{1}{2}c = 1.5 \times 10^8$ m s⁻¹

4. **a.** 2.0×10^{-7} s **b.** 59 m in the lab frame, 12 m in the frame of the particle.

B.1—Thermal energy transfers

1. 531 s

2. 0.024 W m⁻¹ K⁻¹

3. **a.** Silver is the better conductor because it has a higher thermal conductivity. **b.** 76.2 °C **c.** 0.34 W

4. 6.07×10^{-21} J

5. **a.** 500 nm **b.** Visible light **c.** 3.91×10^{26} W **d.** 1 400 W

6. **a.** 21 600 W **b.** This is likely an underestimate, because there will be other heat losses from the room that haven't been accounted for.

B.2—Greenhouse effect

1. **a.** The solar constant is the intensity of solar radiation across all wavelengths on an area above the Earth's atmosphere that is at right angles to the radiation.
   b. The albedo is the energy scattered by a given surface as a fraction of the energy incident on the surface.

   $$\frac{\text{average power scattered}}{\text{area}} = \frac{S}{4} \times a$$

   $$\frac{\text{average power radiated for a black body}}{\text{area}} = \sigma T^4$$

   At equilibrium, $\dfrac{\text{power radiated}}{\text{area}} = \dfrac{\text{power absorbed}}{\text{area}}$

   $$\frac{S}{4}(1-a) = \sigma T^4 \qquad T = \sqrt[4]{\frac{S(1-a)}{4\sigma}}$$

   d. i. The emissivity is the ratio of the power emitted by a radiating object and the power emitted by a black body at the same temperature with the same dimensions. **ii.** 0.6

2. **a.** Methane, CO_2, water vapour and N_2O. **b.** Molecules absorb radiation by being excited from one molecular energy level to another, higher level. The molecular energy levels are often associated with vibration and oscillations of the molecule. The energy of the absorbed photon is equal to the energy difference between energy levels.
   c. The enhanced greenhouse effect is an increase in the greenhouse effect caused by human activities. The increased combustion of fossil fuels (as an energy source) has released extra carbon dioxide into the atmosphere and carbon dioxide is a significant greenhouse gas.

3. **a.** The radiation being received by the Earth was emitted by the Sun. The surface of the Sun is extremely hot. Therefore, much of the radiation that the Sun emits will have short wavelengths—typically in the UV as well as in the visible spectrum. The surface of the Earth is much cooler than the Sun, so the radiation that it emits will have longer wavelengths—typically in the infrared. **b.** The radiation emitted from the Earth's surface is in the infrared region of the electromagnetic spectrum. Some gases in the atmosphere can absorb infrared radiation. These are greenhouse gases: for example, methane, carbon dioxide and nitrous oxide. Having absorbed the IR radiation, these gases can then re-radiate this energy in all directions. As a result, the Earth is further warmed by IR radiation emitted by gases in the atmosphere. The overall result is that the equilibrium temperature of the Earth is increased by the gases in its atmosphere.

4. **a.** 8 700 W m^{-2} **b.** 2 200 W m^{-2} **c.** 2 000 W m^{-2}
   d. 2 000 W **e.** 430 K

5. **a.** Earth scatters 30% of the energy incident on its surface. **b. i.** Snow will have the largest albedo as it is the most reflective. **ii.** Oceans will have the smallest albedo as they absorb most of the energy incident on them. **c.** Snow, deserts, concrete, forests, oceans
   d. Clouds reflect radiation back into space. Therefore, the presence of clouds will cause less power to be received at the Earth's surface. This will increase the Earth's albedo.

B.3—Gas laws

1. **a.** 0.45 m^3 **b.** 12 moles **c.** 1 280 m s^{-1} **d.** 5.8×10^{-22} J
   e. The helium is at a lower temperature so the kinetic energy due to the random motion of the helium molecules must have decreased. Energy must have been lost to the surroundings. **f.** (For example) The helium particles collide elastically with each other and the inside of the balloon. The time of each collision for the helium particles is negligible compared to the time between the collisions.

2. **a.** Macroscopically, an ideal gas is one that obeys the ideal gas equation:
   $$\frac{PV}{T} = \text{constant}$$

   Where P is the pressure, V is the volume and T is the absolute temperature. Real gases depart from this behaviour. Microscopically, an ideal gas is made up of molecules. These molecules:

   - are assumed to obey Newton's laws of motion
   - do not have any intermolecular forces between them (except during collisions)
   - can be treated as points with no volume
   - are in random motion
   - undergo elastic collisions (no energy is lost)
   - have collisions that take place instantly (no time is spent in collisions).

   Real gases experience intermolecular forces and have a non-zero volume.

   b. i. The temperature must be high. **ii.** The pressure must be low. **iii.** The density must be low.
   c. (For example) All the particles have the same mass. The gas particles are in constant random motion.
   The total volume of the particles is negligible compared with the total volume of the gas. **d.** There are no intermolecular forces in an ideal gas, so it has zero potential energy. **e.** 11 cm^3

3. **a.** The ideal gas equation can be rearranged to become $V = nRT \times \frac{1}{P}$. This is in the form $y = mx + c$, so the graph of V against $\frac{1}{P}$ should be a straight line going through the origin. The data does give a straight line, but as the line does not go through the origin, the data cannot be consistent with the ideal gas equation.

   b. The graph does not go through the origin as expected, so every measurement of the volume must have differed from the true value by the same amount (approximately 1 cm^3).

4. **a.** The pressure of a gas is a result of collisions between the molecules and the walls of the container. When a molecule bounces off a wall, its momentum changes (the direction of motion changes). There must have been a force from the wall on the molecule (Newton's second law). There must also have been a force from the molecule on the wall (Newton's third law). This force per unit area of the wall is what we call pressure.
   b. i. The decrease in volume (with the same number of molecules) means that there will be more frequent collisions between the molecules and the walls. The force from any given collision is unaltered, but the number of collisions per unit time has increased. As V decreases, P increases. **ii.** As the gas is compressed, at least one wall of the container will be moving in. When a molecule collides with a moving wall, the velocity after the collision will have increased. Temperature is a measure of the average kinetic energy per molecule. Therefore, the temperature increases.

B.4—Thermodynamics

1. **a. i.** 4.2×10^5 Pa   **ii.**
    iii. 147 000 J
    b. i. 2.1×10^5 Pa
    ii.

    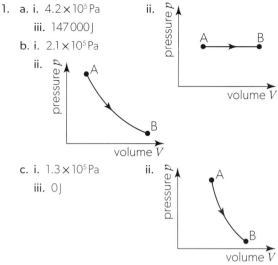

    c. i. 1.3×10^5 Pa   **ii.**
    iii. 0 J

2. An oven operates by converting electrical energy into thermal energy. As a result, the inside of the oven is hotter that the kitchen. When the door is opened, thermal energy will flow from hot (the oven) to cold (the kitchen). The kitchen will warm up. A fridge is a heat pump. It uses electrical energy to move thermal energy from the cold inside of the fridge to the hotter kitchen. The back of a fridge is warm, because the energy taken away from the inside of the fridge is ejected out of the back. As a fridge operates on a Carnot cycle, it cannot be 100% efficient, so the energy ejected from the back of the fridge will be greater than the energy removed from the inside of the fridge. If the door of the fridge is open, the inside of the fridge will be cold, but on average, the temperature of the kitchen will be increased.

3. **a.** 0.25 **b.** The efficiency of a Carnot cycle is the maximum efficiency that a heat engine could achieve. In practice, additional energy must be lost a result of friction in the movement of the engine resulting in the loss of thermal energy to the surroundings and/or the production of sound.

4. **a.** 4.7 J K^{-1} **b.** 610 J K^{-1} **c.** 180 J K^{-1}

5. $3\,900$ W

6. **i.** The definition of the entropy, S, of a system of interacting particles with a number of different possible microstates Ω is given by: $S = k_B \ln\Omega$ Therefore, a change from Ω_1 microstates to Ω_2 microstates means an entropy change of
    $$\Delta S = k_B \ln\Omega_2 - k_B \ln\Omega_1 = k_B \ln\left(\frac{\Omega_2}{\Omega_1}\right)$$
    If the number of microstates increases, then $\Omega_2 > \Omega_1$ and ΔS will be positive. This is an entropy increase. **ii.** At constant temperature, T, the entropy change can be calculated from thermal energy transfer, ΔQ using: $\Delta S = \frac{\Delta Q}{T}$ Therefore, if a system gains thermal energy whilst at a constant temperature, ΔS will be positive. This is an entropy increase. **iii.** The equation in part (ii) cannot be used if the temperature is not constant. There is no simple formula that can be used. Estimations can be made by summing the small entropy changes that take place by assuming that the temperature is approximately constant.

B.5—Current and circuits

1. **a.** 4.0 V   **b.** 3.0 V

2. **a.** $0.5\,\Omega$ **b. i.** 6.0 V   **ii.** $20\,\Omega$
    c. i. 0 A   **ii.** The emf of the cell.

3. **a.** $1.2\,\Omega$ **b.** 12.3 V   **c. i.** 16.3 W   **ii.** 10.0 W

C.1—Simple harmonic motion

1. For motion to be simple harmonic:
    - The force F is a restoring force, acting in the direction against the displacement x from equilibrium.
    - The magnitude of the force is directly proportional to the displacement from the equilibrium.
    - The force is independent of the mass M.

2. **a. i.** $f = \frac{1}{T} = 2.0$ Hz **ii.** $\omega = 2\pi f = 13$ rad s^{-1}
    iii. 79 N m^{-1} **iv.** 1.6 m s^{-2} **b. i.** The spring constant is halved so the time period is multiplied by a factor of $\sqrt{2}$, so $T = 0.7$ s. **ii.** The spring constant is doubled so the time period is multiplied by a factor $\frac{1}{\sqrt{2}}$, so $T = 0.4$ s. **iii.** The only way the gravitational field is involved in the equations of motion is by defining the equilibrium position. There is no change to the time period. **c. i.** 6 cm **ii.** The time period is scaled by a factor $\sqrt{6}$ so 1 s (1.2 s).

3. **a. i.** Moving at a constant velocity has no effect on the period of the pendulum. **ii.** Accelerating upwards in a lift is equivalent to being in a stronger gravitational field. As $T \propto \frac{1}{\sqrt{g}}$, the period is decreased. **iii.** Being in freefall is equivalent to not feeling an acceleration, so there is no oscillation (the time period tends to infinity).

4. **a.** $M = \rho Al$ **b.** $F = mg = 2Ax\rho g$ **c.** $F = Ma = \rho Ala = -2Ax\rho g$, so, $a = -\frac{2g}{l}x$ **d.** The acceleration is proportional to the displacement from equilibrium. The direction of acceleration acts in opposition to the direction of displacement from equilibrium.

5. **a.** 0.04 J **b.** 1.3 m s^{-1} **c.** 8.0 m s^{-2} **d.** 1.0 Hz **e.** ± 0.14 m

6. **a.** $E_K = \frac{1}{2}mx_0^2\omega^2\cos^2(\omega t)$ **b.** $E_P = \frac{1}{2}kx_0^2\sin^2(\omega t)$
    c. $E_{Total} = \frac{1}{2}x_0^2\left(k\sin^2(\omega t) + m\omega^2\cos^2(\omega t)\right)$
    d. $k = m\omega^2$ so $E_{Total} = \frac{1}{2}kx_0^2\left(\sin^2(\omega t) + \cos^2(\omega t)\right)$ and given that $\sin^2(\theta) + \cos^2(\theta) = 1$, $E_{Total} = \frac{1}{2}kx_0^2$ which has no time dependence.

7. 1.1 mm

8. **i.** 0.67 s **ii.** 0.33 m s^{-1} **iii.** 3.1 m s^{-2} **iv.** 0.33 s

C.2—Wave model

1. **a. i.** Sound waves are longitudinal waves, where energy is transferred by the oscillation of particles. **ii.** Electromagnetic waves are transverse waves, where energy is transferred by oscillating electric and magnetic fields. **b. i.** 27.5 m **ii.** 6.0×10^{14} Hz **c.** 8 250 m

2. **a.** 2 cm **b.** 0.67 m s^{-1} **c.** 3.33 Hz **d.** 0.2 m

3. Similarities:
    - Both involve oscillations (either matter or fields).
    - Both transfer energy from source to receiver **without** transfer of mass.

    Differences:
    - Oscillations are in different directions with respect to direction of energy transfer.

- In transverse waves, oscillations are at 90° to energy transfer direction. In longitudinal waves, oscillations are parallel to energy transfer direction.

C.3—Wave phenomena

1. **a.** 600 nm   **b.** 400 nm

2. $d < 2.36 \times 10^{-6}$ m $(\sin\theta_4 < 1)$

3. **a.** 7×10^{-7} m **b.** 55° **c.** There are no longer 1st order maxima, as θ_1 is larger than 90°. Only a central maximum is observed.

4. 600 nm

5. **a.** 0.01 rad   **b. i.**

ii. The fifth-order fringe will be visible.

C.4—Standing waves and resonance

1. **a.** 1.8 m

   b. i. y

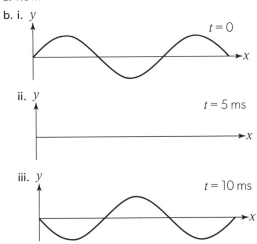

2. The one node standing wave has a length of 0.91 m. The two node standing wave has a length of 1.52 m. The standing waves with zero nodes or greater than two nodes have lengths too short or large respectively.

3. **a.** $\dfrac{7}{8}$ **b.** $\dfrac{6}{7}$

4. For a graph of length against the reciprocal of frequency, speed of sound = 4 × gradient = 337 m s^{-1}

C.5—Doppler effect

1. 410.788 nm, 434.698 nm, 486.864 nm, 657.263 nm

2. **a. i.** Light that has a longer wavelength than the laboratory measurement is redshifted. This indicates that, relative to the observer, the light source is moving further away. **ii.** Light that has a shorter wavelength than the laboratory measurement is blueshifted. This indicates that, relative to the observer, the light source is moving closer. **b.** The left-hand side of the Sun is moving away from the Earth as the Sun rotates (the light has a longer wavelength). The right-hand side of the Sun is moving towards the Earth as the Sun rotates (the light has a shorter wavelength). **c.** 2.18×10^6 s ≈ 25 days

3. **a.**

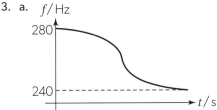

   b. 24 m s^{-1} away from the observer

4. **a. i.** 100 Hz   **ii.** 112 Hz   **b.** 89.2 Hz

D.1—Gravitational fields

1. **a.** 350 N   **b.** 2 800 N

2. **a.** 5.3×10^{30} **b.** The force on the Earth due to the Sun acts as the centripetal force that keeps the Earth in orbit around the Sun.

3. **a.** All the planets orbit the sun on an elliptical path with the sun at one focus. The area swept out by a line between a planet and the Sun is the same for any fixed time. For an orbital time period T and orbital radius r, the ratio $\dfrac{T^2}{r^3}$ is always the same. **b.** Mass of the Sun = 2.0×10^{30} kg

4. **a. i.** The direction of the gravitational field is shown by the direction of the arrows drawn on the field lines. **ii.** The magnitude of the gravitational field at any point is shown by the density of the field lines at that point.

   b. i. 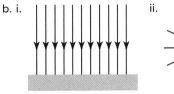   **ii.**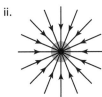

5. 3×10^{-7} N, assuming that the humans both have a mass of 70 kg and their centres of mass are separated by 1 m. Any reasonable distances or masses are acceptable.

6. **a.** 1.1×10^{11} J **b.** -2.1×10^{11} J **c.** -1.1×10^{11} J **d.** A viscous drag force will act to dissipate the energy of the orbiting satellite. This will gradually decrease the velocity and kinetic energy of the satellite. The satellite will fall towards Earth, decreasing its gravitational potential energy.
The total energy of the satellite decreases.

7. **a.** Equate the initial potential energy $-\dfrac{GMm}{r}$,
and the total energy an instance before impact
$\dfrac{1}{2}mv^2 - \dfrac{GMm}{R_E}$. Cancel the mass of the meteorite and
rearrange to make v the subject: $v = \sqrt{2GM\left(\dfrac{1}{R_E} - \dfrac{1}{r}\right)}$

   b. Take the limit as r tends to infinity such that $v = \sqrt{\dfrac{2GM}{R_E}}$. $v = 11.0$ km s^{-1}.

   c. The escape velocity from Earth is $v = \sqrt{\dfrac{2GM}{R_E}}$. $v = 11.0$ km s^{-1}.

   d. It follows by the conservation of energy that the kinetic energy gained by the impacting meteor (falling from rest at infinity) is equal to the minimum energy needed to escape from Earth's surface to approach an infinite distance. This would require the impact velocity to be equal in magnitude to the escape velocity.

8. **a.** The escape velocity can be found by equating the potential energy at the planet's surface $E_\text{p} = -\dfrac{GMm}{r}$ to the kinetic energy of the escaping object $E_\text{K} = \dfrac{1}{2}mv^2$.

The escape velocity from Earth is $v = \sqrt{\dfrac{2GM}{R_\text{E}}}$.

$v = 11.0\,\text{km s}^{-1}$. **b.** To escape the Solar System, the satellite must have sufficient energy to escape not only Earth's gravitational influence, but also the Sun's. This would require a larger initial velocity (closer to $40\,\text{km s}^{-1}$). **c.** Launching rockets have a continuous upwards force accelerating them from rest as they leave Earth. The total work done to escape from Earth is the same in both cases.

D.2—Electric and magnetic fields

1. The charge on each sphere is $1.34 \times 10^{-9}\,\text{C}$, making the total charge shared between the spheres $2.7 \times 10^{-9}\,\text{C}$.

2. **a.** $5.0\,\text{mm}$ **b.** $5.3\,\text{nC}$

3. $625\,\text{V}$ with the positive plate above the drop.

4. **a. i.** $1.10\,\mu\text{m}$ **ii.** Assume that the density of air is very much less that the density of oil, so fluid upthrust can be ignored as negligible. **b. i.** The drop has lost the excess electron and is now neutral. **ii.** $1.74 \times 10^{-5}\,\text{Pa s}$
c. $4.0 \times 10^{-4}\,\text{m s}^{-1}$ upwards

5. **a. i.**

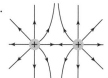

ii.

b. i. Moving between the two electric charges, the density of the field lines decreases, meaning that the field strength decreases in magnitude. Equidistant between the positive charges there are no field lines. The electric fields from the charges cancel out exactly. **ii.** The field lines between the plates are horizontal and equally spaced, meaning that the density of field lines, and therefore the field strength, is uniform between the plates.

6. **a.** $75\,\text{mm}$ away from the larger charge along the line between the two charges. **b.** $144\,\text{V}$

7. $1.87 \times 10^7\,\text{m s}^{-1}$

D.3—Motion in electromagnetic fields

1. $2.9\,\text{m}$

2. 8.2×10^{10}

3. $42°$ ($0.73\,\text{rad}$)

4. **a.** $0.15\,\text{N}$ **b.** Forces on either side of the square produce a turning effect. The coil will end up vertical.

5. **a.** The force on one wire is directly proportional to the product of its current and the magnetic field caused by the other wire. The magnetic field strength caused by the other wire is directly proportional to its current, so the force is directly proportional to the product of the currents. This symmetry means that the force is the same on each wire. **b.** $3.6 \times 10^{-6}\,\text{N}$ **c.** The line pointing in the same direction as the wires that is $60\,\text{mm}$ away from the $4.0\,\text{A}$ wire ($30\,\text{mm}$ from the $2.0\,\text{A}$ wire).

D.4—Induction

1. $0.06\,\text{V}$

2. $5.0 \times 10^{-8}\,\text{V}$

3. **a. i.** $\Phi = BA \cos(\theta)$ **ii.** $\Phi = BA \cos(\omega t)$ **iii.** $E = N\omega BA \cos(\omega t)$
b. i.

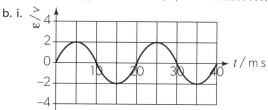

ii. Graph as in part (i) with double the amplitude.
iii. Graph as in part (i) with double the amplitude.
iv. Graph as in part (i) with half the amplitude.

4. **a. i.** Lenz's law in this situation states that the direction of the emf is such that, if a current was to flow, the induced current would oppose the change that caused it. The field of the induced current flowing in the coil would act like a north pole—repelling the approaching north pole of the falling magnet. **ii.** Lenz's law states that the direction of the induced current would oppose the change. The alternative direction of induced current would attract the falling magnet, making it accelerate and generating a larger and larger current. This cannot take place as kinetic energy is being generated from nowhere—this in inconsistent with the law of conservation of energy. Therefore, the direction predicted by Lenz's law is consistent with the conservation of energy. **b.** The rate of change of flux in the coil as a result of the falling north pole is equal and opposite to the rate of change of flux as a result of the falling south pole. Overall, there is no change of flux when the magnet is inside the coil, so no emf is induced. **c. i.** Since the magnet is moving faster, the rate of change of magnetic flux is greater than when it entered the coil. Therefore, the magnitude of induced emf is greater when the magnet is exiting the coil. **ii.** The induced emf is now a result of the south pole moving away from the coil. Therefore, the direction of the induced emf when the magnet exits the coil is in the opposite direction to the direction of the induced emf when the magnet is entering the coil.

d.

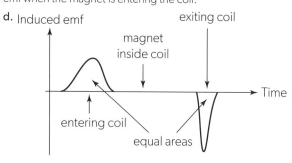

E.1—Structure of the atom

1. **a.** The negative values of the energy levels indicate that energy is required for an electron to move further away from the nucleus. When an electron falls to a lower energy level, it loses energy in the form of a photon. **b.** Longest wavelength: $2.0 \times 10^{-6}\,\text{m}$ Shortest wavelength: $9.7 \times 10^{-8}\,\text{m}$ **c.** 6

d. $E_\text{n} = \dfrac{13.6\,\text{eV}}{n^2}$ $E_2 = \dfrac{13.6 \times 1.6 \times 10^{-19}}{4} = 5.44 \times 10^{-19}\,\text{J}$

2. **a.** As a result of its temperature, the star emits a continuous spectrum (all wavelengths) of electromagnetic radiation. Absorption of some specific wavelengths take place in the

outer layers of the star as a result of the chemical elements present. This wavelength is re-emitted in all directions. The spectrum received on Earth will have these wavelengths "missing". **b.** The specific wavelengths can be used to identify the chemical composition of the outer layers of the star. A star that is moving relative to the Earth will show a Doppler shift in its absorption spectrum. Light from a star that is receding will be redshifted, whereas light from an approaching star will be blueshifted. Analysis of the shift allows the star's velocity (relative to the Earth) to be calculated.

3. **a.** X and Z. X is the chemical symbol and Z is the atomic number. The chemical is defined by the atomic number (the number of protons in the nucleus). **b.** A will be the largest number because it is the total number of protons and neutrons. **c.** $^{235}_{92}U$

4. $\lambda = \dfrac{h}{p} = \dfrac{h}{mv}$ $\therefore h = \lambda mv$

   Units are $m \times kg\,m\,s^{-1} = kg\,m^2\,s^{-1}$

5. $2.7 \times 10^{-12}\,m$

E.2—Quantum physics

1. **a.** The photoelectric effect is the phenomenon whereby when light is shone onto a metal surface, photoelectrons are emitted. Below a certain frequency (the threshold frequency), no electrons are emitted from the metal. The photoelectric effect is evidence for the particle model of light. **b. i.** The stopping potential is the potential at which a photocurrent is no longer observed in an experiment to investigate the photoelectric effect. The stopping potential is a measure of the maximum kinetic energy of the photoelectrons. **ii.** $V_s = 4.5\,V$ **iii.** $h = \dfrac{1.6 \times 10^{-19}}{\text{gradient}} = 6.4 \times 10^{-34}\,J\,s$

2. **a.** Wave–particle duality refers to the nature of light having both wave properties and particle properties. **b. i.** Compton scattering is the effect in which X-rays scattered by a target substance have a higher wavelength than the incident X-rays. **ii.** When X-rays are scattered from an electron, the wavelength increases. The increase in wavelength is consistent with the electron gaining energy as a result giving electrons kinetic energy from a collision. The relationship between change in wavelength and the scattering angle is consistent with the conservation of momentum. Light is behaving like a particle undergoing a collision in which momentum is conserved.

3. **a. i.** $4.9 \times 10^{-12}\,m$ **ii.** $5.0 \times 10^{-15}\,m$ **iii.** $9.5 \times 10^{-36}\,m$ **b.** The de Broglie wavelength of the electrons are of the same order at atomic separations in a crystal, so electron diffraction experiments can experimentally observe diffraction. The de Broglie wavelength for the alpha particle is smaller than typical atomic spacing so diffraction experiments are technically difficult to achieve but possible. The de Broglie wavelength of the person is so small that no diffraction effects could ever be observed.

4. **a.** $1.21 \times 10^{-27}\,N\,s$ **b.** 8.26×10^{20} **c.** Light from the Sun is only made up of photons of wavelength 550 nm. Light from the Sun arrives perpendicular to the Earth's surface. Light photons are absorbed by the Earth's surface.

5. **a.** $8.43 \times 10^{-12}\,m$ **b.** $90°$ **c.** The angle of the final direction of the electron makes the same as the angle of the photon but is in the opposite direction, because momentum must be conserved in all directions.

d. 59.7 keV

E.3—Radioactive decay

1. 70 s

2. **a.** $1.36 \times 10^{-14}\,s^{-1}$ **b. i.** 1005 s **ii.** 8.3%

3. **a.** 2.53×10^{18} **b.** $4.88 \times 10^{-18}\,s^{-1}$ **c.** 12.3 Bq **d. i.** As the half-life of the sample is much larger than 10 years, the activity of the sample will have had no discernible change after 10 years. **ii.** The half-life of the sample in years is 4.50×10^9 years. After 10^9 years, the activity will have decreased by a measurable amount, but will still be greater than half of the initial activity.

E.4—Fission

1. **a.** In the neutron-induced fission of uranium-235, the binding energy of ^{235}U is lower than the total binding energy of the products. Energy is released when the average binding energy per nucleon increases. **b.** The fission reactions in nuclear reactors produce more neutrons. These neutrons then initiate other fission reactions, causing a chain reaction. **c. i.** The fuel rods are long cylinders containing the uranium for the fission reactions. **ii.** Control rods can be lowered into the reactor to absorb neutrons and slow the rate of reaction. **iii.** Moderators reduce the kinetic energy of the neutrons. This slows down the neutrons so that they can initiate further fission reactions. **iv.** The heat exchanger collects the energy from the reactor and transfers it to the water, converting it to steam to drive turbines. **v.** The shielding is a safety mechanism. It surrounds the nuclear reactor and prevents radiation from escaping. **e.** Any radioactive material needs to be secured in lead-lined containers to minimize the radioactive dose received by those working with these materials. Care needs to be taken that radioactive material cannot accidentally leak into the surroundings, so some storage facilities are deep underground in geologically secure locations.

2. **a.** $3.90 \times 10^{-23}\,kg$ **b.** B will release more energy. **c.** Kinetic energy **d.** There is a critical mass that is needed for the chain reaction to be maintained.
   On average, at least one of the neutrons released in the fission reaction needs to go on to cause further fission reactions. The smaller the mass of uranium used, the more likely it is for neutrons to leave the sample without encountering another uranium nucleus.
   e. 174 MeV **f. i.** 8.64×10^{19} **ii.** 1063 kg

E.5—Fusion and stars

1. 0.023 arcseconds

2. **a.**

page 203

b.

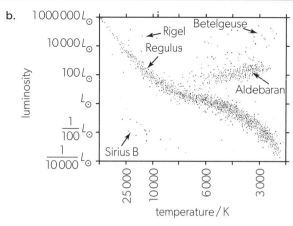

ii.

Star	Stellar type
Aldebaran	Red giant
Betelgeuse	Supergiant
Regulus	Main sequence
Rigel	Blue supergiant
Sirius B	White dwarf

3. A star is in hydrostatic equilibrium. The tendency for the outer layers to expand outwards into space provides an outwards "pressure". There is also an inwards pull of gravity towards the centre of the star because of its mass. A star is in equilibrium and remains fixed in size when these two forces are balance.

4. When hydrogen fusion is no longer possible, larger mass stars can develop into red giant stars, in which oxygen-16 and other heavier elements are created. Any oxygen-16 atoms were created in the fusion process that must have taken place in a red giant star. Iron-56 was also produced in the fusion process in a red giant (or supergiant) star. Energetically, iron is the largest nucleus that can be produced in a fusion process that also releases energy. In the supernova process, larger nuclei than iron can be created, but
this process takes in energy rather than releasing energy. Iodine-127 must have been created in a supernova of a red giant star.

5. a. Nuclear fusion b. i. High density ii. High temperature c. The gravitational collapse of a large cloud of hydrogen brings the atoms together. As they are attracted in, the loss of gravitational potential energy gives rise to an increase in kinetic energy and hence temperature. The gas molecules speed up as they fall in towards the centre of the protostar. With sufficient KE and high enough density, nuclear reactions can take place.

6. a. 3.96×10^{26} W b. 2.1×10^{19} m c. The star is too far away so the parallax effect will be negligible.
d. 7.0×10^{11} m

Tools and inquiry process

1. a. $17 \, g \, cm^{-3}$ b. $\pm 2.3 \, g \, cm^{-3}$ c. $1.93 \times 10^4 \, kg \, m^{-3} = 19.3 \, g \, cm^{-3}$. This is just within the uncertainty limit, so the bar could be pure gold. d. The greatest uncertainty is in the measurement of length
(particularly the measurement of 1.0 cm). A vernier caliper could be used to reduce the uncertainty in the length measurement.

2. a. Random error associated with human reaction time.

b. Human reaction time is approximately 0.2 s. Time can be anticipated so it is unlikely that the uncertainty is this large, but this could be used. A value of ±0.1 s would be reasonable. c. Student B will have a final uncertainty of one thirtieth of the answer given to (b). Student A will have a final uncertainty value of (b). Student B's method will have the lowest uncertainty.

3. a. i. $10.1 \, m \, s^{-2}$ ii. The value for the time ranges from 0.491 s to 0.619 s for the same height. This uncertainty is greater than from the readability of the stopwatch. iii. Range = 0.128 s

$$\therefore \text{uncertainty} \simeq \frac{0.128}{2} \, s = 0.064 \, s$$

iv. 23% v. $g = 10.1 \pm 2.4 \, m \, s^{-2}$ (or $g = 10 \pm 2 \, m \, s^{-2}$)
b. i. $9.70 \, m \, s^{-2}$ ii. 1.7% iii. $g = 9.7 \pm 0.2 \, m \, s^{-2}$ c. The students' values for g overlap within the range of uncertainty, so they agree.

4. a. A random error deviates from the actual "correct" value by different amount for each reading, giving variability. A systematic error always deviates from the actual "correct" value by a fixed amount. b. Repeating readings and averaging will allow random errors to cancel out. c. Accuracy reflects how close a measurement is to the actual "correct" value. Precision reflects how close repeated measurements are to each other. A meter reading with more significant figures is providing a more precise measurement. d. i. The independent variable is the variable that the experimenter chooses to change (and record). ii. The dependent variable is the variable that is affected by changes in the independent variable. The experimenter records matching pairs of the independent variable and the dependent variable. iii. In any experiment, there will be other variables that might affect the dependent variable. These variables are kept, as far as possible, constant. They are known as the control variables.

5. a. m b. i. The graph needs to be linear. A possible plot could be $\frac{1}{v}$ on the y-axis and $\frac{1}{u}$ on the x-axis. ii. y-intercept $= \frac{1}{f}$,

so $f = \dfrac{1}{y - \text{intercept}}$

iii. $f = 4.2 \, cm$. *The error bars are effectively too small to include for many points.*

Index

Page numbers in *italics* refer to question sections.

A

absolute zero 64
absorption lines 56
absorption spectra 138
ac generators 134
acceleration 1, 8
  acceleration–time graphs
    2, 4
  angular acceleration 27
  centripetal acceleration 19,
    28
  equations of uniform angular
    acceleration 27
  equations of uniform motion
    3
  experiment determining
    free-fall acceleration 6
  Newton's laws of motion
    9, 12
  simple harmonic motion
    83, 85, 86
  tangential acceleration 28
  translational and rotational
    motion 27, 28
adiabatic processes 72, 74
albedo 59
alpha decay 151
alpha particles 137, 151, 156
alpha radiation properties 152
alternating current 76, 134
ammeters 79, 170
ampere, definition 130
amplitude
  simple harmonic motion
    83
  stationary and travelling
    waves 103
  wave motion 89
angles, measuring 170
angular acceleration 27
angular displacement vs time
  graph 33
angular impulse 32
angular momentum 32, 141
angular velocity 20, 27
  angular velocity vs time
    graph 33
antimatter 152
antineutrinos 152, 156
antinodes 103
apparent brightness 57
Archimedes' principle 11
artificial transmutations 148
assumptions 174
astronomical unit (AU) 166
atomic spectra 138, 140
atomic structure 137–41, *142*
  atomic energy states 140
  Bohr model 141
  emission and absorption
    spectra 138, 140
  evidence from experiments
    137, 139
  nuclear model 137
  nuclear radii and nuclear
    densities 139
Avogadro constant 66

B

background radiation 152, 192
Balmer series 140
bar charts 184, 185
batteries 77
beta decay 151, 156, 159
beta particles 151, 156
beta plus decay 152
beta radiation properties 152
binding energy 147, 149, 155
black-body radiation 55, 57
black holes 162, 165
blueshift 56, 108
Bohr model of the atom 141
Boltzmann's constant 66
Boyle's law 68
Brackett series 140
buoyancy 8, 10, 11

C

calibration 192
Carnot cycle 74
Carnot engine 74
cathode ray oscilloscope 170
cells and batteries 77
Celsius scale 48
centre of gravity 30
centre of mass 27
centripetal acceleration 19, 28
centripetal force 19
chain reaction 149
Chandrasekhar limit 165
charge 119
charge capacity 77
charge carriers 76
Charles's law 68
circuits 78, *82*
  cells and batteries 77
  current 76
  electrical meters 79, 170
  electromotive force (emf) 77
  internal resistance 77
  investigations 192
  Kirchoff's circuit laws 78
  potential divider circuit 80
  power dissipation 78
  resistance 78, 81
  resistivity 81
  resistors in series/parallel 79
  sensor circuits 80
circular motion 19–20
CNO (carbon–nitrogen–
  oxygen) process 162
collisions 17–18
  molecules of a gas 67
  between photons and
    electrons 145
compound materials 54
compression
  gases 70, 72, 74
  springs 14, 23
  waves 88
Compton effect 145
computer modelling 171–2
conduction 52, 54
  comparison between
    thermal and electrical 54
  conductors and insulators
    52, 54, 119
  electrical conduction in a
    metal 76
conductors 52, 54, 119
conservation of angular
  momentum 32
conservation of charge 119
conservation of energy 22, 72
conservation of momentum
  16–17
continuous wave 88
convection 52
Coulomb's law 119
couples 29
critical angle 95
current 76, 78, *82*
  alternating current 76, 134

coil rotating in magnetic field
  132, 134
  direct current 76
  magnetic field due to
    currents 129–30
  magnetic force on current-
    carrying wire 128, 130
  measuring 79, 170
  root mean square (rms)
    values 134

D

damping 105
data
  collection 171
  determining relationships
    187–8
  graphical analysis 187–8
  measuring variables 168–
    70, 190–1
  outliers 193
  processing 171–2, 193
  range of magnitudes of
    quantities 177
  recording 193
  technology for collection
    and processing 171–2
  uncertainties 182–3
  visual representation 184–6
data loggers 171
databases 171
de Broglie hypothesis 144
deformation 8
degraded energy 24, 73
density 64
diffraction 96, 99
  electrons 144
  light 96, 98, 99, 100, 101
  mathematics 99
  multiple-slit diffraction 101
  single-slit diffraction 99
  Young's double slit
    experiment 98, 100
diffraction gratings 101
diffuse reflection 93
dimensional analysis 181
direct current 76
displacement 1
  displacement–time graphs 2
  simple harmonic motion 83,
    85, 86
  translational and rotational
    motion 27, 28
  wave motion 89
Doppler effect 56, 108–10, *111*
drag 6, 8, 10
  acting on sphere in a fluid 11
  effect on orbiting satellites
    117
drift velocity 76

E

Earth *63*
  albedo 59
  emissivity 59
  global warming 62
  greenhouse effect 61
  incoming solar radiation 60
efficiency 22, 74
Einstein model of light 143
elastic collisions 17–18
elastic potential energy 22
elastic restoring force 8, 10
electric fields 120, *126*
  compared with gravitational
    fields 125
  compared with magnetic
    fields 122

field lines 120
field strength 123
Millikan's experiment 121
motion of a charged particle
  127, 129
potential and potential
  difference 123–4
uniform 125
electric force 8, 10
  conductor moving in
    magnetic field 132
electric potential 123, 124
electric potential difference 76,
  78, 123, 124
  measuring 79, 170
  potential divider circuit 80
  resistors in series/parallel 79
electric potential energy 123
electrical conduction 54, 76,
  119
electrical power production 24
electromagnetic fields 127–30,
  131
electromagnetic force 8, 150
electromagnetic spectrum 53,
  90
electromagnetic waves 90
  Maxwell's equations and
    speed of light 36
  radiation 53
electromotive force (emf) 77
  ac generators 134
  back emf 135
  induced emf 132–5
  Lenz's law and Faraday's law
    133
  transformer-induced emf 133
electron degeneracy pressure
  165
electrons
  atomic structure 137
  conduction electrons 76
  diffraction experiment 144
  drift velocity 76
  energy levels 138, 140, 141
  motion in perpendicular
    electric and magnetic fields
    129
  orbits 141
  photoelectric effect 143
electrostatic force 119
emission spectra 138, 140
emissivity 59
energy 22, *26*
  comparison of energy
    sources 25
  conservation 22, 72
  degradation 24, 73
  energy flow for stars 161
  orbiting satellites 117
  of a photon 143
  and power generation 24,
    158
  range of energies 177
  released in nuclear reactions
    147, 148, 149
  of rotational motion 32
  in simple harmonic motion
    83, 85, 86
  types of 22
  waves 88, 103
energy conversions 24
energy density 25
energy levels 138, 140, 141,
  156
energy sources 25, 158
energy transformations 22
entropy 73